ENGLISH
Language and
Communication Skills
FOR ENGINEERS

Sanjay Kumar

Author, Consultant, and Trainer
English and Soft Skills
Formerly Faculty, BITS Pilani and
Reader and Chairperson, Department of English, CDLU, Sirsa

Pushp Lata

Associate Professor of English
Department of Humanities and Social Sciences
BITS, Pilani

OXFORD
UNIVERSITY PRESS

OXFORD
UNIVERSITY PRESS

Oxford University Press is a department of the University of Oxford.
It furthers the University's objective of excellence in research, scholarship,
and education by publishing worldwide. Oxford is a registered trade mark of
Oxford University Press in the UK and in certain other countries.

Published in India by
Oxford University Press
22 Workspace, 2nd Floor, 1/22 Asaf Ali Road, New Delhi 110002

First published in 2018
Third impression 2025

ISBN-13: 978-0-19-949136-0
ISBN-10: 0-19-949136-4

Typeset in GaramondPro
by E-Edit Infotech Private Limited (Santype), Chennai
Printed in India by Nutech Print Services

Cover image: Bluehousestudio / Shutterstock

For product information and current price, please visit www.india.oup.com

PREFACE

Ours is an age of communication not just because of decisive breakthroughs in communication technology but also because of the impact spoken and written words create in our personal and professional lives. Consequently proficiency, accuracy, and effectiveness in the language we use are considered vitally important. With English becoming a link language worldwide, proficiency in it is considered essential for a person's personal and professional growth. Not surprisingly therefore, it is effective communication in English that not only fetches students their dream jobs, but also defines and redefines them in this competitive world.

About the Book

Written in consonance with the latest curriculum as per NEP for colleges and universities across the country, the book attempts to cover the entire gamut of communication in English—its shades, shapes, colours, and nuances. Besides covering the curriculum completely, the book also includes important aspects related to English language and communication skills for teachers (to teach effectively and rationally) and students (to learn the content thoroughly). Though primarily meant to be a textbook for the undergraduate students of engineering, the book will also serve as a reference guide for working engineers, managers, scientists, teachers, trainees, administrative officers, and other professionals who need to use English as a tool of communication in the professional environment.

Pedagogical Features

Listed below are some pedagogical features that make this book both interesting and highly educative:

Comprehensive text written in an interactive style The comprehensive coverage, annotated examples, and the multiple exercises on each topic are likely to help students approach the variegated communication-related tasks confidently in their professional careers. In order to keep the learners engaged, a warm and interactive style of writing is followed throughout the book.

Practice-oriented approach Each chapter contains a large number of exercises with explanatory answers so that the learners not only gain conceptual clarity but also imbibe these concepts empirically.

Skill development The chapters on written communication include important tips and different elements of professional and sensible writing to help students improve their written communication skills.

Focus on job readiness The unit on communication at workplace discusses job interviews and formal presentations in detail, giving ideas about ways to overcome nervousness and sample questions to help students prepare themselves for interviews and other work-related situations.

Content and Coverage

For the convenience of the reader, the book has been divided into six logical parts, comprising 14 chapters.

The introductory chapter on *English Language and Communication Skills* lays the foundation for learning all the four language skills, namely Listening, Speaking, Reading, and Writing popularly known as LSRW. It discusses the process, importance, features, and types of effective communication. It also highlights the formal and informal flow of communication in an organization.

Unit I: Essentials of Writing Skills, comprising Chapters 2 to 4, focuses on developing the essentials of writing skills of the learners by helping them develop their knowledge of English grammar and usage. This unit also aims at enhancing their vocabulary. *Chapter 2 on Basic Grammar and Usage* covers the essentials of grammar and usage such as nouns, pronouns, adjectives, verbs, adverbs, conjunctions, prepositions, articles, modals, tenses, voice, narration, clauses, and punctuation marks. *Chapter 3 on Common Errors in English* deals with common errors related to subject–verb concord, noun/pronoun agreement, dangling modifiers, etc. The exercises given in the chapter help the learner identify and avoid the errors commonly made in English. *Chapter 4 on Vocabulary Building* aims at helping the students develop their vocabulary by adding new words to make their written and spoken English more effective and powerful. An attempt has been made in this chapter to help the students pick new words through roots, routine sentences, common everyday conversations, situations, context, synonyms, antonyms, etc.

Unit II: Writing Practices is aimed at developing the students' descriptive writing techniques. *Chapter 5 on Nature and Style of Sensible Writing* introduces the learner to the nuances of writing and helps him/her develop the skills required for effective writing. *Chapter 6 on Paragraph Writing* covers the structure, construction, and features of paragraphs and helps students construct effective paragraphs. It also discusses argumentative and analytical paragraphs. *Chapter 7 on Essay Writing* dwells on the dimensions of essay writing discussing in detail narrative, descriptive, reflective, expository, and imaginative essays. *Chapter 8 on Précis Writing* helps the learner understand how to condense effectively a detailed piece of writing and provides ample amount of exercises for developing effective précis writing skills.

Unit III: Listening Skills starts with *Chapter 9 on Listening Skills and Comprehension*, which gives exposure and practice in developing effective listening techniques.

Unit IV: Reading Skills is aimed at developing the art of effective reading techniques in the learner. *Chapter 10 on Effective Reading and Comprehension Skills* gives the students exposure into the art of comprehending a given passage. It helps students learn how, by employing different reading skills, understanding discourse features, and inferring lexical and contextual meanings, the different types of reading comprehension passages can be attempted in an exam.

Unit V: Oral Communication develops effective speaking through various types of tasks. *Chapter 11 on Phonetics and Spoken English* introduces to the learner all the vowel and consonant sounds of English and helps him/her overcome the pitfalls of faulty pronunciation. The chapter stresses on accuracy in pronunciation by introducing the learner to concepts such as syllables, transcription, word stress, weak forms, intonation, rhythm, etc. *Chapter 12 on Conversations and Dialogues: Everyday Speaking Situations* provides tips on improving conversations, and includes sample short conversations, sample telephonic conversations, and situational dialogues.

Unit VI: Communication at Workplace aims at developing professional communication skills in the learner. *Chapter 13 on Job Interviews* discusses the process, stages, and types of job interviews. This chapter also discusses the desirable qualities required in an employee and provides tips for achieving success in interviews. It also discusses the frequently asked questions in an interview and suggests suitable answers and strategies for dealing with them. *Chapter 14 on Formal Presentations* deals with the dynamics of professional presentations. It covers topics such as combating stage fright, and preparing effective PowerPoint presentations.

Acknowledgements

Writing this book has been an arduous as well as exciting journey. It demanded from us a great deal of research, effort, hard work, and commitment. All this required a lot of motivation and professional efficacy which always came from our publishers, Oxford University Press India. We also take this opportunity to thank the reviewers of our book who provided their useful comments, observations, and suggestions, all of which helped us in enriching both the content and the approach for the book.

On the authorial plane, we are grateful to Prof. Sauvik Bhattacharya, Hon'ble Vice-Chancellor, BITS, Pilani for all his support and motivation. We are also indebted to Prof. A.K. Sarkar, Director, BITS, Pilani for his guidance and encouragement.

This book would not have been possible without invaluable inputs from many of our fellow creative intellectuals. In this category, we are indeed grateful to Prof. Krishna Mohan, Prof. Meenakshi Raman, Prof. Sangeeta Sharma, Prof. Binod Mishra, Prof. G.S. Chauhan, Prof. Devika, Prof. S.K. Chaudhary, Prof. Geetha, B., Dr Sushila Rathore, Dr Virender Singh Nirban, Prof. Sanjay Arora, Prof. Rajneesh Arora, Prof. Umed Singh, Prof. Sanjeev Kumar, Dr Satyapaul, and Dr Suman Luhach.

In addition, we thank all our seniors, well-wishers, family members, and friends whose silent but invaluable support we might have failed in appreciating.

Finally, we are grateful to you—our reader—your interest in our book gives us great motivation and satisfaction. Being teachers, we are aware of the fact that in all learning tasks, the learner's participation is of utmost importance. You can ensure your participation and learning by attempting all the exercises in the book conscientiously. We would be delighted to receive your comments, queries, and suggestions for future editions. You can reach us at drarorasanjay@gmail.com.

Sanjay Kumar
Pushp Lata

BRIEF CONTENTS

Preface   iii
Detailed Contents   viii
Road Map to English   xii

1. English Language and Communication Skills: An Overview   1

UNIT I: ESSENTIALS OF WRITING SKILLS

2. Basic Grammar and Usage   15
3. Common Errors in English   95
4. Vocabulary Building   113

UNIT II: WRITING PRACTICES

5. Nature and Style of Sensible Writing   134
6. Paragraph Writing   152
7. Essay Writing   175
8. Précis Writing   190

UNIT III: LISTENING SKILLS

9. Listening Skills and Comprehension   200

UNIT IV: READING SKILLS

10. Effective Reading and Comprehension Skills   210

UNIT V: ORAL COMMUNICATION

11. Phonetics and Spoken English   225
12. Conversations and Dialogues: Everyday Speaking Situations   247

UNIT VI: COMMUNICATION AT WORKPLACE

13. Job Interviews   271
14. Formal Presentations   283

DETAILED CONTENTS

Preface   iii
Brief Contents   vii
Road Map to English   xii

1. **English Language and Communication Skills: An Overview   1**
   - 1.1 Importance of Language and Communication   *1*
   - 1.2 Four Essential Skills—LSRW   *2*
   - 1.3 Communication—An Overview   *2*
   - 1.4 Definition of Communication   *3*
   - 1.5 Process of Communication   *3*
   - 1.6 Features of Successful Professional Communication   *4*
   - 1.7 Importance of Effective Professional Communication   *4*
   - 1.8 Different Types of Communication   *5*
   - 1.9 Communication Flow in an Organization   *5*
     - 1.9.1 Formal Flow of Communication   *5*
     - 1.9.2 Informal Flow of Communication   *6*
   - 1.10 Barriers to Communication   *6*
   - 1.11 Role of Creative and Critical Thinking for Effective Communication   *7*
   - 1.12 Role of Intercultural Communication   *8*
   - 1.13 Verbal Communication   *8*
   - 1.14 Non-verbal Communication   *9*
   - 1.15 Tips for Improvement   *9*

UNIT I: ESSENTIALS OF WRITING SKILLS

2. **Basic Grammar and Usage   15**
   - 2.1 Why Grammar?   *15*
   - 2.2 Fixing Nouns   *15*
     - 2.2.1 Nouns/Noun Problem: Dealing with Problem Areas   *16*
   - 2.3 Possessive Form ('S) or Of   *18*
   - 2.4 Pronouns   *18*
   - 2.5 Adjectives   *21*
   - 2.6 Verbs   *24*
     - 2.6.1 Classification of Verbs   *25*
   - 2.7 Adverbs   *27*
     - 2.7.1 Adverbs: Areas of Concern   *30*
   - 2.8 Prepositions   *31*
   - 2.9 Connectives, Prepositions, and Adverbs as Linkers   *36*
   - 2.10 Determiners and Articles   *39*
     - 2.10.1 Articles   *40*
   - 2.11 Phrases   *43*
   - 2.12 Tenses   *44*
     - 2.12.1 Simple Present or Present Progressive   *47*
     - 2.12.2 Present Perfect or Simple Past   *49*
     - 2.12.3 Simple Past or Past Perfect   *51*
     - 2.12.4 Simple Future or Future Progressive   *52*
     - 2.12.5 Future Perfect   *53*
     - 2.12.6 Present Perfect Continuous   *53*
     - 2.12.7 Past Perfect Continuous   *54*
     - 2.12.8 Future Perfect Continuous   *55*
   - 2.13 Moods of Verbs   *56*
   - 2.14 Active/Passive Voice   *58*
   - 2.15 Direct/Indirect Speech   *63*
   - 2.16 Clause and its Types   *66*
     - 2.16.1 Noun Clauses   *68*
     - 2.16.2 Adjective Clauses   *68*

2.16.3 Adverbial Clauses *69*
2.16.4 Relative Clauses *69*
2.17 Non-finites *71*
2.18 Punctuation Marks *78*
    2.18.1 Full Stop *79*
    2.18.2 Comma *79*
    2.18.3 Dash *80*
    2.18.4 Hyphen *81*
    2.18.5 Semicolon *81*
    2.18.6 Colon *81*
    2.18.7 Single and Double Inverted Commas *81*
    2.18.8 Apostrophe *82*
    2.18.9 Parentheses *82*
    2.18.10 Sign of Interrogation/Question Mark *82*
    2.18.11 Exclamation Mark *83*
    2.18.12 Capital Letters *83*

3. Common Errors in English 95
3.1 Steps for Identifying Errors *95*
3.2 Some Major Types of Errors *95*

3.2.1 Errors Related to Noun/Pronoun Agreement *95*
3.2.2 Errors Related to Subject–Verb Concord *97*
3.2.3 Errors Related to Preposition Usage *102*
3.2.4 Errors Related to Usage of Articles *103*
3.2.5 Errors Related to Misplaced Modifiers *103*

4. Vocabulary Building 113
4.1 Importance of Vocabulary *113*
4.2 Word Formation *113*
4.3 Roots *113*
    4.3.1 Learning through Roots *114*
4.4 Prefixes and Suffixes *118*
4.5 Synonyms *121*
4.6 Antonyms *124*
4.7 Overcoming Confusion in Choice of Words *127*
4.8 Acronyms/Abbreviations *130*

UNIT II: WRITING PRACTICES

5. Nature and Style of Sensible Writing 134
5.1 Tips For Sensible Writing *134*
    5.1.1 Use Simple, Familiar, and Concrete Words *135*
    5.1.2 Prefer Using Verbs to Long Nouns *135*
    5.1.3 Avoid Wordiness and Redundancy *136*
    5.1.4 Provide Complete and Accurate Information *136*
    5.1.5 Judiciously Use Active and Passive Voice *136*
    5.1.6 Follow Emphatic Word Order *137*
    5.1.7 Use Parallel Grammatical Construction *137*
    5.1.8 Avoid Clichés *137*
    5.1.9 Avoid Circumlocution *138*
    5.1.10 Avoid Punctuation and Grammatical Errors *138*
    5.1.11 Use Graphic Aids and Illustrations *138*
5.2 Elements of Professional Writing *139*
    5.2.1 Introducing *139*
    5.2.2 Defining *142*

    5.2.3 Classifying *142*
    5.2.4 Describing *144*
    5.2.5 Providing Evidence or Example *147*
    5.2.6 Analysing and Interpreting *147*
    5.2.7 Concluding *149*

6. Paragraph Writing 152
6.1 What is a Paragraph? *152*
    6.1.1 Structure of a Paragraph *154*
6.2 Topic Sentence *155*
6.3 Construction of a Paragraph *156*
    6.3.1 Narrative Description *156*
    6.3.2 Comparisons and Contrasts *157*
    6.3.3 Sustained Analogy *157*
    6.3.4 Cause and Effect *158*
    6.3.5 Quotations and Paraphrasing *158*
    6.3.6 Enumeration *159*
    6.3.7 Definition *159*
    6.3.8 Expert Testimony *160*
    6.3.9 Facts, Figures, Instances, and Examples *161*
    6.3.10 Episodes *161*
6.4 Using Transitions and Connecting Devices *162*

6.5   Extended Definitions *164*
6.6   Features of a Paragraph *165*
    6.6.1 Unity *165*
    6.6.2 Coherence *166*
    6.6.3 Expansion and Emphasis *167*
6.7   Descriptive Writing Techniques *168*
6.8   Argumentative Paragraph *170*
6.9   Analytical Paragraph *171*

7. Essay Writing 175
7.1   Types of Essays *175*
    7.1.1 Argumentative Essays *175*
    7.1.2 Analytical Essays *176*
    7.1.3 Descriptive Essays *176*

    7.1.4 Expository Essays *177*
    7.1.5 Reflective/Philosophical Essays *177*
7.2   Characteristic Features of an Essay *178*
7.3   Stages in Essay Writing *179*
7.4   Components Comprising an Essay *180*
7.5   Essay Writing—Guiding Principles *182*

8. Précis Writing 190
8.1   Essentials of Précis Writing *191*
    8.1.1 Some Working Principles *191*
8.2   Seven-step Ladder to Writing an Effective Précis *192*
8.3   Writing Précis of Given Passages *193*

UNIT III: LISTENING SKILLS

9. Listening Skills and Comprehension 200
9.1   Why do We Avoid Listening? *201*
9.2   Disadvantages of Poor Listening *201*
9.3   Poor Listening vs Effective Listening *201*
9.4   Advantages of Effective Listening *202*

9.5   Types of Listening *202*
9.6   Barriers to Effective Listening *203*
9.7   Five Steps to Active Listening *204*
9.8   Techniques for Effective Listening *204*
9.9   Practising Listening Activities *204*

UNIT IV: READING SKILLS

10. Effective Reading and Comprehension Skills 210
10.1   Need for Developing Efficient Reading Skills *210*
10.2   Benefits of Effective Reading *210*
10.3   Differences Between Efficient and Inefficient Readers *211*
10.4   Four Basic Steps to Effective Reading *211*

10.5   Getting Acquainted with Major Types of Questions *212*
10.6   Tips to Improve Reading Comprehension Skills *212*
10.7   Stumbling Blocks in Becoming an Effective Reader *213*

UNIT V: ORAL COMMUNICATION

11. Phonetics and Spoken English 225
11.1   Reasons for Incorrect Pronunciation *225*
11.2   Received Pronunciation (RP) *225*
11.3   Misconception about Sounds *226*
11.4   Transcription *226*
11.5   Sounds *226*
    11.5.1 Vowels *227*
    11.5.2 Consonants *229*
    11.5.3 Consonant Cluster (CC) *230*
11.6   Problems of Indian English *230*

11.7   Syllable *231*
    11.7.1 Rules for Counting Syllables *232*
    11.7.2 Dividing Words into Syllables *232*
11.8   Word Stress *234*
11.9   How to Transcribe *236*
11.10 Weak Forms *238*
11.11 Stress, Intonation, and Rhythm *240*
    11.11.1 Rules for Intonation *240*
    11.11.2 Contrastive Stress in Sentences *242*

11.12 Difference between British, American, and Indian Spoken English *242*
    11.12.1 Other Differences in Pronunciation *243*
    11.12.2 Characteristics of Indian English (IE) *244*

12. Conversations and Dialogues: Everyday Speaking Situations 247
12.1 Purpose of General Conversations *247*
    12.1.1 Self-expression and Interaction *247*
    12.1.2 Getting to Know the Other Person Better *247*
    12.1.3 Building Trust and Credibility *247*
12.2 Advantages of Conversations *248*
12.3 Features of a Good Conversation *248*
12.4 Tips for Improving Conversations *248*
    12.4.1 Begin by Using Pleasantries *248*
    12.4.2 Listen More than You Speak *249*
    12.4.3 Reciprocate Warmly *250*
    12.4.4 Ask Open-ended Questions *251*

12.4.5 Be Courteous and Polite *251*
12.4.6 Resist the Urge to Dominate *252*
12.4.7 Listen to Others Attentively *252*
12.4.8 Use Appropriate Body Language *253*
12.4.9 Be Specific and Use Vivid Language *253*
12.4.10 Paraphrase the Speaker's Words *254*
12.4.11 Apply the Three Cs *254*
12.5 Participating in Short Conversations *254*
12.6 Making Requests *256*
12.7 Seeking and Giving Advice *257*
12.8 Agreeing and Disagreeing *259*
12.9 Giving Instructions *260*
12.10 Situational Dialogues *262*
    12.10.1 Definition *262*
    12.10.2 Tips for Writing Dialogues *262*
    12.10.3 Giving Characters Distinct Speech Patterns *263*

UNIT VI: COMMUNICATION AT WORKPLACE

13. Job Interviews 271
13.1 Definition of Interview *271*
13.2 Process of Job Interview *272*
13.3 Stages in Job Interviews *273*
13.4 Types of Interviews and Questions Related to Them *273*
13.5 Desirable Qualities of Candidates *275*
13.6 Preparation for Successful Job Interviews *275*
    13.6.1 Know the Company *275*
    13.6.2 Know Yourself *275*
    13.6.3 Review Common Interview Questions *276*
    13.6.4 Prepare Questions You Want to Ask the Interviewer *280*
13.7 Using Proper Verbal and Non-verbal Cues *280*
13.8 Exhibiting Confidence *281*
13.9 Tips for Success *281*

14. Formal Presentations 283
14.1 Overcoming Nervousness *283*

14.2 Factors that Make a Presentation Work *284*
    14.2.1 Researching the Topic Thoroughly *285*
    14.2.2 Choosing an Appropriate Pattern of Organization *285*
    14.2.3 Starting Innovatively *286*
    14.2.4 Stating Facts to Substantiate Main Ideas *287*
    14.2.5 Using Examples and Instances *287*
    14.2.6 Using Visual Aids Effectively *288*
    14.2.7 Being Witty and Humorous *288*
    14.2.8 Employing Effective Body Language *289*
    14.2.9 Maintaining Appropriate Space Distance *291*
    14.2.10 Employing Paralinguistic Features Effectively *292*
    14.2.11 Ending on an Emphatic Note *296*
    14.2.12 Using PowerPoint Slides Effectively *297*
    14.2.13 Making Effective Group Presentations *297*

ROAD MAP TO ENGLISH

Unit	Topic	Details	Chapter
Unit I	Vocabulary Building	1.1 The concept of word formation 1.2 Root words from foreign languages and their use in English 1.3 Acquaintance with prefixes and suffixes from foreign languages in English to form derivatives 1.4 Synonyms, antonyms, and standard abbreviations	4
Unit II	Basic Writing Skills	2.1 Sentence structures 2.2 Use of phrases and clauses in sentences 2.3 Importance of proper punctuation 2.4 Creating coherence 2.5 Organizing principles of paragraphs in documents 2.6 Techniques for writing precisely	2, 6, 8
Unit III	Identifying Common Errors in Writing	3.1 Subject–verb agreement 3.2 Noun–pronoun agreement 3.3 Misplaced modifiers 3.4 Articles 3.5 Prepositions 3.6 Redundancies 3.7 Clichés	2, 3
Unit IV	Nature and Style of Sensible Writing	4.1 Describing 4.2 Defining 4.3 Classifying 4.4 Providing examples or evidence 4.5 Writing introduction and conclusion	5
Unit V	Writing Practices	5.1 Comprehension 5.2 Précis writing 5.3 Essay writing	6, 7, 8
Unit VI	Oral Communication	6.1 Listening comprehension 6.2 Pronunciation, intonation, stress, and rhythm 6.3 Common everyday situations: Conversations and dialogues 6.4 Communication at workplace 6.5 Interviews 6.6 Formal presentations	9, 11, 12, 13, 14

1

ENGLISH LANGUAGE AND COMMUNICATION SKILLS: AN OVERVIEW

LEARNING OBJECTIVES

After reading this chapter, you will be able to understand
- importance of language and communication
- four essential skills of language—LSRW
- process and types of communication
- features and importance of effective professional communication
- types of communication flow in an organization
- different types of barriers to communication
- role of creative and critical thinking for effective communication
- role of intercultural communication in organizations
- types and importance of verbal and non-verbal communication
- tips for improvement in communication

Language is an important aspect of our day-to-day life because it enables us to communicate. It plays an important role in expressing our thoughts and feelings to the person we talk to. If we look around, we may observe that most of the time in our life, we keep communicating something or the other. For example, when we ask for a cup of tea, talk to a friend over the phone, speak to a fellow passenger while travelling, read the newspaper, watch a documentary, enquire from a passerby someone's address, or listen to the running commentary, we are involved in the process of communication with others through language. Thus, language and communication go hand in hand. When we don't use words, we use and convey through non-verbal forms of language such as gestures, signs, expressions, and symbols to communicate our ideas, thoughts, emotions, and feelings.

Let us see in some detail how important language and communication is in our lives.

1.1 IMPORTANCE OF LANGUAGE AND COMMUNICATION

- It is important in the individual development of the user.
- It enables us to communicate our ideas and emotions to others.
- It helps us understand each other.
- It enhances our social skills.
- It is a means of filtering the beliefs, rituals, and customs of a society.

In the professional world, it is English that is often used as a link language for communication. It is used for a variety of purposes—while conducting meetings and discussions; for managing people, affairs, and tasks; for writing reports, emails, letters, proposals, circulars, notices, and manuals; for giving presentations, delivering public speeches, conducting interviews, holding teleconferences, and tackling negotiations. If we are able to communicate and negotiate successfully with our clients who speak English, it helps our company to conduct business successfully, which will further aid in the robust growth of the enterprise we are associated with. It has also been observed that employees who communicate effectively in English often command higher salaries and get quick career growth.

Keeping in view the importance of developing proficiency in English, we need to understand that there are four basic skills of the language, namely Listening, Speaking, Reading, and Writing (LSRW) that need to be learnt. Therefore, in the following section of the chapter, we will learn how to develop our LSRW skills of English.

1.2 FOUR ESSENTIAL SKILLS—LSRW

In order to become an accomplished communicator, one needs to be proficient in each of the four language skills mentioned above. If you observe carefully, we acquire our first language/mother tongue by first listening to it. Gradually, we start speaking it too, and then go on to develop our reading and writing abilities in it. This is why listening, speaking, reading, and writing are called the four 'language skills' of a language. Figure 1.1 shows the four important language skills.

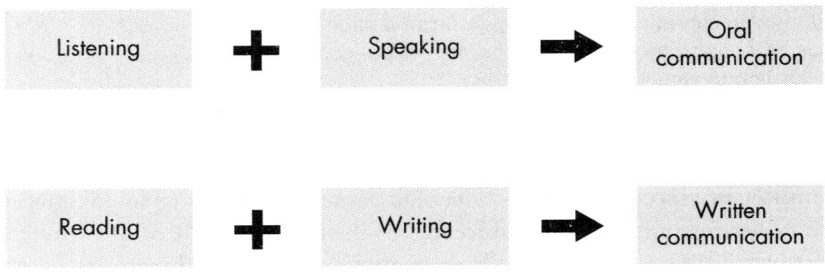

Figure 1.1 LSRW Skills

All the four skills are interrelated and they function in tandem. Therefore, each one of them is crucial for learning a language.

1.3 COMMUNICATION—AN OVERVIEW

As mentioned above, ours is a society that moves on the wheels of communication. Particularly in the professional world, it is communication and its related skills that decide a person's career curve. The better one's communication skills, the higher are the chances for him/her to touch the zenith of success. The poorer one's communication skills, the greater is the possibility of not achieving one's goals.

Actually nothing happens in the professional world without communication, though it is only a means, and not the end. Still it is communication that propels the management process and serves as the lubricant for its smooth operation. It helps professionals in their five major managerial tasks, namely planning, organizing, executing, staffing, and controlling. Since every organization is a social system that involves interaction among people working at different levels, proper communication among them becomes necessary for achieving the goals of an organization.

The necessity and importance of communication skills can be gauged from the fact that professionals spend nearly three-fourth of their working time in communicating their ideas, views, and plans to others. Communication in the professional world occupies such a pivotal position that there hardly exists an activity in business and industry that does not require communication to play any role. Understandably, therefore, while selecting a new recruit, one of the first things that companies look for in an individual is the person's ability to communicate effectively with others. Our communication skill thus has the potential to make or mar our fortune.

It is precisely to address this professional need that we are required to master the various aspects of communication skills. However, before we proceed further, let us make an effort to acquaint ourselves with the other nuances of *communication*, starting with its definition, process, and features.

1.4 DEFINITION OF COMMUNICATION

The term *communication* originates from the Latin word *communico* or *communicare*, which means 'to share'. Various researchers and analysts define the term in their own way. Despite the different versions available, it can be briefly summed up that 'communication essentially means the transfer of ideas, feelings, plans, messages, or information from one person to another'. However, *communication is considered effective only when it gets the desired action or response.*

Let us explore some of the essentials of communication with the help of the discussion that follows.

1.5 PROCESS OF COMMUNICATION

Communication is a process whereby information is encoded, channelled, and sent by a sender to a receiver via a medium. The receiver then decodes the message and gives the sender a feedback. All forms of communication require a sender, a channel, a message, a receiver, and the feedback that effectively winds up the process. Communication requires both the sender and the receiver to have an area of communicative commonality. The process can be well understood with the help of Fig. 1.2.

A plenty of noises may take place in the communication process. Noise can be defined as an unplanned interference in the communication environment, causing hindrance to the successful transmission of the message (Fig. 1.3). It may mainly occur due to two reasons: disturbance in the channel/medium and/or some kind of error in the message sent.

Before we go further, it is important for us to understand how general purpose communication differs from professional communication.

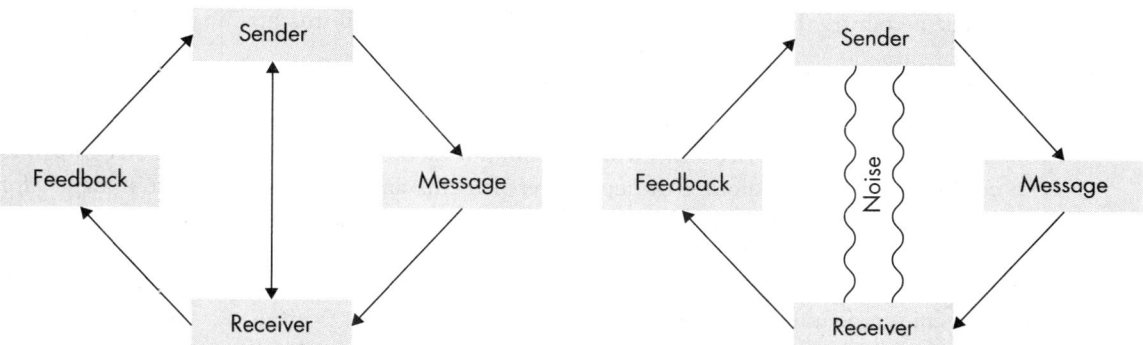

Figure 1.2   The Communication Process   **Figure 1.3**   Noise Hinders Communication Process

The following table highlights the basic differences between these two types of communication.

	General Communication	Professional Communication
Content	Contains general message	Contains a formal and professional message
Nature	Informal in style and approach	Mostly formal and objective
Structure	No set pattern of communication	Follows a set pattern such as sequence of elements in a report
Method	Mostly oral	Both oral and written
Audience	Not always for a specific audience	Always for a specific audience, e.g., customers, banks, etc.
Language	Does not normally involve the use of technical vocabulary, graphics, etc.	Frequently involves jargon, graphics, etc. for achieving the professional purposes

1.6 FEATURES OF SUCCESSFUL PROFESSIONAL COMMUNICATION

Since communication matters a lot in the professional world, it is quite important for us to get acquainted with the most important features of successful professional communication:

- Communication is a two-way process by which information is transmitted between individuals and/or organizations so that an understanding may develop among them.
- Communication is a continuous process of meaningful interactions among persons in an organization that results in meanings being perceived and understood in a desired way.
- The role of the receiver and the sender keeps changing in the entire communication activity.
- Communication broadly includes both verbal and non-verbal forms. Therefore, it also includes lip reading, finger-spelling, sign language, and body language used in face-to-face communication.
- It is a process which transmits and disseminates important ideas, thoughts, feelings, plans, etc.
- Communication skills are generally understood to be an art or technique of persuasion through the use of oral, written, and non-verbal features.

1.7 IMPORTANCE OF EFFECTIVE PROFESSIONAL COMMUNICATION

Let us now see how important communication is in the business world:

- With the emergence of multinational companies, large business houses usually operate both within and outside a country. Effective communication alone can help in maintaining a link among its various branches, offices, and sites.
- All the departments and units of an organization have to go hand in hand to achieve its goals and for that, they need to keep communicating with one another.
- Marketing research suggests that firms which communicate better sell better. Moreover, companies keep competing with one another through advertisements and other propagandist strategies for securing a higher position in the market which involve communication at every step. All of this necessitates effective communication skills.
- Effective communication helps in sustaining a harmonious relationship between salespersons and customers, and trade unions and employees in a company.
- Through effective communication, employees get job satisfaction and develop a sense of belongingness which ultimately helps the organization grow well.

1.8 DIFFERENT TYPES OF COMMUNICATION

Communication is generally classified into the following types:

Types of Communication	Brief Definition
Verbal communication I. Oral communication II. Written communication	Both spoken and written expressions are used in the communication process: I. A face-to-face interaction between the sender and the receiver who use the spoken variety of language II. Sender uses the written mode to transmit his/her messages like reports, proposals, etc.
Non-verbal communication	Communication without using a word through body language and paralinguistic features
Intrapersonal communication	Communication taking place within one's own self during self-reflection, contemplation, and meditation
Interpersonal communication	Written or oral communication that occurs between two or more persons
Extrapersonal communication	Communication with non-human entities, such as animals, birds, etc.
Mass communication	Conveying messages to an entire populace through books, the press, cinema, television, radio, the Internet, etc.
Media communication	Communication through electronic media, such as computer, Internet, cell phones, LCD, video, television, etc.

1.9 COMMUNICATION FLOW IN AN ORGANIZATION

Communication in a professional organization flows at different layers and levels which regulate, guide, and propel its flow. It is both formal and informal in nature. The different types of communication flow in an organization are as follows:

1.9.1 Formal Flow of Communication

The formal flow of communication in an organization can be divided into the types presented in the following table:

Types	Explanation
Horizontal	Takes place among people of the same rank in an organization
Vertical:	Occurs between hierarchically positioned persons and can involve both downward and upward communication:
• Upward	• Happens when information is sent to the people of higher rank—from bottom to top levels in the hierarchy
• Downward	• Exists when information moves from the higher authority to its subordinates—from top to bottom
Crosswise (Diagonal)	Takes place between managers and workers located in different functional divisions/units
Radial (Spiral)	Moves in all directions. For instance, the management circulates a copy of new bonus and incentive scheme among all the employees

1.9.2 Informal Flow of Communication

Informal communication is called ***grapevine***. Such communication is often shorn of all sorts of formalities. For instance, rumours running ripe about the company's expansion, promotion of an employee, discord between top officials, or illicit relations between two colleagues are some of the examples of grapevine. A communication of this variety flows in all directions. Grapevine may create both negative and positive impact on the environment of that organization.

1.10 BARRIERS TO COMMUNICATION

When it comes to effective communication, there are certain barriers that every organization faces. Here are a few of the most commonly-found barriers to communication in an organization:

Perceptual barriers Different people have different perceptions about the same reality. For instance, one room could be big enough for one teacher but the same room could be small for another as s/he has more number of students to teach. This kind of difference in perception leads to miscommunication.

Listening barriers Poor listening often results in incomplete, incorrect, and inconsistent responses. Sometimes people do not listen to others properly and patiently because rather than listening to others' views, they may just be waiting anxiously for the speaker to keep quiet so that they may articulate their own views.

Language barriers Language is a vehicle to effective communication and when two communicators do not share the same language, they encounter difficulty in understanding each other. This problem further aggravates when the second language learners do not use the language with accuracy in a given context. For instance, what is called *sidewalk* in the US, in Britain it is called *pavement*, whereas in India, it is called *platform*. Similarly, it is *apartment* in the US, *flat* in Britain, and *house* in India.

Cultural barriers People across the globe belong to different cultures. A cultural barrier arises when two individuals in an organization belong to different religions, states, or countries. Diverse cultures have different positive and negative meanings associated with colours, signs, designs, shapes, symbols, gestures, and posture.

Physical barriers Research shows that most offices have closed doors and cabins for those at higher levels of the organizational ladder, while the working areas are physically placed far apart. This kind of barrier prevents team members from interacting effectively with each other and authorities.

Psychological barriers Such barriers to communication distort or prevent effective communication within an organization. Subordinates usually have fear and distrust their seniors owing to the latter's dominance, arrogance, or lack of concern for them. Even if they have genuine reasons or plans or suggestions for the working of the organization, they do not feel free to articulate their thoughts due to the authoritarian attitude of their seniors.

Physiological barriers Due to headache, fatigue, or other health reasons, at times people involved in the communication process are not able to send or receive the messages properly. This leads to either complete breakdown of communication or miscommunication between them.

1.11 ROLE OF CREATIVE AND CRITICAL THINKING FOR EFFECTIVE COMMUNICATION

Critical thinking and creative thinking are considered high-order skills which are essential for professionals. ***Critical thinking*** is the active, persistent, and careful consideration of beliefs or knowledge keeping in view the available evidence, whereas ***creative thinking*** is the generation of new ideas. Both are fundamental to human intellectual progress and instrumental in the development of the society. Depending on the context and purpose, critical and creative thinking skills can be interdependent or separately applied.

Critical thinking, in fact, is a self-reflective process that involves elements of conceptualization, reasoning, analysis, interpretation, and evaluation of the available information upon which judgement is based. This involves a wide variety of skills that must be used in order to form that opinion/decision. A few of these include

- making careful observations;
- being inquisitive and asking the relevant questions;
- challenging the beliefs, examining assumptions, and probing opinions which may even be against already established facts;
- recognizing the problems and issues that may appear in future;
- assessing the validity of statements and understanding the logic and strength of arguments given; and
- making workable decisions and finding valid solutions.

The ideal critical thinker is habitually inquisitive, well-informed, dependent on reason, open-minded, flexible, objective in evaluation, honest in resolving biases, prudent in making judgements and willing to reconsider the judgements made earlier. As a professional, you will always come across new problems and aberrations to the existing practices, and your ability to think critically will help you convert the problem into an opportunity. In order to be a critical thinker, you need to be

- Inquisitive
- Systematic
- Analytical
- Open-minded
- Judicious
- Truth seeking
- Confident in reasoning

Creative thinking, on the other hand, is the generation of new ideas within or across domains of knowledge. It requires preparation, incubation, insight, evaluation, elaboration, and communication. In order to develop this, you must try to put aside the common assumptions and look beyond the conditioning that creates stereotypes, prejudices, and parochial thinking. An unconditioned response to a challenge, an inquisitive approach, an insightful penetration, and a passionate commitment to the task help us in

- bringing the existing ideas together into new configurations;
- developing new properties or possibilities for something that already exists; and
- discovering or imagining something entirely new.

Given below are a few basic principles for inculcating creative thinking:

- Be open to new thoughts, ideas, and facts.
- Keep your reading and listening faculty actively engaged in observation.
- Regard the difficulty or a problem as an opportunity.
- Enjoy the process of trying, learning, and evolving.
- Avoid jumping to conclusions; follow deferred judgements.
- Believe in cross-fertilization of ideas.
- Be your worst critic.

Thus, if you sharpen your creative and critical thinking, they will equip you with the skills which later in your professional life will provide you an edge in the competitive world of professionals.

1.12 ROLE OF INTERCULTURAL COMMUNICATION

The way we communicate is determined strongly by the culture we are groomed in. There are several aspects of communication which differ from culture to culture. Such cultural differences may determine how loud or low we talk; the directness with which we speak; the amount of emotions we express in various situations; the use or avoidance of silence; the prevalence or absence of a particular non-verbal or verbal peculiarity; and a series of defining signal which we may emit through our manners, facial expressions, posture, eye contact, tone, and pitch of our speech. Interestingly, all this may be misconstrued in an altogether different manner, depending upon the respondent's own bringing up and cultural variety. It is because of this variegated cultural confluence at workplace that it creates significant challenges to effective communication beyond the obvious barriers.

Today's companies are doing business more and more in a global context. The people that matter in any business including the suppliers, the clients, and the employees may belong to different cultures and may even be located in foreign countries. The need for effective and clear intercultural communication is becoming vital in securing success in today's global workplace. Greater understanding of intercultural differences, etiquette, protocol, and communication will certainly lead to a much higher probability of achieving business goals.

Another interesting aspect of multiculturalism is intercultural interaction between people from both the hemispheres of the earth, which throw up unique communication challenges owing to their diverse cultural nuances. Some of these cultures, such as the English-speaking and the Northern European cultures, may be regarded as belonging to individualistic cultures, with each of them enjoying simultaneous memberships in numerous overlapping, informal, loose groups that they join and leave when convenient. Churches, companies, business associations, social clubs, sports clubs, civic associations, political groups, etc. today actually become manifestation of a culturally kaleidoscopic world. In such a flux, obligations for associations and bonding to other groups are weak, and loyalty is neither required nor highly valued. Common rules of polite behaviour apply equally to group members and non-group members. Relationships with strangers are easily formed and dissolved, and friendship groups are casually replaced and re-formed. Individuals assume as primary their rights to self-expression, self-realization, and self-protection.

On the other hand, highly group-oriented cultures, such as most East and South Asian, South American, Middle Eastern, Eastern European, and sub-Saharan countries, can be seen as a collection of strong groups, starting with close family ties and extending to other blood relatives, school groups, work and military units, and community groups. In-group interaction is heavily circumscribed. Individuals are bound to their groups by heavy obligations and strict rules of intra-group relationships; loyalty is required and highly prized. Friendships exist primarily within groups, are formed with serious intent, and imply increasing reciprocal obligation.

Given such cultural diversity, it becomes important for a professional to be aware of all such culturally triggered behavioural differences and communicate accordingly.

1.13 VERBAL COMMUNICATION

Since a professional has to spend a large amount of his/her working time in speaking and listening to others besides reading and writing, most of the time he/she has to use language as a vehicle of communication. This type of communication is termed as verbal communication.

Verbal communication thus stands both for the spoken and the written word used in the communication process. It can further be divided into oral and written communication.

Oral communication A face-to-face interaction between the sender and the receiver is called oral communication. In this type of communication, there could be two or more than two persons who use spoken language as a medium of communication. For instance, whenever we make presentations, deliver speeches, participate in group discussions, appear for interviews, or simply interact with somebody, we are involved in oral communication.

Written communication In this type of communication, the sender uses the written mode to transmit his/her messages. Reports, proposals, books, handbooks, letters, emails, etc. come in this category. Written communication is routinely used for documentation purposes in business and government organizations.

1.14 NON-VERBAL COMMUNICATION

When a message is communicated without using a word, the process requires non-verbal cues to be transmitted and received. Non-verbal communication forms an important part in the world of professional communication. It can be further categorized into two parts—body language and paralinguistic features. Body language involves aspects such as personal appearance, walk, gestures, facial expressions, hand movements, posture, and eye contact. The paralinguistic features include a person's voice, volume, pitch, rate, pauses, articulation, voice modulation, etc.

1.15 TIPS FOR IMPROVEMENT

Following are some of the ways to overcome the different types of barriers we confront both in our personal and professional lives:
- Send the data only to the people who require it.
- Emphasize the major ideas.
- Delete unwanted details.
- Maintain transparency in policy matters.
- Ensure clarity in message and look for a genuine feedback.
- Understand others' emotions.
- Understand other cultures and language variations and use the appropriate variety in the given context.
- Make sure that information overload does not adversely affect the communication environment.
- Maintain openness and acknowledge that people have different perceptions and views regarding things.
- Encourage innovative ideas and views so that people do not unnecessarily live in fears.
- Listen attentively to others.
- Speak with clarity and conviction.

To sum up, barriers which are caused due to fear, ecstasy, joy, threat, etc. can easily be overcome by increasing self-awareness, careful listening, and a desire to share and build empathy towards others. Moreover, by knowing more about the receiver's background and the level of knowledge or language proficiency, we can achieve the desired result in communication.

EXERCISE 1.1

Identify the type of communication that occurs/exists in the following situations:

1. Feedback given to a student by a teacher about his/her performance in the assignment _____

2. Proposals prepared for submission to the boss _____

3. Communication between managers of various units regarding setting the production target for the next three months _____

4. The General Manager issuing instructions to subordinates _____

5. A subordinate informing the manager about a work-related problem _____

6. Announcement of change of the Eid holiday _____

7. Letter from the CEO _____

8. Chats, conversations, informal talks and the like _____

9. Counselling and training _____

10. Salesman briefing the Sales Manager about the sales of the month _____

EXERCISE 1.2

Choose the correct option from the choices given in each of the sentences:

1. Oral communication is different from written communication as it is
   (a) Spoken and structured
   (b) Spoken and transitory
   (c) Spoken and permanent
   (d) Spoken and time consuming

2. Among the following elements, which element is the medium through which a message is sent?
   (a) Sender   (b) Channel
   (c) Context   (d) Noise

3. In an organization, when a colleague shares official information with another of an equal hierarchical level, this kind of communication is called
   (a) Horizontal
   (b) Vertical
   (c) Radial
   (d) Informal

4. The Sales Manager providing tips to its team for boosting the sales of electronic items during the festive season is _____ communication.
   (a) Informational
   (b) Horizontal
   (c) Radial
   (d) Vertically downward

5. Which of the following statements is correct regarding written communication?
   (a) Written communication enjoys legal status.
   (b) Written communication is more suitable to the immediate needs of organizations.
   (c) Written communication offers immediate feedback.
   (d) Written communication is relatively informal.

6. In communication, the observation of a receiver's response is called
   (a) Feedback   (b) Survey
   (c) Channel   (d) Message

7. Writing diary every day is an example of _____ communication.
   - (a) Extrapersonal
   - (b) Intrapersonal
   - (c) Organizational
   - (d) Interpersonal

8. The Sales Manager, Monte Carlo, Jaipur speaks to the Sales Manager, Monte Carlo, Delhi regarding the sales strategy during Christmas and New Year season this year. This is an example of
   - (a) Grapevine communication
   - (b) Horizontal communication
   - (c) Upward communication
   - (d) Diagonal communication

9. Which of the following is desired for effective communication?
   - (a) Redundancy
   - (b) Clarity
   - (c) Clichés
   - (d) Circumlocution

10. Which one of the following is NOT true about effective professional communication?
   - (a) It projects and promotes a company's image, practices, and goals.
   - (b) It includes the company's manuals, training materials, reports, letters, etc.
   - (c) It is informal in nature.
   - (d) It differs from general communication in its emphasis on clarity, conciseness, accuracy, and usability.

11. Which one of the following is NOT true for written business communication?
   - (a) It is ephemeral.
   - (b) It is formal communication.
   - (c) It serves as a permanent record.
   - (d) It is preferred over oral communication for long reports.

12. Which one of the following component is 'encoded' and 'decoded' in the communication process?
   - (a) Feedback
   - (b) Sender
   - (c) Receiver
   - (d) Message

13. If the management circulates a memorandum regarding new bonus and incentive scheme among all the employees, it will be a case of _____ communication.
   - (a) Downward
   - (b) Upward
   - (c) Radial
   - (d) Grapevine

14. This type of communication takes place within an individual: _____
   - (a) Extrapersonal
   - (b) Intrapersonal
   - (c) Organizational
   - (d) Interpersonal

15. Who encodes a message?
   - (a) Sender
   - (b) Receiver
   - (c) Transmitting medium
   - (d) Both (a) and (b)

16. Mr Jha, Technical Head, Infomin tells his colleague that Mrs Leslie Sebastian, Research Head is likely to be promoted in the coming review. This kind of communication is termed as
   - (a) Horizontal
   - (b) Grapevine
   - (c) Cluster
   - (d) Noise

17. Which one of the following is NOT a feature of grapevine communication?
   - (a) Rapid
   - (b) Formal
   - (c) Multidirectional
   - (d) Voluntary and unforced

18. Which of the following is oral communication?
   - (a) Dictation
   - (b) Brochures
   - (c) Notices
   - (d) Letters

19. No communication is complete without
    (a) Noise　　　　(b) Semantic barrier
    (c) Intrapersonal　(d) Feedback

20. On his retirement day, a senior executive of a leading firm received many sincere tributes during a special dinner hosted in his honour. When finally asked to speak, he got up from his seat, spoke a few words but could not continue. What kind of barrier has occurred in this situation?
    (a) Organizational barrier
    (b) Physical barrier
    (c) Psychological barrier
    (d) Semantic barrier

EXERCISE 1.3

State whether the following statements are true (T) or false (F):

1. Effective communication leads to better work production.

2. When verbal and non-verbal messages clash, receivers tend to believe the non-verbal messages.

3. External communication often consists of emails, memos, and voice messages; internal communication consists of letters.

4. Good listening skills are inherent and cannot be inculcated.

5. To improve communication and to compete more effectively, many of today's companies encourage teamwork and better interpersonal communication.

6. Business communication is both highly formal and unstructured.

7. Before the sender completes his/her message, the listener thinks, 'I know what he/she is going to talk about.' Such type of listener is sharp, intelligent, and good at interpersonal communication skills.

8. Grapevine is a formal communication flow in an organization which has both positive and negative impact on the environment.

9. 'I had personal problems, so I could not prepare the budget efficiently. I am sorry for this. We cannot submit the details to the client today.' Such utterances reflect the lack of commitment and sincerity on the part of a professional.

10. Communication helps management only to make accurate decisions to influence organizational performance positively.

11. The observance of the receiver's reaction to the message is a kind of tool to maintain smooth communication flow between or among individuals.

12. The discussion held between the production manager and the Head, HRD, is a perfect example of horizontal communication.

13. If the management circulates a memorandum regarding change in working hours among all the employees, it will be a case of spiral communication.

14. It is imperative to listen carefully to others in order to avoid confusion regarding instructions, advice, proposals, reminders, etc.

15. Information overload strengthens the communication network in an organization.

16. Every workday, every employee frequently sends and receives messages and, as the size and complexity of the organization increases, so do the number of messages and the possibilities for communication-related problems.

17. Rigidity of thought helps the officer in maintaining a good rapport with his/her subordinates.

18. Badly encoded message leaves its receiver confused and not well-informed.

EXERCISE 1.4

Answer the following questions:

1. What does the term 'communication' imply? Why is effective communication vital in today's world?

2. How important is 'effective communication' in today's business world? Discuss a few aspects of business where communication is very important.

3. Discuss the different levels of communication in detail.

4. Explain the importance of communication in business in about 300 words.

5. What steps would you follow if you have a communication problem?

6. What are barriers to communication? Do you remember any case of poor communication? Specify what went wrong in the case that resulted in poor communication.

7. Discuss any four barriers to communication and substantiate your answer with one example for each.

8. 'A free flow of information ensures the success of an organization.' Elaborate this statement in the light of the flow of communication in any organization.

9. 'Growth and success of an organization broadly lies in continuous, multi-directional, and multi-level flow of communication.' Elaborate the statement citing suitable examples from your own experience.

10. 'Whether an organization is small or large, it is communication that binds the organization together.' Discuss in detail the formal flow of communication in an organization in the light of the above statement.

11. How does a receiver influence the sender's communication skills? Substantiate your answer with appropriate examples.

ANSWER KEY

Exercise 1.1

1. Downward communication
2. Upward communication
3. Horizontal communication
4. Downward communication
5. Upward communication
6. Radial communication
7. Downward communication
8. Grapevine
9. Downward communication
10. Upward communication

Exercise 1.2

1. b   2. b   3. a   4. d   5. a   6. a   7. b   8. b   9. b   10. c
11. a   12. d   13. c   14. b   15. a   16. b   17. b   18. a   19. d   20. c

Exercise 1.3

1. T   2. T   3. F   4. F   5. T   6. F   7. F   8. F   9. T
10. F   11. T   12. T   13. T   14. T   15. F   16. T   17. F   18. T

2

BASIC GRAMMAR AND USAGE

LEARNING OBJECTIVES

After reading this chapter, you will be able to understand
- different parts of speech, namely nouns, pronouns, adjectives, verbs, adverbs, and prepositions
- how connectives, prepositions, and adverbs link different parts of speech in English
- different types of determiners and their uses
- how different phrases work in sentences
- use of different tenses, modals, and active/passive voices in a sentence
- direct and indirect speech and their uses
- clause and its types
- what non-finites are and their types
- types and uses of punctuations

2.1 WHY GRAMMAR?

Grammar helps us develop an efficiency to express ourselves correctly in a language. It also helps us develop the habit of thinking logically and clearly. Therefore, the learning imparted through discussions, examples, practice tests, and exercises in this section aims at developing accuracy of expression and effectiveness of usage. To begin with, let us briefly know the important aspects of English grammar and practise the areas that are problematic and confusing.

2.2 FIXING NOUNS

Let's identify the different types of nouns in the paragraph given below:

Education (Abstract Noun) is often considered a **means** (Common Noun) of **transformation** (Abstract Noun). True **education** (Abstract Noun) is believed to have the **power** (Abstract Noun) to transform the ignorant and innocent **child** (Common Noun) into a knowledgeable, enlightened, happy, and evolved **individual** (Abstract Noun). Modern **education** (Abstract Noun) **system** (Abstract Noun), however, seem to have put all such noble **pursuits** (Abstract Noun) on the backburner. One after another, educational **institutions** (Common Noun) all over the **world** (Common Noun) seem to have capitulated to the **cult** (Abstract Noun) of success (Abstract Noun), as they focus on getting their **students** (Common Noun) **jobs** (Common Noun)—and through it—**money** (Common Noun), **status** (Abstract Noun), **comfort** (Abstract Noun), and **luxury** (Abstract Noun). **People** (Collective Noun) these days seem to have decided to ignore the words of **wisdom** (Abstract Noun) by the great **poet** (Common Noun) **W.B. Yeats** (Proper Noun) who, in his inimitable **way** (Common Noun), once said, 'Education (Abstract Noun) is not the filling of a **pail** (Common Noun) but the lighting of a fire (Common Noun).'

All these types of nouns, namely proper, common, collective, and abstract nouns, can act as the subject, object, or complement in a sentence. Very frequently we use them in combinations with several other kinds of words such as articles (the man), possessives (his book), demonstratives (this article), quantifiers (some rice), adjectives (black sugar), and other nouns (bomb blast). All such noun combinations can be broadly categorized as noun phrases and they too, like nouns, can act as the subject, object, or complement in a sentence. The table given below will help you revise your basic knowledge of nouns:

Noun	Definition	Examples
Proper Noun	Used for specific person, place, or thing; always starts with capital letter	Jodhpur, Taj Mahal, Shanker, Leela, Lord Buddha
Common Noun	Used for naming people, places, and things in general	Furniture, dogs, students, people, park
Collective Noun	Refers to a group of things or persons	Family, bunch, jury, team
Abstract Noun	No physical entity; refers to ideas, emotions, and concepts	Love, honesty, freedom
Compound Noun	Two or more words used as one-word noun; sometimes separated by hyphen	Rainfall, post office, classroom, mother-in-law
Countable Noun	• Singular • Plural	• Book, chair, cow • Bananas, tables, flowers
Uncountable Noun	Refers to liquids, substances, and ideas; cannot be counted	Happiness, iron, beauty, milk, bravery, oil

2.2.1 Nouns/Noun Problem: Dealing with Problem Areas

There are several difficulties that we encounter while using nouns/noun phrases in sentences. In the following section we take up some of these common areas with the help of examples and exercises.

Nouns: Singular or Plural?

Some nouns are mostly used in singular form while some other nouns are always used as plurals.

EXERCISE 2.1

Choose the correct noun forms (singular or plural) in the following sentences:

1. Where are your **belonging/belongings**?

2. The company is planning to buy **furniture/furnitures** for 3 lakh rupees in the next year.

3. Have you broken your looking **glass/glasses** again?

4. He combs his **hair/hairs** backward.

5. Every Diwali, a large amount of pollutants are emitted into the **air/airs**.

6. People interested in a variety of **music/musics** always feel young and energetic.

7. The armed **force/forces** need to be alert all the time.

8. In store we discovered the **equipment/equipments** that was not being used.

9. The **premise/premises** of the building were soon caught in flames.

10. Eventually the new **jean/jeans** got torn in the scuffle.

Nouns: Countable or Uncountable?

While many nouns can be counted and their plurals can be denoted easily by adding an -s or -es at the end such as arm, arms, one arm, both arms, one potato, one kg. potatoes, some of the nouns cannot be treated as countable entities. Attempt the following exercise to figure out how to use such nouns correctly:

 **EXERCISE 2.2**

Cross out the incorrect expressions in the following sentences. Check the right options in the answer key.

1. Give me **two breads/two packets of bread**.

2. Can we have a **coffee/a cup of coffee** to begin with?

3. The **picture gallery/pictures gallery** is to your left.

4. We are planning to buy a lot of **scenery/sceneries** for the new house.

5. **Weather is/Weathers are** usually warm in this part of the country.

6. Wrestlers often take large quantities of **milk/milks** to build their stamina.

7. The police have found some **evidence/evidences**.

8. Can I finally have some **leisures/leisure** in my life?

9. I saw the child trembling with **fears/fear**.

10. A large number of **people/peoples** have gathered to greet the leader.

11. The **goods train/good train** derailed on its way back.

12. Don't take unnecessary **air/airs**; fame is just ephemeral like a perfume.

13. The batsman makes **room/rooms** and hits the ball to the fence.

14. The sculpture was cast in exquisite **stone/stones**.

15. The crowd came to pay their last **respect/respects** to the departed soul.

For denoting plural sense for nouns usually considered uncountable, we at times use some quantifiers such as some, much, both, none, etc.

At times, the plural versions of certain nouns give different meanings from their singular forms:

Singular Noun	Plural Noun
The balloon floated *in the air*.	Don't assume *so much airs*!
I have *great respect* for the leader.	They went to pay their *last respects* to the leader.

Nouns with Unusual Plural Forms

Plurals for some nouns can be denoted by adding an -a or -ses at the end. Take a look at the following sentences:

• The company has signed a number of **memoranda** (~~memorandums~~) with other companies.

• Though a desert land, you will find quite a few **oases** (~~oasises~~) in Rajasthan.

- Suddenly, the company seems to have plunged into multiple **crises** (~~crisises~~).
- What are the **criteria** (~~criterions~~) of selection in your company?
- Several such **phenomena** (~~phenomenons~~) can be witnessed in the universe.

2.3 POSSESSIVE FORM ('S) OR OF

Take a look at the following sentences:

- It is **someone else's mobile**.
- The recommendations **of the report** have been given at the end.
- Why have you torn the **cover of the book**?
- **Dhoni's press conference** eventually silenced the journalists.
- He has fallen in love with **Keats' poetry**.
- By mistake he brought his **classmate's notebook**.

For showing possessive case of nouns, keep in mind the following tips:

- Use ('s) to show possessives of living beings such as **the king's palace, Milton's** *Paradise Lost,* **the friend's residence,** etc. (Not **the palace of the king, Paradise Lost of Milton, the residence of friend**)
- Add just the apostrophe ('s) to denote the possessive case for plural nouns, e.g., **girls' lipsticks, teachers' attitude,** etc. (Not **the girls's lipsticks, teachers's attitude**)
- Use *of* to show possessive with non-living things, e.g., **the front gate of the building, the back of the wall,** etc. (Not **the building's front gate, the wall's back**)
- Use apostrophe ('s) for the last/second noun when a pair of nouns or several nouns come together, e.g., **the monk and the pupil's journey** ended abruptly; that is Tagore, **the poet's house,** etc. (Not **the monk's and the pupil's journey** ended abruptly; that is **Tagore's the poet's house**)
- When two nouns are joined by words such as *in* and *of,* use -s with the first noun to denote plural, e.g., the **commanders-in-chief** (Not **commander-in-chiefs**), **sisters-in-law** (Not **sister-in-laws**)

2.4 PRONOUNS

The words that replace nouns are known as pronouns. Since a pronoun essentially comes in place of a noun, it can be used in subjective, objective, or possessive case. Like nouns, pronouns can also be of various types. Given below is an overview of pronouns and their different types:

Personal Pronouns	he, she, we, you, they, etc.
Impersonal Pronouns	it
Demonstrative Pronouns	this, these, that, etc.
Indefinite Pronouns	one, none, some, none, many, few, we (in general sense), etc.
Distributive Pronouns	each, either, neither, etc.
Reflexive Pronouns	myself, himself, herself, etc. (He fell and hurt himself)
Emphatic Pronouns	myself, himself, herself, etc. (He himself is going to see us)
Relative Pronouns	which, who, that

See further how pronouns can be used in nominative (subjective), objective, possessive, and reflexive/emphatic forms:

Subjective Form	Objective Form	Possessive Form	Reflexive/Emphatic Form
I	me	my, mine	myself
you	you	your, yours	yourself
he	him	his	himself
she	her	her, hers	herself
it	it	its	itself
we	us	our, ours	ourself
you	you	your, yours	yourselves
they	them	their, theirs	themselves
who	whom	whose	

While using pronouns take care of the following grammatical conventions in English usage:

- Use pronouns in subjective form when the pronoun is required to serve as the subject in a sentence:

  He (~~him~~) attended the meeting despite indifferent health.
  She (~~her~~) is planning to visit Kerala in summer holidays.
  We (~~us~~) were shocked to discover the facts.
  They (~~them~~) can be seriously mistaken.

- Use pronouns in objective form when the pronoun is required to serve as the object of a verb or preposition:

  Kanwaldeep told **her** (~~she~~) that he might have to leave the country.
  The receptionist informed **us** (~~we~~) that the forms were not yet printed.
  The policemen assaulted **them** (~~they~~) with canes.
  You cannot fool **me** (~~I~~) like that!

- Use pronouns in objective form when they come after *as, than, except,* and *be* verb:

  She is taller **than me**.
  Nobody knew about it **except us**.
  'Open the door, **it's me**.'
  Her brother was as hospitable **as her**.

- When there are two subjects or objects in a sentence, place them after nouns and arrange them in the third, second, and first person order:

  My friend and I (~~I and my friend~~) went to watch a movie last night.
  You and I (~~I and you~~) will have to sit across the table to sort it out.
  Her friend or she (~~she or her friend~~) is going to be the show stopper.
  My wife has got the coupons for **you and me** (~~me and you~~).

- Use personal and reflexive/emphatic pronouns carefully:

  He hurt himself in the process. **(Hurt no one else, but himself)**
  He hurt him in the process. (Hurt someone else)
  Having reached late, **she eventually found herself** a seat in the auditorium. **(She found the seat for herself)**
  Since she was late, **her friend found her** a seat in the auditorium. **(Someone else found the seat for her)**

- Some idiomatic expressions take reflexive/emphatic form of pronouns:

  '**Look at yourself!** Who do you think you are trying to copy?'
  She should be **ashamed of herself**.
  Leave it, I can **look after myself**.
  See this and **enjoy yourself**.

- Avoid using reflexive pronouns after verbs such as *wash, dress, undress, shave*, etc. unless the action suggests special effort:

  He changed the wig and went to attend the party.
  She dressed up quickly and rushed to office.

But:

  After the accident, **he finds it difficult to dress and shave himself**.
  After the bath, **she managed to dry herself on a towel**.

- Pronouns such as *they, you, we, one, someone*, etc. may refer to people in general and normally follow the following patterns:

  Though the government has been denying it, **we** know what the truth is. (*We* refers to people in general)
  One cannot be so philosophical all the time, **can one**?
  Someone has left **their** mobile here. (Takes singular verb *has* but is referred to in plural possessive *their*.)
  Everyone knows that **they** are supposed to stop at the red light.

Having revised the basics, let's attempt the following exercises to consolidate the concepts:

EXERCISE 2.3

Cross out the incorrect pronoun in each of the following sentences:

1. Yesterday **I/me** went to watch a movie.

2. Don't worry! It's **I/me** in the backyard.

3. Let's distribute the chocolates between you and **I/me**.

4. She does not know what to do with **her/herself**. (Both the pronouns being used for the same person)

5. **That/This** was quite ingenious.

6. We all know that Smita acts better than **him/himself**.

7. While riding, she fell off the horse and hurt **her/herself**.

8. Can she ever figure out what **she/her** is doing?

9. He is likely to drive home **him/himself** today.

10. Leave it, this bag is **our/ours**.

 **EXERCISE 2.4**

Write appropriate pronouns in the blanks of the following sentences:

1. 'What has he been searching for? Has he misplaced _____ mobile again?'

2. All of us have decided to withdraw _____ application from the office.

3. Someone seems to have forgotten _____ library card at the counter.

4. One cannot be too careful in life, can _____?

5. Everyone seems to have invested _____ money in the market.

6. The little parakeet twittered in _____ gleeful squeak.

7. Needless to say that the pleasure is entirely _____!

8. Everybody appears to have packed _____ suitcases.

9. If anyone needs to consult the doctor, _____ can first register at the counter.

10. In India, _____ don't get to learn phonetic symbols at school level.

2.5 ADJECTIVES

Take a look at the following situation and observe carefully the words in bold:

In a generally **hot** country like India, it is only in winters that one can experience the **soothing** comfort that the Sun can provide. When its **mild** and **caressing** rays begin to fill us with **comforting** warmth, happiness in **tiny** hearts begins to experience the **luxuriating** glee.

The words highlighted here are referred to as adjectives. By this time, you must have figured out that the word that describes the quality of a noun or pronoun is known as an *adjective*. There are various types of adjectives. An easy way to categorize them into different types has been suggested below:

Take a look at the following chart and observe the different types of adjectives:

Adjectives Telling Us about	Examples
Perspective, view, opinion, etc.	**Great** victory, **horrible** day, **amazing** feeling, etc.
Age/State	**Old** woman, **new** employee, **latest** rule, etc.
Colour	**Green** pants, **blue** tie, **red** face, etc.
Qualities	**Silent** march, **mild** touch, **dry** skin, **easy** task, etc.
Purpose	**Sick** leave, **eye** drops, **ear** plugs, **washing** machine, etc.
Quantity	**Some** rice, **little** strength, **much** hope, etc.
Number	**Ten** soldiers, **thirty** students, **two** girls, etc.
Size	**Big** room, **small** carpet, **huge** crowd, **long** queue, etc.
Type	**Psychological** problems, **economic** issues, etc.
Origin	**Punjabi** man, **Bengali** woman, **Japanese** child, **Spanish** language, **Indian** culture, etc.

The table given below gives a quick look at adjectives and their types:

Adjectives	Definition	Examples
Quantitative Adjectives	How many and how much	Little, few, any, six
Opinion Adjectives	Attitude, judgments, observations	Delicious, lovely, nice, beautiful
Interrogative Adjectives	Question words that qualify a noun	Which book, what reason
Comparative/Superlative Adjectives	No physical entity; refer to ideas, emotions, and concepts	Better, faster, best, strongest, bigger, eldest, toughest
Classifying Adjectives	Words that tell us type	Classical dance, Indian history, Italian pizza, Kashmiri shawl, goods train
Factual Adjectives	Size, colour, age, shape, etc.	Black, small, big, oval

The most important thing about adjectives is not to worry about their category or type, but to use them accurately. Given below are some of the notable aspects and the usage of adjectives:

- Choose carefully between **-er, -est, -ier, -iest,** and **more, most** for appropriate comparison:

  This room is **bigger than** the adjacent one. (Single syllable words such as *big, short, nice, fit, short, large,* etc. take mostly the **-er, -est** comparative structures.)
  It was the **happiest** day of his life. (Words ending in consonant + y structures such as *happy, lucky, dirty, pretty, silly, funny, easy,* etc. take **-ier, -iest** comparatives.)

- Longer adjectives take **more + adjective** and **most + adjective** structures in comparisons:

  This is the **most advanced** (~~advancest~~) form of technology.
  He was **more comfortable** (~~comfortabler~~) sitting in the cosy room.

- Some adjectives can take **both -er, -est, and more, most** constructions:

  Ramesh is the **most clever (or the cleverest)** boy in this class.
  The **simplest girl (or the most simple)** was actually the **ablest (or the most able)** in the class.

- Some adjectives are **not used in comparative and superlative degrees**:

  In that situation, it was the **perfect decision** (~~more perfect, most perfect~~).
  Given the circumstances it was the **ideal choice** (~~more ideal choice, most ideal choice~~) she could make.

- **The more ... the more** constructions need to be used properly:

  The higher you go, **the cooler** it gets.
  The more positive you are, **the more successful** you can become.
  The richer he grew, **the more impatient** he became for more money.
  The more careful you are in decision making, **the less regrets** you accumulate in life.

- **The + adjective** constructions suggest plural subjects. Use plural verbs for them:

  The poor are always exploited by the rich.
  The young are mostly in a hurry to do things.
  The old find it difficult with the rapid changes in the society.

- Adjective pairs formed with endings **-ing** and **-ed** are confusing. Distinguish them properly:

  We were **amused** to see their antics.
  The teacher narrated an **amusing** anecdote in the class.
  The manager seemed **interested**.
  It was an **interesting** offer to make.

- See the meaning and usage of **few, a few, the few/little, a little, the little** in the following examples:

  Few reporters were seen at the venue.   (Hardly any/no reporters were seen.)
  A few reporters were seen at the venue.   (Some reports were seen.)
  The few reporters who were there too left quickly.   (Whatever small number of reporters)
  There is **little** chance of his survival.   (Hardly any hope of survival = bad news)
  There is **a little** chance of his survival.   (Some chances of survival = good news)
  The little chance that the patient had soon
  vanished as he quickly slipped into a coma.   (Whatever little chance)

- **Compare only the comparable variables.** Errors creep in when incomparable variables are forced into comparison. Avoid such faulty comparisons. Observe the examples given below:

  The population of America is greater **than Canada**.   (Incorrect)
  The population of America is greater **than that of Canada**.   (Correct)

- See examples of **older, oldest** and **elder, eldest** to understand the difference between them:

  Meet my **eldest brother**. (relation in the same family)
  He is the **oldest employee** in our organization. (no family relation)
  The **elder one** is in England.
  The **older couple** looked particularly disappointed.

- Some adjectives take **to** instead of **than** in comparisons:

  In office, she is **superior to me** (~~superior than me~~) in rank.
  In some extremely backward communities, women are regarded as **inferior to** men.

- Use **as … as** or **so … as** judiciously:

  This room is **as spacious as** the one that you have just seen. (Appropriate)
  This room is **so spacious as** the one that you have just seen. (Inappropriate)

  But:

  Shashank is **not so brilliant as** Sarvesh. (Possible)
  Shashank is **not as brilliant as** Sarvesh. (Also possible)

- Read the following examples to know the difference between **last** and **latest**:

  The **last man in the queue** (~~latest man in the queue~~) too collapsed due to oppressive heat.
  The **latest technology** (~~last technology~~) has brought about phenomenal changes in our lives.

EXERCISE 2.5

Rewrite the following sentences using appropriate adjectives:

1. The report is really good; it not only discusses the problem but also gives few suggestions.

   _____

   _____

2. The faster you drive on a serpentine hilly road, poorer are your chances of returning home safely.

   _____

   _____

3. Yesterday he was really sick, but today he is more better.

   _____

   _____

4. This film is so good as the one released last year by the same director.

   _____

   _____

5. Our eldest man in the colony too left the house recently.

   _____

   _____

6. I approached the officer, but he hardly seemed interesting in listening to me.

   _____

   _____

7. You can certainly do it, but you need to exert little more.

   _____

   _____

8. Movies produced in India are more than Iran.

   _____

   _____

9. Ashwin is the most successful spinner than any other spinners in contemporary Indian team.

   _____

   _____

   _____

10. Poors are easily manipulated by rich.

    _____

    _____

2.6 VERBS

The verb is probably the most important component of English language. You can think of a sentence without a subject or an object but you cannot think of a sentence without a verb. Even the shortest sentence contains a verb. You can make a one-word sentence with a verb, for example in day-to-day life; you use some of the following expressions:

Stop!   Come!   Go!   Sit!

However, you cannot make a one-word sentence with any other part of speech.

Verbs are commonly regarded as 'action words' in a sentence. In English language, there are a large number of verbs that denote action, i.e., highlight the idea of 'doing' something. For example, words such as *write, teach, sing, dance,* and *work* convey some action.

But some verbs do not give the idea of action; they give the idea of existence or a state of 'being'. For example, verbs such as *be, appear, exist, seem, feel,* and *belong* convey a state.

A verb always has an explicit or implied subject. For example,

Professor Bhat teaches us English.

Professor Bhat is the explicit subject in this sentence, whereas in the following sentence the subject is implied:

Stop!

You is an implied subject here.

In simple terms, therefore, we can say that *verbs* are the words that tell us what a subject does or is; they describe

1. Action (Siddarth **plays** cricket very well.)
2. State (Mohit **looks** very tired.)

There is something very special about verbs in English. Almost all the verbs in English change in form according to subject and tense. For example, the verbs *sing, dance,* and *cry* have the following forms:

- to sing, sing, sings, sang, singing, sung
- to dance, dance, dances, danced, dancing
- to cry, cry, cries, cried, crying

Now let us learn more about verbs.

2.6.1 Classification of Verbs

Read the following sentences carefully and take a note of the verbs used in them.

- Mr Verma is a doctor.
- The earth revolves round the sun.
- We must pay our taxes in time.

Are the above verbs same in nature? No! In fact, there are many different types of verbs, which are shown in Fig. 2.1 below.

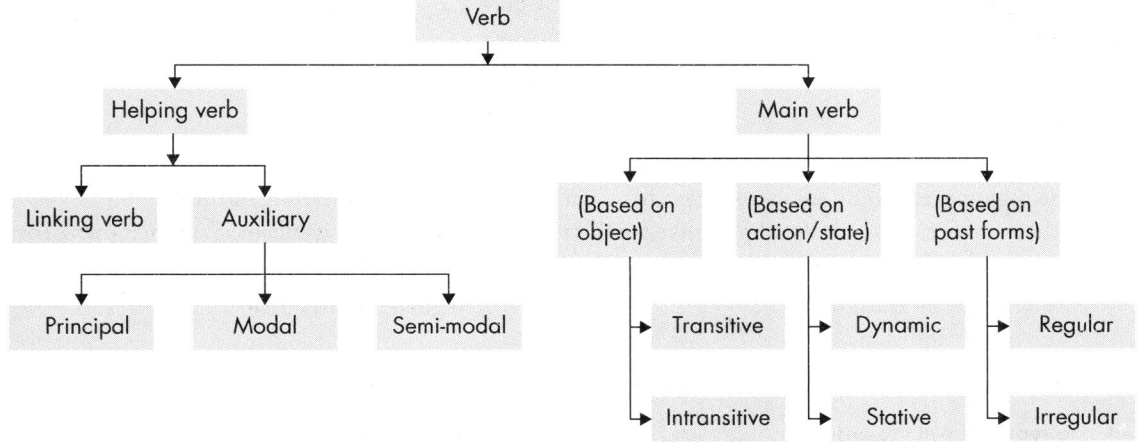

Figure 2.1 Different Types of Verbs

1. **Helping Verbs**: primary/modal
2. **Main Verbs**: transitive/intransitive, dynamic/stative, regular/irregular

Linking verbs or copular verbs Usually, a linking verb shows equality (=) or a change to a different state (→). Linking verbs are mostly used intransitively. Linking verbs such as 'be', 'seem', 'become', and 'look' are quite commonly used in everyday speech. Such verbs are generally followed by complements. For instance, look at the following examples:

- Manisha is intelligent. (Manisha = intelligent)
- Dr Gupta is a surgeon. (Dr Gupta = surgeon)
- Rohit seems tired. (Rohit = tired)
- Ashok sounds greedy. (Ashok = greedy)

- The sky became dark. (the sky → dark)
- The bread has gone stale. (bread → stale)
- His body turned pale. (body → pale)

Auxiliary verbs Auxiliary verbs are the verbs which help to form a tense or an expression. They however cannot form a complete sentence on their own and require main verbs to denote the action. The principal auxiliaries are *to be*, *to have*, and *to do*. However, modals and semi-modals also form auxiliaries since they combine the main verb to convey a distinct sense. Figure 2.2 shows the different types of auxiliary verbs.

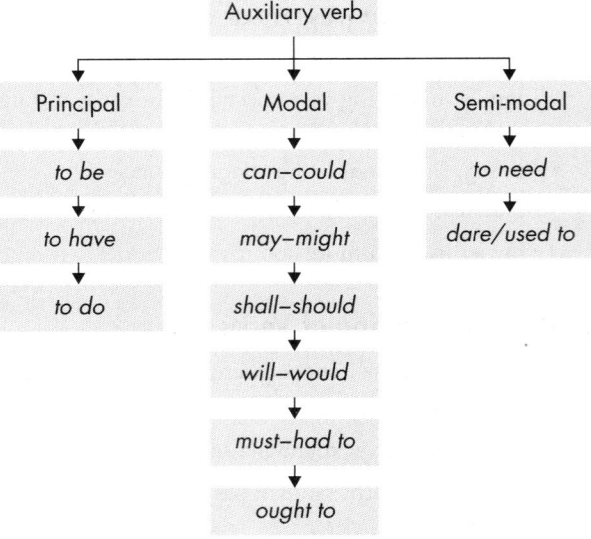

Figure 2.2 Different Types of Auxiliary Verbs

Let us read the following examples:

- I am waiting for you. (to be auxiliary)
- My father has deposited that money in the bank. (**to have** auxiliary)
- You can do this project in time. (**can** auxiliary)
- They used to visit us quite often (**used to** auxiliary)

Main Verbs

Read the following sentences:

- I **write**.
- Children **play**.

- They **run**.
- We **laugh**.

These highlighted words are *main verbs*; they denote action and have meaning of their own. Main verbs are also called lexical verbs. Unlike auxiliary verbs, main verbs have meaning on their own. There are thousands of main verbs and we can classify them in the following ways:

- Transitive and intransitive
- Dynamic and static

- Regular and irregular

Transitive and intransitive verbs Read the following sentences carefully:

- He **read** a novel yesterday.
- My mother has **planned** a trip to Mumbai.

- Snigdha **loves** swimming.
- Maria **wrote** a letter to Peter.

The verbs in the above sentences—read, planned, loves, wrote—require objects in order to complete the sentences. Such verbs are called transitive verbs.

A *transitive verb* takes a direct object. For example, *Somebody killed the snake*. An *intransitive verb* does not require a direct object. For example, *He died*. However, many verbs can be used transitively as well as intransitively.

Now look at the following examples:

- I am reaching shortly.
- My friend speaks fast.
- We are flying high in the sky.

- The letter reached us last night.
- They speak English fluently.
- Children are flying kites today.

Dynamic and stative verbs The verbs which describe actions are called 'dynamic verbs'. For example, *hit, kill, fight, run, go, throw, explode, write*, etc. These can be used with continuous tenses. There are other verbs which describe a state or a situation and are called 'stative'. For example, *like, love, prefer, impress, hear, see, sound, belong to, consist of, need, resemble, seem*, etc. They cannot normally be used with continuous tenses (though some of them can be used with continuous tenses with a change in meaning).

Regular and irregular verbs This is another classification which you need to understand regarding verbs. The only real difference between regular and irregular verbs is that they have different endings for their past tense and past participle tense forms. For regular verbs, the past tense ending and past participle ending is always the same: *-ed*. For irregular verbs, the past tense and the past participle endings are variable; so it becomes essential to learn them by heart.

Regular verbs The following examples give the base, past tense, and past participle forms of a few regular verbs:

- Cook, cooked, cooked
- Clean, cleaned, cleaned
- Water, watered, watered
- Turn, turned, turned

- Smile, smiled, smiled
- Wash, washed, washed
- Smoke, smoked, smoked
- Work, worked, worked

Irregular verbs The following examples give the base, past tense, and past participle forms of some irregular verbs:

- Do, did, done
- Eat, ate, eaten
- Drink, drank, drunk
- Cut, cut, cut
- Sleep, slept, slept

- Write, wrote, written
- Sing, sang, sung
- Be, was, been
- Throw, threw, thrown
- See, saw, seen

2.7 ADVERBS

While adjectives modify a noun or pronoun, adverbs add meanings to a **verb**, an **adjective**, and **another adverb**. See the following examples and observe the functions of adverbs:

- Children **performed brilliantly**.   **(Verb + Adverb)**
- It was **meticulously planned**.   (Adverb + Verb)
- It was **very meticulously planned**.   (Adverb + Adverb + Verb)
- They were **really good friends**.   (Adverb + Adjective + Noun)

EXERCISE 2.6

Taking a clue from the examples above, identify whether the words highlighted in the sentences below are adjectives or adverbs. Also write, in the space, the structure of the words given in bold. The first sentence has been solved for you:

1. The thief *walked briskly* through the groove. **briskly (Adv); (Verb + Adverb)**

2. The speaker was **really nervous**. _____

3. The speaker spoke **rather nervously**. _____

4. The food served in the party was not **good enough.** _____

5. How can you be **so mean?** _____

6. We reached the airport **quite early**. _____

7. Father's sudden death **terribly shook** him. _____

8. For the meeting, he seemed **elegantly poised**.

9. It was **rather surprising** that she did not scream at him. _____

10. The shuttler was **quite excited** at having achieved a milestone in her career. _____

Many a time we form adverbs from adjectives and complements. See the following examples:

It was an **easy** victory.	The contest was **easily** won.
He seemed **furious.**	He paced about the room **furiously**.
Nobody was prepared for the leader's **sudden** death.	**Suddenly,** a visitor appeared from nowhere.
Why are you being so **unreasonable**?	Why are you behaving so **unreasonably?**
Last year, we bought an **automatic** washing machine.	It **automatically** washes all types of clothes.

EXERCISE 2.7

Given below is a passage about a visit to some fort. Choose either the adjective or the adverb from the options given for each blank:

Visiting Amer Fort in Jaipur was a _____ **(wonderful/wonderfully)** experience. Having crossed the crowded wall city area, our bus moved _____ **(slow/slowly)** as we began to mount the road leading to the fort. It was an _____ **(extreme/extremely)** cold day. The bus left us right in front of a hill at the top of which the fort stood _____ **(majestic/majestically)**. The road in front of it was _____ **(heavy/heavily)** crowded. Scores of tourists both from India and abroad had thronged the place. As a result, the _____ **(narrow/narrowly)** road in front of it was swarmed with multiple city buses, tourist buses, cars, auto-rickshaws, and two wheelers. The young and the age, men and women, all of them kept getting off their respective vehicles and began to move closer to the fort's _____ **(glorious/**

gloriously) inviting aura. All of them seemed _____ **(excited/exciting)** at having been given an opportunity to witness one of the ageless monuments of Indian history. Among all age groups the children began their upward march

quite _____ **(energetic/energetically).** The young kept them good company while the age trudged behind _____ **(leisure/leisurely).**

Just as there are various types of nouns, pronouns, and adjectives, adverbs too are of various kinds. Take a look at the table given below to understand the different types of adverbs:

Adverbs	Examples
Adverb of Time	Now, soon, always, still, yet, etc.
Adverb of Manner	Poorly, brilliantly, leisurely, elegantly, etc.
Adverb of Place	Here, there, everywhere, inside, etc.
Adverb of Frequency	Usually, often, occasionally, never, etc.
Adverb of Degree	Quite, very, extremely, rather, etc.
Adverb of Affirmation or Negation	Certainly, definitely, absolutely, etc.

An important thing to learn about adverbs is to place them accurately in a sentence. Take a look at the following examples and see how a change in the position of the adverb can change the meaning of the sentence:

- **Only** a fool like you will do such a thing!   (**Nobody else** but only a fool will do.)
- A fool like you will do such a thing **only**!   (A fool will do **nothing else** but only such a thing.)
- **Clearly**, he did not answer the question.   (**It is clear** that he **did not answer**.)
- He did not answer the question **clearly**.   (He tried but **could not give a clear answer**.)

1. Usually, the type of adverb can decide its placement in a sentence. For instance, Adverbs of Manner are generally placed in the beginning or at the end of a sentence.
2. Adverbs of Time and Place are placed after the verb or the object.
3. Adverbs of Frequency are placed between the subject and the verb.

See the examples below to understand the positioning of adverbs:

- Murad entered the room quite **excitedly**.   (Adverb of Manner)
- Rimika **never** visits us now.   (Adverb of Frequency)
- He hasn't come **yet**.   (Adverb of Time)

Note At times, the type of verb can decide the position of adverb in a sentence. For example:

- **Rohan is never** late for school.   (Subject + Verb + Adverb)
- **Smita never fails** to answer the question.   (Subject + Adverb + Verb)

EXERCISE 2.8

Rewrite the following sentences placing the adverbs correctly in each of them:

1. He could sense the problem always.

   _____

2. Rub gently the old man's leg.

   _____

3. The plane landed somehow safely.

   _____

4. Last month sharply the sales fell.

   _____

5. Nearly he was dead in the accident.

   _____

6. This man speaks the truth always.

7. Nadal pumped aggressively the air.

   _____

8. The newly recruited marketing manager quietly sat in the meeting.

   _____

   _____

9. Place there the book.

   _____

10. You could see him rarely reaching late.

    _____

2.7.1 Adverbs: Areas of Concern

Errors creep in as we often overlook the minute differences in the meaning and usage of some adverbs. Therefore, take care of the following confusing pairs of adverbs:

Quite and Rather **Quite** is usually used in positive remarks. **Rather** is used in negative remarks.

- Food was **quite good**.   (Positive Remark)
- Movie was **rather boring**.   (Negative Remark)
- They spoke to us **quite nicely**.   (Positive Remark)
- They handled the drunk **rather shabbily**.   (Negative Remark)

Note The adverb **quite** can be used to convey both positive and negative ideas but **rather** is normally used to convey a negative sense:

- It was **quite strange** that they did not think of it in advance.   (Correct)
- Keats' poetry is **rather pictorial**.   (Incorrect)

Quite suggests 'completely' and 'fairly' with some adjectives:

- *Waiting for Godot* was written **quite absurdly**.
- Don't expect her to turn up in time; she is **quite hopeless** in this sense.
- At the end of the day, I felt **quite exhausted**.
- The younger son's parking sense is **quite horrible**.

Still and Yet **Still is** used in both positive and negative statements. **Yet** is used mostly in negative statements.

- Have you received any reply? No, not **yet**.
- Are you **still** waiting for the reply?

- After holidays, he hasn't joined office **yet**.
- You are nearly twenty and you **still** can't manage even your wardrobe!

Too and Enough **Too** is placed before an adjective or adverb for negative connotations and is not appropriate for conveying appreciation and or positive attributes. **Enough** is placed after an adjective or adverb for both positive and negative connotations.

- The thief was **too short** to jump the wall.   (too + negative attribute)
- The thief was **tall enough** to easily jump the wall.   (positive attribute + enough)
- The thief was **not strong enough** to jump the wall.   (not + positive attribute + enough)

2.8 PREPOSITIONS

Take a look at the examples given below and observe carefully the highlighted words:

- Our train is passing **through** a tunnel.
- Are you still confused **about** the career options?
- Majestic, the super boar, is speaking **at** the top of his voice.
- Mr Vats is travelling **by** plane.
- Is he junior to you **in** the department?
- The river is flowing **above** the danger mark.
- The child was running **towards** me.
- I am waiting for you **at** the railway station.

The small words highlighted in all these sentences are known as prepositions and are placed before a noun or pronoun to establish their relation with other parts of the sentences. However tiny they might be, prepositions can completely change the meaning of a sentence. See how small prepositions change meanings in the following sentences:

- Casper, the little cat, is sitting **on** the moving car.
- Casper, the little cat, is sitting **underneath** the moving car.
- Casper, the little cat, is sitting **in** the moving car.
- Casper, the little cat, is sitting **beside** the moving car.

Therefore, in order to express ourselves correctly, we need to use prepositions accurately while speaking English. Let's learn how with the understanding of standard practice, these prepositions can be used appropriately. **In, on, at, under, inside, underneath** are used to denote a position:

- Mother is **inside** the room.
- The suitcase is **on** the trunk.
- The keys are **in** the drawer.
- I am waiting for you **at** the doctor's.
- A slimy lizard slid **underneath** the carpet last night.

Since all of these denote position, understanding which preposition is to be used to communicate ourselves appropriately is crucially important. To discover their distinctive meanings, take a look at the following expressions:

- In Delhi, in garden, in US, in the queue, in 1972, in the morning, in winter, in the month, in class, in lesson, in photographs, in films, in hospital, etc.
- On the road, on sixth floor, on page 46, on the beach, on the rooftop, on Monday, on the tree, on Sunday morning, on that day, etc.
- At her desk, at the bus stand, at 458/2 Mandir Marg, at the function, at the bottom, at home, at the moment, at night, at two o'clock , etc.

Note: **In** and **at** are both used for buildings. Observe the difference:

- Just five spectators were there **in** the theatre.   (inside the building)

- Where are you? I am waiting for you **at** the theatre.　(reference is to venue)
- There was chaos all around, so we waited **in** the hotel.　(inside the building)
- We were **at** the hotel.　(taking food probably)

Since prepositions depend a lot on collocations, remember to pick the right preposition by following the commonly practised grammatical conventions. Given below are some of the areas where such grammatical conventions can resolve our confusion:

In, On, or *By* **for Transport** **By** without a/an/the is used to denote means of transport. **On** and **in** too are possible with a/an/the.

- We are going to Jodhpur **by train**.　(*by* suggests mode of transport)
- The keynote speaker will come **by air**.　(not *by the air*)
- The salesman often comes **on his bike**.　(not *in* or *by his bike*)
- The passengers are sitting even **on the coach**.　(on top of it)
- There were thirty passengers **in the coach**.　(inside the coach)

In Time **or** *On Time?*

- Starting sharp at 6, we were quite **in time** for the flight.　(early enough)
- Don't worry, we are **on time**.　(at the right time)
- These days, many trains reach **on time**.　(at the scheduled time)
- We reached the station **just in time**.　(at the last moment)

In the Way **or** *On the Way, In the End* **or** *At the End*

- **On the way**, we observed fascinating sights.　(while journeying)
- The tree fell **in the way** and we could not move for a while.　(blocking the road)
- **At the end**, however, the hero makes the villain realize his folly with mighty punches on his face.　(when the movie gets over)
- Clara keeps rejecting suitors only to choose the worst of them **in the end**.　(after a long time, finally)

By, Until, **or** *Till*

- The applications must reach the office **by 31st January 2017**.　(not later than)
- The university website will not be open **until 10th January 2017**.　(not before)
- We will need the report **by next Friday**.　(not later than)
- I'll not be able to look at your report **until next Friday**.　(not before)
- Wait, **till I come back**.　(somewhat informal)

Into, Onto **and** *To* **for suggesting movement**

- On hearing this, she went **into the room**.　(inside)
- I am going **to the meeting**.　(purpose)
- Pour water **into the jug**.　(direction)
- He barged **into the room** flustered and angry.　(enter)
- I wonder how his name got **onto the list of awardees**.　(something added to a list, etc.)

Beside or *Besides*

- The bridegroom sat **beside** (not besides) the groom.

  (**beside** is a preposition meaning **by the side of**)

- **Besides** these, the company can also adopt other measures to preempt such accidents in future.

  (**besides** is a conjunction meaning **apart from, in addition to**)

For or *Since*

- It has been raining **since morning**. (since – point of time)
- It has been raining **for the last two hours**. (for – period of time)

Before or *In front of*

- The famous statue is right **in front of the museum**. (for non-living objects)
- The actress has been asked to appear **before the jury**. (for living beings)
- The students were waiting for the Principal **in front of the college gate**. (for non-living objects)
- How many more people are standing **before you**? (for living beings)

With and *Within*

- Can I come **with you**? (suggesting togetherness)
- We'll have to submit the assignment **within a fortnight**. (before the end of …)
- You can do wonders **with such a team**. (suggests company togetherness)
- The flower began to wither **within a week or so**. (before the end of …)

For and *From*

- I have come **for the interview**. (purpose)
- The candidate had come **from Patna**. (indicates the place)
- Madhubala is still revered **for her beauty**. (implied)
- **From East to West**, you observe variegated shades of culture in this country. (indicates direction)

To or *With*

- On this issue, I **agree with her**. (to share a point of view)
- I don't get along well with her even though most of the time I **agree to her suggestions**. (to accede to)

Above or *Over*

- The river is flowing **above** the danger mark. (higher than)
- They have built a bridge **over** the river. (indicates position)

Below or *Under*

- Pesky, the little pet, is sitting quietly **under the table**. (covered by)
- After the snowfall, the temperature recorded **below freezing point**. (less than)

About and *Of*

- Do you wish to **talk about** your marriage? (more informal)
- Do you ever **think of** your marriage? (plan)

- The singer was **talking about** *ragas* when the radio went off. (discuss)
- Last night I **dreamt of** parachuting to an alien land and meeting strangers. (phrasal verb)
- The report discusses the problem exhaustively. (**not discusses about the problem**) (common error)

Further, let's learn more about prepositions by the grammatical structures that precede or follow them. In order to accommodate more such collocations small expressions have been written instead of full sentences:

Collocations: Verbs + Prepositions

endowed with	accustomed to	filled with
consist of	apprised of	laughed at
pay for	belong to	enquire about
suffer from	accused of	discourage from
thank for	grateful to	compare with/to
suspected of	aimed at	refer to
besotted with	spend on	translate into
add to	blamed for	critical of
criticized for	split into	invited to
provided with	alarmed at	situated at
robbed of	armed with	judged by
accessible to	confined to	addicted to
worried about	fond of	reflected on

Going further, attempt the following exercises to learn more about prepositions:

EXERCISE 2.9

Fill in the blanks with appropriate prepositions:

1. Are you listening _____ me?

2. We are waiting _____ the train.

3. Can you do it _____ me?

4. He is going _____ present a paper there.

5. The couple is seen living _____ the first floor.

6. _____ such situations all you need is grit and determination.

7. He always confuses _____ Sarita and her sister.

8. Stop it! You have been fooling around _____ quite some time now.

9. The sandalwood thief slipped _____ the thick dark grove of trees.

10. These two girls keep whispering _____ each other's ears all the time!

EXERCISE 2.10

Pick correct prepositional expressions from the options given for each of the following sentences:

1. He is _____ his neighbours.
   (a) sick with   (b) sick of

2. I saw him standing and _____ the mirror.
   (a) looking into   (b) looking at

3. Mostly, the dejected writer remains _____ _____ himself.
   (a) confined to   (b) confined with

4. Mr Singh has often been _____ for his poor verbal skills.
   (a) criticized with   (b) criticized for

5. Gradually, she was _____ receiving visitors in evenings.
   (a) accustomed to   (b) accustomed with

6. _____! Why can't you start all over again?
   (a) come on   (b) come in

7. The book _____ twenty chapters.
   (a) consists with   (b) consists of

8. My grandmother generally gets _____ small happenings around.
   (a) alarmed at   (b) alarmed with

9. Anita Desai has often been _____ Virginia Woolf.
   (a) compared for   (b) compared with/to

10. Unfortunately, she married someone who was _____ drugs and ruined himself within two months of their wedding.
    (a) addicted on   (b) addicted to

EXERCISE 2.11

Cross out the incorrect prepositions/prepositional phrases in the following sentences:

1. I am **concerned about/concerned with** what is going to happen to the programme.

2. The poor in this country are even **deprived of/deprived for** two square meals a day.

3. Caught up in adverse circumstances, he is **fighting with/fighting for** his survival.

4. Desperately, she moved from window to window, **enquiring from/enquiring about** the plane.

5. You are not supposed to hit your opponent **under the belt point/below the belt point**.

6. A lot **depends on/depends at** how the middle order performs.

7. Initially, the producer was not **interested with/interested in** the script.

8. After the sudden demise of their father, they have to **fend for/fend at** themselves.

9. The fault is entirely yours! You were standing right **in the middle of the road/on the middle of the road**!

10. All these monuments were damaged **with the fanatic intruder/by the fanatic intruder**.

EXERCISE 2.12

Read the extract below and fill in the blanks with appropriate prepositions:

I reached the cinema hall well _____ time to be right _____ front _____ the queue _____ the ticket-window. I kept standing there _____ a long while, the window remained shut, but the queue _____ me kept growing all the time. More and more people joined ____ and the long queue swell even ____ the boundary wall. Thrilled ____ the idea ____ leading such a large contingent ____cinegoers, I really felt flattered ____ my achievement. Meanwhile, two eager boys ____ me started talking _____ what was so great about the movie. They first began _____ how good the acting _____ their favourite movie star was. One ____ one, they analysed his dancing, romancing, fighting, cavorting, and jumping skills. Then their discussion drifted _____ how the villain too had emerged as potent adversary ____ the protagonist. Having discussed the exploits of the hero and the villain, they went _____ describe how wonderful had their favourite heroine looked ____ each frame ____ the movie and how charming she looked ____ her dancing sequence! Silently cursing them ____ ruining all my interest ____ the movie, I kept waiting ____ the ticket-window to open.

2.9 CONNECTIVES, PREPOSITIONS, AND ADVERBS AS LINKERS

In English, we use several connectives, prepositions, and adverbs to link different parts of speech, clauses, and sentences. Broadly, they can be referred to as linkers and discourse markers. In this section, we'll learn how to use such linking devices accurately and effectively so that the errors that arise of them can be avoided.

Given below are some examples and usage based exercises on such linkers so that you can use them correctly:

Broad Classification of Linkers

Purpose of Linkers	Examples
To add	and, also, too, as well, as well as, in addition, besides, furthermore, further, moreover, moving further, furthermore, again, and so on and so forth
To illustrate	for example, for instance, in fact, etc.
To highlight time...event sequence	when, while, after, now, once, after, until, before, till, as soon as, no sooner ... than, hardly had/scarcely had ... when, the moment, from the time, since, even as, etc.
To compare and contrast	but, although, though, on the other hand, still, even then, however, nevertheless, nonetheless, on the opposite, all the same, on the other hand, after all, on the contrary, anyway, since, while, whereas, etc.
To underline reasons	because, so, consequently, furthermore, therefore, as a result
To indicate conditions	if, in case, unless, until, as long as
To establish purpose	to, in order to, so that, so as to, for
Pair and choice linkers	or, neither, either, nor, either ... or, neither ... nor, both ... and, not only ... but also
To concede and disagree	even if, even do, in spite of, despite, anyhow, somehow

To conclude ideas	to end, in the end, coming to the end, to wind up, to sum up, in short, before I close, briefly, in a nutshell
Other linkers	as if, as though, even if, even though, even so, indeed, and speaking of, while coming to describe, regarding, as regards, with regard to, by the way, as far as, as for that, to begin with, on the whole, quite frankly, admittedly, understandably, obviously, I guess, I reckon, I am afraid, or rather, actually, at least, sort of, talking/speaking about/of, all right, right, OK, to a great extent, to some extent, in general, broadly speaking, mind you, I mean, you know, in my view/opinion, I/suppose/feel, well, actually, to tell the truth, herein, herewith, hereby, by and by, whereupon, wherein, henceforth, erstwhile, then on, from that time/day/month/moment, etc.

Now, let's see how some of these linkers are used in sentences:

But and *Although*

- I wanted to attend the party, **but** was not feeling well.
- **Although** I wanted to attend the party, I was not feeling well.
- **Though** I wanted to attend the party, I was not feeling well. (*though* is a bit informal)

Even if and *Even though*

- **Even though** the movie is boring, people will go and watch it. (the movie is boring)
- **Even if** the movie is boring, people will go and watch it. (the movie may be boring)

In spite of and *Despite* for concession

- **Despite injury**, Kapil Dev took a five-wicket haul to dismiss the mighty Aussies on a paltry 81 way back in 1981–82.
- **Inspite of injury**, Kapil Dev took a five-wicket haul to dismiss the mighty Aussies on a paltry 81 way back in 1981–82.

To, For, In order to, So that, So as to, So as not to, In order not to, etc. for purpose

- I'll send you an alert **so that** you don't forget about it.
- I hurried up **so as not to** miss the bus. (I hurried up not to miss the bus.)
- Why don't you join us **for** lunch?
- See, now you are beginning to dye your hair **to** look young! (**to** is a bit informal than **in order to**)

While and *Whereas* for comparison; *While* for simultaneous action

- I saw a snake **while** coming back home.
- Dr Vishakha is an expert **while/whereas** her husband is just a naïve.

Because and *So* for reason

- I had to take back the charge from her **because** she was just very casual.
- She was very casual, **so** I had to take back the charge from her.

In case, If, Unless, Until, etc. for condition

- **In case** he comes, tell him that I am not there.
- **Unless** you improve your handwriting, you are not going to score well in exam.
- **If** you listen to me patiently now, you may not have to regret in future.

And* and *As well as **And** is sometimes confused with **as well as**. **And** is additive (This + That). **As well as** is parenthetical; similar to **with, alongside, besides,** and **in addition to**. The first noun decides whether the noun is singular or plural.

- **The owner as well as** the servant **is** (~~are~~) in the showroom.
- **The boys as well as** the Principal **are** (~~is~~) standing in the field.
- The Principal **as well as** the boys **are** (~~is~~) standing in the field. (Better option)

EXERCISE 2.13

Choosing from linkers and discourse markers such as *by the way, while, whereas, because, as if, as though, either... or, neither ... nor, whether ... or,* and *as*, fill in each of the following blanks appropriately:

1. _____ you talk sense, _____ you keep your mouth shut!

2. Women at the club kept gossiping _____ their husbands played cards.

3. He talks to me _____ he were my boss.

4. _____ you allow me _____ not, I am going to the rave party.

5. The application cannot be submitted now _____ the last date was 13 October 2016.

6. Our company backs itself on customized

   products _____ they thrive on their gross turnover.

7. You are telling me _____ I keep doing it repeatedly.

8. The boy _____ called up _____ sent the pen drive.

9. _____, when is your flight?

10. _____ you don't hold the membership card, we cannot consider giving you the discount.

EXERCISE 2.14

For each of the blanks in the following sentences some options are given. Choose the appropriate linkers for them:

1. I know it may just be a futile journey. _____, I am going to give it a try.
   (a) By all means   (b) Nevertheless

2. _____ your story sounds interesting, I don't think I am sufficiently impressed!
   (a) As though   (b) Even though

3. _____ the backlog issue is concerned, we are going to clear it up in the next week.
   (a) As far as   (b) Though

4. The imaginative captain kept rotating his

   bowlers _____ the batsmen did not settle into a rhythm.
   (a) So as not to   (b) So that

5. I searched for him everywhere, _____ he was not seen anywhere.
   (a) In fact   (b) but

6. _____ the impact of globalization on our culture, let's understand what has our culture been.
   (a) Coming to   (b) About

7. _____ is the situation, you need not lose heart.
   (a) Whatever (b) Whoever

8. _____ she spotted the assailant in the kitchen, she let out a stifled scream.
   (a) While (b) As soon as

9. _____, the company has increased the number of working hours per week.
   (a) On the other hand (b) With regard to

10. _____, the officer was transferred to some distant location.
    (a) As a result (b) As

EXERCISE 2.15

Choose the correct option and cross out the irrelevant linkers and discourse markers for each of the following sentences:

1. _____ let me explain what we understand by the term 'surfeit economy'. **(First of all, Coming to, As regards, With reference to)**

2. Think properly before taking this decision. _____, it is the question of your career. **(Before, By all means, After all)**

3. I am quite particular about my health and don't overstep my limits. _____, I don't take more than three cups of coffee in a day. **(By the way, For example, By all means)**

4. I saw her coming back _____ I was coming out of the class. **(Even as, even if, even though)**

5. The long queues in front of ATMs and banks are continuing; workers are finding it difficult to get any work; and everybody seems to be facing some financial crunch. _____, we are witnessing quite a chaotic situation all around. **(On the contrary, On the whole, By and by)**

6. _____, let me summarize the points we have discussed so far. **(To wind up, To begin with, Turning to)**

7. _____, we all need holidays, but these days we are really struggling to meet the deadlines. **(Of course, By all means, Certainly)**

8. _____ if you don't want to go, leave it; I'll manage somehow. **(Just as, Since, Look)**

9. _____, the price per unit is also beyond our budget. **(Moreover, Therefore, It seems)**

10. Sir, _____ the ink cartridge got over and we could not get any printouts for nearly three hours. **(As, Actually, Since)**

2.10 DETERMINERS AND ARTICLES

The words that add to the meaning of nouns, noun phrases, and adjectives are generally referred to as determiners. Broadly speaking, determiners can be divided into the following categories:

Determiners	Examples
Articles	a, an, the
Possessives	my, his, our, their, her, etc.
Demonstratives	this, that, those, these, etc.
Quantifiers	all, each, every, either, some, any, no, much, many, etc.

Since we have already learnt a few things about possessives, demonstratives, and quantifiers, let's focus on articles in this section.

2.10.1 Articles

Take a look at the following paragraph:

> When Sunil Gavaskar came to open **the innings** for India against **the West Indies** in 1983, he was under tremendous pressure to perform. India had already lost **the first** test in Ahmedabad and he had scored just seven runs in two innings. In fact, in one of the innings, Malcolm Marshall's fiery pace had sent **the little master's bat** flying out of his hands. It brought about **an all-round criticism** from all across and many of his bitter critics started writing him off. So, when Gavaskar walked on to bat for **the second test** in Delhi, there was **a lot** at stakes for him besides **the expectations** of millions of his fans to score **the 29th test century** of his career. But **the great opener** rose to **the occasion** and started assaulting **the mighty pacers** straight-away. Batting with great determination, technique, and class, **the champion opener** went on to script **an amazing chapter** in **the history** of Indian cricket.

The words such as *a*, *an*, and *the* that you see in the above paragraph are known as articles. Read further to understand how to use them appropriately:

A or An

- Megha is studying in **a college** in Canada. (*a* is being used for words starting with a consonant sound)
  More examples: **a match, a laptop, a large church, a good book, a terrorist, a tiny shop**, etc.
- She is **an Indian**. (*an* is being used for words starting with a vowel sound)
  More examples: **an attitude, an old institute, an inkpot, an interesting story,** etc.

EXERCISE 2.16

Choose the article *a* or *an* according to your understanding so far:

1. Next year, she will go to _____ (a/an) university in Netherlands.

2. _____ (A/An) woman was seen pushing the cart along the street.

3. Will you be getting _____ (a/an) M.B.B.S. degree for this?

4. Seeing the ghost approaching her, she closed her eyes in _____ (a/an) fearful expression.

5. Though she appears to be _____ (a/an) Chinese, she is _____ (a/an) Indonesian.

Going further, try to figure out how the choice between *a*, *an*, and *the* is made in different structures given below:

- **A sound** was heard outside.   (the sound is not known)
- **The sound** was heard quite distinctly. (we know what sound we are talking about)
- We took **a taxi**. (we are not speaking to any particular taxi)
- **The taxi** longer than expected. (the taxi we have referred to earlier)
- **An envelope** was dropped at his doorstep. (we don't know which envelope)
- When **the envelope** was opened, anthrax was found in it. (the envelope that has already been referred to)

Notes
- Use *a/an* when the context is generalized and not specific.
- Use *the* when the context is specific.

Sometimes, it is not required to use any of the articles. See the following examples:

- **Milk** (a/an/the milk) is sold here in bulk.
- He goes to **school** (a/an/the school) everyday.
- I love **cricket** (the cricket).
- **France** (the France) is a culturally vibrant country.
- They are travelling **by train** (by the train).
- You can send the cheque **by Friday** (by the Friday).
- **Women** (the women) are generally more expressive than men (the men).

In order to use articles properly, bear in mind the following grammatical conventions:

- Don't use *the* before routine meals.

  I usually go for a walk **after dinner** (after the dinner). (routine meals in the night)

  But: **The dinner** (dinner) served was stale and tasteless. (refers to some particular dinner)

- Don't use *the* before the names of countries and languages.

  China (the China) has started focusing **on English** (on the English) recently.

  But: English is the mother tongue of several Western countries including the United States of America. (country made of small states/parts/islands)

- Don't use *the* before days, months, years, seasons, days, parts of day and night, etc.

  Indira Gandhi was assassinated **in 1984** (in the 1984).
  Christmas (the Christmas) is celebrated with great fanfare in this country.
  We can conduct this programme **on Friday** (on the Friday).
  At night (at the night) you can hear some peculiar sound in the room.

- Don't use *the* before nouns such as *church, school, office, hospital, home,* etc. for specific routine business:

  When I was in **hospital** (the hospital) for fifteen days, I really missed home.
  I usually go to **office** (the office) at 10 a.m.
  Quite religiously he visits **Church** (the Church) on every Sunday.

  But: **The hospital** remains quite crowded. (some specific hospital)
  People in this village fetch water from **the temple**. (temple being used for some other purpose)
  We are going to **the school** to deposit the fee of our ward. (not for studying)

- Use *the* in structure where an adjective follows a proper noun:

  Alexander, **the famous conqueror**, died a sadder but wiser man.
  Sachin, the little master, is revered by cricket lovers.

- Retain *the* in the reverse order as well:

  The famous conqueror Alexandar died a sadder but wiser man.
  Cricket lovers revere Sachin, **the little master**.

- Use *the + adjective* structure when you wish to denote an entire class or type through it:

  The wise (wise) know the truth.

The **poor** always find it difficult to make **the rich** realize the extent of **their** suffering. (~~the poor always finds it difficult to make the rich realize the extent of his/her suffering.~~)

- Use *the* before superlative degrees of adjectives:

  It was **the most frightening experience** (~~most frightening experience~~) of my life.
  Madhubala was often regarded as **the most beautiful actress** (~~most beautiful actress~~) of Hindi Cinema.

- Avoid *the* in comparative degrees:

  After Rio Olympics, PV Sindhu is **more popular** than many other sportspersons in the country.
  The poor are generally **more contended** than the rich.

- However, use *the* also with comparative degrees of adjectives if they are repeated in the same sentence and not followed by *than*:

  The slower you drive, **the safer** it is for you.
  The more you read, **the more knowledgeable** you become in life.

- Avoid *the* with the second noun if two or more nouns refer to the attributes of the same person:

  Tagore, **the poet and thinker**, is known all over the world. (~~Tagore, the poet and the thinker…~~)
  Bertrand Russell, **the philosopher and humanist**, is also a brilliant essayist.

- **But** use *the* if two nouns refer to different attributes or designations of different people:

  The captain and the deputy were both injured in the match.
  The cashier and the accountant are still working out the financial details.

- Use *the* with common nouns if the reference is to some abstract attribute of the person:

  Finally, **the rebel** in him is stirred and he walks out of the gathering.
  The crusader in him could not be a silent spectator to the situation.

- Use *the* with ordinal numbers:

  The **first person** to emerge out of the plane was none else but him.
  The **fifth chapter** of the book deals with Optimization Techniques.

But: **The fifth and sixth chapters** discuss the different aspects related to Juvenile Delinquency.
  The sixth and seventh students in the left row were copying.

- *The* is not used for titles and if we intend to convey that somebody has got some unique position (the only one in the organization):

  President Bush enjoyed good friendly relations with **Prime Minister Tony Blair**.
  Narender Modi was sworn in as **Prime Minister of India** in 2014.

- Names of universities, institutions, airports, and many other similar organizations are written without *the* in usual order:

  He aspires to go to **Delhi University** for his postgraduation.
  I'll be landing at **Mumbai airport** at about five in the morning.
  But: Garima took a Bachelor's degree from **the University of Rajasthan**.
  Even **the Jaipur airport** looked so neat and clean that day!

- Names of newspapers and many other publications such as books, magazines, and journals are preceded by *the*:

  The Times of India is widely circulated all across the country.
  The Sunday Express often comes up with some very engaging cover stories.

2.11 PHRASES

A phrase is a group of related words that complements the overall meaning of a sentence. It makes partial sense, but not complete sense. It is part of a sentence but is not a complete sentence in itself. A phrase may function as a noun, an adjective, a preposition, or an adverb. Depending upon its function, a phrase can be noun phrase, verb phrase, adjective phrase, adverb phrase, gerund phrase, and infinitive phrase. While identifying the type of phrase, you should look for its main/head word.

See the examples given below to understand how different phrases work in sentences:

I bought a rainbow-coloured umbrella.

(a rainbow-coloured umbrella) ⟶ **Noun Phrase**

In this kind of phrase, the head word is a noun and the entire phrase acts as the subject or object of the verb.

The teacher wrote a poem on the blackboard.

(on the blackboard) ⟶ **Prepositional Phrase**

A prepositional phrase starts with a preposition and mostly ends with a noun or pronoun. A prepositional phrase works as an adjective or adverb in a sentence.

The man with a red hat is a detective.

(with a red hat) ⟶ **Prepositional Phrase**

This prepositional phrase is functioning as **Adjective Phrase**. An adjective phrase is a group of words that works like an adjective in a sentence.

He drives his car very fast.

(very fast) ⟶ **Adverb Phrase**

Like an adverb, it modifies a verb, an adjective, or another adverb.

She has been watching a film for two hours.

(has been watching) ⟶ **Verb Phrase**

A verb phrase is a combination of the main verb and its auxiliaries (helping verbs) in a sentence.

She likes to eat waffles.

(to eat waffles) ⟶ **Infinitive Phrase**

An infinitive phrase consists of a to-infinitive (to + base form of verb) and a noun or adverb; it acts mainly as a subject or object of the verb.

I like reading detective novels.

(reading detective novels) ⟶ **Gerund Phrase**

A gerund phrase consists of a gerund (verb + ing) and other words associated with the gerund; it works as a subject or object of the verb.

Children ran around making a lot of noise.

(making a lot of noise) ⟶ **Participle Phrase**

A participle phrase consists of a present participle (verb + ing), a past participle (verb + ed) and modifies a noun like an adjective.

2.12 TENSES

Read the following sentences:

1. I take lessons in English language skills.
2. I took lessons in English language skills last year.
3. I shall take lessons in English language skills next month.

What do you notice in the above sentences? Yes, in sentence 1, *take* refers to the present. In sentence 2, *took* refers to the past. And, in sentence 3, *shall take* refers to the future. Thus, a verb may refer to any of the following:

- Present time
- Past time
- Future time

A verb that refers to a time in the present is said to be in present tense. For example:

- I often write a letter to my friend.
- He loves his younger brother.

A verb that refers to a time in the past is said to be in past tense. For example:

- Rita washed her sweater.
- They prepared fried rice for dinner.

A verb phrase that refers to a time in the future is said to be in future tense. For example:

- I shall visit my friend today.
- We shall discuss our future plans.

The above sentences might not have been really challenging for you mainly because they all are related to simple time frames in the present, past, and future. However, the varied human actions do not necessarily relate to simple time frames and hence we are required to learn in detail all the possible ways in which the different time frames related to the present, the past, and the future should be employed while we speak and write English.

Therefore, let us learn all the tenses in English in detail. To begin with, take a look at the following set of sentences:

I get up at five o' clock in the morning. I go for a walk with my father. After returning from the walk, I study for half an hour and get ready for my college. My father drops me there in his car. I get back from college at 4 p.m.

When do you think we write like this? We do it when we want to express the actions that happen in a general or routine manner. This means that the action may not be happening at the time of speaking. The statements given above merely suggest a routine activity usually followed. The tense used in these sentences is known as **present indefinite tense** or **simple present tense**. While using Simple Present Tense, we use the following structure:

Subject + Base Form of Verb + s/es + Object

See the following examples:

- She likes soft toys. (III Person Singular + Base Form of Verb + s + Object)
- We fight with each other. (I Person Plural + Base Form of Verb + Object)

By using the above structure of sentences you can express the following:

- The actions that are done as habits in everyday life
- General facts
- Universal truths or facts

Read the following sentences carefully and see how this structure helps us express various actions in the present:

- The earth revolves round the sun. (**Universal truth**)
- Mr Arora watches a movie on Sunday. (**Habitual action**)
- I usually get up at five in the morning. (**Habitual action**)
- Horses run faster than donkeys. (**General fact**)
- We go to some hill station during summer holidays. (**Habitual action**)

The following table should help you observe the structure of the simple present tense/present indefinite tense.

Subject	Verb	Object/Adverb/Complement
I	do not play (do not + base form of verb with I, we, you, they, plural subject)	football.
Do we (Interrogative (Do/Does) + Subject)	sing (Base form of verb)	well?
She	cooks (Base form of verb + s/es with he, she, it, singular subject)	food.
Doesn't he (Interrogative + Negative (Don't/Doesn't) + Subject)	obey (Base form of verb)	his parents?
My teacher	teaches (Base form of verb + s/es with singular noun)	English.

EXERCISE 2.17

Fill in the blanks with appropriate verbs in simple present tense:

1. My mother _____ (**buy**) vegetables from the Reliance Fresh store.

2. Normally he _____ (**walk**) very fast.

3. She _____ (**rebuke**) her children for playing computer games.

4. We _____ (**not find**) the solution of such problems on the Internet.

5. They _____ (**not trust**) their employees.

6. Girls _____ (**not like**) wrestling.

7. The chief librarian usually _____ (**purchase**) new books and journals for the library in July.

8. Snigdha _____ (**dance**) skilfully.

9. Siddharth _____ (**take**) coffee after dinner.

10. It _____ (**rain**) frequently in London.

Read the following sentences and see how the actions are expressed:

- Priya **is learning** French from the American Institute of Foreign Languages.
- We **are celebrating** the fourth marriage anniversary of my brother today.
- He **is toying** with the idea of creating a new robot with emotions.
- The cost of living **is increasing** day by day.

What do you observe in these sentences? In these sentences, the action is not a routine activity; in fact, it is going on even at the time of speaking. The action in all these sentences seems to be in progress at the time of speaking. This is called **present continuous** or **present progressive tense**. The structure for this tense is as follows:

Subject + is/are/am + (Base Form of Verb + ing) + Object

Rule Singular subject takes *is*; plural subject takes *are*; and the subject *I* takes *am*.

Subject	Verb
I person singular (I)	am
I person plural (we)	are
II person (you)	are
III person singular (he, she, it)	is
III person plural (they)	are

The following table should help you understand the structure of the present continuous or present progressive tense.

Subject	Verb	Object
I	am writing	a letter.
She	is watching	a movie.
We	are discussing	a problem.
Boys	are laughing at	the joke.

EXERCISE 2.18

Fill in the blanks with appropriate verbs. Look for the clues that should help you choose between simple present and present progressive tenses:

1. I _____ **(work)** hard for my GRE test these days.

2. We _____ **(face)** an acute problem in power supply these days.

3. Since Mr Smith _____ **(go)** to France, he _____ **(learn)** French these days.

4. Due to recession, many companies _____ **(downsize)** their operations.

5. Look! Anne _____ **(relish)** orange juice and French fries in the sun.

6. Our institute _____ **(plan)** to bring a change in its promotion policy.

7. Our government _____ (not cut) down the prices of petroleum and gas.

8. The patient _____ (wear) a blanket because he is feeling very cold.

9. The watchman normally _____ (bring) tea and snacks for the hostel inmates from outside.

10. That great man always _____ (donate) a lot of money for poor children.

In the above exercise the expressions such as *these days, always, normally,* etc. helped us choose the tenses correctly. Now, the following section helps you understand where to use simple present tense and where to opt for present progressive tense.

2.12.1 Simple Present or Present Progressive

Look at the following sentences:

1. The cake **is smelling** sweet.

2. I **am thinking** that the idea given by you is quite good.

3. I **am loving** it.

4. He **is owning** a very big bungalow in the heart of the city.

5. Somehow he **is** always **disliking** my suggestions.

6. When I went to the party last night, I **was not recognizing** my uncle.

7. Sorry, I **am not understanding** your point.

8. These days, I **am not having** any vehicle.

9. He **is not believing** in God.

10. He **is never trusting** his neighbours.

It is not difficult to observe that all the above sentences are written incorrectly. Let us see how we can use them correctly:

1. The cake **smells** sweet.

2. I **think** that the idea given by you is quite good.

3. I **love** it.

4. He **owns** a very big bungalow in the heart of the city.

5. Somehow he always **dislikes** my suggestions.

6. When I went to the party last night, I **could not recognize** my uncle.

7. Sorry, I **do not understand** your point.

8. These days, I **don't have** any vehicles.

9. He **does not believe** in God.

10. He never **trusts** his neighbours.

In all the above sentences, the verbs of perception, thoughts, emotions, senses, or possession are used. None of these verbs are usually expressed in continuous form as they are suggestive of more stable emotions, thoughts, perspectives, beliefs, and feelings.

Look at more such verbs which normally do not appear in the continuous form:

Incorrect Usage	Correct Usage
I **am not agreeing** to your point of view.	I **don't agree** to your point of view.
The committee **is consisting** of three members.	The committee **consists** of three members.
He **is appearing** to be sad today.	He **appears** to be sad today.
Normally, I **am preferring** tea to coffee.	Normally, I **prefer** tea to coffee.
He **is seeming** to be all right now.	He **seems** all right now.
I **am feeling** for the poor.	I **feel** for the poor.
We **are not meaning** this.	We **don't mean** this.
Are you minding moving a little?	**Do you mind** moving a little?
We **are hoping** to see you sometime.	We **hope** to see you sometime.
We all **are wishing** to be happy in life.	We all **wish** to be happy in life.

So, be cautious and use a simple present tense when the verbs to be chosen are any of the following:

1. **Verbs of emotion**, e.g., wish, desire, like, love, hate, want, refuse, etc.
2. **Verbs of thought**, e.g., think, believe, agree, understand, mean, mind, know, etc.
3. **Verbs of senses**, e.g., see, hear, taste, feel, smell, touch, etc.
4. **Verbs of perception**, e.g., recognize, notice, perceive, imagine, remember, etc.
5. **Verbs of appearance**, e.g., appear, seem, look, etc.
6. **Verbs of possession**, e.g., own, possess, belong, contain, have, consist, etc.

EXERCISE 2.19

Pick the correct options in the following sentences:

1. Why **are you/do you** always come late?
2. He **is likely/likes** to visit our school during vacation.
3. 'Look, how glorious **is appearing/appears** the Sun today!'
4. He **is going to resume/resumes** his innings on a nervous 99 after lunch.
5. Why **are you informing/do you inform** me about that now?
6. Sometimes it **is raining/rains** here quite torrentially.
7. He **is writing/writes** his poems in Urdu.
8. We **are waiting/wait** for the signal to clear.
9. Normally, the temperature **is ranging/ranges** between 10 and 20 degrees in this region.
10. He **is conducting/conducts** a meeting right now in his chamber.

2.12.2 Present Perfect or Simple Past

Moving further, now read the following sentences carefully:

- He **gave** me a watch.
- My friend **asked** for help.
- The tourist **went** around the city.
- His uncle **asked** him to bring a laptop for his daughter.

What have you observed? In these sentences, the action is completed in the past. For expressing such actions, we use simple past/past indefinite tense and use the following structure:

Subject + Past Form of Verb + Object/Complement/Adjunct

Now go through the following set of sentences and observe how the simple past tense is used:

- Parimal **decided** to leave his job.
- She **did not understand** the problem.
- Sukumar **disclosed** the secret.
- **Did** you **enjoy** your trip?

EXERCISE 2.20

Complete the following sentences by using the structure for simple past tense:

1. Earlier, I _____ (**cannot contact**) you.

2. _____ the officer _____ (**inform**) you about that?

3. My children _____ (play) badminton while I _____ (**sleep**).

4. _____ your company _____ (**plan**) to start something in Kashmir earlier this year?

5. Last month, my wife _____ (**visit**) New York for attending a meeting.

6. His father _____ (**drive**) us back home very fast.

7. Mr Batra _____ (**deposit**) five thousand rupees in his son's account.

8. They _____ (**open**) new branches in all the cities but surprisingly _____ (**close**) each of these one by one.

9. Since she was not well, she _____ (**consult**) a doctor.

10. The teachers at the conference _____ (**identify**) the innovative methods of teaching.

Moving on to the next tense, let's now read the following set of sentences:

- India **has contributed** immensely in the field of science and technology.
- The gardener **has planted** a few more shrubs and trees this month.
- Sunil Gavaskar **has redefined** cricket in our country.
- The journalist **has brought** the unsung heroes to light.

All the above sentences use the present perfect tense as each of these follows the following structure:

Subject + has/have + Past Participle Form of Verb + Object

Note The present perfect form of the verb is preferred when the focus is on the completion of action and the immediacy of the past. Attempting the practice tests that follow should help you understand when to use the present perfect form of the verb.

EXERCISE 2.21

Complete the following sentences with appropriate verbs in present perfect tense:

1. I am not feeling hungry, I _____ (take) a heavy breakfast.

2. It is nice to see you again; we _____ (not meet) each other for such a long time!

3. Recently, the state government _____ (pass) a bill for free college education for girls.

4. Though she loves going on long drives, she _____ (not learn) how to drive.

5. _____ you ever _____ (think) how stressful life _____ (become) these days.

6. I know I _____ (leave) no stone unturned to pass the CAT exam.

7. The music band _____ (display) a stupendous show this time.

8. The film director _____ (develop) the plot of the story and used the camera and lights skilfully.

9. He is not aware of the legal implications as he _____ (not purchase) any land before.

10. The policy _____ (come) as a result of the scathing attack from the media.

Since the present perfect tense is at times confused with simple past tense, a careful use is desirable. Remember that we can go wrong not only in choosing between the simple present and the present progressive, but also in choosing between the present perfect and the simple past tense.

EXERCISE 2.22

In the following sentences, identify the places where the present perfect and the simple past tenses are either mixed or chosen not so judiciously and correct them:

1. Sir, I have passed my B.Tech in 2003.

2. We finished our assignment just now.

3. Don't worry; I already informed her about that.

4. We have seen a tiger five years ago.

5. I have spoken to him last night.

6. Wait; I did not yet finish my work.

7. I have read that story in Class IX.

8. We have spent a very enjoyable evening yesterday.

9. She has submitted her project this morning.

10. Last year, we have conducted several workshops for our teachers.

None of these sentences chooses the correct tense. Whenever a particular particle of time such as *yesterday, this morning, the year 2002, last month, couple of hours back*, etc. appears, we normally choose simple past tense. The expressions such as *just now, recently, already, yet,* etc., on the other hand, should make us choose the present perfect tense.

EXERCISE 2.23

Choose the correct tense in the following sentences:

1. Call the doctor, I think he **broke/has broken** his toe.

2. Now that you **came/have come**, why don't you stay with us for a while?

3. They **questioned/have questioned** the actor at the airport before they **let/have let** him go.

4. We **spent/have spent** the entire weekend worrying about his whereabouts.

5. Research **showed/has shown** that exercises help people remain cheerful.

6. Shakespeare **wrote/has written** his last play possibly in 1613.

7. Don't worry, I **informed/have informed** his parents about his illness.

8. Earlier he **made/has made** some comedies but for some time now he **produced/has produced** only serious movies.

9. I am sure I **read/have read** about that episode in some magazine.

10. You **grew/have grown** so big ever since I saw you last.

2.12.3 Simple Past or Past Perfect

Now read the following set of sentences.

- I **had finished** my lunch before the kids came from school.
- The students **had checked** their pre-comprehensive marks before their final exams.
- After we **had identified** the areas of improvement, we commenced the training programme.
- Mr Jones **had gone through** the manuscript several times before sending it to the publisher.

In the above sentences, both the actions happen in the past time but one action takes place earlier than the other. To demarcate the earlier action from the succeeding one in the past, you are required to use the past perfect tense as shown in the above examples. This tense is formed by using **had** with the **past participle form** of the verb. So the basic structure of this tense is as follows:

Subject + had + Past Participle Form of Verb + Object/Complement/Adjunct

Now let us understand where we should use simple past tense and where to use past perfect tense.

EXERCISE 2.24

Check if the past perfect and simple past tense in the following sentences are used correctly and correct them wherever required:

1. The British had ruled over India for nearly two hundred years before they had handed it over to us.

2. We had walked all the way to the station only to know that the train had already left.

3. When the police had interrogated the criminal, they had put him behind the bars.

4. My neighbour had told me that his father died.

5. By the time the doctor had reached, the patient had died.

6. We thought of raising your pay, but had not been able to get enough funds.

7. After he finalized the deal, he had signed it.

8. The movie already began when we had entered the hall.

9. He planned to retire at the age of sixty-five, but he had died much before that.

10. I just entered the building, when the bomb had gone off suddenly.

Of course, none of these sentences is correct. Choosing between the simple past and past perfect tense is at times difficult. To avoid confusion, choose past perfect (had + past participle form of the verb) for the action that precedes the other action in the past. Choose simple past for the action that follows. In other words, choose **past perfect** for the **earlier action** and **simple past** for the **later action**.

Thus, it is important to distinguish two actions of the past if one of them takes place before the other. However, when two actions of the past happen successively and also when we want to emphasize that the second event is the result of the first, we choose simple past tense in both the clauses. Look at the following sentences:

- The thief **broke** (not had broken) into the shop and stole jewellery.
- Rushdie **shot** (not had shot) to fame after he wrote *Midnight's Children*.
- The cow **entered** (not had entered) the farm and walked over the plants.
- When fog **cleared** (not had cleared), we resumed our journey.
- When we **reached** (not had reached) the station, we found them waiting for us.

2.12.4 Simple Future or Future Progressive

Let us read the following sentences:

- My brother **will come** tomorrow.
- We **shall abide** by the rules of the institute.
- They **will go** on strike if there is a hike in petroleum prices.
- I **shall visit** my friend since he is not keeping fine these days.

What do you observe? These sentences express an action or a situation that will occur in the future. This tense is formed by using **will/shall** with the **base form** of the verb. So, the basic structure for **simple future/ future indefinite tense** is as follows:

Subject + will/shall + Base Form of Verb + Object/Complement/Adjunct

Going back to the past tense, look at the following sentences:

- We **were waiting** for the class to be over.
- The children **were playing** cricket in the garden.
- They **were patrolling** the territory when the bomb went off.
- When my friend called me, I **was trying** to figure out the crossword puzzle.

In all the above sentences, the structure that is followed can be grammatically summed up as follows:

Subject + was/were + Base Form of Verb + ing + Object/Complement/Adjunct

The tense that follows this structure is called **past continuous/past progressive tense** and is chosen to represent a progressive action in the past.

Now let us go through the following set of sentences:

- Praveen **will be going** to Mumbai for cancer treatment.
- We **shall be completing** our degree next year.
- My uncle **will be joining** me for dinner tonight.

Future progressive tense is also chosen to express the actions that will take place in future. The basic structure for this tense is as follows:

Subject + will be/shall be + Base Form of Verb + ing + Object/Complement/Adjunct

2.12.5 Future Perfect

Future perfect tense describes an action that will occur in future before some other action. This tense is formed by using **will have** with the **past participle form** of the verb.

- By the time summer approaches, I **shall have finished** my exams.
- When their son turns 16, they **will have decided** where they will build a house.

As you can make out from the above sentences, the basic structure of the **future perfect tense** is as follows:

Subject + will have/shall have + Past Participle Form of Verb + Object/Complement/Adjunct

2.12.6 Present Perfect Continuous

Let us read the following set of sentences:

- We **have been waiting** for you all day.
- She is tired. She **has been working** all day.
- They **have been studying** since 5 o'clock.

What do you observe? In these sentences, actions start sometime in the past and they continue in the present. This is called **present perfect continuous tense**. Since present perfect continuous tense refers to an action that started in the past but has continued in the present, it needs to be chosen judiciously.

Read the following sentences:

1. We **are waiting** for you for the last two hours.
2. He **is making** a fool of us for such a long time!
3. We **are not seeing** them for the last couple of days.

None of these sentences is appropriate because all these sentences choose present continuous tense while denoting an action that has started in the past and is still continuing at the time of speaking. Hence, always use present perfect continuous tense in such situations.

Observe how the revised versions of these sentences seem appropriate:

1. We **have been waiting** for you for the last two hours.
2. He **has been making** a fool of us for such a long time!
3. We **have not been seeing** them for the last couple of days.

Here are a few more examples:

- It **has been raining** since morning.
- Though I **have been reading** the novel all afternoon, I have not finished it.
- I **have been sleeping** in this bed since morning.

The basic structure of **present perfect continuous tense** is as follows:

Subject + has been/have been + Base Form of Verb + ing + Object/Complement/Adjunct

Remember, mostly there is a mention of time in this tense and it is denoted through either of the following:

(a) **For**—a length of time
(b) **Since**—a point in time

Read the following sentences carefully:

- I have been working at BITS, Pilani, **since 1994**. (a point in time)
- Deevan Knitwares has been exporting to China and Korea **since its inception**. (a point in time)
- It has been snowing in Shimla **for one week**. (a length of time)
- My brother has been dealing in tyres **for the past twenty-five years**. (a length of time)

2.12.7 Past Perfect Continuous

Read the following sentences:

- We **had been talking** since morning.
- I **had been walking** on the road for two hours.
- The girls **had been dancing** on stage for three hours tirelessly.

The past perfect continuous tense is used to express actions that started and continued over a period of time in the past with some part of the action having been completed.

See the following examples:

- We found them waiting at 9 a.m. The doctor arrived at 11 a.m. When the doctor arrived, they **had been waiting** for two hours.
- Suddenly, my car broke down. I was not surprised. It **had not been running** well for a long time.

The **past perfect continuous tense** is generally formed this way:

Subject + had been + Base Form of Verb + ing + Object/Complement/Adjunct

Let us see a few more examples:

- Milkha Singh was very tired. He **had been running**.
- I could smell cigarettes. Somebody **had been smoking** there.

- They went to watch a movie. They **had been working** very hard for their final exams for the past one and a half months.
- **Had** the pilot **been trying** to give some signal of helplessness before the crash?

2.12.8 Future Perfect Continuous

Read the following sentences carefully:

- I **will have been working** here for three years by the end of next month.
- Shane Bond **will have been playing** international cricket for nine years by next March.
- Siddharth **will have been studying** for tomorrow's exam for eleven hours by seven o'clock next morning.

The future perfect continuous is used when we wish to emphasize the duration of some activity in continuation at a particular point in future.

The basic sentence structure for **future perfect continuous tense** is as follows:

Subject + will/shall + have been + Base Form of Verb + ing + Object/Complement/Adjunct

See the following examples:

- She **will have been raising** all speculations by the time she becomes the dean of her unit.
- By the time she finishes this semester, Susheela **will have been studying** about parasites for four years.
- By next Thursday, I **will have been working** on this project for three years.

In brief, let us revise what we have learnt so far with the help of the verb *write.*

Structure of Verb Phrases

Tense	Simple	Continuous	Perfect	Perfect Continuous
Present	Write(s)	Am/Is/Are writing	Have/Has written	Have been/Has been writing
Past	Wrote	Was/Were writing	Had written	Had been writing
Future	Will/Shall write	Will/Shall be writing	Will have/Shall have written	Will have been/Shall have been writing

Finally, to recapitulate what we have learnt in this section, let us remind ourselves how a sentence can be written in different tense forms.

An Action Expressed in Different Tenses

Examples	Tense
I read novels during holidays.	Present indefinite tense
I am reading a novel at the novel.	Present continuous tense
I have recently read that novel.	Present perfect tense
I have been reading novels since my childhood.	Present perfect continuous tense

Examples	Tense
I read that novel last week.	Past indefinite tense
I was reading a novel at that time.	Past continuous tense
I had read that novel before I lent it to a friend of mine.	Past perfect tense followed by past indefinite tense
I had been reading that novel before it was stolen.	Past perfect continuous tense followed by past indefinite in the passive
I'll read that novel during my holidays.	Future indefinite tense
I will be reading that novel in a couple of days.	Future continuous tense
I will have read this novel by then.	Future perfect tense
I'll have been reading this novel for a month or so.	Future perfect continuous tense

EXERCISE 2.25

Select the appropriate verb from the choices given below and choose their correct forms so as to fit in the blanks:
(grow, have, decide, watch, work, paint, rain, write, want, keep, put)

1. I did my homework when I _____ television.

2. Since it _____, we cannot go to beach.

3. Yesterday, I _____ breakfast at 7.30 a.m.

4. Where's my wallet? It was on the table. Probably, somebody _____ it somewhere else.

5. We _____ (not) to bother them. So we stopped asking them stupid questions.

6. After finishing his work he _____ to go out.

7. Don't disturb me I _____ an essay.

8. I'm very tired today. I _____ all day.

9. Unemployment _____ at an alarming rate for the past two years because of economic depression.

10. This room was white. Now it is blue. He _____ it blue.

2.13 MOODS OF VERBS

Don't you feel that verbs can also be moody! After all, they express actions. Hence, they have all the swings of temperament! Verbs do have different ways and manners of expressions which we refer to as their **moods**.

There are three moods of verbs in English. To understand them, look at the following expressions:

- He speaks wonderful English.
- Learn from him.
- If I were him, I would not have been all that fluent.
- I wish I knew how to speak that well.

The first sentence makes a statement. So we say that the verb is in an **indicative mood.** The verb chooses to be in this mood to make a statement of facts, ask a question, or express a supposition which is taken for granted. Look at the different expressions in which the verb appears to be in the indicative mood:

- The movie was quite impressive. (Statement)
- Have you finished your meal? (Question)
- I am a great admirer of Brian Lara. (Statement)
- If he is the project leader, I shall blame the failure of the project. (Supposition taken for granted; the speaker knows him for that the person referred to as *he* is the project leader)
- Am I audible to you? (Question)
- Mr Smith taught us English. (Statement)
- If it rains, I shall stay back. (Supposition taken for granted)
- He gets up by six in the morning. (Statement)

The other most commonly observed mood of verb is **imperative mood.** The verb chooses to be in this mood to express a *command, request, order, caution, exhortation, prayer, entreaty,* etc. Whenever the verb acquires this mood, the subject of verb (you) is omitted. Look at the following sentences and see the different expressions of the verbs in their imperative mood:

- Please listen to me. (Request)
- Don't leave us, please! (Entreaty)
- Avoid chewing tobacco. (Suggestion/Caution)
- Don't park your vehicle here. (Order)
- O God! Give us our daily bread. (Prayer)
- Come here. (Command/Request)
- Be careful in life. (Caution)

The third and most unusual mood of verb is **subjunctive mood**. It is in this mood that the verb chooses to express itself in peculiar grammatical structures. Look at the following sentences and see how unusually they are structured:

- We recommend that the director be removed.

  (Not **we recommend that the director should be removed**)
- I wish I knew her name.

  (Not for the present situation; replaces **I wish I know her name**)
- He talks to me as though I were his servant.

  (Not **he talks to me as though I am his servant**)
- I would rather you kept your mouth shut.

  (Not **I would rather you keep your mouth shut**)
- It is high time we did something about corruption.

  (Not **it is high time we do or should do something about corruption**)
- If I were to be the captain, I would not make that error.

  (Not **if I was the captain, I would not make that error**)
- I wish I were a superstar.

  (Not **I wish I am/was a superstar**)
- The landlord demanded that the boys vacate the house.

  (Not **the landlord demanded that the boys should vacate the house**)

The subjunctive mood of verb is expressive of formal expressions, which is used more frequently in American English. The subjunctive mood of the verb is often chosen in a that-clause following words such as *demand, insist, recommend, suggest, vital, propose,* etc. In such clauses, present subjunctive mood is chosen, for instance,

- The workers got together and demanded that the union leader be released immediately.
- The company insisted that the employee withdraw his claims.

The past subjunctive is chosen to express the following:

(i) After the verb *wish* to express a desire contrary to the reality, for instance,

- I wish I were the Prime Minister of India.
- She wishes she were a lot more educated.

(ii) After expressions such as *if, as if, as though* to express some improbability, for instance,

- The rookie behaves as though he were the greatest bowler around.
- If I were you, I would accept that offer.
- She tells me as if this were the only thing for me to do in life.

(iii) After the expression *it is time/it is high time + subject*, for instance,

- It is time we moved back.
- It is high time we listened to our children.

(iv) To express a preference in expressions with *would rather*, for instance,

- They would rather you kept out of it.
- She would rather you stayed back home.

EXERCISE 2.26

Write whether the verbs in the following sentences are in indicative, imperative, or subjunctive mood:

1. I move that Ms Slipslop be appointed the Managing Director.
2. Steve craves for Stella as though she were his beloved.
3. Don't speak to me like that!
4. I wish I knew how to drive a car.
5. The sun rises in the east.
6. Save some money.
7. It is high time we left the party.
8. Please don't be so rude!
9. If I were you, I would never speak to her like that.
10. Shut up!

2.14 ACTIVE/PASSIVE VOICE

Read the following sentences:

- The committee cut the budget.
- The budget was cut by the committee.

You can see that the second sentence is the passive form of the first sentence. As you must know, we make the passive voice of a sentence by interchanging the position of the subject and the object in the sentence. In the above sentence, *the committee* is in the subject position, whereas *the budget* is in the object position. The case is reversed in the second sentence.

The agent of the action has been shown with the help of the preposition *by*. Further, the simple past *cut* becomes *was cut* in the passive form.

Let us first see how to convert active voice into passive in the following table.

Converting Active Voice into Passive Voice

Active Form	Tense Employed	Original Structure	Passive Form	Recast Structure	Focuses on
Geeta writes a letter.	Present indefinite/simple present tense	Base form of the verb + s/es with III Person singular	*A letter is written by Geeta.*	Is/Am/Are + Past participle form of the verb	**A letter is written**.
Geeta is writing a letter.	Present progressive/ Continuous tense	Is/Am/Are + Base form of the verb + ing	*A letter is being written by Geeta.*	Is/Am/Are + Being + Past participle form of the verb	**A letter is being written**.
Geeta has written a letter.	Present perfect tense	Has/Have + Past participle form of the verb	*A letter has been written by Geeta.*	Has been + Past participle form of the verb	**A letter has been written**.
Geeta wrote a letter.	Past indefinite/ Simple past tense	Past form of the verb	*A letter was written by Geeta.*	Was/Were + Past participle form of the verb	**A letter was written**.
Geeta was writing a letter.	Past continuous/ Past progressive tense	Was/Were + Base form of the verb + ing	*A letter was being written by Geeta.*	Was/Were + Being + Past participle form of the verb	**A letter was being written**.
Geeta had written a letter.	Past perfect tense	Had + Past participle form of the verb	*A letter had been written by Geeta.*	Had been + Past participle form of the verb	**A letter had been written**.
Geeta will write a letter.	Simple future/ Future indefinite tense	Shall/Will + Base form of the verb	*A letter will be written by Geeta.*	Will be + Past participle form of the verb	**A letter will be written**.
Geeta will have written a letter.	Future perfect tense	Will have/Shall have + Past participle form of the verb	*A letter will have been written by Geeta.*	Will have been + Past participle form of the verb	**A letter will have been written**.

Apart from the other structural changes, an important change in passive from active *is the shift of emphasis*. The last column in the above table illustrates how the focus in the passive shifts *from the doer or agent* of the action *to the action* itself. That is why, in many passive forms, we see the agent of the action being dropped altogether.

Going back to the opening sentence, can you now figure out the difference between these two versions of the same sentence? Look at them once more:

- **The committee** cut the budget.

  (The focus is on who cut the budget.)

- **The budget** was cut by the committee.

  (The focus is on what was done.)

Actually, the focus in the passive is generally on the action part. Therefore, in most cases, it can be written without mentioning the agent.

Since this aspect is not usually stressed, we end up using active voice where the passive would be most suitable.

EXERCISE 2.27

Look at the sentences given below and suggest whether it is an active or a passive that is required to suit the occasion and also change it accordingly:

1. We are sorry to inform you that **we cannot do anything** about your problem.
   (Sounds like a real bad news; prefer passive voice in case the active sounds too blunt)

2. **Accidents kill** thousands of people every year.
   (Normally what happens should be more important in such statements; the focus in this sentence, however, is what/who kills thousands of people)

3. **The newscasters telecast** the news at 8.00 p.m.
   (It is not important who telecast them but the action)

4. **You have not** yet informed me.
   (Sounds blunt and accusatory)

5. **They held** the gathering near the temple.
   (The focus should be on the action and not on the agent)

6. **The nurse has given** the medicine to the patient.
   (The fact that the medicine has been given should be highlighted and not who has done that)

7. **The agitators handed** a memorandum to the district collector.
   (The action should be stressed in such statements and not the agent)

8. As we started walking, **a small cab was seen coming** from the other direction.

Note By suggesting you to prefer using passive to active voice in such situations, we do not intend to suggest that the active versions of these sentences are incorrect. However, the passive voice puts the focus on the right place in the above sentences, hence, recommended by us.

EXERCISE 2.28

Read the following passage and rewrite it choosing passive voice wherever required:

They did not invite me to the party. Still, I was determined to attend the same. So, I reached the place uninvited. What I saw was something really forgettable. What was happening around was strange. Waiters were supplying wine openly to the guests. The guests were consuming that unashamedly. That was not enough. I could also see the young girls dancing with their suitors. The attendants were coming again and again and filling their wine glasses with more wine. Later on, I observed these devotees of god Bacchus inserting their fangs into the non-vegetarian dishes which the other set of waiters were supplying at a frantic pace.

In the above passage, the narrator chooses active voice throughout the description of his/her experience. While seeing the revised version in the Answer Key that mostly chooses a passive voice, you can make out that passive voice suits the occasion much better than active voice.

Further, passive voice is also preferred when we tend to describe a procedure or method.

Passive voice is also preferred when the focus is on a generalized notion. Read the following expressions:

1. **People regard Shakespeare** to be the greatest playwright of all times.

2. **People require water** for everything.

Don't you feel that both these expressions will sound better in passive voice? Of course, unless otherwise the focus is entirely on **people**. In normal circumstances, you feel like saying the same thing this way:

1. **Shakespeare is regarded** as the greatest playwright of all times.

2. **Water is required** for everything.

In the above sentences, we not only use the passive form of voice but also eliminate the agent when the focus is rested firmly on the action and the agent is irrelevant. Read the following expressions and decide which option you would choose:

- You should apply by 31st December. (OR)

  Applications must be sent by 31st December.

- We are providing this service as per our contract. (OR)

  This service is being provided as per our contract.

- Someone stole my mobile. (OR)

  My mobile was stolen.

Of course, the options in the passive voice seem far more relevant and appropriate.

The passive is usually chosen also for writing sentences with expressions *get/got, it is said/reported/thought/ believed, said to be*, etc. Look at the sentences given below:

- They got married last June.

  (Not **they married each other last June**)

- I got selected for the armed services twice.

  (Not **the armed forces selected me twice**)

- These forts are believed to be built in the twelfth century.

  (Not **they are believed to have built these forts in the twelfth century**)

- It is said that animals can quite well make out what we want from them.

  (Not **people say that animals can quite well make out what we want from them**)

- The prisoner is known to have assaulted the inmate earlier too.

  (Not **we know that the prisoner has assaulted the inmate earlier too**)

Moving further, let us see another aspect of active and passive voice. We trust you know that some verbs can have two passives. See the following examples:

1. She gave me a book. (Active)

   I was given a book by her. (Passive)

   A book was given to me by her. (Passive)

2. The academy gave the scientist the prestigious award. (Active)

The scientist was given the prestigious award by the academy. (Passive)

The prestigious award was given to the scientist by the academy. (Passive)

On the other hand, certain expressions with verbs *lack, resemble, suit, let*, etc. cannot be converted into passive. See the following examples:

- I have three jackets in the wardrobe.

  (Not **three jackets are had by me in the wardrobe**)

- The dress does not suit you.

  (Not **you are not suited by the dress**)

- He resembles his father.

  (Not **his father is resembled by him**)

- Our new boss lets us have a little chat in the office.

  (Not **we are let to have a little chat in the office**)

But see the following example:

We are allowed to have a little chat in the office.

(The verb **allow** can have a passive form but not the verb **let**.)

EXERCISE 2.29

Rewrite the following sentences using passive voice:

1. We advise the patients of swine flu to wear a mask.

2. We can prove that Darwin's theory has some chinks in the armour.

3. They will organize the function in the auditorium.

4. You have not yet reported to me.

5. The attendants change bed sheets every day in this hotel.

6. They pay me monthly.

7. The producers are likely to offer a staggering signing amount to the star.

8. For many centuries we did not know that plants can breathe.

9. Translators the world over have translated Premchand's stories into different languages.

10. People mostly consider learning a language to be a difficult task.

11. In the meeting, the members agreed that new norms be brought into effect.

12. The minister announced that he will give pension to all the old people in the state.

13. They shifted a large number of victims to the relief camps.

14. Dr Samuel Johnson compiled the first English dictionary.

15. The government has announced that it will introduce the new Act in the next parliamentary session.

16. The captain desires that they should play the game in the positive spirit.

17. The glass broke as you walked over it.

18. I always service my car at this service station.

19. Earlier people believed that AIDS spreads by touch.

20. Fans expected our team to win, but we lost.

2.15 DIRECT/INDIRECT SPEECH

To begin with, let us see what Julia's teacher announces in her class:

Girls, on 15 December, we are going to organize a speech competition. Those of you who are interested in delivering a speech may give their names to me. Girls, you can choose any topic for your speech. You can give your speech on a great person, great event, great achievement, great movement, or any other thing that interests you. You will be required to speak at least for five minutes and the maximum time you can take will be seven minutes. Those of you who come first, second, and third would be given attractive prizes.

Now, Julia has to inform her mother about what the teacher told her. Read her version carefully and find out where she goes wrong. This is what she told her mother:

Mom, **our teacher today said** that on 15 December, **we** are going to organize a speech competition. **Those of you** who are interested in delivering a speech may give **their names to me**. **You can** choose any topic for **your speech**. She also told **you can** give **your speech** on a great person, great event, great achievement, great movement, or any other thing that interests **you**. **You will be** required to speak at least for five minutes and the maximum time **you can take** will be seven minutes. **Those of you** who come first, second, and third would be given attractive prizes.

What do you think of Julia's version of the announcement? She did try well but at certain places, she went wrong. The expressions highlighted above are to be changed. Let us start from the very beginning. In indirect speech, *told* replaces *said* if the reporting verb has an object. Since the announcement was made to the students by the teacher, Julia should have chosen *our teacher told us* instead of our *teacher said*.

Further, in indirect speech, the pronouns used are changed according to the subject of the verb in the reporting speech; *we* should be replaced by *they* or *the school*. Similarly, some other changes should have been employed.

This is how actually Julia should have informed her mother about the announcement made by her teacher:

Mom, our teacher today told us that on 15 December, the school is going to organize a speech competition. Those of us who are interested in delivering a speech may give our names to her. We can choose any topic for our speech. She also told us that we can give our speech on a great person, great event, great achievement, great movement, or any other thing that interests us. We would be required to speak at least for five minutes and the maximum time we can take would be seven minutes. Those of us who come first, second, and third would be given attractive prizes.

Hence, while using indirect speech, we change the tense, person, and time according to the subject. To learn further, let us see how the changes are affected in indirect narration:

Direct Narration

1. Mildred said, 'I am busy today.'
2. The teacher said, 'God is everywhere.'
3. 'You have come first in your class,' my friend told me.
4. 'I am feeling hungry,' the little boy said to his mother.
5. Jack said to Rose, 'You look nice in this dress.'
6. Wilber said to Agatha, 'I am leaving tomorrow.'
7. 'You shall come back by eleven,' my father told me.
8. 'It may rain this evening,' said Jane to Jasper.

9. Kate said to me, 'I know the way.'

10. Scott's mother told him, 'You must not forget your tiffin in your class.'

Indirect Narration

1. Mildred said that she was busy that day.

   (**I am** becomes **she was** and **today** becomes **that day**.)

2. The teacher said that God is everywhere.

   (Universal statements are not changed in indirect structure/narration.)

3. My friend told me that I had come first in my class.

   (**You** becomes **I**; **your** becomes **my**; **have** becomes **had**; **have** can be retained if the statement is still relevant.)

4. The little boy told his mother that he was feeling hungry.

   (**I am** becomes **he was**; **said to** becomes **told**.)

5. Jack told Rose that she looked nice in that dress.

   (**Said to** becomes told; **you look** becomes **she looked**; **this** becomes **that**.)

6. Wilber told Agatha that he was leaving the next day.

   (**Said to** becomes **told**; **I am** becomes **he was**; **tomorrow** becomes **the next day**.)

7. My father told me that I should come back by eleven. (OR)

   My father asked me to come back by eleven. (OR)

   My father advised me to come back by eleven.

   (Instead of quoting the exact words we can report the meaning in our own words. Hence, **asked/cautioned/suggested/advised** are also possible.)

8. Jane told Jasper that it might rain that evening.

   (**Said to** becomes **told**; **may** becomes **might**; and **this evening** becomes **that evening**.)

9. Kate told me that she knew the way.

   (**Said to** becomes **told**; **I** becomes **she**; **know** becomes **knew**.)

10. Scott's mother asked/warned him not to forget his tiffin in his class.

    (The sense of the sentence can make us choose **warned** and **asked** in place of **told**.)

    (OR)

    Scott's mother told him that he must not forget his tiffin in his class.

    (**Said to** becomes **told**; **you** becomes **he**; **your** becomes **his**.)

Remember that some verbs should be followed by an indirect object. For instance,

- The principal **promised us** a holiday.

  (Not 'The principal promised a holiday.')

- The chairman **informed us/everyone/the members** that the meeting would start at three.

  (Not 'The chairman informed that the meeting would start at three.')

- His teacher **told him** that he should be serious in the class.

  (Not 'His teacher told that he should be serious in the class.')

Remember that if the direct speech is in simple past tense, it is changed to past perfect. For instance,

I said to my friend, 'I **saw the Taj** when I was eight years old.'

I told my friend that I **had seen the Taj** when I was eight years old.

The use of past perfect in place of simple past indicates that the monument was seen further in the past. However, when it becomes clear that something happened long before, past perfect is not required. Also when the reference is to something improbable or unreal, simple past is chosen.

See the following examples:
- 'I felt awful,' she told me.

  She told me that she felt awful.
- She said to the police, 'If I knew, I'd tell you.'

  She told the police that if she knew, she would tell them.
- 'I wish I had a girlfriend!' Stephen said.

  Stephen wished he had a girlfriend.

If the reported speech puts a question, question verbs such as **ask, enquire, wonder, want to know,** etc. can be used. If the reported speech starts with a yes/no question, **if** or **whether** is used in the indirect narration.

See the following examples:
- 'Is some more time left?' spoke the student.

  The student asked if some more time was left.
- 'Who is there?' she spoke in a surprised voice.

  She was wondering who was there.
- He asked, 'Lisa, do you have any answer?'

  He enquired/wondered if Lisa had any answer.

To put a request or order into indirect speech, the verbs **tell** and **ask** are commonly chosen. For example,
- 'Please go out of the room,' the teacher said to the students.

  The teacher asked the students to go out of the room.
- 'Would you move a little to your left,' he said to his fellow passenger.

  He asked/requested his fellow passenger to move a little to his left.
- 'Just keep quiet,' the teacher told us.

  The teacher asked us to keep quiet.

Since the focus is on the emotion or idea expressed, we can certainly use an alternative pattern while using indirect speech. Look at the following examples:
- 'I am sorry,' he said.

  He apologized.
- 'I am not going to help you,' he told me.

  He refused to help me.
- 'Well done for playing so well,' the coach said to his players.

  The coach complimented the players on playing well.
- 'You have to reach office in time!' the director told the officials.

  The director insisted that the officials reach office in time. (OR)

  The director asked his officials to reach office in time.

- 'Be careful,' the road is meandering.

  He warned/cautioned us that the road was meandering. (OR)

  He warned about the meandering road that was ahead.

- 'I am sorry, I lost your notebook,' he said.

  He regretted losing my notebook.

Thus, it becomes really important for us to correctly recapture the mood, tone, and tenor in indirect speech.

EXERCISE 2.30

Given below is an exercise to find out whether you can guess the emotion/idea appropriately. Hence, choose the verb that you feel would adequately express the idea in the context:

1. He **told/warned** us not to be rude with him next time.

2. The plumber **warned/informed** us that there was a leakage in the pipeline.

3. My doctor **advised/wanted** me to cut down on sweets.

4. The clerk **refused/advised** to help us.

5. The teacher **requested/asked** us to be silent.

6. She **cautioned/reminded** me that it was our marriage anniversary that day.

7. He **criticized/complained** us for being sloppy in our attitude.

8. He **reassured/reminded** me that we would get a seat.

9. Roberts **worried/wondered** why he should always be neglected for promotion.

10. The captain **warned/thanked** the players for winning him the crucial match.

EXERCISE 2.31

Change the following expressions into indirect speech:

1. 'Why do you always vex me like that?'

2. 'May we leave now?'

3. 'I'm afraid we can't do anything about that.'

4. 'Don't worry; I'll help you.'

5. 'We are not going to speak to the journalists.'

6. 'Be careful; he is a clever fellow.'

7. 'Why can't I get the same appreciation?'

8. 'Thank you very much.'

9. 'Let's watch a movie.'

10. 'You really need to see a doctor.'

Note: There may be more than one way of converting these sentences into an indirect speech.

2.16 CLAUSE AND ITS TYPES

In simple words, a clause is a group of words that forms part of a sentence and has a subject and a predicate of its own. Read the following expression:

Take this or leave it.

In this sentence, we have two different sentences:

- Take this.

- Leave it.

Now, both these sentences are combined with a coordinating conjunction *or*. Hence both—*take this* and *leave it*—are coordinate clauses. They both can stand on their own and are thus **independent clauses**. Now, look at this sentence:

Take an umbrella because it is going to rain.

In this sentence we have two clauses—**take an umbrella** and **because it is going to rain**. Out of these two clauses, *take an umbrella* is an **independent clause**. It can stand on its own. The other clause—*because it is going to rain*—has to depend on the other clause. Thus, it is a **subordinate clause**.

Therefore, clauses can be divided into two broad categories:

1. Independent or main or principal clause

2. Dependent or subordinate clause

Dependent clauses can be of various types. Read the following sentences and see how the dependent/ subordinate clause can be distinguished from the main clause:

1. When I read her letter, I realized my mistake.

2. Since you say so, I must look into the matter.

3. She lives as Americans do.

4. I could not buy the ticket as I had no money.

5. You may go wherever you like.

6. Though he is rich, he has no friends.

7. As soon as the thief heard the noise, he jumped over the fence.

8. If I see him, I will inform him.

9. I don't know what you are trying to prove.

10. This is the place where the battle of Panipat was fought.

This is how you can separate the main clause from the subordinate clause (highlighted in bold):

1. **When I read her letter**, I realized my mistake.

2. **Since you say so**, I must look into the matter.

3. She lives **as Americans do**.

4. I could not buy the ticket **as I had no money**.

5. You may go **wherever you like**.

6. **Though he is rich**, he has no friends.

7. **As soon as the thief heard the noise**, he jumped over the fence.

8. **If I see him**, I will inform him.

9. I don't know **what you are trying to prove**.

10. This is the place **where the battle of Panipat was fought**.

Dependent clauses can function as nouns, adjectives, and adverbs. Therefore, we can name them noun clause, adjective clause, and adverb clause. Now let us learn about such clauses a little more so that we may sharpen our writing skills in a systematic manner.

2.16.1 Noun Clauses

Read the following sentences and identify what kind of function the subordinate clauses perform:

- The child wondered **if his parents bought him what he wanted for Diwali**. (Object of the verb *wondered*)
- **What I want for dinner** is a pizza. (Subject of the predicate)
- The stranger told us **how he escaped the militants' clutches**. (Object of the verb *told*)
- Vacation is **what I need most**. (Complement of the subject *vacation*)
- Give it to **whoever requires it the most**. (Object of the preposition *to*)

So you can notice that all the above subordinate clauses are functioning as subjects, objects, or complements. All these clauses are noun clauses.

Note A noun clause can replace any noun in a sentence, by functioning as a subject, object, or complement.

2.16.2 Adjective Clauses

Let us read the following set of sentences and see what kind of function the subordinate clauses perform here:

- I listened to the song that you told me about.
- The novel that won the Pulitzer Prize had not sold well when it was first published.

In the first sentence, the clause 'that you told me about' functions as the modifier of the noun phrase 'the song'. Similarly, in the second sentence, the clause 'that won the Pulitzer Prize' can't stand by itself and modifies the noun phrase 'the novel'. Such dependent and modifying clauses are known as adjective clauses.

Note An adjective clause mostly modifies a noun or a pronoun that appears in the subject or the object position of a sentence.

See a few more similar examples:

- The building that they built on Juhu Beach in Mumbai is worth seven thousand dollars.
- The ceremony, which several celebrities attended, received intense coverage.

Now read the sentences given below:

- I'll do the laundry when I'm out of clothes.
- Radha brushed her long hair while she waited for her husband to come.

In the above two sentences, we observe that both the subordinate clauses are an answer to the 'when' part of the action. Since they function as adverbs, they are called adverb clauses.

Note Like all adverbials, adverb clauses express when, where, why, and how something occurs. A dependent clause is an adverb clause if it can be replaced by an adverb.

We hope by now you must be in a position to distinguish the subordinate clause from the main clause.

Go ahead and identify the subordinate clauses in the following sentences:

1. We asked whomever we saw for a reaction to the play.
2. We asked whoever called us to call back later.
3. They gave the money to whoever presented the winning ticket.

4. While we saw fumes in the air, we drove away as quickly as we could.

5. The group of tourists decided to have lunch in the village because the van needed repairs.

This is how you can separate the main clauses from the subordinate ones. The clauses highlighted below are the subordinate clauses:

1. We asked **whomever we saw** for a reaction to the play.

2. We asked **whoever called us** to call back later.

3. They gave the money to **whoever presented the winning ticket**.

4. **While we saw fumes in the air**, we drove away as quickly as we could.

5. The group of tourists decided to have lunch in the village **because the van needed repairs**.

2.16.3 Adverbial Clauses

An adverbial clause is a subordinate clause that acts as an adverb in a sentence. It may denote time, place, purpose, condition, concession, cause, reason, or result. See the following sentences:

- My daughter was playing with her friends **while I was busy in the kitchen**. (Adverbial clause of time)
- **Since it was raining heavily**, I could not attend my friend's wedding. (Adverbial clause of reason)
- **When the boss entered the conference hall**, all stood up and clapped. (Adverbial clause of time)
- **Although what you say might be right**, I can't change my decision. (Adverbial clause of concession)
- **If you go to Delhi**, bring some new books for me. (Adverbial clause of condition)
- Sit **wherever you like**. (Adverbial clause of place)
- Take medicine **so that you get well soon**. (Adverbial clause of purpose)

2.16.4 Relative Clauses

A relative clause is a subordinate clause that begins with a question word (e.g., who, which, where) or that. You can use it to modify a noun or a pronoun. A relative clause helps to identify or at times gives more information about a noun or a pronoun in a sentence.

Read the following set of sentences:

- Students who have critical listening and thinking skills often achieve good academic results.
- There is a new novel that highlights the pangs of the recent Mumbai terrorist attack.
- A university is a place where students can pursue advanced studies in specific disciplines.
- This is the banquet hall in which my niece's marriage will take place next week.

Words such as **who**, **that**, and **when** are often referred to as relative pronouns when they are used to introduce relative clauses.

They are used for the following:

Who	$\longrightarrow$	for people
Which	$\longrightarrow$	for things
That	$\longrightarrow$	for both people and things
Whom	$\longrightarrow$	as the object of a relative clause (in more formal English), though it is increasingly common to replace it with **who**
Whose	$\longrightarrow$	to indicate possession, as a determiner before nouns

See the following examples:
- Can you tell me the name of the person who first landed on the moon?
- All the students whose registration was done last month will continue attending the classes.
- In this conference I will be meeting Professor David Crystal, a renowned Professor of Linguistics whom I wanted to meet for a long time.

Types of relative clauses There are two types of relative clauses:
- Defining (or restrictive)
- Non-defining (or non-restrictive)

Defining/Restrictive clauses We use a defining (or restrictive) relative clause to 'identify' or 'restrict the reference of' a noun. We do not separate it from the rest of the sentence by commas (in text) or pauses (in speech). Let us read the following sentences:
- The student who scores highest marks in this essay competition will get a cash prize of five thousand rupees.
- The computer games and movies that involve fighting leave a negative impact on young children.

Non-defining/Non-restrictive clauses We use a non-defining (or non-restrictive) relative clause to provide additional information about the noun, whose identity or reference is already established.
- Albert Einstein, **who put forward the theory of relativity**, is considered by many as the most intelligent person in human history.
- The CIEFL, **which provides opportunities for advanced research in teaching of English**, is located in Hyderabad.

Note You should not use the relative pronoun *that* in non-defining relative clauses.

Reduction of relative clauses You can sometimes reduce a relative clause to create a more concise style. Read the examples given below:
- The training session (that was) arranged for middle level managers has been postponed for fortnight.
- The girl (who/whom) you met at the party last night is my cousin.

 EXERCISE 2.32

Combine the following sentences by using a coordinating or subordinating conjunction:

1.	You invited me.	I came.
2.	Children played.	Mother slept in the afternoon.
3.	Walk fast.	You should miss the train.
4.	Give me this purse.	I shall snatch it away from you.
5.	We found the lock broken.	We reached back home.
6.	They tried to win the race.	They lost the race.
7.	You are a genius.	You cannot solve this puzzle.
8.	Keep quiet.	Get lost.
9.	He is a complete idiot.	His brother is a wizard.
10.	I can do this.	I won't do this.

EXERCISE 2.33

Choose the adverbial clauses in the following sentences and identify their types:

1. Before you leave, tell me the whole story.

2. Since you say so, I must believe it.

3. If I want it, I'll let you know.

4. Search for it, where you kept it.

5. Don't turn on the television, until you finish your homework.

6. Though the exercise seems difficult, it has its own advantage.

7. They were asked to wait till they fainted in the sun.

8. Had I seen him, I would have informed him.

9. Some of us live so that we may accumulate more wealth.

10. Since you were not there, I left the letter with your sister.

EXERCISE 2.34

Complete the following sentences with a clause:

1. Since we wanted to watch a movie, _____ _____.

2. I went to Delhi so that _____.

3. We discussed our problems with our teacher _____.

4. _____, the teacher had already started teaching the lesson.

5. They tried their best _____.

6. The man _____ was my uncle.

7. Give me some money, otherwise _____ _____.

8. The officer asked me not to go home unless _____.

9. Had they worked hard, _____ _____.

10. Pay your taxes in time or _____ _____.

2.17 NON-FINITES

Read the following sentences:

1. I **play** in the evening.
2. I **have been playing** since morning.
3. I **was playing** yesterday.
4. I **will play** tomorrow again.
5. In the morning, I **played** for more than two hours.
6. I **had played** for half an hour or so before the bell rang.

In all the above sentences, the verb *play* has been contextualized with the help of the auxiliary verbs *have been*, *was*, *will*, *had*, etc. These auxiliaries are chosen according to the tense that is intended to be communicated. That is why, when the purpose is to suggest a continuation of an action over a period of time in the present, *have been playing* has been used. For a continuous action in the past, *was playing* has been chosen and in order to show future, *will play* is written. And for a routine action, simply *play* is chosen. Similarly, for some action that took place in the past, *played* is used and finally to refer to the earlier action (of playing) in the past, in comparison to the later one (the ringing of the bell) *had played* is used. Therefore, we see the verb *play* being used in different forms—*play, have been playing, was playing, will play, played,* and *had played.* Thus, *play* is a finite verb. A finite verb changes according to the tense that it has to denote. Now, to see the other side of the coin, look at the following sentences:

1. I plan to play in the evening.
2. I have been planning to play since morning.
3. I was planning to play yesterday morning.
4. I will plan to play tomorrow again.
5. In the morning, I planned to play with my friend.
6. I had planned to play before the bell rang.

Do you observe how the verb *to play* remains as such throughout all the above sentences? It has not changed its construction regardless of the tense employed, whereas the other verb *plan* in these sentences keeps on changing as it becomes *plan, was planning, have been planning, will plan, had planned,* etc. In this sentence, *plan* is a finite verb, whereas *play* is used as a to-infinitive. Thus the verb that gets changed according to the tense and time is a finite verb and the one that does not get affected is a non-finite verb.

There are three types of non-finite verbs—**infinitive**, **gerund**, and **participle**. Let us see the following set of sentences to understand them in detail:

1. My friend, John, wants **to swim**.
2. Not just that, John simply loves **swimming**.
3. **Swimming** is his absolute passion.
4. His girlfriend, Jane, however dislikes **swimming**.
5. Because of this, Jane never learnt how **to swim**.
6. So, whenever Jane finds him **swimming**, she goes nuts.
7. This does not affect John who just keeps **swimming**.
8. Even yesterday, Jane found John in the **swimming** pool.
9. When she came in the morning, John was **swimming** and when she left in the afternoon, he was still **swimming**. It became too much when she found him **swimming** again in the evening.
10. Angry and distraught, Jane decided to walk out on John, leaving him in the sweet company of his not so sweet hobby—**swimming**.

Probably, the expression *to swim* in the first and fifth sentences is not a problem now. It is similar to the expression *to play* that occurred in the examples that preceded this set of sentences. So *to swim*, like *to play*, is a **to-infinitive**. It has a *to* and the base form of the verb. So the expressions, such as *to swim, to dance, to speak, to kill*, and so on and so forth are examples of **to-infinitives** which consist of *to* and the base form of the verbs. In the other type of infinitive, only the base form of the verb is used. Such infinitives are known as plain/bare infinitives. For example:

They made me **laugh**.

In all the remaining sentences, the word *swimming* occurs.

Let us see all the remaining sentences one by one:

1. Not just that, John simply loves **swimming**.

The verb *loves* in this sentence answers *what John loves,* i.e., *swimming.* If you see it carefully, this sentence has a structure which is similar to the structure of the sentences given below:

1. John loves her.

2. John loves coffee.

3. John loves this house.

Now, what are these words—*her, coffee, this house?* These are nouns and pronouns. Hence, in the sentence *John loves swimming,* the word *swimming* replaces other nouns or pronouns such as *her, coffee, this house,* etc. Seen thus, the class of the word *swimming* appears to be similar to that of a noun or a pronoun. However, *swimming* is not exactly like *her, coffee,* and *this house* because it embodies some action *swim* also, which other words such as *her, coffee,* and *this house* do not embody. Therefore, *swimming* in this sentence is a gerund which though appears to be a verb but is used as a noun.

Further, since a noun or a pronoun can take the subject and the object positions in a sentence, the word *swimming* in both the second and the third sentences takes exactly these positions. So, we write the following:

1. John loves swimming.

    (John (subject) loves (verb) swimming (object))

2. Swimming is his absolute passion.

    (Swimming (subject) is (verb) his absolute passion (subject complement))

Similarly, in the fourth sentence observe that the word *swimming* becomes the object as it answers what Jane, the subject, dislikes:

His girlfriend, Jane, however, dislikes swimming.
((His girlfriend, Jane (subject), however dislikes (verb) swimming (object))

In the sixth sentence, however, the word *swimming* is used in an entirely different way. Look at it:

So, whenever Jane finds him swimming, she goes nuts.

The word *swimming* here seems to qualify the object *him* doing something. The word *swimming* in this sentence has the qualities both of a verb, as it denotes some action, and that of an adjective, for it also acts as a modifier. This is what a *participle* is. Look some more examples of participles:

1. **Thinking** all was safe, she decided to take risk.

2. **Driven** by passion and desire, Dr Faustus falls headlong into the hell.

3. **Studded** with armour, he approached the battlefield.

4. **Pining** for more, man keeps **hankering** after material possessions.

Look carefully to observe that all the words here—*thinking, driven, studded,* and *pining*—suggest some action but at the same time, they also qualify the subjects—*she, Dr Faustus, he,* and *man,* respectively. So, the words *thinking, driven, studded,* and *pining* are participles. *Thinking* and *pining* are present participles and *driven* and *studded* are past participles. *Hankering* in the last sentence, however, functions as a gerund.

In the next sentence, the word *swimming* is again a gerund. In the eighth sentence, the word *swimming* qualifies *pool* and hence is a **participle adjective** that is formed from verbs with -ing and -ed or -en endings;

e.g., interesting story, tired face, broken toy, etc. and act as adjectives. In the ninth sentence, *swimming* is used twice and both the times, it is a **pure verb** in the progressive tense. In the tenth sentence, swimming is used as a participle and in the last sentence, it is a gerund.

Believing that you now can make out the difference between a gerund, a participle, and a to-infinitive, we put you through the task of making such distinction. Go ahead and identify the non-finites, namely gerunds, participles, and to-infinitives in the following sentences:

1. Believing people seldom doubt.
2. This is not the time to fight with each other.
3. Singing gives me immense pleasure.
4. Crooning an old tune, she picked up the phone.
5. We are terribly sorry to hear this.
6. Beating the door wildly, the girl screamed for help.
7. He is fond of playing cricket.
8. Jumping over the fence, the thief escaped.
9. He saw a clown standing on his head.
10. His dejected look won't make him a good public speaker.

See how we can make out these three non-finites:

1. **Believing** people seldom doubt.

   (Those people who believe qualifies people besides showing action, hence present participle)

2. This is not the time **to fight** with each other.

   (to + the base form of the verb, hence to-inifinitive)

3. **Singing** gives me immense pleasure.

   (What gives me pleasure—singing—a verbal noun, hence gerund)

4. **Crooning** an old tune, she picked up the phone.

   (She picked up the phone doing what—crooning; hence *crooning* qualifies *she* besides denoting action; hence a verbal adjective; therefore, present participle)

5. We are terribly sorry **to hear** this.

   (to + base form of the verb, hence *to hear* is a to-infinitive)

6. **Beating** the door wildly, the girl screamed for help.

   (*Beating* qualifies the person besides denoting action hence adjective verb—participle)

7. He is fond of **playing** cricket.

   (He is fond of what—*playing*. Hence, *playing* is an object + verb = noun + verb = gerund)

8. **Jumping** over the fence, the thief escaped.

   (Adds to the meaning of the action by qualifying the person doing it; hence, a participle)

9. He saw a clown **standing** on his head.

   (The clown was seen doing what—standing on his head. Hence, a participle)

10. His **dejected** look won't make him a good public speaker.

    (What type of look—dejected; hence participle adjective)

EXERCISE 2.35

Figure out the gerunds, participles, to-infinitives, and verbs in progressive tense in the following expressions:

1. Making a lame excuse, he sounded quite cheap.
2. Children love making mud castles.
3. Seeing is believing.
4. Seeing, he believed.
5. Waving their hats and handkerchiefs, the crowd cheered the king.
6. Asking questions is easier than answering them.
7. Making food is not difficult.
8. You are making a fool of yourself.
9. Making tea, she answered the call on her cell.
10. He died in the waiting room.
11. Waiting is often painful.
12. He died waiting for the train.
13. King Lear decides to divide his kingdom.
14. The thief entered through the broken widow.
15. We live to succeed.

At times, we make errors in using participles. Read the following sentences and decide if participles are correctly chosen:

1. **Crying** over a broken toy, the mother consoled her child.
2. **Blinded** by the fog, the bike rammed into a tree.
3. **Sitting** in the park, a snake bit him.
4. **Driven** by greed, valuables were pinched.
5. **Upon landing** at the airport, the company sent a Toyota to pick her up.
6. **Being corpulent and overweight**, the hill could not be mounted.
7. **Having flooded** the street, she could not reach home.
8. **Going** up the hill, the old ramparts became visible.
9. **Entering** the room, the darkness was quite blinding.
10. **Being built** on the rock, the experts predicted that the building would not settle.

Can you figure out what goes wrong with these sentences? Actually, the participle beginnings such as **crying over the broken toy, blinded by the fog, sitting in the park, driven by greed, upon landing, being corpulent and overweight, having flooded, going up the hill, entering the room,** and **being built on the rock** are all modifying in nature. They all add to the meaning of the word that they modify.

Now, as a norm, the modified and the modifier need to be placed close to each other to avoid ambiguity in expression. For example, the participle beginning—*crying over a broken toy*—is followed by *the mother*. Now, is it the *mother* who is *crying over the broken toy* or *her child*? Of course, the child.

Thus, the wrong positioning of the participle beginning makes these sentences amusingly ambiguous. Therefore, remember to keep the participles close to the words they are required to modify. The above sentences can be recast in a meaningful manner as follows:

1. The mother **consoled her child who was crying over a broken toy**.
2. **As the biker was blinded by the fog,** the bike rammed into a tree.

3. A snake bit him **while he was sitting in the park**.

4. **Driven by greed, they** pinched the valuables.

5. **Upon her landing at the airport**, the company sent a Toyota to pick her up.

6. **As they were corpulent and overweight**, they could not mount the hill.

7. **As the street was flooded, she could** not reach home.

8. **As we went up the hill, the old ramparts** became visible.

9. **As we entered the room, the darkness** was quite blinding.

10. The experts predicted that the **building would not settle because it was being built on the rock**.

Wrong placement of participle is not the only type of error that we commit while dealing with non-finites. At times, gerunds and to-infinitives are wrongly used in place of each other making the entire grammatical structure go haywire. Look at the following sentences and decide whether they are grammatically correct:

1. The school authorities failed in informing the parents of the sick child.

2. Avoid to copy others!

3. When he realized that smoking causes cancer, he stopped to smoke.

4. The rich refuse accepting the poor in their fold.

5. To err is human; still, we should avoid to make the same error in life.

6. When you finish to read the book, would you lend me that for a couple of days?

7. We hope achieving the target by the year end.

8. If you have some doubt, don't hesitate calling me.

9. They have managed completing their task in time.

10. Though he has to stay in a city, he has always missed to be in his village.

Can you make out what went wrong? Gerunds and to-infinitives have been wrongly chosen in these constructions. In fact, there are some verbs, such as *agree, manage, aim, demand, fail, offer, decline, want, wish, prepare, tend*, etc., which are normally followed by a *to-infinitive*, that is, to + verb's base form.

On the other hand, there are certain other verbs, such as *avoid, dread, deny, feel like, imagine, consider, suggest, consider*, etc., which are usually followed by a *gerund*, that is, -ing with the base form of the verb. The above sentences are rewritten correctly as follows:

1. The school authorities **failed to inform** the parents of the sick child.

2. Avoid **copying** others!

3. When he realized that smoking causes cancer, he **stopped smoking**.

4. The rich **refuse to accept** the poor in their fold.

5. To err is human; still, we should **avoid making** the same error in life.

6. When you **finish reading** the book, would you lend me that for a couple of days?

7. We hope **to achieve** the target by the year end.

8. If you have some doubt, don't **hesitate to** call me.

9. They have managed **to complete** their task in time.

10. Though he has to stay in a city, he has always **missed being** in his village.

Even when some of the non-finite verbs such as *come, try, regret, remember, stop,* etc. take both **to-infinitive** and **-ing forms**, they don't mean the same thing. Look how the meaning communicated with to-infinitive is different from the one communicated through -ing construction in the following sentences:

1. He **stopped to take** a cup of tea on the way.

   (He stopped so that he could take a cup of tea.)

2. He **stopped taking** a cup of tea in the morning.

   (The practice of taking a cup of tea in the morning was stopped.)

3. The child **came running** with a kite in his hand.

   (It describes the manner in which the child came, i.e., running.)

4. Every child **has to come** to realize that he/she (or it) cannot afford to be a child any longer.

   (It highlights the gradual change that takes place in every child's life.)

5. **Remember to** take your umbrella if you go out; it is going to rain today.

   (The action of remembering precedes the other action.)

6. I don't **remember having seen** him all these days.

   (The other action precedes the action of remembering.)

7. **Stop telling** me that you are always right!

   (It focuses on what needs to be discontinued.)

8. **He stopped to have** a closer look at the report before resuming further.

   (It highlights an action completed in the past.)

9. I **regret having spoken** to you so rudely at that moment.

   (Not happy about what the speaker had done in the past.)

10. We **regret to inform** you that despite our best efforts, we are unable to accommodate your request.

    (Not happy about what the speaker regrets doing now.)

 EXERCISE 2.36

Find out whether the expressions written in bold in the following sentences act as gerunds, participles, participle adjectives, or verbs:

1. **Challenging** the enemy, he threw his handkerchief on the floor.

2. **Challenging** someone's beliefs is not always pleasant.

3. He was chucked out for he was **challenging** the authorities.

4. **Speaking** over the phone, he sounded like a moor.

5. Don't disturb, I am **speaking** to my boss over the phone.

6. He avoids **speaking** to me directly.

7. We don't need inarticulate fools, we require **speaking** people.

8. **Reading** is a wonderful habit.

9. **Reading** newspaper in the morning is a matter of routine for many.

10. The parents were shocked to find the child **reading** an erotica.

11. Last night, I broke my **reading** glasses.

12. Men are often seen **reading** at the breakfast table while women are seen **talking** incessantly.

13. **Seeing** a snake in the room, she shouted at the top of her voice.

14. You cannot avoid **seeing** the truth.

15. Why are you **telling** me this?

16. He gave his enemy a **telling** blow.

17. **Crying** inconsolably, children take their **broken** toys to their elders.

18. **Pampered** children are not those who are told a story by their grandmothers.

19. The **told** story needs to be retold.

20. **Exuding** confidence, he did not try to conceal his **vaulting** ambition.

 **EXERCISE 2.37**

Rewrite the following sentences using appropriate gerunds, participles, or to-infinitives:

1. Stop to talk to me in such a rude manner!

2. I want going through the whole exercise all over again.

3. The members resented the idea to invite her to the meeting.

4. I don't feel like to tell you that I am not happy with your performance.

5. Avoid to be late all the time!

6. He admitted to be there at the time of the crime.

7. The speaker failed making a proper impression on the audience.

8. We all detest to face difficult situations.

9. To our surprise, she declined helping us even in those circumstances.

10. How can you imagine to do such a thing!

2.18 PUNCTUATION MARKS

Punctuation marks are visual indicators used in a written or printed text in order to separate sentences or a part of a sentence from another. They are used to make an idea readable. Look at the following example:

I can't do it he said speaking at the top of his voice she listened to it and said ok go to hell

Would you like to read something of this sort? Of course, it would be quite a challenge to read a thing like that. Can you make out what is wrong with the above expression? The sentence does not have any commas, inverted commas, full stop, or exclamation marks; in brief, the signs that are known as **punctuation marks**.

In this section, we shall learn how to use punctuation marks correctly. Given below are the important punctuation marks which are normally used in written English:

1. Full stop (.)
2. Comma (,)
3. Dash (—)
4. Hyphen (-)
5. Semicolon (;)
6. Double inverted commas (" ")
7. Single inverted commas (' ')

8. Colon (:)
9. Apostrophe (')
10. Parentheses ( )
11. Sign of interrogation/Question mark (?)
12. Exclamation mark (!)
13. Capital letters

Let us see all these punctuation marks in detail.

2.18.1 Full Stop

The **full stop** (.) is used in the following cases:

1. It is used to mark the end of an affirmative, negative, or imperative sentence.
- Marie Curie was a great scientist.
- She did not know the way to the market.
- Listen to me.
2. It is also used in abbreviations, such as the following.
- He is an M.B.B.S. doctor.
- She works for I.D.B.I.
- Our teacher is pursuing his Ph.D.

Not long ago, it was customary to write *Mr.* and *Mrs.* in English, that is, with a full stop at the end of these words. In current usage, however, we write these abbreviations as *Mr* and *Mrs*, that is, without a full stop since they are now seen as full spellings.

2.18.2 Comma

Just as a full stop marks the end of a sentence, a **comma** (,) suggests a pause in writing. Following are the main uses of a comma:

1. It indicates omission of a word, especially a verb.
- You can do that; I, never.
- Her mother was an English; her father, an American.
- She got her prize; I, my punishment.
2. It separates the co-ordinate clause(s) in a compound sentence.
- I came, I saw, I conquered.
- Father is in the office, mother is in the kitchen.
- Men may come and men may go, but I go on for ever.
3. It separates the subject and the long preceding phrase that characterizes it.
- Harassed and distraught right from the early days of her marriage, she decided to embark on a journey of her own.
- Contrary to the notion that it consumes a lot of your time and gives you only a little, reading gives you an opportunity to look not just beyond but inside you as well.
4. It separates the same parts of speech used in the same sentence.
- She was tall, slim, and beautiful.
- Books, chairs, tables, desks, and settees could be seen in the lawn.
- Unwilling to go to school, the child whined, cried, groaned, and protested whichever way he could.
5. It separates the parenthetical ideas from the core ideas in a sentence.
- Your suggestion, however, is quite tempting.
- The villain, having trapped the hero, gave a malicious smile.
- No such efforts, therefore, are going to yield fruit.

6. It marks a non-defining clause. It is used to contribute to the original idea in a parenthetical way and can be omitted without doing any harm to the core meaning of the sentence.

- My friend, who is a journalist, doesn't think so.
- The poet, the one who always defied the system, decided not to comply with the king's orders.
- His book, the one that he wrote at the fag end of his career, is likely to create a stir.

7. It is used to separate two or more nouns in apposition.

- Shakespeare, the greatest dramatist of all times, was born in 1564.
- Indira Gandhi, the only woman Prime Minister of India so far, was a great politician.
- Sam, my uncle, is returning from England.

8. It is used to address people.

- Sir, I am indebted to you.
- How are you, my dear?
- Come here, little girl.

9. It marks off direct quotations from the rest of the sentence.

- Mother said to her children, 'Have your food.'
- 'What do you think,' said he, 'is the cause of your failure?'
- 'Come in and tell what happened,' the fat man said and moved away from the door.

10. It is used to separate an adverbial clause from the principal clause.

- When we came back, we found the doors opened.
- If you do not work hard, you cannot succeed.
- Though it is none of my business, I cannot force myself into aloofness on this issue.

11. It is used before and after words, phrases, or clauses that are introduced to the main thought in a parenthetical way.

- This, in no way, is my problem.
- The poor little children, when they first saw him, thought he was an angel.
- Your story, in all probability, is fairy tale.

2.18.3 Dash

A **dash** (—) indicated by a long horizontal line is often used in place of a colon or parenthesis. Here are its uses:

1. It is used to emphasize the idea anticipated in the sentence.

- Finally, we got what we had all along desired—our first television set at home.
- He is what you expect him to be—the greatest fool on earth!
- They told us whatever was to be told—nothing could be done.

2. At times, much like a comma, a dash is used to separate an expression from the rest of the sentence.

- He is—after all—his mother's son.
- In the end—to be precise—I would say that all that shines is not gold.
- We are—generally speaking—people of short memories.

3. It is also used after the colon to indicate something that follows.
- These are some of the views—
- He says—*frailty thy name is woman*!
4. It is also used to indicate an abrupt change of idea.
- Had he not boarded the plane—but what is the use of thinking like that?
- Once you reach here—but wait, you are coming, aren't you?
- Only if we were a little more educated—but how would that have changed our lives?

2.18.4 Hyphen

A **hyphen** (-) is a shorter line than a dash. It is used to join two or more words in a compound word.
- She was truly tormented by her daughter-in-law.
- The commander-in-chief refused to sanction any leave to the sergeant.
- The ex-director of the company is paying a visit this afternoon.
- These days, in the name of scholars, you will see jack-of-all-trades but master-of-none.

2.18.5 Semicolon

A **semicolon** (;) stands for a longer pause than a comma. Following are the uses of a semicolon:

1. It is used to separate clauses.
- Reading maketh a full man; conference a ready man; and writing an exact man.
- Man proposes; God disposes.
- Not that I loved Caesar less; but that I loved Rome more.
- It is easy to be difficult; but difficult to be easy.
2. It is used to express different ideas without writing a new sentence.
- Today, we don't do anything regarding global warming; tomorrow there is nothing we can do about it.
- In the morning, he fought with his wife; in the afternoon, he reconciled with her.
- One man kept her in good humour; the other kept her in the need of the first.

2.18.6 Colon

A **colon** (:) is used to list examples and enumeration.
- Following are the examples of parts of speech: noun, pronoun, adjective, adverb, etc.
- These are the points to be kept in mind: …
- The team consists of eleven players: Sachin Tendulkar, Rahul Dravid, V.V.S. Laxman,…

2.18.7 Single and Double Inverted Commas

Double inverted commas (" ") are used to quote the exact words of the person being quoted.
- He said, "You are my friend."
- "One cannot fool oneself for a long time," cleaning his glasses he spoke, "but you have tried to keep yourself foolish enough for a pretty long time."
- Eliot begins by saying, "April is the cruelest month."

Single inverted commas (' ') are used to cite a quotation within another quotation.

- "There is no point in keeping a pulled face", said he, "even if you are perturbed by the 'to be or not to be' conundrum."
- "What sort of movie was that—so loud and so pompous?" felt she, "they seem to have forgotten that 'art lies in concealing art'."

Many publications, including this book, follow the exact opposite of the rules mentioned in the examples, as per their individual house-style guidelines:

2.18.8 Apostrophe

The **apostrophe** (') is used in the following cases:

1. It is used to indicate the possessive of a noun. If the noun is singular, the apostrophe is followed by an **s**; if the noun is plural, the **s** is followed by the apostrophe, except when the plural does not end in **s**, as in the case of a few irregular nouns, e.g., children's.

- The children's books are lying there.
- Brown's house is next to ours.
- Waugh's captaincy is still appreciated.
- The girl's purse was lost. (the purse of a girl)
- The girls' purses were stolen. (purses of many girls)

2. It is also used to show words in a contracted form.

- I feel it's time to move out of the house. (*it's* stands for *it is*)
- It's been ages since we met her. (*it's* stands for *it has*)
- Let's go and watch some play. (*let's* stands for *let us*)
- You're just a complete fool. (*you're* stands for *you are*)
- Won't you come inside? (*won't* stands for *will not*)
- Don't you dare speak to him like that! (*don't* stands for *do not*)

3. It is sometimes also used to show the letters and figures in the plural form to avoid confusion.

- In 1970's was seen the first wave of Parallel Hindi Cinema.
- Articulate your s's and sh's properly.
- Round off all the 0.25's and 0.50's in the final total.

2.18.9 Parentheses

Parentheses ( ) are used by writers to indicate an afterthought by introducing some words, a phrase, or a clause:

- The great man (this is how he is seen to be in the area) is reported to have killed his wife.
- The development (so it seems) was achieved by turning the poor out of their huts.

2.18.10 Sign of Interrogation/Question Mark

The **sign of interrogation/question mark** (?) is used after a direct question or a tag question that is appended to a statement:

- Do you understand what I say?

- Shall we take some rest?
- You are stupid, aren't you?

Remember that a question mark is not used after an indirect question.

- I am not sure what to do in life.
- The inspector could not make out if she was telling a lie.
- They asked their children whether they are doing good parenting.

2.18.11 Exclamation Mark

The **exclamation mark** (!) is used in phrases and sentences that express sudden, strong emotion or a wish:

- May you live long!
- What a terrible sight!
- Hamlet, speak no more!
- Oh, you fool! Listen to me first and then decide.

2.18.12 Capital Letters

Capital letters are used for various purposes, which are as follows:

1. To begin with, we start a sentence with a capital letter.
- We can't do anything about it.
- No problem.
- Has he come?
2. They are used to begin a sentence inside inverted commas.
- It is said, 'To err is human.'
- Shakespeare says, 'One may smile and smile, and still be a villain.'
3. They normally begin a proper noun and the adjectives we form from it.
- Pinter is known for his theatre language popularly known as Pinteresque idiom.
- Italy is a place of intellect; the Italian thinker Machiavelli is still well known.
- Though *Maqbool* does try to recreate Shakespeare's classic *Macbeth*, the sweep of imagination and grandeur of spectacle is hardly Shakespearean.
4. They are used to refer to a person's title or degree.
- Pandit Nehru was the first prime minister of India.
- Sir V.S. Naipaul is visiting India next year.
- Dr R.P. Pareek, an MD, is an expert in diabetics.
5. They are used to refer to the names of festivals.
- Christmas falls on 25th December.
- Diwali is the single most important festival in our family.
6. They are used to refer to the names of days, weeks, months, and events.
- On Sundays, we generally get up quite late.

- North India is quite cold in January.
- The Trojan War has acquired mythical significance in our collective unconscious.

7. They are used to mark the important words in a title. Normally, the head words, such as nouns, pronouns, adjectives, verbs, and adverbs, are written in capital letters, whereas conjunctions, prepositions, and articles are written in small letters.

- 'Ode on a Grecian Urn' is a great poem by John Keats.
- The title of my book, *Language as Stratagem in Pinter's Plays,* has won me laurels on many occasions.
- His sister is pursuing her research and is currently busy in the writing of a project entitled *Rediscovering Indian Diaspora: A Study of Postmodern Fiction in English with Special Reference to the Works of Jhumpa Lahiri, Rohinton Mistry, and Jaishree Mishra.*

8. They are chosen to refer to the word *God* and the pronouns replacing it.

- God is great.
- No one knows His ways.
- Don't worry; He knows that you are innocent.

9. They are used in words of exclamations.

- Oh! You are back.
- This is the solution, Eh!
- Ugh! I forgot to call you.

10. The personal pronoun *I* is always written in capital letter.

- I can't see you.
- 'It is doubtful,' I said to her.
- I will not say I have won the battle unless I am convinced that I have done it.

 EXERCISE 2.38

Punctuate the following choosing appropriate punctuation marks at appropriate places:

1. That he was alone and wanted to be alone was a matter of concern for all

2. If you want to be healthy in life do this get up early work hard lead a natural life

3. When I heard a knock at the door I turned around

4. It is however not all that important to speak all the time

5. When he was young Shakespeare who went on to become the greatest writer of all times married a woman eight years his senior

6. God made women beautiful so that men may love them and men foolish so that they may return the favour

7. His attitude to say the least was really horrible

8. America England and France got together and went after Germany

9. Milton the great Puritan poet went blind at the age of forty-four

10. He told his wife 'Learn to live with my silence'

ANSWER KEY

Exercise 2.1

1. Belongings
2. Furniture
3. Glasses
4. Hair
5. Air
6. Music
7. Forces
8. Equipment
9. Premises
10. Jeans

Exercise 2.2

1. Two packets of bread
2. A cup of coffee
3. Picture gallery
4. Scenery
5. Weather Is
6. Milk
7. Evidence
8. Leisure
9. Fear
10. People
11. Goods train
12. Airs
13. Room
14. Stone
15. Respects

Exercise 2.3

1. Yesterday **I/~~me~~** went to watch a movie.
2. 'Don't worry! It's **I/me** in the backyard.
3. Let's distribute the chocolates between you and **I/me**.
4. She does not know what to do with **~~her~~/herself**. (Both the pronouns being used for the same person)
5. **That/~~this~~** was quite ingenious. (refers to the past)
6. We all know that Smita acts better than **him/~~himself~~**.
7. While riding, she fell off the horse and hurt **~~her~~/herself**.
8. Can she ever figure out what **she/~~her~~** is doing?
9. He is likely to drive **~~him~~/himself** home today.
10. Leave it, this bag is **~~our~~/ours**.

Exercise 2.4

1. His
2. Our
3. Their
4. One
5. Their
6. Its
7. Ours
8. Their
9. They
10. We

Exercise 2.5

1. The report is really good; it not only discusses the problem but also gives **a few** suggestions.
2. **The faster** you drive on a serpentine hilly road, **the poorer** are your chances of returning home safely.
3. Yesterday he was really sick, but today he is **much better**.
4. This film is **as good as** the one released last year by the same director.
5. The **oldest** man in the colony too left the house recently.
6. I approached the officer, but he hardly seemed **interested** in listening to me.
7. You can certainly do it, but you need to exert **a little** more.
8. Movies produced in India are more than **those produced in Iran/those in Iran/the number of movies produced in Iran**.

9. Ashwin is the **most successful among all spinners** in contemporary Indian team.

   OR

   Ashwin is **more successful** than **any other spinner** in contemporary Indian team.

10. **The poor** are easily manipulated by **the rich**.

Exercise 2.6

1. Briskly (Adverb); (Verb + Adverb)
2. Really (Adverb); (Adverb + Adjective)
3. Rather (Adverb); (Adverb + Adverb)
4. Good (Adjective); (Adjective + Adverb)
5. So (Adverb); (Adverb + Adjective)
6. Quite (Adverb); (Adverb + Adjective)
7. Terribly (Adverb); (Adverb + Verb)
8. Elegantly (Adverb); (Adverb + Adjective)
9. Rather (Adverb); (Adverb + Adjective)
10. Quite (Adverb); (Adverb + Adjective)

Exercise 2.7

Wonderful; Slowly; Extremely; Majestically; Heavily; Narrow; Gloriously; Excited; Energetically; Leisurely

Exercise 2.8

1. He could always sense the problem.
2. Gently rub the old man's leg.

   OR

   Rub the old man's leg gently.
3. The plane somehow landed safely.
4. Last month, the sales fell sharply.

   OR

   The sales fell sharply last month.
5. He was nearly dead in the accident.
6. This man always speaks the truth.
7. Nadal pumped the air aggressively.
8. The newly recruited marketing manager sat quietly in the meeting.
9. Place the book there.
10. You could rarely see him reaching late.

Exercise 2.9

1. To	2. For	3. For	4. To	5. On
6. In	7. Between	8. For	9. Through	10. Into

Exercise 2.10

1. b	2. a	3. a	4. b	5. a
6. a	7. b	8. a	9. b	10. b

Exercise 2.11

1. I am getting **concerned about/~~concerned with~~** what is going to happen to the programme.
2. The poor in this country are even **deprived of/~~deprived for~~** two square meals a day.

3. Caught up in adverse circumstances, he is ~~fighting with~~/**fighting for** his survival.
4. Desperately, she moved from window to window, ~~enquiring from~~/**enquiring about** the plane.
5. You are not supposed to hit your opponent ~~under the belt point~~/**below the belt point**.
6. A lot **depends on**/~~depends at~~ how the middle order performs.
7. Initially, the producer was not ~~interested with~~/**interested in** the script.
8. After the sudden demise of their father, they have to **fend for**/~~fend at~~ themselves.
9. The fault is entirely yours! You were standing right **in the middle of the road**/~~on the middle of the road~~!
10. All these monuments were damaged ~~with the fanatic intruder~~/**by the fanatic intruder**.

Exercise 2.12

I reached the cinema hall well **in** time to be right **in** front **of** the queue **at** the ticket-window. I kept standing there **for** a long while; the window remained shut, but the queue **behind** me kept growing all the time. More and more people joined **in** and the long queue swell even **beyond** the boundary wall. Thrilled **at** the idea **of** leading such a large contingent **of** cinegoers, I really felt flattered **by** my achievement. Meanwhile, two eager boys **behind** me started talking **about** what was so great abou⁻ the movie. They first began **with** how good the acting **of** their favourite movie star was. One **by** one, they analysed his dancing, romancing, fighting, cavorting, and jumping skills. Then their discussion drifted **towards** how the villain too had emerged as potent adversary **of** the protagonist. Having discussed the exploits of the hero and the villain, they went **on to** describe how wonderful had their favourite heroine looked **in** each frame **of** the movie and how charming she looked **in** her dancing sequence! Silently cursing them **for** ruining all my interest in the movie, I kept waiting **for** the ticket-window to open.

Exercise 2.13

1. **Either** you talk sense, **or** keep your mouth shut!
2. Women at the club kept gossiping **while** their husbands played cards.
3. He talks to me **as though** he were my boss.
4. **Whether** you allow me **or** not, I am going to the rave party.
5. The application cannot be submitted now **because** the last date was 13 October 2016.
6. Our company backs itself on customized products **whereas** they thrive on their gross turnover.
7. You are telling me **as if** I keep doing it repeatedly.
8. The boy **neither** called up **nor** sent the pen drive.
9. **By the way**, when is your flight?
10. **As** you don't hold the membership card, we cannot consider giving you the discount.

Exercise 2.14

1. b	2. b	3. a	4. b	5. b
6. a	7. a	8. b	9. a	10. a

Exercise 2.15

1. First of all, ~~Coming to, As regards, With reference to~~
2. ~~Before, By all means~~, After all
3. ~~By the way~~, For example, ~~By all means~~
4. Even as, ~~Even if, Even though~~
5. ~~On the contrary~~, On the whole, ~~By and by~~
6. To wind up, ~~To begin with, Turning to~~
7. Of course, ~~By all means, Certainly~~
8. ~~Just as, Since,~~ Look
9. Moreover, ~~Therefore, It seems~~
10. As, Actually, ~~Since~~

Exercise 2.16

1. Next year, she will go to **a** university in Netherlands.
2. **A** woman was seen pushing the cart along the street.
3. Will you be getting **an** M.B.B.S. degree for this?
4. Seeing the ghost approaching her, she closes her eyes in **a** fearful expression.
5. Though she appears to be **a** Chinese, she is **an** Indonesian.

Exercise 2.17

1. My mother **buys** vegetables from the Reliance Fresh Store.
2. Normally he **walks** very fast.
3. She **rebukes** her children for playing computer games.
4. We **do not find** the solution of this problem on the Internet.
5. They **do not trust** their employees.
6. Girls **do not like** wrestling.
7. The chief librarian usually **purchases** new books and journals for the library in July.
8. Snigdha **dances** skillfully.
9. Siddharth **takes** coffee after dinner.
10. It **rains** frequently in London.

Exercise 2.18

1. I **am working** hard for my GRE test these days.
2. We **are facing** an acute problem in power supply these days.
3. Since Mr Smith **is going** to France, he **is learning** French these days.
4. Due to recession, many companies **are downsizing** their operations.
5. Look! Anne **is relishing** orange juice and French fries in the sun.
6. Our institute **is planning** to bring a change in its promotion policy.
7. Our government **is not cutting** down the prices of petroleum and gas.
8. The patient **is wearing** a blanket because he is feeling very cold.
9. The watchman normally **brings** tea and snacks for the hostel inmates from outside.
10. That great man always **donates** a lot of money for poor children.

Exercise 2.19

1. Why **do you** always come late?
2. He **is likely** to visit our school during vacation.
3. 'Look, how glorious **appears** the Sun today!'
4. He **is going to resume** his innings on a nervous 99 after lunch.
5. Why **are you informing** me about that now?
6. Sometimes it **rains** here quite torrentially.
7. He **writes** his poems in Urdu.
8. We **are waiting** for the signal to clear.
9. Normally, the temperature **ranges** between 10 and 20 degrees in this region.
10. He **is conducting** a meeting right now in his chamber.

Exercise 2.20

1. Earlier, I **could not contact** you.
2. **Did** the officer **inform** you about that?
3. My children **played** badminton while I **slept**.
4. **Did** your company **plan** to start something in Kashmir earlier this year?
5. Last month, my wife **visited** New York to attend a meeting.
6. His father **drove** us back home very fast.
7. Mr Batra **deposited** five thousand rupees in his son's account.
8. They **opened** new branches in all the cities but surprisingly **closed** each of these one by one.
9. Since she was not well, she **consulted** the doctor.
10. The teachers at the conference **identified** the innovative methods of teaching.

Exercise 2.21

1. I am not feeling hungry, I **have taken** a heavy breakfast.
2. It is nice to see you again; we **have not met** each other for such a long time!
3. Recently, the state government **has passed** a bill for free college education for girls.
4. Though she loves going on long drives, she **has not learnt** how to drive.
5. **Have** you ever **thought** how stressful life **has become** these days?
6. I know I **have left** no stone unturned to pass the CAT exam.
7. The music band **has displayed** a stupendous show this time.
8. The film director **has developed** the plot of the story and used the camera and lights skilfully.
9. He is not aware of the legal implications as he **has not purchased** any land before.
10. The policy **has come** as the result of scathing attack from the media.

Exercise 2.22

1. Sir, I **passed** my B.Tech in 2003.
2. We **have finished** our assignment just now.
3. Don't worry; I **have** already **informed** her about that.
4. We **saw** a tiger five years ago.
5. I **spoke** to him last night.
6. Wait; I **have not** yet **finished** my work.
7. I **read** that story in Class IX.
8. We **spent** a very enjoyable evening yesterday.
9. She **submitted** her project this morning.
10. Last year, we **conducted** several workshops for our teachers.

Exercise 2.23

1. Call the doctor; I think he **has broken** his toe.
2. Now that you **have come**, why don't you stay with us for a while?
3. They **questioned** the actor at the airport before they **let** him go.
4. We **spent** the entire weekend worrying about his whereabouts.

5. Research **has shown** that exercises help people remain cheerful.
6. Shakespeare **wrote** his last play possibly in 1613.
7. Don't worry; I **have informed** his parents about his illness.
8. Earlier he **made** some comedies but for some time now he **has produced** only serious movies.
9. I am sure I **have read** about that episode in some magazine.
10. You **have grown** so big ever since I saw you last.

Exercise 2.24

1. The British **had ruled** (the action that precedes) over India for nearly two hundred years before they **handed** (the action that follows) it over to us.
2. We **walked** (later action) all the way to the station only to know that the train **had already left** (earlier action).
3. When the police **had interrogated** (earlier action) the criminal, they **put** (later action) him behind the bars.
4. My neighbour **told** (later action) me that his father **had died** (earlier action).
5. By the time the doctor **reached** (later action), the patient **had died** (earlier action).
6. We **had thought** of raising your pay (earlier action), but **could not get** (later action) enough funds.
7. After he **had finalized** the deal (earlier action), he **signed** it (later action).
8. The movie **had already begun** (earlier action) when we **entered** the hall (later action).
9. He **had planned** to retire at the age of sixty-five (earlier action), but he **died** much before that (later action).
10. I **had just entered** the building (earlier action), when the bomb **went off** suddenly (later action).

Exercise 2.25

1. Was watching	2. Is raining	3. Had	4. Put
5. Did not want	6. Decided	7. Am writing	8. Have been working
9. Has been growing	10. Has painted		

Exercise 2.26

1. Subjunctive	2. Subjunctive	3. Imperative	4. Subjunctive	5. Indicative
6. Imperative	7. Subjunctive	8. Imperative	9. Subjunctive	10. Imperative

Exercise 2.27

1. We are sorry to inform you **that nothing much can be done about your problem**.
   (The passive highlights the lack of control over the circumstances and hence communicates the situation to the reader in a better way)
2. **Thousands of people are killed** in accidents every year.
   (Highlights the tragic reality. In such expressions, what happens is more important than who causes it)
3. **The news was telecast** at 8.00 p.m.
   (The focus is rightly placed on the action that took place)
4. **I have not yet been informed**.
   (Correctly implies the wait/disappointment/impatience without sounding blunt and full of accusations)
5. **The gathering was held** near the temple.
   (The focus properly shifts to the **action conducted**)
6. **The patient has been given the medicine**.
   (The passive correctly highlights that what was important, has been done)

7. **A memorandum was handed** to the district collector.

(The action is properly stressed through the passive)

8. As we started walking, **a small cab was seen** coming from the other direction.

(What was seen has been given more importance than who saw it)

Exercise 2.28

They did not invite me to the party. Still, I was determined to attend the same. So, I reached the place uninvited. What I saw was something really forgettable. What was happening around was strange. **Wine was being openly served and consumed** by the guests. That was not enough. **Young girls were/could be seen dancing** with their suitors. Their glasses of **wine were being filled** again and again. Later on, these devotees of god Bacchus **were observed** inserting their fangs into the non-vegetarian dishes **which were being supplied** at a frantic pace.

Exercise 2.29

1. The patients of swine flu **are advised** to wear a mask.
2. It **can be proved** that Darwin's theory has some chinks in the armour.
3. The function **will be organized** in the auditorium.
4. I **have not yet been reported**.
5. Bed sheets **are changed** every day in this hotel.
6. I **am paid monthly**.
7. The star **is likely to be offered** a staggering signing amount.
8. For many centuries it **was not known** that plants can breathe.
9. Premchand's **stories have been translated** into different languages the world over.
10. Learning a language **is mostly considered** to be a difficult task.
11. In the meeting, **it was agreed** that new norms be brought into effect.
12. The minister announced that all the old people in the state **would be given** pension.
13. A large number of victims **were shifted** to the relief camps.
14. The first English dictionary **was compiled** by Dr Samuel Johnson.
15. The government has announced that the new Act **will be introduced** in the next parliamentary session.
16. The captain desires that the game **should be played** in the positive spirit.
17. The glass **was broken** as you walked over it.
18. I always **get my car serviced** at this service station.
19. Earlier it **was believed** that AIDS spreads by touch.
20. We **were expected** to win, but we lost.

Exercise 2.30

1. He **warned** us not to be rude with him next time.
2. The plumber **informed** us that there was a leakage in the pipeline.
3. My doctor **advised** me to cut down on sweets.
4. The clerk **refused** to help us.
5. The teacher **asked** us to be silent.
6. She **reminded** me that it was our marriage anniversary that day.
7. He **criticized** us for being sloppy in our attitude.
8. He **reassured** me that we would get a seat.

9. Roberts **wondered** why he should always be neglected for promotion.
10. The captain **thanked** the players for winning him the crucial match.

Exercise 2.31

1. She complained about being vexed like that.
2. They sought permission before leaving.
3. The man expressed regret/felt sorry for not being able to help us.
4. He promised to help me.
5. The duo decided not to/refused to speak to the journalists.
6. They warned us to be careful for the man was a clever fellow.
7. She complained about not getting the same appreciation.
8. They thanked us.
9. He suggested watching a movie.
10. He advised me to see a doctor.

Exercise 2.32

1. I came because you invited me.
2. Children played while mother slept in the afternoon.
3. Walk fast lest you should miss the train.
4. Give me this purse otherwise I shall snatch it away from you.
5. When we reached back home, we found the lock broken.
6. They tried to win the race but lost.
7. Unless you are a genius, you cannot solve this puzzle.
8. Keep quiet or get lost.
9. He is a complete idiot, whereas his brother is a wizard.
10. Though I can, I won't do this.

Exercise 2.33

1. Before you leave (Adverbial Clause of Time)
2. Since you say so (Adverbial Clause of Cause or Reason)
3. If I want it (Adverbial Clause of Condition)
4. Where you kept it (Adverbial Clause of Place)
5. Until you finish your homework (Adverbial Clause of Time)
6. Though the exercise seems difficult (Adverbial Clause of Concession)
7. Till they fainted in the sun (Adverbial Clause of Time)
8. Had I seen him (Adverbial Clause of Condition)
9. So that we may accumulate more wealth (Adverbial Clause of Purpose)
10. Since you were not there (Adverbial Clause of Cause or Reason)

Exercise 2.34

1. Since we wanted to watch a movie, we left the office early.
2. I went to Delhi so that I could visit a few libraries and collect material for my research.

3. We discussed our problems with our teacher while Sahil kept playing game on his cell.
4. When we reached our classroom, the teacher had already started teaching the lesson.
5. They tried their best but failed miserably.
6. The man whom you met yesterday was my uncle.
7. Give me some money, otherwise I will not be able to buy medicine for my mother.
8. The officer asked me not to go home unless I had finished the report.
9. Had they worked hard, they would have cleared the exam.
10. Pay your taxes in time or you will be behind bars.

Exercise 2.35

1. **Making** a lame excuse, he sounded quite cheap. (Participle)
2. Children love **making** mud castles. (Gerund)
3. **Seeing** is **believing**. (Gerund, Gerund)
4. **Seeing**, he believed. (Participle)
5. **Waving** their hats and handkerchiefs, the crowd cheered the king. (Participle)
6. **Asking** questions is easier than **answering** them. (Gerund, Gerund)
7. **Making** food is not difficult. (Gerund)
8. You are **making** a fool of yourself. (Verb)
9. **Making** tea, she answered the call on her cell. (Participle)
10. He died in the **waiting** room. (Participle Adjective)
11. **Waiting** is often painful. (Gerund)
12. He died **waiting** for the train. (Participle)
13. King Lear decides **to divide** his kingdom. (to-infinitive)
14. The thief entered through the **broken** widow. (Participle Adjective)
15. We live **to succeed**. (to-infinitive)

Exercise 2.36

1. Participle	2. Gerund	3. Verb
4. Participle	5. Verb	6. Gerund
7. Participle Adjective	8. Gerund	9. Gerund
10. Participle	11. Participle Adjective	12. Participle, Participle
13. Participle	14. Gerund	15. Verb
16. Participle Adjective	17. Participle, Participle Adjective	18. Participle Adjective
19. Participle Adjective	20. Participle, Participle Adjective	

Exercise 2.37

1. Stop talking to me in such a rude manner!
2. I want to go through the whole exercise all over again.
3. The members resented the idea of inviting her to the meeting.
4. I don't feel like telling you that I am not happy with your performance.
5. Avoid being late all the time!
6. He admitted being there at the time of the crime.

7. The speaker failed to make a proper impression on the audience.
8. We all detest facing difficult situations.
9. To our surprise, she declined to help us even in those circumstances.
10. How can you imagine doing such a thing!

Exercise 2.38

1. That he was alone and wanted to be alone was a matter of concern for all.
2. If you want to be healthy in life, do this: get up early; work hard; lead a natural life.
3. When I heard a knock at the door, I turned around.
4. It is, however, not all that important to speak all the time.
5. When he was young, Shakespeare, who went on to become the greatest writer of all times, married a woman eight years his senior.
6. God made women beautiful so that men may love them; and men foolish so that they may return the favour.
7. His attitude, to say the least, was really horrible.
8. America, England, and France got together and went after Germany.
9. Milton, the great Puritan poet, went blind at the age of forty-four.
10. He told his wife, 'Learn to live with my silence.'

3 COMMON ERRORS IN ENGLISH

LEARNING OBJECTIVES

After reading this chapter, you will be able to understand
- steps for identifying errors in English
- major types of errors committed in English

While going through this book, there is one thing that you are certain about: we all aim at becoming an effective communicator. For this purpose, you need to learn the art of speaking and writing error-free English. This can be done only when you develop an eye to spot errors in your own utterances or any other communicator's message. The obvious reason behind this is that people, who are well versed in English and its usage, may also falter at times. Moreover, in order to get through the English language proficiency test in competitive exams such as SSC, Banking, Railways, SAT, CAT, GRE, IELTS, and TOEFL, you need to develop the ability to identify the errors related to grammar and usage. In this part of the test, you are asked to attempt questions related to spotting errors. Keeping the accuracy of usage in mind, let's take a systematic approach in identifying common errors in sentences:

3.1 STEPS FOR IDENTIFYING ERRORS

1. Read the entire sentence—even if you feel confident about identifying the error at first glance, you should read the sentence till the end and prevent yourself from making mistakes.
2. Check each underlined section or given options individually.
3. Quickly look over the other answer choices to confirm that none of them contain an error.
4. Always make sure you can explain to yourself what the solution is for the error you have identified.

3.2 SOME MAJOR TYPES OF ERRORS

In the preceding chapter you have learnt about the subtle nuances of usage related to different parts of speech and other grammatical concept. Let us now study a few problematic areas with the help of examples and exercises so that we can avoid them in our speaking and writing tasks.

3.2.1 Errors Related to Noun/Pronoun Agreement

Following are some examples that will help you understand how speaking and writing skills get affected with limited knowledge of noun/pronoun agreement:
- Where are my jeans? Well, they are on the bed. (Where is my jeans? Well, it is on the bed.)
- What have you done with the scissors? They are not able to cut even a single piece of paper! (What have done with the scissor? It is not able to cut even a single piece of paper!)

- The jury were at sixes and sevens. They could not decide a thing. (~~The jury was at sixes and sevens. It could not decide a thing.~~)
- The committee settled the matter without getting up from their seats. (~~The committee settled the matter without getting up from its seats.~~)
- Why did you have to buy such expensive goggles? They don't even suit you! (~~Why did you have to buy such expensive goggle? It doesn't even suit you!~~)
- One of the major findings of the research relates to the connection between thinking and physical health. It clearly observes a parallel pattern in a person's thinking process and his/her physical health. (~~One of the major findings of the research relates to the connection between thinking and physical health. They clearly observe a parallel pattern in a person's thinking process and his physical health.~~)
- The committee is planning to give its recommendations by next month. (~~The committee is planning to give their recommendations by next month.~~)
- Majority of people in the country believe that they are not getting their due. (~~Majority of people in the country believe that it is not getting its due.~~)
- A large chunk of India's population lives in slums. It is believed to be in millions. (~~A large chunk of India's population lives in slums. They are believed to be in millions.~~)
- Every child must bring their geometry box to the class. (~~Every child must bring his/her geometry box to the class.~~)

EXERCISE 3.1

Cross out the inappropriate options in the following sets of sentences maintaining the correct noun/pronoun agreement:

1. (a) Researches conducted in the past have never been convincing; they are either subjective or not properly substantiated.
   (b) Researches conducted in the past have never been convincing; it is either subjective or not properly substantiated.

2. (a) A group of visitors has decided to take the matter to higher authorities. It is demanding an impartial enquiry into the matter.
   (b) A group of visitors has decided to take the matter to higher authorities. They are demanding an impartial enquiry into the matter.

3. (a) The lady and her dog are going for a walk.
   (b) The lady and her dog is going for a walk.

4. (a) One must not lose his temper all the time!
   (b) One must not lose one's temper all the time!

5. (a) Someone has left their mobile on the desk.
   (b) Someone has left his mobile on the desk.

6. (a) Everyone was asked to take his seat.
   (b) Everyone was asked to take their seats.

7. (a) A group of scientists is working on this project. Each of them is in their twenties.
   (b) A group of scientists are working on this project. Each of them are in his twenties.

8. (a) Everyone started laughing, but soon he realized that the jester was actually not joking.

   (b) Everyone stated laughing, but soon they realized that the jester was actually not joking.

9. (a) We cannot expect anything more than that; everyone seems to have done their best.

   (b) We cannot expect anything more than that; everyone seems to have done his best.

10. (a) One of the girls could not mark their attendance.

    (b) One of the girls could not mark her attendance.

11. (a) Everyone has come, haven't they?

    (b) Everyone has come, hasn't he?

12. (a) Someone has called you just now, hasn't he?

    (b) Someone has called you just now, haven't they?

13. (a) One cannot be too careful, can one?

    (b) One cannot be too careful, can he?

14. (a) Somebody is knocking at the door; who could he be?

    (b) Somebody is knocking at the door; who could they be?

15. (a) I am a fool, am I not?

    (b) I am a fool, aren't I?

3.2.2 Errors Related to Subject–Verb Concord

At times we make errors in using appropriate verb (singular or plural) for the subject. Therefore, we need to understand how to choose verbs correctly in consonance with subjects. Let's learn this aspect of English usage in some detail. Take a look at the following sentences:

- The **girl is dancing** in the park.   (*is dancing* because *girl* is singular)
- The **girls are dancing** in the park.   (*are dancing* because *girls* is plural)

Choosing *is* with *girl* and *are* for *girls* is suggestive of a pattern in English grammar. It is called **agreement** or **concord** between the subject and the verb in a sentence. Usually it is easy to decide if a subject is singular or plural. However, there are a larger number of expressions in English which cause confusion in terms of whether the subject will take a singular or a plural verb. Take a look at the following examples to figure out how to maintain correct subject–verb concord:

- The CEO as well as his secretary **is** (are) reaching in an hour.
- Walking for ten miles in a day **is** (are) a child's play.
- Almost half of the cosmetics **were** (was) washed away in the flood.
- Furniture really **costs** (cost) a lot these days.
- The majority **is** (are) happy with the decision.
- The majority of people **believe** (believes) in rituals.
- **Is** (Are) everyone listening to me?

- A lot of our customers **are** (~~is~~) complaining about the services.
- Performing well at gymnastics **demands** (~~demand~~) a lot of practice.
- The officer along with her subordinates **is** (~~are~~) just about to reach.

For maintaining proper subject–verb concord, keep in mind the following grammatical conventions:

- When two nouns refer to just one idea, the verb used is singular:

  Bread and butter **is** (~~are~~) his staple food.
  Madam, the horse and carriage **is** (~~are~~) ready.

- When phrases such as *with, along with, besides, in addition to, as well as* combine two nouns, the verb relates to the first noun:

  The film director, as well as the entire unit, **reaches** (~~reach~~) the city in the afternoon.
  The film directors, as well as the entire unit, **reach** (~~reaches~~) the city in the afternoon.
  Besides the decked-up wife, the unkempt husband **was** (~~were~~) seen.

- When two nouns are joined by the coordinating conjunction *not only … but also,* the verb needs to agree with the nearest noun/noun phrase:

  Not only the child, but the **parents are** also responsible for lack of togetherness in the family.
  Not only the parents, but the **child is** also responsible for lack of togetherness in the family.

- Units of measurement and titles with plural forms take singular verbs:

  The Sound and Fury **is** (~~are~~) a brilliant novel by William Faulkner.
  Five thousand rupees **is** (~~are~~) a paltry sum today.

- Subjects comprising or denoted through *any, no, every, each, everyone, someone, somebody, one, none, what, which,* etc. usually take a singular verb:

  Everyone **is** (~~are~~) required to attend the meeting tomorrow.
  Someone **has** (~~have~~) left the letter for you.
  No answer **was** (~~were~~) available in the books.
  One **needs** (~~need~~) to be responsible in life.
  Who really **bothers** (~~bother~~) about cleanliness?
  What **is** (~~are~~) going on here?

- Two singular nouns joined by *either … or, neither … nor* take a singular verb. However, when one of these nouns is plural, the verb chosen is plural which is placed closer to it as well:

  Either the farmer or the **son has** destroyed the crop.
  Either the farmer or the **sons have** destroyed the crop.

- When the subject of a sentence is complex, the main noun decides whether the verb will be singular or plural:

  Many **members** of the opposition **feel** (~~feels~~) that such reforms would help the society.
  'The only **answer** that we can think of today to your multiple questions **is** (~~are~~) that we will try playing better in the next match,' said the captain of the losing team.

- Nouns connected with *one of, a large amount of, a huge quantity, a portion of,* etc. take singular verbs:

  One of the brothers is (are) retiring next year.
  A large population of India still **lives** (live) below poverty line.
  A large amount of rain water **is** (are) wasted due to poor water management.

- Nouns connected with *a lot of, lots of, number of, majority of,* normally take a plural verb:

  A lot of our customers **have given** (has given) positive feedback about the product.
  Majority of people in this country still **believe** (believes) in hero worship.

- Collective nouns such as *jury, group, committee, team, opposition,* etc. take a singular verb if the reference is to their togetherness and a plural verb when the purpose is to suggest their division, discord, or lack of togetherness:

  The **jury were** divided over the quantum of punishment.
  The **committee is** of the opinion that the controversy arose due to lack of caution.

- Pair nouns such as *scissors, spectacles,* etc. take plural verbs:

  My **trousers are** missing from the suitcase.
  Be careful! There **are scissors** in the drawer.

- Certain nouns, which end in -s in spellings like *news*, names of some games and sports, names of some subjects, etc., take a singular verb:

  His **physics is** very poor.
  Athletics is an exciting sport.
  TV **news has** become quite loud these days.

EXERCISE 3.2

Choose the appropriate verbs in the sentences given below:

1. Nowadays, a number of students **is/are** returning to humanities and commerce streams.

2. What actually scared us **was/were** the fact that there was no one around to help us.

3. All the riches of the world **has/have** not helped man feel happy and contented.

4. Waiting for five hours for the interview **was/were** a big waste.

5. Each of the boys **has been/have been** given the necessary instructions.

6. At the last moment there **was/were** a change in the venue of the event.

7. All the corrupt politicians and their cronies **is/are** simply at a loss after the demonetization of 500 and 1000 rupee notes.

8. Either the student or the teachers **is/are** to blame for his performance in the final exams.

9. Multiple crises **seem/seems** to have ruffled them up.

10. One of our employees **is/are** retiring today.

EXERCISE 3.3

Rewrite the sentences given below, after carefully observing the underlined verbs and making necessary corrections, if required:

1. Driving for five hundred kilometers in a day **are** a tiring proposition.

   _____

   _____

2. Linguistics **are** an interesting subject.

   _____

   _____

3. I don't think the criteria for selection in this company **is** fair enough.

   _____

   _____

4. **Is** each one of you speaking the truth?

   _____

5. One of the passengers **were** seriously injured in the accident.

   _____

   _____

6. The actor as well as his assistants **were** seen in the party.

   _____

   _____

7. The majority here **feels** that the decision was not in favour of them.

   _____

   _____

8. What truly **surprise** us is the fact that a political rookie can upset an inexperienced politician even in America.

   _____

   _____

   _____

9. *City Lights* **are** a wonderful movie.

   _____

10. Some of them still **feels** that they both are at fault.

    _____

EXERCISE 3.4

Choose the correct verbs for the subjects by crossing out the incorrect ones in each of the sentences given below:

1. In a funny sequence, the clown's trousers **was/were** pulled down.

2. Besides the minister, the bodyguard too **was/were** killed.

3. Either of the sisters **is/are** responsible for the rift in the family.

4. Every girl and boy **was/were** informed well in time.

5. One of the presents sent by you **was/were** really fascinating.

6. Neither the teacher nor the student **knows/know** about how to behave in class.

7. A large number of people still **live/lives** below poverty line in our country.

8. Both of the parents **is/are** equally responsible for the child's upbringing.

9. Sir, my particulars **has been/have been** given in the résumé.

10. Which of these girls **is/are** your sister?

EXERCISE 3.5

Choose the correct options by maintaining correct subject–verb concord:

1. Holidays _____ **(is/are)** just round the corner.

2. Mills and Boons once _____ **(was/were)** a popular series.

3. Two thirds of the goods _____ _____ **(was/were)** destroyed in the accident.

4. Some of the boys _____ _____ **(was jogging/were jogging)** in the field.

5. _____ **(Is/Are)** anyone inside the room?

6. Some patients _____ **(was/were)** waiting outside the doctor's cabin.

7. In addition to the mistakes, the report also _____ **(has/have)** several anomalies.

8. One of the girls _____ **(was/were)** wearing a yellow frock.

9. Which of the days _____ **(suit/suits)** you the most?

10. The news _____ **(was/were)** rather depressing.

EXERCISE 3.6

Rewrite the following sentences choosing the correct subject–verb agreement:

1. The majority of our primary teachers is not well trained.

   _____

2. Either Vikram or Anita have left the room unlocked.

   _____

3. One of the actors were seriously injured in the incident.

   _____

   _____

4. None of it really matter.

   _____

5. The boy who is moving with that group of students are my brother.

   _____

   _____

6. Quite a few singers finds it difficult to sing well to classical tunes.

   _____

   _____

7. The delegation consisting of thirty scholars are arriving tonight.

   _____

   _____

8. These days, only a few students pays attention to what teachers tell in the class.

   _____

   _____

9. What generally interest me is light movie with some humour.

10. It seems as though neither the government nor the people is serious about the cleanliness drive.

   _____

   _____

EXERCISE 3.7

Cross out the incorrect verb so as to maintain correct subject–verb concord in the following sentences:

1. A delegation comprising nearly half a dozen solar experts **is/are** visiting our institute.

2. Even after several long hearings, the jury **was/were** sharply divided on the verdict.

3. Despite the pressing needs for modernization, cost effectiveness **remain/remains** one of our key concerns.

4. One of our main batsmen **has continuously been/have continuously been** out of form.

5. A majority of India's population **has always been/have always been** quite hard working.

6. The manager as well as the team **is/are** required to defend this proposal in the board meeting.

7. Two thousand rupees, something that the ATMs successively cough up these days, **is/are** a meagre amount after all.

8. Despite their best effort, the police **is/are** unable to achieve any breakthrough in the case.

9. It seemed everybody **was/were** enjoying themselves.

10. Are you crazy! Fifteen kilometers **is/are** quite a distance!

3.2.3 Errors Related to Preposition Usage

Please refer to *Chapter 2: Basic Grammar and Usage* for understanding the common errors related to use of prepositions. In addition, attempt the following exercise and also those given at the end of this chapter.

EXERCISE 3.8

Choose the correct prepositions in the following sentences:

1. We arrived in this city thirty years _____ **(ago/before/by)**.

2. Don't you know _____ **(between/since/during)** holidays all schools remain closed?

3. The little kid was run _____ **(on/over/above)** by the speeding vehicle.

4. The Banerjee family lives _____ **(in/on/at)** 242, Circular Road, Dehradun.

5. We need the entire payment _____ **(in/for/with)** advance.

6. Let's not worry about anchoring; we have Shrankhala, who is really good _____ **(for/at/with)** it.

7. Unfortunately, he got involved _____ **(in/into/on)** some controversy which led to this crisis.

8. Will you do me a favour? I am really hard _____ **(at/by/on)** cash these days.

9. All forms need to be submitted _____ **(within/by/on)** 30 December, 2016.

10. Though whatever happened was unavoidable, we are sorry _____ **(for/from/with)** the inconvenience it may have caused you.

3.2.4 Errors Related to Usage of Articles

Please refer to *Chapter 2: Basic Grammar and Usage* for understanding the common errors related to use of articles. In addition, attempt the exercises given at the end of this chapter.

3.2.5 Errors Related to Misplaced Modifiers

Modifiers are the words, phrases, and clauses used to modify some word or group of words in a sentence. Since modifiers are used to add to the meaning of the words or expressions modified, they should be placed closer to each other. Wrong placement of the modifier can create ambiguity and confusion in meaning. See the examples given below. The ambiguity has been highlighted within brackets in each of the sentences:

- Crying over the broken toy car, the mother consoled the little girl. (Who was crying—the child or the mother?)
- Playing in the garden, the snake bit the child. (Who was playing in the garden—the snake or the child?)
- The husband shot himself dead after bidding his wife goodbye with a gun. (What did the husband do with the gun—bid his wife goodbye with it or shot himself dead?)

See the corrected version of these sentences:

- The mother consoled the **child who was crying** over the broken toy.
- The snake bit the **child while he/she was playing** in the garden.
- After bidding his wife goodbye, **the husband shot himself dead** with the gun.

EXERCISE 3.9

Rewrite the following sentences by properly placing the modifier and the modified together:

1. The worker was run over by the speeding car, sleeping on the pavement.

   _____
   _____

2. With leaking pipes the woman found it hard to water her plants.

   _____
   _____

3. The movie star finally decided to consult a psychiatrist suffering from emotional turmoil.

   _____

4. The witness told the court quite often that the politician used to visit the dancer.

   _____
   _____

5. Being raised in the sand, the parents knew that the castle would not settle.

   _____
   _____

EXERCISE 3.10

Rewrite the following sentences to express the intended idea in them:

1. This is soup which I made with rice and barley.

2. I have heard these news right in the morning.

3. My younger brother had not wanted to listen to my advices.

4. Please credit this amount to my name.

5. I like her childish face.

6. The convict stood in front of the judge.

7. On his birthday, I gave Rohan with a green colour tee shirt.

8. The lab being build on rock, the scientists knew that it would not settle.

9. Pinter has left Portia so that he can paint in Paris.

10. While playing in the garden, a wasp string him.

EXERCISE 3.11

Rewrite the following sentences to express the intended idea in them:

1. Each boy and each girl were given a book.

2. The news had been broadcast at 2.00 p.m.

3. I have passed my B.Tech in 2007.

4. He shook hand with his beloved.

5. One half of the women thinks high heels make their feet look smaller.

6. On my way, I have seen a girl of five years.

7. There was an accident yesterday on the corner of the street.

8. He picked up a quarrel on his way.

   _____

9. God forbade Adam not to eat the apple.

   _____

10. If she has been crying, she must been very upset.

    _____

    _____

EXERCISE 3.12

In the following sentences, the same idea has been expressed in different ways. Choose the one that conforms to standard English usage for each set of sentences:

1. (a) The poet and philosopher are dead.
   (b) The poet and the philosopher is dead.
   (c) The poet and philosopher is dead.
   (d) Poet and philosopher is dead.

2. (a) The captain as well as their soldiers are dead.
   (b) The captain as well as his soldier are dead.
   (c) The captains as well as his soldiers is dead.
   (d) The captain as well as his soldiers is dead.

3. (a) Neither he nor his secretary were present.
   (b) Neither he nor his secretaries was present.
   (c) Neither his secretary not he were present.
   (d) Neither he nor his secretary was present.

4. (a) Either of the two sisters are at fault.
   (b) Either of the two sisters is at fault.
   (c) Either of the two sister are at fault.
   (d) Either of the two sister is at fault.

5. (a) The economics of the government has always baffled me.
   (b) The economic of the government has always baffled me.
   (c) The economics of the government has baffled me always.
   (d) The economics of the government have always baffled me.

6. (a) Mother Teresa's aim and objective in life was to provide relief to the poor.
   (b) Mother Teresa's aims and objectives in life was to provide relief to the poor.
   (c) Mother Teresa's aim and objective in life was to provide relief to poor.
   (d) Mother Teresa's aim and objective in life were to provide relief to the poor.

7. (a) Chair's legs are broken.
   (b) The chair's legs are broken.
   (c) The legs of the chair are broken.
   (d) Legs of chair are broken.

8. (a) The star and orator have arrived.
   (b) The star and the orator have arrived.
   (c) The star and orator have been arrived.
   (d) Star and orator have arrived.

9. (a) Sorry, I am not understanding your point.
   (b) Sorry, I don't understand your point.
   (c) Sorry, I am cannot understand your point.
   (d) Sorry, I cannot be able to understand your point.

10. (a) I am loving it.
    (b) I am in love with it.
    (c) I love it.
    (d) I have loved it.

EXERCISE 3.13

Choose the best way to express the idea from each set of sentences given below:

1. (a) Either of the sister is coming today.
   (b) Either of the sisters are coming today.
   (c) Either of the sisters is coming today.
   (d) Either of the sisters could have been coming today.

2. (a) Had we bowled well, we would won the match.
   (b) Had we bowled well, we would have won the match.
   (c) Had we bowled well, we will win the match.
   (d) Had we bowled well, we shall win the match.

3. (a) The officer along with his secretaries have come.
   (b) The officer along with his secretaries has come.
   (c) The officer along with his secretaries is come.
   (d) The officer along with his secretaries are come.

4. (a) These days, I am reading a detective story.
   (b) These days, I have been reading a detective story.
   (c) These days, I had read a detective story.
   (d) These days, I read a detective story.

5. (a) When I was young, I can walk ten miles.
   (b) When I was young, I shall walk ten miles.
   (c) When I was young, I could walk ten miles.
   (d) When I was young, I could have been walked ten miles.

6. (a) Prepare well lest you should not fail the test.
   (b) Prepare well lest you should fail the test.
   (c) Prepare well lest you will not fail the test.
   (d) Prepare well lest you will fail the test.

7. (a) Hardly had I entered the room, than the mobile started ringing.
   (b) Hardly had I entered the room, when the mobile had started ringing.
   (c) Hardly had I entered the room, when the mobile will have started ringing.
   (d) Hardly had I entered the room, when the mobile started ringing.

8. (a) When the master came home, the dog wagged it's tail.
   (b) When the master comes home, the dog wagged its tail.
   (c) When the master had come home, the dog wagged its' tail.
   (d) When the master came home, the dog wagged its tail.

9. (a) John and I often study together.
   (b) John and me often study together.
   (c) I and John often study together.
   (d) Me and John often study together.

10. (a) The farmer reaped the crop and sold it in the market.
    (b) The farmer had reaped the crop and had sold it in the market.
    (c) The farmer reaped the crop and had sold them in the market.
    (d) The farmer had reaped the crop and sold it in the market.

EXERCISE 3.14

Read the following sets of sentences and choose the structure that expresses the idea in the best possible manner:

1. (a) The girl who sat besides my friend is his sister.
   (b) The girl who sat beside my friend is his sister.
   (c) The girl who sat beside my friend was his sister.
   (d) The girl besides my friend was his sister.

2. (a) After he had written the mail, he sent it to his partner.
   (b) After he wrote the mail, he sends it to his partner.
   (c) After he has written the mail, he sent it to his partner.
   (d) After he wrote the mail, he had sent it to his partner.

3. (a) He is too clever to solve this problem.
   (b) He is clever enough not to solve this problem.
   (c) He is not too clever to solve this problem.
   (d) He is clever enough to solve this problem.

4. (a) There are so many as 1000 small activities involved in this whole process.
   (b) There are as many as 1000 small activities involved in whole process.
   (c) There are as many as 1000 small activities involved in this whole process.
   (d) There are as many as 1000 small activities in this whole process involved.

5. (a) Even as he stops taking sugar, he will not lose weight.
   (b) Even though he stops taking sugar, he will not lose weight.
   (c) Even while he stops taking sugar, he will not lose weight.
   (d) Even if he stops taking sugar, he will not lose weight.

6. (a) Let me read the report and decide the matter.
   (b) Let I read the report and decide the matter.
   (c) Let me read the report and decide about the matter.
   (d) Let I read the report and decide about the matter.

7. (a) The peacock is one of the most beautiful bird in the world.
   (b) The peacock is one of the beautiful bird in the world.
   (c) The peacock is one of the most beautiful birds into the world.
   (d) The peacock is one of the most beautiful birds in the world.

8. (a) At his arrival, the spectators greeted the superstar.
   (b) On his arrival, the spectators greeted the superstar.
   (c) With his arrival, the spectators greeted the superstar.
   (d) In his arrival, the spectators greeted the superstar.

9. (a) Thirty security personnel are reported to have been injured in the blast.
   (b) Thirty security personnels are reported to have been injured in the blast.
   (c) Thirty security personnel have reported to be injured in the blast.
   (d) Thirty security personnels have reported to have been injured in the blast.

10. (a) Hope for the best, but be prepared for worst.
    (b) Hope of the best, but be prepared for the worst.
    (c) Hope for the best, but be prepared for the worst.
    (d) Hope for best, but be prepared for worst.

EXERCISE 3.15

Choose the best option in the following sets of sentences:

1. (a) The tiny, timid girl spoke in so low a voice that she was almost inaudible.
   (b) The tiny, timid girl spoke in such a low voice that she was almost inaudible.
   (c) The tiny, timid girl spoke in so much low voice that she was almost inaudible.
   (d) The tiny, timid girl spoke in such low a voice that she was almost inaudible.

2. (a) The book is either written by Shakespeare or one of his contemporaries.
   (b) The book is written either by Shakespeare or one of his contemporary.
   (c) The book is written by Shakespeare either or by one of his contemporary.
   (d) The book is written either by Shakespeare or by one of his contemporaries.

3. (a) Either the actors or the director are to be blamed for the failure of the show.
   (b) Either the actors or the director is to be blamed for the failure of the show.
   (c) Either the director or the actors are to blame for the failure of the show.
   (d) Either the directors or the actor is to be blamed for the failure of the show.

4. (a) Due to information technology people across the globe are exposed to each other's cultures as never before.
   (b) Due to information technology people across the globe are exposed to each other's cultures like ever before.
   (c) Due to information technology people across the globe are exposed into each other's cultures like never before.
   (d) Due to information technology people across the globe are exposed to each other's culture like never before.

5. (a) How can he be promoted? After all, he is junior to me.
   (b) How can he be promoted? After all, he is junior than me.
   (c) How can he be promoted? After all, he is junior than I.
   (d) How can he be promoted? After all, he is junior than I am.

6. (a) He stopped smoking once he realized that it can cause cancer.
   (b) He stopped to smoke once he realized that it can cause cancer.
   (c) He stopped for smoking once he realized that it can cause cancer.
   (d) He stopped the smoking once he realized that it can cause cancer.

7. (a) The doctor prohibited him to take sugar once he was diagnosed for diabetes.
   (b) The doctor prohibited him from taking sugar once he was diagnosed for diabetes.
   (c) The doctor prohibited him from taking sugar once he was diagnosed with diabetes.
   (d) The doctor prohibited him not to take sugar once he was diagnosed with diabetes.

8. (a) Of the two most exciting tennis players, you seem to like the most glamorous one.
   (b) Of the two most exciting tennis players, you seem to like the more glamorous one.
   (c) Of the two most exciting tennis players, you more seem to like the glamorous one.
   (d) Of the two most exciting tennis player, you seem to like the more glamorous one.

9. (a) If I had gone with my friends to Pehalgam, I could take skiing lessons.
   (b) If I had gone with my friends to Pehalgam, I could have taken skiing lessons.

(c) If I would had gone with my friends to Pehalgam, I could have taken skiing lessons.

(d) If I had gone with my friends to Pehalgam, I would have taken skiing lessons.

10. (a) The students of today needs to be trained about cultural diversity as this will facilitate constructive learning outcomes.

(b) The students of today need to be trained about cultural diversity as this will facilitate constructive learning outcomes.

(c) The students of today need to be trained for cultural diversity as this will facilitate constructive learning outcomes.

(d) The students of today need to be trained about cultural diversity since this will facilitate constructive learning outcomes.

ANSWER KEY

Exercise 3.1

1. (a) Researches conducted in the past have never been convincing; they are either subjective or not properly substantiated.

   (b) ~~Researches conducted in the past have never been convincing; it is either subjective or not properly substantiated.~~

2. (a) ~~A group of visitors has decided to take the matter to higher authorities. It is demanding an impartial enquiry into the matter.~~

   (b) A group of visitors has decided to take the matter to higher authorities. They are demanding an impartial enquiry into the matter.

3. (a) The lady and her dog are going for a walk.

   (b) ~~The lady and her dog is going for a walk.~~

4. (a) ~~One must not lose his temper all the time!~~

   (b) One must not lose one's temper all the time!

5. (a) Someone has left their mobile on the desk.

   (b) ~~Someone has left his mobile on the desk.~~

6. (a) ~~Everyone was asked to take his seat.~~

   (b) Everyone was asked to take their seats.

7. (a) A group of scientists is working on this project. Each of them is in their twenties.

   (b) ~~A group of scientists are working on this project. Each of them are in his twenties.~~

8. (a) ~~Everyone stated laughing, but soon he realized that the jester was actually not joking.~~

   (b) Everyone started laughing, but soon they realized that the jester was actually not joking.

9. (a) We cannot expect anything more than that; everyone seems to have done their best.

   (b) ~~We cannot expect anything more than that; everyone seems to have done his best.~~

10. (a) ~~One of the girls could not mark their attendance.~~

    (b) One of the girls could not mark her attendance.

11. (a) Everyone has come, haven't they?

    (b) ~~Everyone has come, hasn't he?~~

12. (a) ~~Someone has called you just now, hasn't he?~~

    (b) Someone has called you just now, haven't they?

13. (a) One cannot be too careful, can one?

    (b) ~~One cannot be too careful, can he?~~

14. (a) ~~Somebody is knocking at the door; who could he be?~~

    (b) Somebody is knocking at the door; who could they be?

15. (a) ~~I am a fool, am I not?~~

    (b) I am a fool, aren't I?

Exercise 3.2

1. are	2. was	3. have	4. was	5. has
6. was	7. are	8. are	9. seem	10. is

Exercise 3.3

1. Driving for five hundred kilometers in a day **is** a tiring proposition.
2. Linguistics **is** an interesting subject.
3. I don't think the criteria for selection in this company **are** fair enough.
4. **Is** each one of you speaking the truth? (No error)
5. One of the passengers **was** seriously injured in the accident.
6. The actor as well as his assistants **was** seen in the party.
7. The majority here **feels** that the decision was not in favour of them. (No error)
8. What truly **surprises** us is the fact that a political rookie can upset an inexperienced politician even in America.
9. *City Lights* **is** a wonderful movie.
10. Some of them still **feel** that they both are at fault.

Exercise 3.4

1. In a funny sequence, the clown's trousers ~~was~~/**were** pulled down.
2. Besides the minister, the bodyguard too **was**/~~were~~ killed.
3. Either of the sisters **is**/~~are~~ responsible for the rift in the family.
4. Every girl and boy **was**/~~were~~ informed well in time.
5. One of the presents sent by you **was**/~~were~~ really fascinating.
6. Neither the teacher nor the student **knows**/~~know~~ about how to behave in class.
7. A large number of people still **live**/~~lives~~ below poverty line in our country.
8. Both of the parents ~~is~~/**are** equally responsible for the child's upbringing.
9. Sir, my particulars ~~has been~~/**have been** given in the résumé.
10. Which of these girls **is**/~~are~~ your sister?

Exercise 3.5

1. are	2. was	3. were	4. were	5. is
6. were	7. has	8. was	9. suits	10. was

Exercise 3.6

1. The majority of our primary teachers **are** not well trained.
2. Either Vikram or Anita **has** left the room unlocked.
3. One of the actors **was** seriously injured in the incident.
4. None of it really **matters**.
5. The boy who is moving with that group of students **is** my brother.

6. Quite a few singers **find** it difficult to sing well to classical tunes.
7. The delegation consisting of thirty scholars **is** arriving tonight.
8. These days, only a few students **pay** attention to what teachers tell in the class.
9. What generally **interests** me is light movie with some humour.
10. It seems as though neither the government nor the people **are** serious about the cleanliness drive.

Exercise 3.7

1. A delegation comprising nearly half a dozen solar experts **is/~~are~~** visiting our institute.
2. Even after several long hearings, the jury **~~was~~/were** sharply divided on the verdict.
3. Despite the pressing needs for modernization, cost effectiveness **~~remain~~/remains** one of our key concerns.
4. One of our main batsmen **has continuously been/~~have continuously been~~** out of form.
5. A majority of India's population **has always been/~~have always been~~** quite hard working.
6. The manager as well as the team **is/~~are~~** required to defend this proposal in the board meeting.
7. Two thousand rupees, something that the ATMs successively cough up these days, **is/~~are~~** a meagre amount to many.
8. Despite their best effort, the police **~~is~~/are** unable to achieve any breakthrough in the case.
9. It seemed everybody **~~was~~/were** enjoying themselves.
10. Are you crazy! Fifteen kilometers **is/~~are~~** quite a distance!

Exercise 3.8

1. ago	2. during	3. over	4. at	5. in
6. at	7. in	8. on	9. by	10. for

Exercise 3.9

1. Sleeping on the pavement, the worker was run over by the speeding car.
2. The woman found it hard to water her plants with leaking pipes.
3. Suffering from emotional turmoil, the movie star finally decided to consult a psychiatrist.
4. The witness told the court that the politician used to visit the dancer quite often.
5. As the castle was being raised in the sand, the parents knew that it would not settle.

Exercise 3.10

1. This is the soup that I made with rice and barley.
2. I heard this news in the morning.
3. My younger brother didn't want to listen to my advice.
4. Please credit this amount to my account.
5. I like her childlike face.
6. The convict stood before the judge.
7. On his birthday, I presented Rohan with a green coloured tee shirt.
8. As the lab was being built on rock, the scientists knew that it would not settle.
9. Pinter has left Portia so that he can paint in Paris. (No error)
10. While he was playing in the garden, a wasp stung him.

Exercise 3.11

1. Each boy and each girl was given a book.
2. The news was broadcast at 2.00 p.m.

3. I passed my B.Tech in 2007.
4. He shook hands with his beloved.
5. One half of the women think high heels make their feet look smaller.
6. On my way, I saw a five-year-old girl.
7. There was an accident yesterday at the corner of the street.
8. He picked a quarrel on his way.
9. God forbade Adam to eat the apple.
10. If she was crying, she must have been very upset.

Exercise 3.12

| 1. (c) | 2. (d) | 3. (d) | 4. (b) | 5. (d) |
| 6. (a) | 7. (c) | 8. (b) | 9. (b) | 10. (c) |

Exercise 3.13

| 1. (c) | 2. (b) | 3. (b) | 4. (a) | 5. (c) |
| 6. (b) | 7. (d) | 8. (d) | 9. (a) | 10. (a) |

Exercise 3.14

| 1. (b) | 2. (a) | 3. (d) | 4. (c) | 5. (d) |
| 6. (a) | 7. (d) | 8. (b) | 9. (a) | 10. (c) |

Exercise 3.15

| 1. (b) | 2. (d) | 3. (c) | 4. (d) | 5. (a) |
| 6. (a) | 7. (c) | 8. (b) | 9. (b) | 10. (b) |

4 Vocabulary Building

LEARNING OBJECTIVES

After reading this chapter, you will be able to understand
- importance of vocabulary
- how words are formed
- importance of studying and knowing the roots of words to improve vocabulary
- how adding prefixes and suffixes can change the meaning of words
- importance of knowing synonyms and antonyms of words to enhance vocabulary
- significance of knowing meanings and usage of confusing words

Language is the vehicle of communication and words form the basic component of a language that we use for conveying our ideas. Words can have different grammatical categories such as nouns, pronouns, adjectives, adverbs, connectives, etc. In order to make our utterances meaningful, we need to know their meaning as well as their category. Therefore, let us learn their importance first and then learn the ways of enriching our vocabulary.

4.1 IMPORTANCE OF VOCABULARY

Our world is a world of words. We need words for conveying our every single ideas, beliefs, emotions, sentiments, feelings, and thoughts. Words colour our lives; they empower us; they distinguish us from one another. In a way, they define us. Indeed without words, humans are just like any other animal—dumb, drab, and inexpressive. In all walks of life, we need to have words to keep us meaningfully engaged in our human affairs.

When it comes to the professional front, the importance of words grows manifold. In a fiercely competitive professional world, what distinguishes us from others is our ability to use words—the powerful words. It is in this sense that a professional requires powerful words much more than other common mortals do. However, it is not just the power of words but also their appropriate usage that is required for us to be good communicators.

4.2 WORD FORMATION

One simple way to define, understand, and utilize a word is by studying its formation—the root that it comes from and the various prefixes and suffixes that change not only the shape of a word but also its shade, meaning, and usage.

4.3 ROOTS

English is an Indo European Germanic language and is spoken by more than one-fourth of the global population. According to research, words originating from French, Greek, and Latin make up 29% of the English language. English has also assimilated words from Urdu, Sanskrit, and Hindi languages. Additionally, from the 1000 most commonly used words, almost 50% have French origins. Therefore, understanding the meanings of the common word roots can really help us deduce the meanings of many new words that we may encounter while reading a book or listening to a lecture. But be careful; though different words may emanate from the same root, they will each have a distinct meaning of their own. Further, each of these words may have different meanings in different contexts. In addition, words that look similar may also come from different roots. So, when you come across a new word, be sure to refer to a dictionary to establish its meaning and usage correctly. Nevertheless, an understanding of roots helps us enrich our vocabulary.

4.3.1 Learning through Roots

See how through one root, we can reach out to more words that stem from it:

1. *am/ami* = **Love**

   Related words: Amiable, Amicable, Amorous, Amity, Amateur, Amalgamate, Ameliorate, etc.

2. *bell* = **War, Fight**

   Related words: Belligerent, Bellicose, Rebellious, etc.

3. *ben/bon* = **Good**

   Related words: Benevolence, Benign, Benediction, Bonafide, Bonhomie, Bon-voyage, Bon-vivant, etc.

4. *burs* = **Money, Purse**

   Related words: Reimburse, Disburse, Bursary, etc.

5. *carn* = **Flesh**

   Related words: Incarnate, Incarnation, Reincarnation, Carnivorous, Carnal, etc.

6. *cide* = **Kill**

   Related words: Homicide, Suicide, Patricide, Parricide, Fratricide, Sororicide, Genocide, Regicide, etc.

7. *circ/circum* = **Around**

   Related words: Circumlocution, Circumscribe, Circumspect, etc.

8. *corp* = **Body**

   Related words: Corpulent, Corpse, Corporal, Corporeal, etc.

9. *cred* = **Belief, Trust**

   Related words: Credulous, Credence, Credentials, Credibility, Credo, Creed, Credible, Incredible, Creditable, etc.

10. *eu* = **Good, Well**

    Related words: Eulogy, Euphony, Euhemerism, Euphoria, Euphemism, Eudemonia, Euthanasia, Eugenics, etc.

11. *grad/gress* = **To Step, To go**

    Related words: Gradual, Degradation, Progress, Digress, Regress, Ingress, Egress, Retrograde, Retrogressive, Transgress, etc.

12. *ject/jet* = **Throw**

    Related words: Eject, Reject, Inject, Project, Jettison, Object, Abject, Dejected, Conjecture, Projectile, etc.

13. *neo/nov* = **New**

    Related words: Innovate, Renovate, Naïve, Novel, Novitiate, Neophyte, Neologism, Novice, etc.

14. *phil* = **To love**

    Related words: Philology, Anglophile, Philanderer, Bibliophile, etc.

15. *phon* = **Sound**

Related words: Telephone, Euphonious, Cacophonic, Symphony, etc.

16. *phob* = **Fear**

Related words: Claustrophobia, Agoraphobia, Ergophobia, Xenophobia, Astraphobia, etc.

17. *morph* = **Shape**

Related words: Metamorphose, Amorphous, Morphology, Polymorphous etc.

18. *sacr/sanct* = **Sacred, Holy**

Related words: Sacrosanct, Sanctuary, Sanctimonious, etc.

19. *scrib/scrip* = **Write**

Related words: Scribble, Inscribe, Prescribe, Proscribe, Ascribe, Transcribe, Script, Manuscript, Postscript, etc.

20. *seq/sec* = **Follow**

Related words: Sequence, Obsequious, Sequel, Consequent, Consequentially, Subsequent, etc.

21. *spic/spec* = **Look, See**

Related words: Perspicacious, Retrospective, Introspective, Spectator, Perspective, Prospective, Prospectus, etc.

22. *surg/surrect* = **Rise, Surge, Flow, Gush, Pour, Heave**

Related words: Insurgent, Resurrect, Resurgent, Insurgency, Insurrectionary, etc.

23. *theo/thei* = **God**

Related words: Theist, Atheist, Theology, Theocracy, etc.

24. *turb* = **Shake**

Related words: Disturb, Perturb, Perturbation, Turbid, Turbulent, etc.

25. *un/uni* = **One**

Related words: Unanimity, Unify, Unity, Unison, Unilateral, Unanimous, etc.

26. *vac* = **Empty**

Related words: Vacant, Vacancy, Vacuous, Evacuate, Vacate, etc.

27. *ver* = **True**

Related words: Veracity, Aver, Verification, Verify, etc.

28. *vert/vers* = **Turn**

Related words: Vertigo, Avert, Revert, Convert, Divert, Subvert, Pervert, etc.

29. *voc/voca/vok/vow* = **Call, Word**

Related words: Equivocal, Vocal, Evoke, Invoke, Revoke, Provoke, Vociferous, etc.

30. *vor* = **Eat**

Related words: Voracious, Carnivorous, Omnivorous, Herbivorous, Panivorous, etc.

Moving ahead, read the following sentences and guess the meaning of the words in bold:

- When people feel vulnerable, they become more **circumspect**.
- If you want to become a good speaker, try to avoid **circumlocutions** in your speech.
- No soon had the bell gone than all the children came out running in a **euphoric** mood.
- The organizers kept uttering **eulogies** in praise of the chief guest while the latter slept in his armchair.

- 'She can't be let off! She has committed a **culpable** crime by letting her Mercedes run over the sleeping labourers,' the inspector told the lawyer.
- The minister was first **inculpated** in the scam but was later **exculpated** as there wasn't enough evidence available.
- 'Please don't leave home!' the mother spoke to her son in a **placating** tone.
- The Aussies seem to have become **complacent** about their champions' status.
- God is supposed to be **omnipotent, omniscient,** and **omnipresent**.
- Couple of days back I bought a Hardy **omnibus**.

Let's try and get a closer look at all these words again:

- A **circumspect** approach is cautious and careful.
- If you write with **circumlocutions**, you beat around the bush a lot.
- If people are **euphoric**, they are happy and excited about something.
- When you **eulogize** someone, you praise them.
- A **culpable** crime is the one that calls for punishment.
- When people are accused of having committed a crime they are **inculpated** and when they are set free they are **exculpated**.
- When someone speaks in a **placating** tone, they try to appease you.
- When you are **complacent** about something, you are self-satisfied and don't want to improve further.
- God can do all, see all, and is present everywhere. Hence, God is seen as **omnipotent, omniscient**, and **omnipresent**.
- An **omnibus** contains the collected works of an artist.

This is how we can associate these words with their roots:

- **circ** = around; Circumspect, Circumlocutions
- **eu** = good; Euphoric, Eulogize
- **culp** = punish; Culpable, Inculpate, Exculpate
- **plac** = please, peace; Placating, Complacent
- **omnis** = all; Omnipotent, Omniscient, Omnipresent, Omnibus

Can you think of more such words which have similar root structures and can fit into the blanks in the following sentences?

 EXERCISE 4.1

Based on your understanding of the words associated with the roots mentioned in the list and the box above, fill in the blanks with the root words as per the context. The intended sense is conveyed within parentheses. Refer to the Answer Key at the end of the chapter to tally your answers with those given:

1. When annoyed, James becomes completely _____ (not ready to be pleased).

2. It was too _____ (peaceful) a place to be liked.

3. When you say he is no more, you are only _____ (in a polite and good manner) telling that the person is dead.

4. First he _____ (sailed around) the entire world and then settled down to run his business empire.

5. Most of us fail to grow as we live in crippling, _____ (limiting from all sides) situations all the time.

6. In South, he always projected himself to be an _____ (all powerful) leader.

7. How can you _____ (set free)

someone who is clearly the offender of the law?

8. It will still probably take years for us to accept the concept of _____ (mercy killing; good, painless death).

9. Bertrand Russell is known to be a _____ (peacemaker).

10. The Chief Guest dozed off in the sofa chair as the anchor kept showering _____ (song of praise).

EXERCISE 4.2

Based on your understanding of the root words given above, fill in the blanks in the following exercise. Use the beginning of the word as a clue to get to the target word:

1. Because of the accident ahead, vehicles were **div**_____ to a different route.

2. The jury could not decide anything **unan** _____ and the matter could not be resolved.

3. Hypocrite people often appear far too **sanc** _____ in their actions and words.

4. He is such a **bib**_____! He loves all types of books.

5. Instead of getting to hear **euph**_____ music, what we mostly get to hear in weddings is a raucous, cacophonic noise.

6. Don't sound so **equi**_____! Come out clearly on whose side you are!

7. It is so unfortunate that our politicians sound too **retr**_____ to be appreciated.

8. He was such a **cred**_____ man! He believed whatever anyone said.

9. Despite all modern thinking, a woman's career and position in our society remains often **circ**_____ and stunted.

10. One cannot make out what he writes! He just **scr**_____ so illegibly on the paper!

EXERCISE 4.3

Using your understanding of the roots discussed above, fill in the blanks in the following exercise. Use the ending of the word as a clue to get to the target word:

1. Good researchers often need to be _____**cious** readers of their subject.

2. _____**lent** weather conditions kept us waiting under the groove for a long time.

3. Don't throw yourself beneath your grace. There is absolutely no need for you to be so _____**quious** in the company of your boss.

4. The _____**gent** Indian hockey team has done so well in the recent past.

5. Everything seemed to have _____ **phosed** so completely that it was difficult to recognize places in the city that was my home for such a long time.

6. If you really want to grow in life, you cannot become _____**cent** at any stage of your life.

7. The company will _____**urse** all the expenses that you incur on the tour.

8. Most of the people today push themselves only for worldly and _____**real** drives.

9. Winning and losing is part of the game. But such an _____**ect** surrender was so humiliating.

10. Despite all odds, both P.V. Sindhu and Saina Nehwal seemed to have scripted an _____**ble** chapter in the Indian sports history in the recent past.

4.4 PREFIXES AND SUFFIXES

Just as it is important to understand the root of a word to understand its meaning, it is also worthwhile to learn how certain small additions at the beginning and ending of words can add to the meaning or change the existing meaning of certain words. It is so because we form words by adding prefixes and suffixes to different words. Therefore, it is not only the roots but also the prefixes and suffixes which help us add more words to our vocabulary.

In fact, if you study the shape of a word, you can broadly divide it into three parts—the prefix, the suffix, and the root word. Since we have already studied some roots and the related words, let us now study some prefixes and suffixes and see the words that can be formed by using them:

in- **Negative Prefix (denotes the opposite)**

Examples:

Insufficient	(in + sufficient)
Insane	(in + sane)
Invalid	(in + valid)
Inappropriate	(in + appropriate)

un- **Negative Prefix (denotes the opposite)**

Examples:

Unpleasant	(un + pleasant)
Unproductive	(un + productive)
Unadvisable	(un + advisable)
Unhappiness	(un + happiness)

im- **Negative Prefix (denotes the opposite)**

Examples:

Impolite	(im + polite)
Improper	(im + proper)
Imperfect	(im + perfect)
Impious	(im + pious)

-fy **Verb Suffix (Nouns/Adjectives converted into Verbs)**

Examples:

Class	Classify
Pure	Purify
Note	Notify
Terror	Terrify

-ation **Noun Suffix (Verbs converted into Nouns)**

Examples:

Educate	Education
Indicate	Indication
Authenticate	Authentication
Purify	Purification

-er **Noun Suffix (Verbs converted into Nouns)**

Examples:

Teach	Teacher
Inform	Informer
Lead	Leader
Manage	Manager

-ment Noun Suffix (Verbs converted into Nouns)

Examples:

Involve	Involvement
State	Statement
Enjoy	Enjoyment
Entertain	Entertainment

-ion Noun Suffix (Verbs converted into Nouns)

Examples:

Provide	Provision
Decide	Decision
Illustrate	Illustration
Appreciate	Appreciation

-ness Noun Suffix (Adjectives converted into Nouns)

Examples:

Kind	Kindness
Small	Smallness
Useful	Usefulness
New	Newness

-less Adjective Suffix (Nouns converted into Adjectives)

Examples:

Value	Valueless
Mercy	Merciless
Worth	Worthless
Effort	Effortless

-ful Adjective Suffix (Nouns converted into Adjectives)

Examples:

Mind	Mindful
Disdain	Disdainful
Fear	Fearful
Regret	Regretful

-able Adjective Suffix (Nouns and Verbs converted into Adjectives)

Examples:

Objection	Objectionable
Achieve	Achievable
Identify	Identifiable
Favour	Favourable

-ental Adjective Suffix (Nouns converted into Adjectives)

Examples:

Judgment	Judgmental
Sentiment	Sentimental
Instrument	Instrumental

-ly Adverbial Suffix (Adjectives converted into Adverbs)

Examples:

Loud	Loudly
Cheap	Cheaply
Suggestive	Suggestively
Imaginative	Imaginatively

 EXERCISE 4.4

Use the following words in your own sentences:

1. Disdainful
2. Purify
3. Judgmental
4. Imaginatively
5. Effortlessly
6. Regrettably
7. Incremental
8. Illustrate
9. Identify
10. Unproductive

EXERCISE 4.5

Choosing the Right Word at the Right Place:

Each of the following words can be used as different parts of speech. The statements given below use each of them in one specific form such as noun/adjective/verb/adverb, etc. Reading how each has been used in one particular way, form more sentences so that the word can be used in other forms as well:

1. **Ambivalent/Ambivalence/Ambivalently**

   One can never be sure of his decisions; he is so **ambivalent (Adj)**.

   _____

   _____

   _____

   _____

2. **Resent/Resentment**

   As a young child, he always **resented (V)** his father's authoritarian attitude.

   _____

   _____

   _____

3. **Imperious/Imperiously**

   Haughty and grumpy, he moves across the stage **imperiously (Adv)**.

   _____

   _____

   _____

4. **Meticulously/Meticulous**

   Don't worry, my wife plans everything so **meticulously (Adv)** that we she never gets late.

   _____

   _____

   _____

   _____

5. **Inadvertent/Inadvertently**

   It was an **inadvertent (Adj)** error that cost him his job.

   _____

   _____

   _____

6. **Extravagance/Extravagant/Extravagantly**

   Mindless **extravagance (N)** can lead us to financial crisis.

   _____

   _____

   _____

   _____

7. **Redundantly/Redundant**

   In order to compose good reports, we need to delete all **redundant (Adj)** expressions that we at times use while writing.

   _____

   _____

   _____

8. **Vivid/Vividly**

   Throughout his presentation, he put across his ideas quite **vividly (Adv)**.

   _____

   _____

   _____

9. **Insanely/Insanity/Insane**

   We need to do something about him; his **insanity (N)** is increasing day by day!

   _____

   _____

   _____

   _____

10. **Superficial/Superficiality/Superficially**

Though the leader tried to impress the crowd, his **superficial (Adj)** knowledge exposed him quite bitterly.

11. **Obsessive/Obsessed/Obsessively**

Throughout the novel, the villain keeps chasing the heroine quite **obsessively (Adv)**.

12. **Triumphantly/Triumphant/Triumph**

After kissing it ardently, the veteran raised the trophy **triumphantly (Adv)**.

13. **Malicious/Maliciously**

The **malicious (Adj)** look on the wicked man's face sent a shiver down her spine.

14. **Resilience/Resilient/Resiliently**

Amidst all odds and difficulties it was his **resilience (N)** that kept him going all these years.

15. **Indolence/Indolent/Indolently**

I don't understand what's wrong with you! Such **indolence (N)** I have never seen in anyone else!

4.5 SYNONYMS

A synonym is a word or expression that has the same or almost the same meaning as another word or expression. The word 'synonym' is a composite of two Greek words: the prefix 'syn' means 'together' and 'onym' is 'name'; so, synonym can mean 'together naming the same thing'. The English language has an enormous vocabulary; almost all words have more than one synonym. Let us see a few examples of words with their synonyms in the list given below:

List of Synonyms

Amazing	astounding, surprising, stunning
Ancient	antique, dateless, immemorial, old
Destruction	annihilation, extinction, demolish, raze
Benefit	profit, revenue, yield
Courageous	brave, valiant, heroic

Destitute	bankrupt, impoverished, poor
Deterioration	pollution, defilement, adulteration
Decide	determine, settle, choose, resolve
Huge	enormous, gigantic, massive
Reply	answer, respond, acknowledge
Bad	evil, wicked, vile, malicious
Fertile	productive, fruitful, abundant, evil
Obtain	secure, procure, gain, accumulate
Dwelling	abode, domicile
Hungry	ravenous, empty
Wounded	injured, damaged, harmed
Intelligent	clever, brilliant, knowledgeable
Look	glance, see, gaze, stare
Old	elderly, aged, senior
Organization	institution, management
Create	originate, invent, design, fabricate
Partner	associate, colleague, companion
Polite	courteous, cordial, gracious
Quick	fast, swift, speedy, rapid
Risky	dangerous, perilous, treacherous
Sleepy	drowsy, listless, sluggish
True	correct, right, accurate, exact
Move	plod, creep, crawl, inch, poke, drag
Under	below, beneath, lower
Vacant	empty, deserted, uninhabited
Abandon	desert, leave, forsake, depart from
Woman	lady, female, girl
Afraid	aghast, alarmed, fearful, horrified
Damp	moist, soaked, soggy, wet
Enormous	big, huge, massive, giant, immense
Drill	exercise, hone, practice, tune up, work out
See	watch, observe, notice, envisage, spot

By learning various synonyms of words you will be able to increase your word power, which will surely help you improve your writing skills.

EXERCISE 4.6

Write the synonyms of the following words:

1. Infallible
2. Impeccable
3. Interminable
4. Illicit
5. Intractable
6. Impregnable
7. Impertinent
8. Incorrigible
9. Ignoble
10. Intrepid

EXERCISE 4.7

Pick out the word closest in meaning to the head word:

1. **Gentle**
   (a) Rectifiable   (b) Docile
   (c) Composed   (d) Indigent
   (e) None of the above

2. **Composure**
   (a) Coexist   (b) Cohabit
   (c) Join   (d) Poise
   (e) None of the above

3. **Moan**
   (a) Criticize   (b) Groan
   (c) Shout   (d) Wail
   (e) None of the above

4. **Retrograde**
   (a) Recess   (b) Revive
   (c) Regressive   (d) Reproduce
   (e) None of the above

5. **Slender**
   (a) Poor   (b) Scanty
   (c) Slim   (d) Weak
   (e) None of the above

6. **Diminutive**
   (a) Short   (b) Stunted
   (c) Titanic   (d) Hefty
   (e) None of the above

7. **Deceitful**
   (a) Dreadful   (b) Drab
   (c) Deceptive   (d) Delightful
   (e) None of the above

8. **Adore**
   (a) Adulate   (b) Understand
   (c) Admire   (d) Appreciate
   (e) None of the above

9. **Disparage**
   (a) Discourage   (b) Distrust
   (c) Disapprove   (d) Deprecate
   (e) None of the above

10. **Prudent**
    (a) Sensible   (b) Prudish
    (c) Disrespectful   (d) Prolific
    (e) None of the above

11. **Ghastly**
    (a) Ghostly   (b) Horrific
    (c) Livid   (d) Terrific
    (e) None of the above

12. **Imposter**
    (a) Impoverished   (b) Imbalanced
    (c) Dissembler   (d) Pleasing
    (e) None of the above

13. **Berserk**
    (a) Incorrigible   (b) Wild
    (c) Battered   (d) Betrayed
    (e) None of the above

14. **Perish**
    (a) Disturb
    (b) Dismiss
    (c) Disappear
    (d) Disbelieve
    (e) None of the above

15. **Impeccable**
    (a) Flawless
    (b) Flawed
    (c) Imprisoned
    (d) Implacable
    (e) None of the above

 EXERCISE 4.8

Find out the word that is closest in meaning to the given head word:

1. **Punctilious**
   (a) Meticulous   (b) Casual
   (c) Perfunctory   (d) Final
   (e) None of the above

2. **Opulence**
   (a) Poverty   (b) Penury
   (c) Affluence   (d) Indigence
   (e) None of the above

3. **Stolid**
   (a) Stupid   (b) Stylish
   (c) Impressive   (d) Impassive
   (e) None of the above

4. **Buoyant**
   (a) Energetic   (b) Blissful
   (c) Tedious   (d) Enticing
   (e) None of the above

5. **Momentous**
   (a) Mesmerizing   (b) Stormy
   (c) Memorable   (d) Significant
   (e) None of the above

6. **Stultify**
   (a) Stupefy   (b) Chalk
   (c) Choke   (d) Chaff
   (e) None of the above

7. **Profligate**
   (a) Prolific   (b) Proliferate
   (c) Extravagant   (d) Exaggerate
   (e) None of the above

8. **Babble**
   (a) Talk   (b) Scribble
   (c) Believe   (d) Sight
   (e) None of the above

9. **Retaliate**
   (a) Reveal   (b) Repeal
   (c) Respect   (d) Retort
   (e) None of the above

10. **Superfluous**
    (a) Redundant   (b) Superficial
    (c) Essential   (d) Superb
    (e) None of the above

4.6 ANTONYMS

Just as it is possible to learn new words by seeing their synonyms, it is also worthwhile to understand their antonyms—the words opposite in meaning—to understand their usage. Antonym is a word which has the opposite meaning of a particular word, although not necessarily in all its shades.

Look at the following list which consists of a few words with their antonyms in the next column.

List of Antonyms

Achieve	fail, fall short (of), miss, skimp
Afraid	confident, adventurous, audacious, bold, daring
Ancient	modern, new, recent, contemporary, novel
Arrive	depart, check out, clock (out), flee, leave
Arrogant	humble, lowly, modest, unpretentious
Ascend	descend, decline, dip, drop, fall (off), plunge
Attack	defend, evade, shun, dawdle, fiddle (around)
Blunt	sharp, circuitous, edgy, ground, honed
Brave	cowardly, chickenhearted, timorous, fearful
Cautious	careless, heedless, incautious, unmindful
Complex	simple, no-frills, unsophisticated, uncomplicated
Compliment	insult, put-down, slight, affront, barb
Crazy	sane, realistic, reasonable
Crooked	straight, direct, linear
Decrease	increase, boost, enlargement, gain
Demand	supply, nonessential, non-necessity
Destroy	create, restore, resurrect, resuscitate, revive
Divide	unite, join, link, unify, blend, combine
Enormous	dwarf, puny, small, undersized
Expand	contract, abbreviate, abridge, condense, shorten
Freeze	boil, heat
Gloomy	cheerful, blissful, buoyant, chipper, delighted
Guilty	innocent, shameless, remorseless, unapologetic
Idle	active, alive, busy, operative, working
Innocent	guilty, devil, knave
Lavish	stingy, bare, minimal, scant, spare
Like	hate, dislike, detest, loathe, despise
Sharp	blunt, dull, even, moderate, blurred, dim, slow, stupid

Knowing antonyms will help you not only learn the difference between words but also equip you improve your expression while writing and speaking. Given below is one example which will help you understand how to do it in examination.

Truncate

(a) Inflate   (b) Curtail   (c) Abridge   (d) Shorten   (e) None of the above

Key: All the words except **(a) Inflate** relate to the action that cuts and reduces the size of something. Something *inflated*, however, is enhanced and exaggerated; for example, *inflated ego*, hence the choice.

Sometimes by removing the prefix, we can get the word opposite in meaning. Look at the following words and see how we can figure out their antonyms or words opposite in sense by doing away with the prefixes or suffixes attached to them:

- Ignoble: Noble
- Incorrigible: Corrigible
- Impertinent: Pertinent
- Intractable: Tractable
- Illicit: Licit
- Infallible: Fallible
- Interminable: Terminable

- Inextricable: Extricable
- Impotent: Potent
- Improvident: Provident
- Harm: Harmless
- Use: Useless
- Speech: Speechless
- Fear: Fearless

Task I Read the following paragraph paying special attention to the words highlighted and attempt the exercises that follow:

Despite their **staggering** achievements in all walks of life, being a girl in Indian society is a difficult preposition to deal with. It takes all the **grit, determination, audacity,** and **perseverance** for a girl to **attain irreproachable** and **dignified** place for herself. In the past couple of decades education and sports seem to have contributed significantly in this **demanding odyssey** of Indian girls who seem to be striding towards their **emancipation** all the more **resolutely** and **belligerently**. Therefore though **delighted** we were, it was not at all shocking when Harmanpreet Kaur **bludgeoned** down a **swashbuckling** and **historic** 171 against Australian women cricketers and when PV Sindhu **crowned herself** with another silver medal at World Badminton Championship while Saina Nehwal **added another feather to her crown** by **grabbing** the bronze at the same event.

Going ahead, attempt the exercise given below on the basis of your understanding of the words highlighted.

EXERCISE 4.9

Mark the words that do not match the rest:

1. **Persevere**
   (a) Continue
   (b) Sustain
   (c) Squander
   (d) Maintain

2. **Belligerently**
   (a) Cowardly
   (b) Aggressively
   (c) Courageously
   (d) Bravely

3. **Staggering**
   (a) Stunning
   (b) Moderate
   (c) Noticeable
   (d) Remarkable

4. **Irreproachable**
   (a) Beyond guilt
   (b) Blameless
   (c) Accused
   (d) Faultless

5. **Resolutely**
   (a) Firmly
   (b) Ambivalently
   (c) Earnestly
   (d) Strongly

6. **Emancipate**
   (a) Incarcerate
   (b) Liberate
   (c) Exonerate
   (d) Release

7. **Grab**

   (a) Capture   (b) Relinquish

   (c) Snatch   (d) Seize

8. **Odyssey**

   (a) Quest   (b) Peregrination

   (c) Pilgrimage   (d) Procrastination

9. **Dignified**

   (a) Decorous   (b) Gauche

   (c) Graceful   (d) Stately

10. **Demanding**

   (a) Exacting   (b) Arduous

   (c) Facile   (d) Challenging

EXERCISE 4.10

Find out the word that is closest in meaning to the word/expression given in the question:

1. A **fragile** object is

   (a) Strong   (b) Weak

   (c) Narrow   (d) Robust

2. If a meeting is **stalled**,

   (a) it is disrupted and stopped

   (b) it is resumed

   (c) it turns violent

   (d) it is abandoned

3. If you find someone's presence **stultifying**, you consider it

   (a) Confusing   (b) Suffocating

   (c) Encouraging   (d) Harrowing

4. A **solemn** speech is

   (a) Entertaining   (b) Hilarious

   (c) Informative   (d) Serious

5. **Plausible** explanation is

   (a) Descriptive   (b) Baseless

   (c) Convincing   (d) Conducive

6. A **wistful** look on one's face is suggestive of

   (a) Excitement

   (b) Pensive emotion

   (c) Happiness

   (d) Subdued presence

7. If someone has **penetrative** eyes, they are quite

   (a) Absorbing   (b) Observant

   (c) Petulant   (d) Haughty

8. An **inscrutable** design is

   (a) Difficult to decode   (b) Difficult to form

   (c) Difficult to copy   (d) Difficult to dictate

9. When different elements are **synchronized**, they are

   (a) Stirred   (b) Separated

   (c) Spoiled   (d) Mixed

10. An **inconsequential** meeting is often

   (a) Fruitless   (b) Fulfilling

   (c) Fruitful   (d) Fractious

4.7 OVERCOMING CONFUSION IN CHOICE OF WORDS

In English language a large number of words seem or sound similar to one another. Because of similarity in shape or sound of words, confusion at times arises about their correct usage. See the sentences below to understand the meaning and usage of the words generally confused:

1. **Contemptible/Contemptuous**
   - Despite all our growth and development, the **contemptible** discrimination on the bases of caste, colour, and creed continues to bedevil us.
   - The **contemptuous** look on his face clearly revealed that he did not like my presence any longer.

2. **Coarse/Course**
   - His **coarse** manners drew sneers and mocking giggles from the girls around.
   - Komal is doing a **course** on *Effective Public Speaking* to improve her communication skills.

3. **Verbal/Verbose**
   - The poet creates an outstanding **verbal** imagery to create an environment of suspense and mystery.
   - If you wish to write well, stop being **verbose**.

4. **Ingenuous/Ingenious**
   - 'You cannot deal with complexity of the business world with a direct, **ingenuous** approach,' told the legendary business tycoon to the gathering.
   - The little girl surprised everybody with her witty and **ingenious** reply.

5. **Eminent/Imminent/Immanent**
   - The **eminent** actor kept the entire production unit waiting for three hours. However, when he arrived, he gave a perfect shot within minutes.
   - The dark brooding clouds and fierce winds were clearly indicative of an **imminent** disaster.
   - You can try your level best, but it is the **immanent** will of God that will eventually decide their destiny.

6. **Defy/Deify**
   - Youngsters today have developed a tendency to **defy** their elders.
   - The way Virat Kohli is playing, it seems that the next generation is going to **deify** him as a cricketing God.

7. **Sculptor/Sculpture**
   - The **sculptor** kept working all through the night and his hands did not rest even for a while.
   - An exhibition of art and **sculpture** is being organized in the city on 11 September 2018.

8. **Collision/Collusion**
   - The head-on **collision** inflicted untold miseries on the passengers.
   - Without their **collusion** with the staff, the thieves could not have robbed the painting.

9. **Incite/Insight**
   - The leader kept **inciting** the crowd throughout his speech.
   - What guided the poet was not the worldly ambition but a subtle, poetic **insight**.

10. **Judicial/Judicious**
    - The **judicial** enquiry in the case is likely to bring forth new facts.
    - A woman has to very **judiciously** create a balance between her professional and home life.

11. **Historic/Historical**
    - It was left to MS Dhoni to hit a majestic six and take India to a **historic** win.
    - The **historical** account of the king's tenure and achievements is quite flimsy.

12. **Coach/Couch**
    - Greg Chappell turned out to be a controversial **coach** for the Indian cricket team.
    - One of the **coaches** that derailed was hers.
    - 'Rather than just reclining on the **couch** all day long and watching idiotic movies, you should do something fruitful in life!' the woman told the man.

13. **Loss/Loose/Lose**
    - The company has suffered heavy **losses** in the last couple of years.
    - He entered the presentation area wearing a long, **loose** apron.

- 'Just as winning is a habit, **losing** too is a tendency; so, let's work together not only to develop a winning habit but for overcoming the tendency to lose,' said the captain.

14. **Indigent/Indignant**
    - It is such an irony that one of the brothers in Raheja family is so rich while others are so **indigent**.
    - The tourist was clearly upset and **indignant** at the type of facilities provided for her stay.

15. **Spacious/Specious**
    - He has a large and **spacious** bungalow to live in.
    - 'Don't give me any more of your **specious** details; I have already had enough of them!'

EXERCISE 4.11

Fill in the blanks with relevant options from brackets in the following sentences:

1. Everybody was terribly moved as the body of the _____ (diseased/deceased) solider arrived wrapped in the national flag.

2. As a strangely coercive strategy, interactions between teachers is being _____ _____ (prescribed/proscribed) by the management of some schools.

3. The historical fort of Amer attracts _____ (hoards/hordes) of tourists to Jaipur every year.

4. Despite all his innocence, the poor deer eventually falls _____ (prey/pray) to the wily tactics of the wolf.

5. 'It's a dream come true; it is well and truly the most _____ (momentous/memorial) occasion of my life,' exulted the new nearly crowned Miss World in all her glee and excitement.

6. Coming from his fierce opponents, the Director took all his appreciation only as a back-handed _____ (complement/compliment).

7. The Director kept favouring the very ordinary actress simply because of his _____ (illicit/elicit) relationship with her.

8. The bowler started by pitching some _____ (loose/lose) deliveries.

9. We simply cannot depend on evidence all the time; we do need really a _____ (judicial/judicious) panel of jury to give fair judgement.

10. Regardless of all logic and justification, violence remains a _____ (contemptible/contemptuous) deed.

EXERCISE 4.12

Choose the correct option in the following sentences:

1. Both the parties have arrived at an **amiable/amicable** solution.

2. 'Why don't you want to accept the facts? What kind of **illusions/allusions** you wish to stick to all through your life!' said the poet's wife to her husband.

3. The education system should aim at developing the **imaginative/imaginary** faculty of students.

4. 'Don't be so **childish/childlike**, it is irritating to see you behave so stupidly!'

5. The criminal is being **prosecuted/persecuted** in the court.

6. Life has a strange way of teaching us lessons; those very situations that you wish to **invade/evade** confront you time and again in your life.

7. She entered the room very elegantly and shut the door quite **discretely/discreetly**.

8. Opportunities knock at everybody's door; it is for us to **seize/cease** the moment and use them to our advantage.

9. Spiritual quest requires us to transcend our **corporal/corporeal** pursuits and experience reality at a different level.

10. After the blast, the militants seemed to have taken **refuge/refuse** in the safe havens of dark hills.

4.8 ACRONYMS/ABBREVIATIONS

The difference between an *acronym* and an *abbreviation* is that an acronym is a shortened phrase and an abbreviation is a shortened word. According to answers.com, this difference may be true, but it is a debatable point. More succinctly, an acronym is an abbreviation for a series of words, and which is *pronounceable*. An abbreviation is commonly the first letter of each of a series of words *without considerations whether it is pronounceable*. An example of an abbreviation is 'FDIC'. An example of an acronym is 'AFLAC' (as uttered by the company's mascot duck). So, an acronym can be an abbreviation and an abbreviation can be an acronym, but not all abbreviations are acronyms. However, you need to understand that in official documents, we should not use abbreviations and acronyms generously. If you are using, define them in full parenthetically at the first place and later use them. Besides, if you are using abbreviations which have more than one expansion, define them in the glossary.

List of Common Abbreviations

approx.—*approximately*	ib./ibid.—Latin *ibidem* = in the same place
constr.—construction	i.e.—Latin *id est* = that is
contd.—continued	jr.—junior
def.—definition	jour.—journal
dept.—department, deputy	ltd.—limited
dir.—director	mech.—mechanical, mechanics
doz.—dozen	non seq.—Latin *non sequitur* = it does not follow
ed.—edited, edited by, edition, editor	op. cit.—Latin opere citato = in the work cited
e.m.u.—electromagnetic unit	pct.—percent
enc.—enclosed	quot.—quotation
fac./fax—facsimile	rps—revolutions per second
ff./fol.—folios, following	rpt.—reprint
fig.—figure	sym.—symbol
fwd.—foreword	sup.—superior, supplement, supply, (Latin *supra* = above), supreme

gen.—gender, genera, general, genus	tbs./tbsp.—tablespoon
geol.—geologic, geologist, geology	vet.—veteran, veterinary
geog.—geographer, geographical, geography	v.p.—vice president, vice principal
gloss.—glossary	v.s.—Latin *vide supra* = see above
govt.—government	vs./v.—Latin *versus* = against
gr—grain(s), gram(s)	wpm—words per minute
3M—Minnesota Mining and Manufacturing	GNC—General Nutrition Centers
3PL—Third Party Logistics	HP—Hewlett Packard
ADP—Automatic Data Processing	IBM—International Business Machines Corporation
B2B—Business to Business	ILM—Industrial Light and Magic
B2C—Business to Consumer	IMR—Information Management Research
BBB—Better Business Bureau	IREA—Intermountain Rural Electric Association
BOI—Business Object Interface	JOA—Joint Operating Agreement
CEO—Chief Executive Officer	KPI—Key Performance Indicator
CFO—Chief Financial Officer	MOH—Message/Music On Hold
CK—Calvin Klein	MSI—Multiple Streams of Income
COB—Close Of Business	MSN—Microsoft Network
COGS—Cost of Goods Sold	OPM—Other People's Money
COLA—Cost of Living Adjustment	OPR—Other People's Resources
COO—Chief Operating Officer	OPT—Other People's Time
CRM—Client Relationship Management	PE—Printer Error (a publishing term)
CSP—Certified Speaking Professional	PL—Profit and Loss
CTO—Chief Technology Officer	PO—Purchase Order
DBA—Doing Business As	POP—Point of Purchase
DSO—Days Sales Outstanding	PT—Part Time
DSW—Discount Shoe Warehouse	QA—Quality Assurance
EA—Electronic Arts	QC—Quality Control
FLP—Family Limited Partnership	QSC—Quality, Service, Cleanliness (Ray Kroc's motto for McDonald's)
FSB—Fortune Small Business	REI—Recreational Equipment, Inc
FT—Full Time	RFP—Request for Proposal
FTE—Full Time Equivalent	SFI—Six-Figure Income
FUBU—For Us, By Us	SKU—Stock Keeping Unit
GE—General Electric	SOHO—Small Office, Home Office
GEICO—Government Employees Insurance Company	SYSTEM—Save YourSelf Time, Engergy, and Money
GM—General Motors *or* General Mills	TM—Trademark

ANSWER KEY

Exercise 4.1

1. Implacable
2. Placid
3. Euphemistically
4. Circumnavigated
5. Circumscribing
6. Omnipotent
7. Exculpate, Acquit
8. Euthanasia
9. Pacifist
10. Eulogies, Paeans

Exercise 4.2

1. Diverted
2. Unanimously
3. Sanctimonious
4. Bibliophile
5. Euphonic
6. Equivocal
7. Retrogressive
8. Credulous
9. Circumscribed
10. Scribbles

Exercise 4.3

1. Voracious
2. Turbulent
3. Obsequious
4. Resurgent
5. Metamorphosed
6. Complacent
7. Reimburse
8. Corporeal
9. Abject
10. Incredible

Exercise 4.4

1. He maintained a **disdainful** look all through the meeting.
2. 'First **purify** your thoughts, and then claim to have achieved salvation!' shouted the woman in the foyer.
3. 'Don't be so **judgmental** all the time! After all there is a generation gap between us and them.'
4. The novelist **imaginatively** descends into the working of the mind and lays bare the inner conflicts of the protagonist.
5. 'Meryl Streep is such a wonderful actress! She slips into the characters she plays so **effortlessly**!' said the chief guest on the occasion.
6. **Regrettably**, the son went on the ask his parents to vacate his house.
7. Dhoni has been **instrumental** in the Indian cricket team's triumph both on the home grounds as well as on foreign trips.
8. **Illustrate** your points with the help of citations from the text.
9. There were so many mobiles of the same look, shape, and colour that for a long while, I struggled to **identify** the one that was mine.
10. Though she tried to make amends for her errors, her efforts remained **unproductive** as her husband refused to relent.

Exercise 4.5

Check your answers with your teacher.

Exercise 4.6

1. Infallible: Unerring, Trustworthy, Unfailing
2. Impeccable: Perfect, Consummate, Irreproachable, Faultless
3. Interminable: Endless, Continuous, Ceaseless, Perennial
4. Illicit: Illegal, Unlawful, Secret, Clandestine
5. Intractable: Unmanageable, Uncontrollable, Ungovernable, Restive
6. Impregnable: Invincible, Unconquerable, Indomitable
7. Impertinent: Insolent, Impudent, Disrespectful, Irreverent
8. Incorrigible: Beyond Redemption, Irreclaimable, Intractable
9. Ignoble: Vile, Base, Knavish, Wicked
10. Intrepid: Fearless, Undaunted, Courageous, Audacious

Exercise 4.7

1. b 2. d 3. b 4. c 5. c 6. a 7. c 8. c 9. d 10. a
11. b 12. c 13. b 14. c 15. a

Exercise 4.8

1. a 2. c 3. d 4. a 5. d 6. c 7. c 8. a 9. d 10. a

Exercise 4.9

1. c 2. a 3. b 4. c 5. b 6. a 7. b 8. d 9. b 10. c

Exercise 4.10

1. b 2. a 3. b 4. d 5. c 6. b 7. b 8. a 9. d 10. a

Exercise 4.11

1. Deceased 2. Proscribed 3. Hordes 4. Prey 5. Momentous
6. Compliment 7. Illicit 8. Loose 9. Judicious 10. Contemptible

Exercise 4.12

1. Amicable 2. Illusions 3. Imaginative 4. Childish 5. Prosecuted
6. Evade 7. Discreetly 8. Seize 9. Corporeal 10. Refuge

5

UNIT II: WRITING PRACTICES

NATURE AND STYLE OF SENSIBLE WRITING

LEARNING OBJECTIVES

After reading this chapter, you will be able to understand
- important tips for sensible writing
- different elements of professional writing

Professional writing is a functional type of writing. It includes several types of writing tasks—from writing a simple message in an email to writing persuasive sales letters; from writing about an issue in an article to writing technical descriptions of a machine or process; from writing business reports to writing technical proposals; from writing memorandum to writing the minutes of a meeting; and from writing class assignments to writing project reports.

Writing professionally differs from writing for fun, expression, or self-exploration, where the focus is on what the writer wishes to convey. Writing professionally requires us to keep the reader and the message in mind while crafting the message. Therefore, all professional writers are required to make their writing easy and sensible for their readers. Before discussing how to make our manuscripts more sensible and professional in spirit, let us discuss how sensible writing is different from insensible writing.

Sensible Writing	Insensible Writing
Grammatically accurate	Grammatically inconsistent
Culturally and contextually appropriate language	Inappropriate language
Authenticity of information	Lack of authenticity in information
Written in a lucid style	Improper style and delivery of message
Audience centric	Writer centric
Devoid of unnecessary verbiage and ostentations	Replete with superfluity and pomposity
Coherent and focused	Lack of unity and coherence

5.1 TIPS FOR SENSIBLE WRITING

In order to write sensibly, one needs to follow the *7 Cs* of writing, namely Completeness, Conciseness, Concreteness, Consideration, Courtesy, Clarity, and Correctness.

For achieving the 7 Cs of writing, keep the following tips in mind:
- Choose simple, familiar, and concrete words.
- Prefer using verbs to long nouns.

- Avoid wordiness and redundancy.
- Provide complete and accurate information.
- Judiciously use active and passive voice.
- Follow emphatic word order.
- Use parallel grammatical construction.
- Avoid camouflaged expressions.
- Avoid excessive use of jargons.
- Avoid clichés.
- Avoid circumlocution and ambiguity.
- Use graphics and illustrations.
- Avoid punctuation and grammatical errors.
- Make your writing more culturally relevant.

By following the above tips, you can write in such a way that with minimum effort and time it will lead to maximum understanding of your message. Let's see some of these points with some examples:

5.1.1 Use Simple, Familiar, and Concrete Words

Professional writings require us to use simple, familiar, and concrete words. Avoid ostentation and flowery language as far as you can. Also, prefer using concrete words rather than choosing abstract expressions for maintaining clarity and precision in your writings. See the following examples:

Original In all probability, we are likely to launch a mobile set that is bound to have a resounding repercussion on the way mobiles are designed.

Revised Our new mobile set is likely to change the existing mobile designs.

Original The committee will *decipher* the factors responsible for lack of *synergy* between the two departments.

Revised The committee will find out causes for the lack of cooperation between the two departments.

Original The *ramifications* of the experiment done in the laboratory should be *corroborated*.

Revised The results of the lab experiment should be verified.

5.1.2 Prefer Using Verbs to Long Nouns

Psychologically, it is easier for us to remember actions than objects. In language, action is often described through verbs while objects are denoted through nouns. Preferring verbs to nouns, particularly the longer nouns, helps us express ourselves in an emphatic, clear, and forceful way. Consider the following examples to understand how the use of verbs in the revised versions expresses the idea more lucidly and appropriately:

Original After a careful revision of the suggestions made, a consideration for their implementations is likely to follow.

Revised We are likely to implement the suggestions after carefully considering and revising them.

Original Please make an approbation of the recommendations only after a meticulous observation thereof.

Revised Please approve the recommendations only after meticulously observing them.

Original A new procedure has achieved its full realization. All the members of the staff are requested to make a utilization of the new procedure for obtaining short leaves during office hours.

Revised A new procedure for obtaining short leaves during office hours has been implemented. All the members of the staff are requested to follow that.

5.1.3 Avoid Wordiness and Redundancy

After you have decided on the meaning you are trying to convey, work on putting it in a concise language. Be brief, whenever possible. Avoid wordiness and unnecessarily long words. When you use more number of words to convey the same meaning, it is called *redundancy*. Strive for clarity in your writing and avoid vagueness. See the following examples:

Original Tsunami had the effect of a destructive, disparaging and caustic impact on the manufacturing plant.

Revised Tsunami destroyed the manufacturing plant.

Original Keeping in mind the objective of facilitating and having smooth operation for timely processing of rebate requests, it appears that more employees are required.

Revised To fulfil the rebate requests quickly, we need six more employees.

5.1.4 Provide Complete and Accurate Information

The writings which provide incomplete information are likely to create vagueness in the mind of the reader in some aspect or the other. Consequently, the reader interprets the data differently from the way the writer intended it. Take a look at the following examples:

Original The sales force will meet at 6 pm on Wednesday.

Revised The sales force will meet at 6 pm on 30 June 2018, Wednesday in the Senate Hall.

Original This year the firm has incurred high profits.

Revised This year the firm has incurred 4.8% more profit as compared to the last year.

5.1.5 Judiciously Use Active and Passive Voice

In general, active voice is preferred to express ideas in professional write-ups. The unnecessary use of passive voice sometimes makes us write more than required. However, passive voice is preferred in order to avoid curtness or give prominence to the action rather than the agent. See the following examples:

Original Because Mr Thareja, Accounts Officer, forgot to include the correct budget projections with the bid, we lost the client.

Revised The correct budget was accidentally left out of the bid due to which we lost the client.

Original You have not yet informed me about the latest marketing strategies you are likely to follow from this month onwards.

Revised I have not yet been intimated about the latest marketing strategies you are likely to follow.

Thus, there are times when judicious use of passive voice can enhance the subtlety and tactfulness in your writing.

5.1.6 Follow Emphatic Word Order

Since a professional write-up is a concise presentation of facts, an emphatic word order is required to arrest the attention of the reader. For a reader, what comes in the beginning and at the end has an extra emphasis in meaning and idea. Therefore, try and supply the most important part of your message either in the beginning or at the end of a sentence and let it not be lost somewhere in the middle of a sentence. See the following examples:

Original When he returned to the production unit, the Production Manager tried to implement the strategies he had learnt about in the training programme attended in the previous month.

Revised On his return from the training programme, the Production Manager tried to implement the strategies recently learnt.

Original Individual preferences in the decision to allocate the division work among employees would be considered before making a final decision on this.

Revised Before allocating the division work among employees, individual preferences would be considered.

5.1.7 Use Parallel Grammatical Construction

While writing, remember to follow parallel grammatical structures. Grammatically, a gerund is parallel to a gerund while a to-infinitive is parallel to a to-infinitive. Look at the following examples and learn to use parallel grammatical structure as suggested:

Original Reading in the conference hall may be accommodated to some extent but to cook there seems weird and strange.

Revised Reading in the conference hall may be accommodated to some extent but cooking there seems odd and strange.

Original While you speak to inform, remember to use slides for carrying conviction.

Revised While speaking to inform, remember using slides for carrying conviction.

Original The Manager asked for improving the marketing strategy and to introduce attractive schemes for enticing more customers.

Revised The Manager asked for improving the marketing strategy and introducing the schemes to entice more customers.

5.1.8 Avoid Clichés

Just as overusing a machine makes it groan, overusing an expression makes it sound clichéd and hackneyed. Therefore, while writing a report, try to avoid expressions which sound drab and repetitive. See the following examples:

Original We assure you that we would spare no stone unturned in helping the company achieve its objectives.

Revised We are committed to doing our best in order to help the company achieve its objectives.

Original Last but not the least, let me thank the management.

Revised Finally, I would also like to thank the management.

Besides clichés, avoid overusing jargons and excessive use of foreign words. Doing this unnecessarily confuses the reader and leads to ambiguity which certainly is not a desirable trait.

5.1.9 Avoid Circumlocution

Since professional writing is all about being concise and precise, do not bury your message in the labyrinth of the words. Not arriving at the point of discussion early is almost like a criminal offence in the professional world. Remember that more number of words in professional situations means more money, time, and energy; and an extravagant use of any of these is certainly suggestive of an amateurish and unprofessional approach towards work. Therefore, avoid circumlocutory expressions and be pointed and straight while writing professionally. Look at the following examples to understand the point better:

Original In the given circumstances, it would hardly augur well if the company decides to retrench its tried and trusted employees especially when suitable replacements of theirs would not be easy to come by. Hence, our suggestion is to forestall the process of termination of employees, particularly those who are quite tried and trusted and would be hard to replace.

Revised We don't suggest retrenchment of experienced and trusted employees for it is generally difficult to replace them.

Original All in the present moment of time, mobile industry has witnessed a mad scramble for more customer orientation with all the major players in the field readily making frequent announcements and thereby securing their clientele as the inducements they offer that are far too luring for the average customer in India to put a resistance to.

Revised At present all the major mobile companies are trying to attract customers and are trying to secure clientele by launching attractive schemes and offering tempting inducements which are difficult to be resisted by an average customer in India.

5.1.10 Avoid Punctuation and Grammatical Errors

Grammatical and punctuation errors can jolt your credibility severely in the professional world. Therefore, you need to be correct in terms of grammar and usage in your professional writings. In the grammar section of the text, you have already been instructed about how to avoid grammatical and punctuation errors. Make good use of these instructions and try to make your writings as error-free as possible. Many a time, errors are caused simply because of insufficient proofreading of the document. Therefore, before you release a professional document, you must proofread it thoroughly.

5.1.11 Use Graphic Aids and Illustrations

Using illustrations provides a professional flair to your writing. If done in a professional and methodical manner, it surely helps your reader grasp the content easily. For example, most of the reports include complex, voluminous data which can be presented in a better way by including graphic aids (e.g., tables, charts, diagrams, etc.). Graphic aids supplement the text and help you communicate the message and the content much more engagingly. The use of graphic aids makes your writings more interesting and readable. Similarly, these aids can be used when you have to draft a proposal, manual, handbook or prepare PPTs for your presentation.

EXERCISE 5.1

Rewrite the following sentences to make them simple, clear, and precise:

1. Our experience suggests that who listen to others with dwindling attention, fail to ever speak properly. It is so because listening is the mother of all speaking.

2. Though we all pretend to listen to others while sitting in a meeting or attending some oral presentation, we usually are subtly occupied with the impulsive idea of speaking at the earliest opportunity.

3. It is commonly observed as charging on their emotional intensity, youngsters are prone to hasty and often miscalculated guess usually much to the chagrin of their officers.

4. Taking feedback from employees helps them in the removal of the unnecessary cobwebs arising out of the ills of hierarchy and achieves a commonality of purpose within an organization.

5. The task of laying off employees is a daunting one and needs subtleties of expressions to be employed deftly and strategically in order to keep the right-minded employees hooked to the goals of the organization.

6. In professional environment, listening acquires a monumental importance as without listening to the others' views, no corporate communication would attain the precision and authenticity desired in such circles.

7. Inspiring the employees to come out with a genuine feedback, processing the public perceptions received and emitting a positive signal continuously requires monumental communicative talent.

8. Most of us have had experiences as harrowing, traumatic, and distressing as this one, to some extent at least.

9. He seemed at first to conscientiously and carefully try to carry out the captain's instructions.

10. Michael successfully underwent on the third of last month a surgery at the Ray Hospital.

5.2 ELEMENTS OF PROFESSIONAL WRITING

Having understood the guiding tips for sensible writing, let us learn what the different elements of professional writing are and how to write them in a sensible and effective manner.

Given below are major elements of professional writings:

- Introducing
- Defining
- Classifying
- Describing
- Providing evidence and example
- Analysing
- Concluding

5.2.1 Introducing

Regardless of the type of professional write-up we are preparing, introducing the central idea, concept, notion, and thought plays a significant role. A manuscript, speech, letter, email, or conversation that does not begin well fails to create a lasting impact. For different types of professional write-ups, different introductions are required. Take a look, for example, at the following introduction and observe whether this makes for a good beginning of a report:

Hi, Sir, I have written this report for you. This is a great report. It talks about the problems that students face in our hostels. In our hostels, there are many types of problems and this report talks about all those problems. We need to improve hostels' situations. Otherwise there will be strikes in hostels.

Obviously, the paragraph written above is amateurish, incoherent, and hence unsuitable for a professional document such as a report. See how the revised version presents the same idea in a more organized and effective manner:

The present report discusses the problems faced by students in the hostels of the university. It analyses the various types of difficulties they face while living in the hostels of our university. Besides highlighting the problems and analysing the causes that lead to these problems, the report offers suggestions following which some of these problems can be solved.

See the opening sentences of the following speech and decide whether this makes the beginning interesting, systematic, and captivating—something that the beginning of a speech should do:

Hi friends, I am Dr Alok Srivastava. I am here to deliver a talk. The topic of my talk is 'How to Deal with the Problem of Hypertension?' Now, what is hypertension? Friends, hypertension is a common disease. Why is it so common? Is hypertension genetically induced? Is hypertension related to obesity? Does it relate to mental stress? Well, in our talk today, I'll discuss all these aspects related to hypertension and I will also tell you how to control hypertension.

Take a look at the following introduction and see how the same ideas can be articulated in a more imaginative and captivating manner:

Good morning, Ladies and Gentlemen! I am Dr Alok Srivastava and today I am going to discuss a disease that is considered to be a silent killer. Yes, it is a silent killer. Never taken much seriously because of its commonness, it keeps ticking in us, giving rise to several other diseases and eventually killing us. Can you guess which disease am I talking about? Yes, I am talking about hypertension—something that we commonly refer to as blood pressure. So, today I'll discuss what hypertension is; how it is caused; whether it is genetically induced or environmentally, psychologically, or physiologically produced; and what the possible remedies to curb, control, or cure it are.

At times, unnecessary verbiage takes away the impact of a good sensible beginning. See the following example:

We are thankfully in receipt of your letter no. SGL/VTK 033/131 dated 23-7-2017.

Observe how the revised version makes it succinct and effective:

Thank you very much for your letter no. SGL/VTK 033/131 dated 23-7-2017.

Emails can also start rather abruptly and unprofessionally such as:

Hi, all! A meeting at 4.30 with the CEO! Land up in time and fasten your seatbelts!

See, how the revised version makes the message more appropriate professionally:

Please note that a meeting with the CEO is scheduled in the Conference Room at 4.30 p.m. Please report in time and take your seat.

Let's now read the beginning of a speech on Kleptomania and observe how the imaginative and creative opening of the speech makes for an interesting beginning:

Situation: A Speech on Kleptomania

These days I dread Sundays. Not that I am a workaholic and don't want to rest. Given a choice, all I would do is rest. But then, come Sunday and my roommate wants me to accompany her to the 'newest shopping mall' in the city. Since I can never say *no* to her, I trudge my way behind her. With a thumping heart I watch her slipping into one shopping corner after another. It starts pounding faster when she gapes at a fascinating trinket for a longer while and certainly skips a beat when she, not knowing that she is a kleptomaniac, sends it into the depths of her pocket. This is what happens to kleptomaniacs; they steal on impulse. Ladies and Gentlemen, today, I am here to discuss with you what kleptomania is, why people suffer from it, and how it can be cured.

EXERCISE 5.2

Imagine that as Member of Lions Club of the city, you are required to make a speech on Intellectual Property Rights. Write the beginning of the speech.

EXERCISE 5.3

Read the introduction of the following report. Observe carefully the expressions that seem to be insensible or ineffective to you and revise the content so as to make it sensible and effective:

This report has been written to deal with the problem of absenteeism in the company. It has been seen that a large number of employees in the company do not turn up in time for office work and meetings. In the meeting recently convered by the CEO, this trend remained unabated. This got the company administration rather worried and frustrated. They have ordered an inquiry into the matter. I have, therefore, been asked to submit a report on the problem of absenteeism in the company. It studies the patterns of absenteeism in different departments of the company. The method chosen for collecting data has been the observation and personal interviews. Questionnaires have also been used for gathering the required information. Office record has also been handy in giving us the required information. The main problem has been lack of proper control at the division level. Poor delegation of work and inadequate number of biometric machines are also responsible for the widespread absenteeism. In a way, the overall monitoring system needs to be refurbished. The report has been divided in six chapters; they study the trends of absenteeism in different departments such as purchase, production, marketing, and quality control. The chapters on introduction and conclusion are any way the necessary chapters in every report and hence they have been included. The significance of the report lies in the fact that by observing the major trends of absenteeism and identifying the loopholes in the system, we can plug in the gaps in time. It can in turn lead to greater productivity, better sales, improved administration, and an overall growth in the market. This report has been authorized by the General Manager of the company and is meant to be read by him and the CEO, Sir.

5.2.2 Defining

Defining is one of the important methods for developing effective writing. By taking the reader through the definition of a particular word, the author is generally able to prepare his/her readers to follow the intended line of argument or thought. See how the author in the following passage attempts to define the term 'insomnia' for a specific purpose:

> The term *insomnia*, derived from the Latin root *somn*, refers to the *chronic and habitual inability to fall asleep or remain asleep for an adequate length of time*. Though insomnia can strike people of any age group, old people are more prone to it. However, owing to a stressful life and unhealthy food habits, a large number of young people today suffer from it. In a mechanical, alienated, frantic, and guilt-ridden life, there are other sleep-related disorders, as some people become *somnambulists*, that is, they begin to walk in their sleep. Almost all patients of *insomnia* feel *somnolent*, that is, sleepy or drowsy during their waking hours and some others become *amnesiac*, that is, they start losing their memory.

By defining the term 'insomnia' and other related words, the author is able to make things clear to his/her reader. Look how the speaker, by introducing a little known expression 'anorexia nervosa', through its dictionary meaning, immediately establishes a rapport with the listeners in the following extract from a speech:

> Friends, today we are going to talk about the rise of a very peculiar health disorder in young girls. In medical terms it is known as *anorexia nervosa* which stands for a psychological disorder, mainly afflicting adolescent girls and young women, characterized by a significant decrease in body weight, deliberately induced by refusal to eat because of an obsessive drive to lose weight. In this age of glamour, an urge to look smart and presentable is very common and we see a large number of young girls trying to shed their weight at a frantic pace. Therefore, a frequent food evasion or massive cuts in food intake often becomes a way of life for them. While doing so, however, little do they seem to realize that by indulging in such weight loss obsessions, they are likely to fall victim to a debilitating health disorder known as anorexia nervosa.

Having already defined the term 'anorexia nervosa', the speaker makes it convenient for him/her to refer to the term as and when required in the subsequent part of the speech, without causing ambiguity or confusion in the mind of the listeners.

5.2.3 Classifying

Just as defining and introducing the concept, classifying the information into smaller units too is an important part of writing strategy. For classifying the information, we need to keep in mind the following principles:

Logical arrangement In professional writings, logical arrangement of ideas is crucial. Depending upon their preference, different writers arrange the information from least important to most important ideas or vice-versa.

Coordination While we classify, we need to remember to join two related ideas of equal importance and give them equal status in our writing.

Subordination We also need to align subordinating ideas underneath the main ideas.

Parallel grammatical structure While dividing and classifying the matter into smaller segments, we need to phrase ideas in parallel grammatical structures.

Suitable numbering system Sections and sub-sections in professional writings are required to be structured in a suitable numbering system. Of the various numbering systems, the decimal numbering system is the most commonly preferred as the sections and sub-sections of the content are denoted through digits.

While composing certain professional documents such as reports and proposals, classification of the content is almost mandatory for writing properly. In reports, such division and classification of the content is known as outline, which needs to be written as per the principles given above.

Keeping the above principles for division and classification of matter in mind, see whether the following outline of a report is in proper order:

Fatal Road Accidents

1. Introduction
2. Accidents: Causes and Reasons
   2.1 Negligence
   2.2 Impact
   2.3 Youngsters don't Follow Traffic Rules
   2.4 Driving Rashly
   2.5 Roads—Poor Conditions
   2.6 Safety Measures are Not being Followed
3. Impact of Accidents
   3.1 Loss of Life
   3.2 Multiple Injuries
   3.3 Government also Loses Money
   3.4 Families cannot Recover from Emotional and Financial Loss
4. Strict Monitoring System
   4.1 Strict Implementation of Traffic Rules
   4.2 Speed Control through Mechanical Devices
   4.3 Introduction of Remedial measures
   4.4 Construction and Repair of Roads
5. Conclusion

The above outline is not appropriate. It does not adhere to the principles of logical arrangement, proper coordination, logical subordination, parallel grammatical construction, and decimal numbering system.

See how the same outline can be reframed in the following manner:

Fatal Road Accidents

1. Introduction
2. Causes of Accidents
   2.1 Negligence
   2.2 Rash Driving
   2.3 Violation of Traffic Rules
   2.4 Over Speeding
   2.5 Poor Condition of Roads
   2.6 Avoidance of Safety Measures
3. Impact of Accidents
   3.1 Loss of Life
   3.2 Injuries and Amputations
   3.3 Loss to Government Exchequer
   3.4 Emotional and Financial Setback to Families
4. Remedial Measures
   4.1 Strict Implementation of Traffic Rules
   4.2 Speed Control through Mechanical Devices
   4.3 Introduction of Latest Monitoring Systems
   4.4 Construction and Repair of Roads
5. Conclusion

EXERCISE 5.4

Assume that you are the Chief Librarian of the Radha Krishnan Community Centre, Chandigarh. Nirman Organization, a non-profit group, raises funds and provides volunteers to support your centre. Every February, you send a report of the previous year's activities and accomplishments to this group, as it provides an annual grant of fifty lakh rupees. Now write an Outline containing the details of the previous year's activities and including the new activities you are planning to introduce in the coming year.

5.2.4 Describing

Of all the writing techniques, descriptive writing is the one that is most commonly employed by us. It is quite extensively used for describing an idea, object, process, procedure, event, product, features, functions, etc. Regardless of the profession, all of us have to use descriptive writing in order to make an idea, object, process, event, feature, or function known to others. Since we all have to employ descriptive writing techniques, it won't be out of context for us to learn them in some detail.

Given below are the tips for making your descriptive writing effective:
- Create a picture of the object/person/place/thing in your mind.
- Memorize the object of description.

- Visualize its features intimately.
- Employ memory and imagination.
- Create an intimate image in your mind.
- Provide verbal structure to the object imagined.
- Make your description interesting and innovative.
- Use vivid and lucid language to communicate the idea.
- Choose words which strike clear, unambiguous images in the mind of the reader.
- Be intimate and warm in your approach.
- Use catchy, informal phrases to capture the attention of the reader.
- Use humour and wit, if possible.

See how descriptive writing techniques can help you provide effective descriptions such as the one given below:

Description of a Toaster

One of the most compact and the best performing oven-toaster-grill (OTG), the bake-all oven continues to perform life long for the satisfaction of its owner. The Bake All oven is fitted with special and powerful sheathed heaters made of chrome nickel steel tube for fast, even cooking. Special pilot lamps are provided to give you an indication of upper lower Heater. The bake-all oven also has two level fixed shelf support along with a fork. A special toughened see-through glass front window allows you to actually observe the food being cooked. The thermostatically controlled oven uniformly heats up to 300 degree centigrade to suit the individual requirement of each item you would like to cook. With its unique features and extraordinary design, this lovely appliance which can be kept on your dining table, provides you with a variety of 5-Star menus. Sleek and functional, your bake-all oven is an ideal saver of fuel, time, and space. Literally, the OTG warms up your lifestyle.

EXERCISE 5.5

Keeping in view the instruction provided above, write a technical description for a fully-automatic washing machine.

Describing a Table/Chart/Graph

In the business world you may need to refer to numbers, statistics, and other data and may have to discuss the information on graphs. Here are a few useful tips for discussing a graph:

- Use specific vocabulary to describe graph trends. For example, for a rising trend, you can use *went up, increased, grew;* for a decreasing trend, you can use words such as *fell, dropped, declined,* etc. And for no change you can use expressions such as *remained constant, levelled off, stabilised,* etc.; for showing a fluctuating trends you can use *zigzagged, fluttered, undulated.* For discussing the small changes you can use expressions such as *gradual change, slight change,* or *steadily moved;* for discussing drastic changes you can use adverbs such as *suddenly, sharply, dramatically,* and *steeply.*

- You should use the correct use of tenses when describing a chart. If the charts deals with facts in the present (as in our example), use Simple Present Tense; if the facts are related to the past, then use Simple Past Tense. If there is a connection between the past and the present, use Present Perfect Tense.

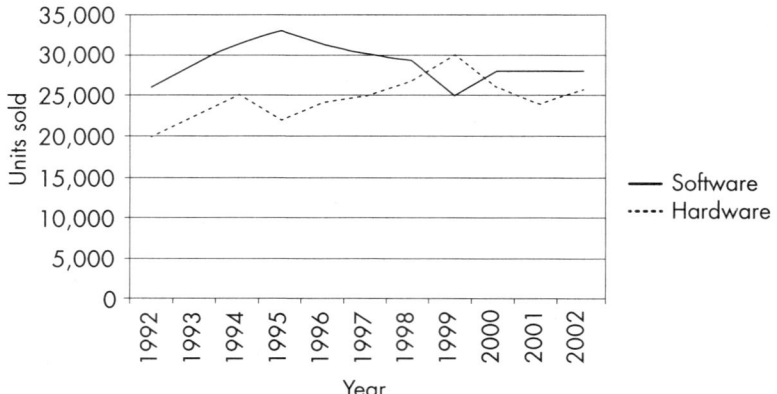

Figure 5.1 Annual Sales of Hardware and Software

The above multiple line graph reflects the annual sales of the company's hardware and software during 1992 to 2002. It shows that the sale of the software was highest in 1995 with 33,000 units sold and lowest in 1999 with just sale of 25,000 units getting sold. This 16.66% decline in the sale of software was caused because of the enhanced competition in the market. On the other hand, the sale of hardware has been fluctuating as just 20,000 units were sold in 1992 and the figure of sales went up in 1994 by 25% due to the introduction of technology in education sector. However, in the very next year (1995) the sale went down by 12%. After that, there was a steady increase till 1999 when the sales of hardware touched its highest with the sale of 30,000 units getting sold. In the next two years, the sale again went down and came to the sale of 24,000 units in 2001. The graph seems to show that sales figures have fluctuated over the period described. It also reflects that there is not much correlation between the sales of software and hardware.

EXERCISE 5.6

Read the following excerpt from an essay and comment on the strategies employed to augment the idea:

Rice is eaten in a variety of ways all across the country. However, the frequency, quantity, and type of dish in which rice is consumed differs from state to state. For example, in South India, it is the single most important ingredient and it is used in a variety of ways; apart from being eaten as cooked rice, it is also used in making different Indian dishes such as *pulao, dosa, idli, murukku,* etc. In Bengal, Bihar, and Uttar Pradesh, it is eaten with curry, in *biryani* and also with mango. In several states such as Rajasthan and Haryana it is eaten with curry and also with sugar or *khand,* and *bura.* In several other states including Madhya Pradesh and Gujarat, it is eaten as *poha,* i.e., as beaten rice. It is not just the quantity, frequency, and variety of dish made from rice that differs from state to state but also its cultural significance and social relevance in a particular context. For instance, in northern states, people prefer rice to chapatti when they wish to have something light, whereas in Orissa it is avoided and chapatti is preferred when they wish to eat something light.

5.2.5 Providing Evidence or Example

Evidence and examples form an integral part of sensible writing. In fact, without evidence, examples, quotations, and facts, figures and illustrations, whatever we write gives the impression of being subjective, personal, or opinionated. Since professional writings are supposed to be factual, it is important for us to use textual evidences, statistical data, factual details, and illustrative and corroborative material in our writings. See the paragraph given below and observe how the example helps to render the entire argument augmented and convincing:

Let us see how in the following example the writer has provided an evidence from Frantz Fanon's *The Wretched of the Earth* while talking about an analysis of the relationship between the colonized and the colonizers:

> The colonizers dehumanize the colonized. They reduce them to the state of an animal. This is evident when they use zoological terms to refer to the colonized. Their vocabulary consists of terms and phrases like 'this explosive population growth, those hysterical masses, those blank faces, those shapeless, obese bodies, and this headless, tailless cohort' (Fanon, *The Wretched of the Earth*, p. 8). They use these terms to put the humans on the same pedestal as the animal. By reducing their state to animals, colonizers argue that the colonized are uncultured, uncivilized beings.

Observe how again the examples in the following paragraph augment the idea properly:

> It is generally believed that Americans are very good speakers of English. Their articulation, however, does not really seem to support such beliefs. In fact, observed closely, it seems that Americans use sloppy articulation for quite a few expressions. For example, *I did not* for them becomes *I dint*, whereas the true contracted form for *I did not* should be *I didn't*. Similarly, *you ought to* in American English sounds like *you oughta* or *you otta* and *you have to* becomes *you hafta*. The forceful and intense *yes* in British English is always a sloppy *yeah* for them and *I don't know* sounds like *I dunno*.

 **EXERCISE 5.7**

Going further, read the following extract from a professional report and rewrite it to make it sensible and effective:

The present report is the result of a survey. The report talks about the changing preferences of the youth towards the fashions. The report highlights that the there is a shift in the preference of the youth. Most of the young boys and girls prefer wearing jeans and tee shirts. The exhibits from 3.4 to 3.9 show the different clothing patterns chosen by the youngsters. Preference for trousers and shirts is quite less. Similarly, footwear choice has also changed. Mostly they wear sports shoes (see Exhibit 3.10–3.14). Even girls prefer wearing shoes (see Exhibit 3.15–3.20). Even working women wear saris and shoes! (see Exhibits 3.21–3.25). In professional setting—mainly academic institutions—too men walk in wearing jeans and *kurtas* (see Exhibits 3.26–3.30) while women wear jeans and top (see exhibits 3.31-3.35). We feel a lot of such changes are brought in by print and visual media. They show popular images and thus trends are established.

5.2.6 Analysing and Interpreting

Just as defining, describing, and illustrating, analysing and interpreting facts and figures, data and statistics, and situations and contexts is an important part of writing skills. As a professional writer, we are quite often required to interpret and analyse data, facts and figures, to draw inferences and arrive at certain conclusions. A lot of factual information is often presented through graphic aids such as tables, graphs, charts, etc. As a professional writer, we need to cultivate the skill to analyse the given facts objectively and impartially. Given below are a couple of examples to help you understand how to interpret and analyse facts and figures:

As regards the composition of respondents, the questionnaire was filled by 26.7% first-year students, 20.4% second-year students, 19.1 % third-year students, 28 % by fourth-year students, and 5.8% fifth-year students. This shows that the issue of fee hike is being taken seriously by the students studying from first to fourth years. The low response from the fifth year reflects their indifference due to the fact they are in the last semester and are about to complete their degree. Since the increased fee is not likely to hit their pocket for a long time, they seem to be least concerned about this issue. Further, nearly half of the students are getting scholarships from the university which comfortably

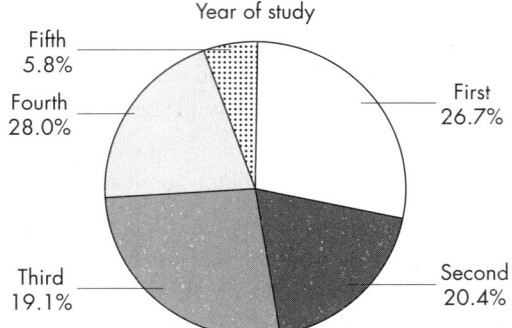

Figure 5.2 Distribution of the year of study of the respondents

sets off the impact of the fee hike for them. The highest level of response from the fourth year students brings to the fore their concern about the fee hike. It also subtly reflects their dissatisfaction at not getting placed at a higher package. It may be recalled here that the pay packages offered to our students by the recruiting companies have only been average.

Going further, see the bar graph given below and observe how it can be integrated with the remaining text through analysis:

As can be observed through the bar graph cited below, as many as 85 respondents think that they aren't comfortable in interacting with people from foreign cultures. In the era of globalization, such a response makes for a worrying proposition. There can be various reasons for it such as lack of knowledge, rural background of students, and an insufficient exposure to cosmopolitan culture. However, as we are aware of the fact that the modern corporate culture is increasingly becoming cosmopolitan and multicultural, the discomfort with a foreign culture, mannerism, language, religion, or region is likely to severely cripple the placement opportunities of our students. We need to sensitize our students about the cross-cultural issues in the corporate world as it is important for a successful global manager to be able to interact, work, and co-exist comfortably with people from other cultures. Keeping all these factors in mind, courses on cross-cultural competence need to be incorporated in our curriculum.

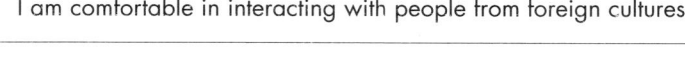

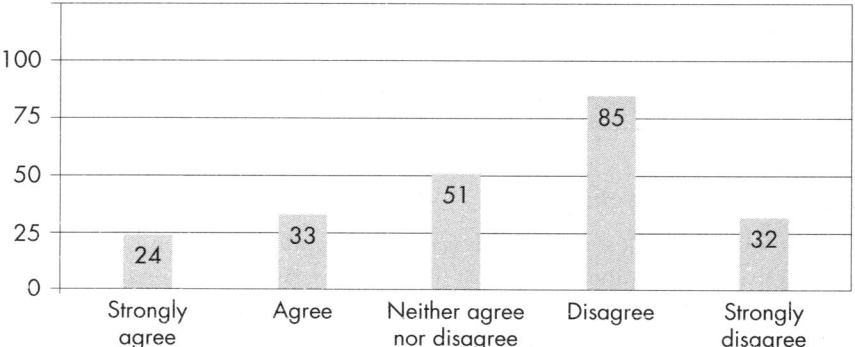

EXERCISE 5.8

Moving ahead, interpret and analyse the following bar graph that exhibits trends of preference for different disciplines in higher education:

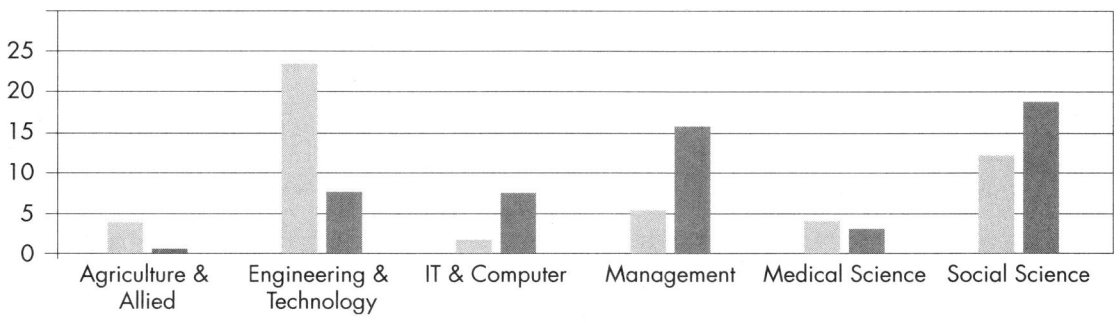

5.2.7 Concluding

Though brief, the concluding part of any professional writing is as important as its other sections. The nature, style, and tone of conclusion differ in different types of professional writings. In professional reports, the concluding part consolidates all the major inferences arising out of the discussion section; in a speech it provides the gist of the entire argument; in a debate it is shaped as a rebuttal of the opponent's argument; and in a sales letter it attempts to induce action in the reader by reinforcing the product or service being marketed. Therefore, while writing the conclusion in a professional writing, we should see to it that it falls in consonance with the specific requirement of the subject.

Keeping in view the above principle, see whether the conclusion of the following report is appropriate:

It has been often seen that the youths are the principal violators of traffic rules. As the survey suggests, 60% boys don't wear helmets while going to nearby markets. Young girls too do not prefer wearing helmets and nearly 40% of them admitted to having breached the traffic signal while driving. In terms of speed also, boys prefer driving their bikes quite fast. Only 12% of boys conceded to the idea of driving their bikes at 60 km per hour. As many as 88% boys felt that the speed limit for them should be 80 km per hour. Lack of awareness was common in people coming from nearby villages. They did not seem to know that pavements were for pedestrians. Around 70% of milkmen bringing milk from nearby villages every morning are not used to wearing helmets while driving. The overall situation seemed to be bleak and disheartening.

More than deriving conclusions, the above paragraph seems to be focusing on analysing the situation. Moreover, the above paragraph also indiscriminately mixes the present and the past tense, which is not appropriate grammatically. See the revised version below to understand how to write in a more appropriate manner:

Based on the analysis done in the preceding chapters, it can be concluded that carelessness, over speeding, ignorance, and violation of traffic rules are the major reasons for most of the fatal road accidents. As the preceding discussion reveals, 60% boys and 33% girls do not mind breaching traffic signal and seem disinclined to wearing helmets. Reports substantially establish the fact that lack of safety measures on roads and violation of traffic norms leads to fatal accidents quite often. Over speeding is another factor that causes 27% of the fatal road accidents as young bike riders drive their vehicles faster than the rule permits. Ignorance of traffic rules is yet another factor and a large number of villagers commuting to cities from nearby villages neither wear helmet while driving nor use pavements while walking on busy roads. As chapter four reveals, this has led to 12% of the road accidents in Jaipur alone. Thus, it can be concluded that in terms of negligence, over speeding, violation of traffic rules, condition of roads, and ignorance about the safety norms, the situation poses a grave challenge.

Since different types of professional write-ups are prepared to serve different purposes, they differ not only in terms of content, but also in style and tone. The following example denotes how the content, style, and tone of the text would change dramatically if it were to be the conclusion of a speech:

A Speech on Fatal Road Accidents

Conclusion

As you can see Ladies and Gentlemen, it is not some external, supernatural agency that is pushing us to our tragic, untimely, painful deaths on roads; it is we, you, and I, and our young boys and girls, who are cooking this disaster recipe on roads. Our study ostensibly reveals the fact that majority of accidents occur due to rashness, over speeding, violation of traffic signals, ignorance about the safety measures on roads, and a complete apathy towards the value of human life. The situation is so alarming that it is difficult to imagine a newspaper edition in our country without an accident story in some part of the country or the other. So, who is conspiring it against us? Is it God? Is it our destiny? Or the government? No my dear friends, it is we who are the authors of this awful, woeful tale of ours. Of course, the system and poor conditions of roads do contribute to the number of accidents. But if we are cautious and disciplined enough; if we follow traffic rules; if we drive within the prescribed limits and remain alert while driving; and—in short—if we care for our and others' life, most of these terrible tragedies can be avoided. So, friends, let's stop blaming destiny or government every time a fatal road accident takes place; let's take responsibility of our actions; let's live and let others live on roads.

By comparing the conclusion of a speech with that of a report, one can easily observe how different professional writings require different approach, style, and tone. However, incorporating the essentials of basic writing skills such as clarity, consistency, courtesy, and precision are a prerequisite in all types of professional writings in order to render your writing sensible and effective.

 **EXERCISE 5.9**

The Chairman of Oasis Computers Ltd, Ludhiana has felt the need for an intensive HR training programme for its entry-level and middle-level managers. Hence he has asked you, being the Director of the company, to analyse the various areas in which training is required for them. You have collected data for this purpose which is tabulated below:

Table showing training needs in percentage:

Level of Managers	Soft Skills	Mangerial Skills	Software Skills
Middle Level	39.8	26.2	34
Top Level	34.4	23.3	43.3

Now, write the introduction and the conclusion of this report.

 **EXERCISE 5.10**

Imagine that as the Human Resource Manager of New Era Visions, New Delhi, you have been asked to deliver a keynote address on *Positive Thinking*. Write the introduction and ending of your speech, inventing the necessary details.

6 PARAGRAPH WRITING

LEARNING OBJECTIVES

After reading this chapter, you will be able to understand
- meaning and structure of a paragraph
- ways to construct an effective paragraph
- importance and use of different transitional and connecting devices
- use of extended definitions
- features of a good paragraph
- techniques required to construct descriptive paragraphs
- importance of argumentative and analytical paragraph writing

Writing skill is an important part of professional communication. Good writing skills allow you to communicate your messages with clarity, ease, and precision. To equip yourself with better and faster writing skills, you need to practise different types of writing assignments. In this chapter, you will learn how to write one such descriptive piece of writing, which is paragraph writing.

6.1 WHAT IS A PARAGRAPH?

Take a look at the paragraph that follows:

Rabindranath Tagore was a great poet. He is known for the lyrical quality in his poems. Rabindranath Tagore was a multifaceted individual. His poems are wonderful for their musical appeal. Tagore was born in Bengal. His whole life was dedicated to the service of society and literature. Tagore, however, was not just a poet. In his poetry, we observe not just melody but also the commitment to eradicate the social taboos. Tagore was a poet who had great associations with other great Indians. Even today, his songs are sung and heard by many. In fact, you cannot imagine Bengal and its culture without imagining Tagore. Mahatma Gandhi was one of those Indians with whom Tagore shared a lot of his intellectual perspectives. When Tagore died, he left millions of hearts crying behind.

Can you figure out what is wrong with this passage? Would you describe it as a well-written passage? No. This is so, because most of the readers of this passage are not going to go beyond the third or the fourth line, as the passage does not really make much sense. Why?

Actually, the passage lacks continuity, focus, coherence, and unity. When we read this passage, it is difficult to keep track of the thought process of the writer, as he keeps jumping from one idea to another.

The passage starts by introducing *Tagore as a great poet*. It quickly adds that *Tagore's poetry is known for its lyrical quality*. This opening sentence makes the reader subconsciously anticipate something more about Tagore's poetry. What we are, however, told is that *Tagore was a multifaceted individual*. Somewhat confused, we look for some details about Tagore's versatility, but are told that his *poems are wonderful for their musical appeal.* With some effort, we start feeling that after all, the passage is about Tagore the poet, and the lyrical and musical quality of his poetry. However, some kind of an introductory idea—*Tagore was born in Bengal* confronts us. This is followed by another introducer—*his entire life was dedicated to the service of society and literature.* Then we are made to read a transitional sentence—*Tagore, however, was not just a poet.*

The paragraph continues to drift into incoherence in telling the reader about Tagore's contribution to Bengali culture—*In fact, you cannot imagine Bengal and its culture without imagining Tagore.* But then it changes gear all too suddenly and finally, when the writer ends the passage on a supposedly emotive note—*When Tagore died, he left millions of hearts crying behind*—we heave a sigh of relief. Such passages can actually test the tolerance of the readers.

Though it is impossible to really figure out what the writer actually intended to communicate to us by writing such a hopeless passage, we can make a valiant attempt to carve out some method of this madness. Here is an improved version of the above paragraph:

> Born in Bengal, Rabindranath Tagore was a great poet. He is known for the lyrical quality of his poems. His poems are wonderful for their musical appeal. Tagore, however, was not just a poet. He was a multifaceted genius whose whole life was dedicated to the service of society and literature. Therefore, in his poetry, we observe not just melody but also a commitment to eradicate taboos from the society. Because of his intellectual eminence, Tagore enjoyed a great association with other great Indians. Mahatma Gandhi was one of those Indians with whom Tagore shared a lot of his intellectual perspectives. When Tagore died after years of service to the domain of knowledge, intellect, art, music, and culture, he left millions of crying hearts behind. Tagore's influence on Bengali culture is so significant that even today one cannot imagine Bengal and its culture without remembering Tagore.

We admit that rescuing a badly constructed paragraph is an exacting task. Even then, you probably can figure out that the second version of the paragraph is decidedly better than the first one. It starts with an introducer: *Born in Bengal, Rabindranath Tagore was a great poet.* Having introduced the idea that Tagore was a great poet, the passage sets out to highlight the lyrical and musical quality of his poetry—*He is known for the lyrical quality of his poems. His poems are wonderful for their musical appeal.* Following this, we are introduced to the other side of the poet's personality—*Tagore, however, was not just a poet. He was a multifaceted genius whose whole life was dedicated to the service of society and literature.* A developer that follows—*Therefore, in his poetry, we observe not just melody but also a commitment to eradicate the social taboos*—augments and substantiates the idea proposed through the transition.

Emphasizing Tagore's intellectual prowess further, the next sentence in the paragraph cites his association with other great Indians of his time: *Because of his intellectual eminence; Tagore enjoyed a great association with other great Indians.* The next sentence immediately illustrates the idea by referring to the fact that *Mahatma Gandhi was one of those Indians with whom Tagore shared a lot of his intellectual perspectives.*

Honestly speaking, the paragraph needs further development as the idea of Tagore's genius, as a poet, lyricist, intellectual, and social reformer—though perfunctorily referred to in the passage—is not satisfactorily developed. But then we have not been given any other details on these aspects of Tagore's versatility. In the want of that, the passage makes its way out by putting together both the terminators—*When Tagore died after years of service to the domain of knowledge, intellect, art, music and culture he left millions of crying hearts behind. Tagore's influence on Bengali culture is so significant that even today, one cannot imagine Bengal and its culture without imagining Tagore.*

The two versions of the passage throw up some vital points, necessary to write well-structured and hence well-understood paragraphs. This exercise also makes us construct a loose definition about what a paragraph is; as we can say that *a paragraph is a group of sentences that introduces, presents, develops, and winds up one main idea on a topic.* It is an argument or a stand-alone piece of writing that usually has one controlling idea. Ideally speaking, if you have more than one main idea to communicate, you need to write as many paragraphs. Put to this test, the original paragraph falls short of our expectations as it tries to yoke together many differing ideas all at one place.

Therefore, a paragraph has a group of sentences rather than a group of ideas. The idea in a paragraph should actually be one, and the different types of structural devices should help it come out clearly. Though the paragraph cited originally presents an unusual example of messy structure, the mistake committed is not all that unusual. In fact, to some extent, quite a few of us tend to lose the structural sense of the paragraph. By and large, the entire problem arises due to the fact that people start writing without understanding the structure of a paragraph. Therefore, it is quite vital for us to understand the essential components of a paragraph and how they function, so that while writing we can use them properly in a paragraph.

Let us first study how a paragraph is structured.

6.1.1 Structure of a Paragraph

Broadly speaking, a paragraph is made up of three major parts:

- Topic sentence/introducer
- Supporting details/developers
- The concluding sentence/terminator

Introducer An *introducer* generally lays the foundation for the rest of the argument to follow. It raises hopes and makes promises that the remaining sentences in a paragraph are required to fulfil. In fact, the much sought after concept of unity in a paragraph is measured in terms of how far the expectations raised by the topic sentences of the passage are fulfilled by the remaining sentences in a paragraph.

Developer The sentences that aim at fulfilling the promise made by the introducers are called *developers*. Just as the function of the introducer is to introduce and emphatically place the central idea in a passage, the job of developers is to substantiate, augment, and authenticate the claims made by the introducer. In fact, if the developers fail to relate to the introducer, the paragraph continues to exhibit chinks in the argument and may not seem convincing to the reader.

Terminator The third category of sentences is known as *terminators*. The purpose of terminators in a paragraph is to wind up the discussion in a manner that is fulfilling and satisfies the reader in a psychological way. Though coming at the end of a paragraph, the importance of terminators in a paragraph can never be underestimated. They leave on the reader the final impression about the crux of the entire paragraph.

Having acquainted ourselves with the three different types of sentences used, read the following paragraph and figure out these three different types of sentences:

Beauty Lies in the Eyes of the Beholder

The concept of beauty is an ambiguous phenomenon. Some find beauty to be a physical attribute while others regard it as a matter of intellectual comprehension. For an epicurean, beauty never filters underneath human skin whereas for a thinker, it is always skin-deep. It can always be argued as to which of these two perspectives is worth assimilation in life. I feel we cannot choose one and discard the other altogether. This is so because we are neither only a physical entity nor are we just a brooding sage. We are both—the mind and the body. So, if we say we can turn a blind eye to physical beauty, we end up deceiving ourselves. On the other hand, if we focus obsessively only on physical beauty, we are unable to comprehend the other, and at times, far more subtle vistas of beauty. Hence, there is no harm in believing the dictum that beauty lies in the eye of the beholder, for, after all, it gives you an opportunity to appreciate the beauty of all that your eye beholds and mind observes.

The first sentence in the paragraph introduces to us the central idea. It is therefore the *topic sentence* or the *introducer* in the passage. The second to the ninth sentences constitute the main body of the passage, and hence are the *developers* in the paragraph. The last sentence winds up the discussion and hence is the *terminator*.

Thus, a good paragraph generally has a beginning, a middle, and an ending which can always be denoted through *introducer*, *developers*, and *terminator* in a well-structured paragraph.

EXERCISE 6.1

Read the following sentences and identify whether they are introducers, developers, or terminators:

1. Further, it is also important for a manager to be punctual and methodical.

2. Man is born free but he finds himself in chains everywhere.

3. To sum up, suffice to say that corruption has corroded our country.

4. Although there are many ways to achieve success, none of them leads to happiness.

5. But it is not possible for us to forget the sacrifice of our forefathers.

6. Poetry developed as an art form much later than drama that has its roots in religious conventions.

7. Therefore, all we can do is just sit silently and pray.

8. Surprisingly enough, the police kept aloof throughout the incident.

9. Meanwhile, his business had started taking a downward slide.

10. Of course, there is no point in overlooking the advantages of democratic governance.

6.2 TOPIC SENTENCE

The sentence that introduces the main idea in a paragraph is called the *topic sentence*. Generally, it appears in the beginning of the paragraph but sometimes it does appear towards the end of the paragraph. At times, however, the topic sentence can also be seen hidden somewhere in the middle of the passage. Since the purpose of the topic sentence is to emphasize the main idea of the passage, it is not generally suggested or practised to keep the topic sentence hidden under the debris of other details. This provides the core idea(s) that run throughout the paragraph like an underlying thread. The topic sentence guides the readers and lets them know what it is all about. So it performs two major functions. They are as follows:

Structural topic sentences Structural topic sentences may shape the openings such as these:

- There are three main reasons for the high inflation rate in Indian economy at present.
- Positive thinking has several benefits.

- Meditation, which is an intensely personal and spiritual experience, leads to three major important results.
- There are various causes for underemployment in urban areas.
- Distance education in the past one decade has had the following results.

These examples demonstrate how the structural topic sentences guide the readers to anticipate and move with the rest of the paragraph that unfolds as outlined by such introducers. Using structural topic sentences like these will help you follow your argument easily, as long as you link your ideas together.

Interpretive topic sentences An interpretive topic sentence not only introduces the reader to the main idea but also acquaints the reader to the author's perspective on the issue. The interpretive topic sentence, hence, becomes more valuable than the structural topic sentence. In order to use interpretive topic sentences effectively, you can employ some of the following strategies:

i) Use descriptive words such as **high, low, widespread, limited, half**, etc.

ii) Interpret/wind up the idea using words such as **suitable, beneficial, unsuccessful, serious**, etc.

iii) You can even express your opinion by using expressions such as **shocking, disheartening, disturbing,** etc. if you want your reader to share your perspective on the issue.

Some examples:

- Many communicable **diseases of man are known to be** caused by microorganisms. Some of these microorganisms are …
- In education, **girl children drop out earlier than boys**. Girls' enrolment is just 61 per cent, compared to …
- A recently released report by the Ministry of Human Resource Development (MHRD) shows a **nationwide decline** in school dropout rates. In Maharashtra too, the number of students …
- **Almost 49 per cent of the children** fail to complete primary level education. In a recent study in 11 districts of Rajasthan, it was found that …
- Access to basic services is **extremely limited**. It was found that …

Going further, let's learn how to construct a good paragraph.

6.3 CONSTRUCTION OF A PARAGRAPH

Just as it is important to understand the structure of a paragraph, it is also very important for us to learn ways to construct a good, emphatic, and effective paragraph. Let us learn how to use different strategies with the help of which paragraphs are constructed effectively.

6.3.1 Narrative Description

Look at the following paragraph and figure out the technique employed:

We kept moving upwardly. The incline required us to put in more than we were capable of producing. The scorching shining sun above posed another challenge. Within moments we broke into a sweat. More than once, we toyed with the idea of giving up on our expedition. Every time, however, we thought of covering a little bit more before dropping the anchor for the day. And it went on for hours together; and when we did finally stop, we were literally on our last legs. Panting and sweating, we looked at each other and smiled—the smile of satisfaction and accomplishment.

This small paragraph is quite catchy. Can you guess what makes it interesting? It actually is the narrative description of the passage that makes us read this. In this paragraph, the writer ventures to tell a story to the reader so that the message is communicated in an engaging manner.

Narrative descriptions best suit the paragraphs that have an intense emotion to express. Moving further, see how deftly the author in the following paragraph sustains our interest in the details that are structured through a narrative:

It was such a beautiful feeling, so ennobling, so liberating! Something that I had cherished forever, dreamt forever, craved forever was finally here. And it caused numbness in me, so I could not say anything; even though I wanted to say a lot. Emotions floated to the brim inside me, but words required to convey them deserted me. Valiantly, I groped for the right words to express what I was going through, but it wasn't possible. All of sudden, speechlessness descended on me as Rio stood in front of me on its four legs. Its two little eyes evoked compassion; its tail wagged perpetually announcing its love for all. Finally, when senses were revived in me, I hugged Daddy in unspeakable joy and gratitude. My best birthday ever had arrived and it had brought with it an exquisite moment of love, happiness, and pride!

6.3.2 Comparisons and Contrasts

We can construct a large number of paragraphs with this device. For developing paragraphs on these lines, two similar things are compared or two dissimilar things are contrasted to make the entire argument appear forceful and emphatic.

For instance, look at the paragraph given below. See how the speaker brings to the fore the significance of the changed perspective that characterizes a teacher's life in modern times:

India has changed a lot, and so has the teacher's life in this country. From being a *Guru* and *Acharya* in the Vedic times, our teacher is now beginning to look more like a trainer, some coach, or an expert of some kind. No doubt that even now the teacher holds an important position in the society. Even today, students come to him/her for guidance. But unlike in the past, a teacher is not expected to be the gospel of truth who could guide his/her disciples through the journey of their life; he/she is supposed to merely share with them his/her expertise in the relevant field. In coaching institutes, a teacher is treated as an instrument in ensuring success to his/her students. Here he/she is supposed to share skills, tips, methods, or some tricks that help the students crack a decisive entrance exam; beat the fierce competition around him/her; and grab a place of pride in the list of successful candidates.

By saying that in ancient times it was the student who used to help the teacher in the times of the latter's need, the speaker puts the entire complexity in a proper perspective. The comparisons drawn by the speaker help him sound authentic and unbiased. Thus, through comparisons and contrasts, we can carry conviction and authenticate our perspectives in an objective and emphatic manner.

6.3.3 Sustained Analogy

Using analogies is another way to draft emphatic passages. Comparisons and contrasts are carried out also through analogies. However, in its impact and appeal, this approach is more figurative and literary. Unlike simple comparisons and contrasts, analogies are used to compare things which are generally not from the same class. When such comparisons are used extensively, the device is termed as *sustained analogy*. Look at the paragraph given below and observe how through a sustained analogy, the author compares life to a journey:

> Life is a journey. Just like any other journey—that starts with a single step—our life also starts with a single breath or cry. During our journey, we come across new people, places, and experiences. Some of these are bitter, others sweet, and some others bitter-sweet. Sometimes we are made to tread a jerky, bumpy road and at times, we keep marching ahead on a silken, smooth road! In journeys, it is common to confront deserts, oceans, and mountains. However, once on journey, you cannot call it quits. Once committed to the journey, one has to keep moving. So stop not till your journey is over.

6.3.4 Cause and Effect

Cause and effect is an important device with which we construct paragraphs on a variety of topics. Through this method, the paragraph attempts to establish a relationship between certain events and the reasons behind them. While using this method, authors are able to convince their readers in a scientific and logical manner. Read the following paragraph and see how this device is used effectively:

> The effect of guilt in a person's life can easily be observed throughout his/her life. Those who are constantly gnawed by a deep-seated guilt often blame themselves for all the problems around them. Such people are never optimistic or excited about anything in their life. Most of the time, they are sad and gloomy. They keep lamenting their actions of the past, and their present too keeps drifting away from them. It leads to multiplication of guilt, as the guilt of lost opportunities gets combined with the mistakes committed in the past. This vicious circle of guilt hence never allows its victims to succeed or be happy in life. It is so because guilt saps all enthusiasm, energy, and an urge to survive or excel. The result is that a guilt-ridden individual tires quickly. Not being able to enjoy life or carry out their responsibilities in full measure, such people retreat into an apathetic, dull, listless condition and are even prepared to bring their life to an end.

By relating the feelings of guilt to an apathetic, dull, and listless condition, the author provides to us the psychological perspective through which one can observe why the underperformers in life lead a life of little activity as they constantly wriggle under the weight of a constantly tormenting sense of guilt.

6.3.5 Quotations and Paraphrasing

Quoting authorities is an excellent way to develop a paragraph. Read the following paragraph:

> Isn't it surprising that despite so many schemes announced by the government, nothing much changes in the life of the poor? Probably it isn't. Knowing how deep-rooted corruption has become in our country, it really seems the only natural outcome of all government policies. Modern day capitalism and the contiguous narcissism have added to the culture of corruption in our country. People feel like accumulating money; by hook or crook. Understandably therefore, the gap between the poor and the rich is widening. Sometimes, I feel like reminding all the corrupt people about Gandhi who once said, 'Recall the face of the poorest and the weakest man whom you may have seen, and ask yourself, if the step you contemplate is going to be of any use to him. Will he gain anything by it? Will it restore him to a control over his (her) own life and destiny? In other words, will it lead to *swaraj* for the hungry and spiritually starving millions? Then you will find your doubts and your self-melting away.'

By quoting Gandhiji, the passage drives home the point that a life of purpose is basically the one that is not obsessively self-centred. It is not essential that the quotations are cited only from eminent personalities.

Even common people are quoted to substantiate a point of view. When the words of the commoners are used, it is known as *peer testimony*.

Take a look at how a paragraph on a similar issue can authenticate itself even by quoting common people:

Isn't it surprising that despite so many schemes announced by the government, nothing much changes in the life of the poor? Probably it isn't. Knowing how deep-rooted corruption has become in our country, it really seems to be the only natural outcome of all government policies. Modern day capitalism and the contiguous narcissism have added to the culture of corruption in our country. People feel like accumulating money, by hook or by crook. Understandably, therefore, the gap between the poor and the rich is widening. Corrupt people have no time to listen to story of a poor peasant who says, 'I have two children who are given food on alternate days. I cannot feed both of them everyday. It is really painful to see them hungry. But what can I do? I don't have enough to make both ends meet everyday.'

6.3.6 Enumeration

At times, we list a series of ideas in order to substantiate the topic sentence. This device, used quite often to construct a paragraph, is known as *enumeration*.

Read the following example to see how enumeration leads to not just authentication but also coherence in a paragraph:

Despite all the growth and development registered in post-independent India, our country continues to be tormented by a large number of social evils. Some of the most disturbing ills prevalent in our society are casteism, communalism, corruption, dowry system, hooliganism, untouchability, intoxication, and child labour. It is difficult to say which of these are worse than the rest of them. Though all such ills and problems can be categorized as bad, worse, or worst, the impact that they leave on the social milieu is always only worst.

By enumerating the evils in the society, the writer is able to highlight the number of problems that beset our lives even amidst the times of all-round growth and development. Look at the following paragraph and see how through enumeration, the author builds up the paragraph:

No rules are required for you to lose your life on the road. But if you want to be safe on the road, go by the following: While driving your vehicle on the road: keep to your left; always stick to your lane; never try to overtake from the wrong side; drive within the prescribed speed-limit; stop at every red-light; use dippers at night; use your seat belt while driving a four-wheeler; and wear your helmet while riding a two-wheeler.

6.3.7 Definition

Another way to develop a paragraph is to use *definition*. This method for developing a paragraph is particularly employed in those situations where the author intends to take up some topic, term, issue, or argument in a particular way. By taking the reader through the definition of a particular word, the author is able to prepare his/her readers to follow the intended line of argument or thought. See how the author in the following passage attempts to define the term 'insomnia' for a specific purpose:

The term *insomnia*, derived from the Latin root *somn* refers to the *chronic and habitual inability to fall asleep or remain asleep for an adequate length of time*. Though insomnia can strike people of any age group, old people are more prone to it. However, owing to a stressful life and unhealthy food habits, a large number of young people today suffer from it. In a mechanical, alienated, frantic, and guilt-ridden life, there are other sleep-related disorders, as some people become *somnambulists*, that is, they begin to walk in their sleep. Almost all patients of *insomnia* feel *somnolent*, that is, sleepy or drowsy during their waking hours and some others become *amnesiac*, that is, they start losing their memory.

By defining the term 'insomnia' and other related words, the author is able to make things clear to his/her reader. Take a look at how the speaker, by introducing a little known expression 'anorexia nervosa', through its dictionary meaning, immediately establishes a rapport with the listeners in the following extract of a speech:

Friends, today we are going to talk about the rise of a very peculiar health disorder in young girls. In medical terms it is known as *anorexia nervosa* which stands for a psychological disorder, mainly afflicting adolescent girls and young women, characterized by a significant decrease in body weight, deliberately induced by refusal to eat because of an obsessive drive to lose weight. In this age of glamour, an urge to look smart and presentable is very common and we see a large number of young girls trying to shed their weight at a frantic pace. Therefore, a frequent food evasion or massive cuts in food intake often becomes a way of life for them. While doing so, however, little do they seem to realize that by indulging in such weight loss obsessions, they are likely to fall victim to a debilitating health disorder known as anorexia nervosa.

Having already defined the term 'anorexia nervosa', the speaker orients the audience to the subsequent part of the speech, without causing ambiguity or confusion in their mind.

Reading further, take a look at how by defining the multi-layered term *Positive Thinking*, the author, in the following paragraph, prepares the reader to approach the subject of discussion:

Friends, of every ten books written today, one is surely on *Positive Thinking*; of every five workshops in a metro city, one is on *Positive Thinking*. There are lecturers, seminars, discussions, and discourses on *Positive Thinking*. Professionals are discussing about it, celebrities are prescribing it, mascots of success are preaching it, and spiritualists are discoursing it. However, for each of these different people, the term *positive thinking* acquires different meaning. For one, it is the absence of negative thinking; for the other, it is being optimistic and hopeful; and for some other, it is being happy in all situations.

6.3.8 Expert Testimony

Giving testimony is another way to develop a paragraph. Testimony can be of two types—*peer testimony* and *expert testimony*. Just as *peer testimony*, cited earlier in the discussion, expert testimony also lends credibility to the author's opinion. See how in the following paragraph, the author uses expert testimony, to drive his/her ideas home:

A deeper look into the problem helps us observe that a neurotic and anxious person is going to think more about death, than the one who is positive, optimistic, and generally cheerful. In fact, modern psychology finds a direct connection between someone's neurotic outlook and their preoccupation with death. 'The more neurotic and anxious you are, the more preoccupied you'll be with death and unable to focus on meaningful life changes,' says Laura Blackie, an assistant professor of psychology at the University of Nottingham.

By citing expert comments, the author succeeds in augmenting the information.

6.3.9 Facts, Figures, Instances, and Examples

Besides carrying conviction and substantiating the point of view through narrations, comparisons, quotations, enumeration, and testimony, paragraphs can also be developed through facts, figures, and examples. It is done so in order to sound authentic and convincing. Read the following paragraph and see how it is constructed successfully with the help of facts and figures:

> The Indian woman continues to live on the periphery. And this, despite the fact that she is now more self-reliant, more conspicuous in social circles, and well rooted in the professional world. Though in modern times, she earns well, this does not ensure equality for the Indian woman. According to a survey conducted by an NGO based in Mumbai, it is suggested that more than 50 per cent newly married males are uncomfortable with the idea of not having a son born to them, while 65 per cent resented the idea of their wives getting a job and financial independence at their expense. Not only this, nearly 35 per cent of them felt that it is better to have a less educated girl for a wife as she would be easy to be tamed. So much so, that nearly 15 per cent of men were not against using violence against their women, for, *if nothing else works, this does!*

By citing factual data from the findings of an NGO research, the above paragraph builds up the entire edifice of the argument in a convincing manner. The figures that follow the topic sentence clearly illustrate the central idea that even today, women in India continue to lead a life of secondary existence in the patriarchal Indian social structure.

Look how again the examples in the following paragraph construct it well:

> It is generally believed that Americans are very good speakers of English. Their articulation, however, does not really seem to support such beliefs. In fact, observed closely, it seems that Americans use sloppy articulation for quite a few expressions. For example, *I did not* for them becomes *I dint*, whereas the proper contracted form for *I did not* should be *I didn't*. Similarly, *you ought to* in American English sounds like *you oughta* or *you otta* and *you have to* becomes *you hafta*. The forceful and intense *yes* in British English is always a sloppy *yeah* for them and *I don't know* sounds like *I dunno*.

By citing relevant examples, the author of this paragraph tries to bust the myth that Americans are very good speakers of English.

6.3.10 Episodes

Like facts, figures, instances, and examples, episodes also help the construction of a paragraph. At times, situations require writers to talk about various episodes in order to drive home their ideas in a convincing and emphatic manner. Look at the following paragraph and note how through episodic illustrations, the paragraph is constructed in a neat and convincing manner:

> I trembled as I boarded the train the next time. Could this be my last ride in life? Will I too die, blown away by some bomb? I thought and thought. Should I get off the train? Catch an auto and reach office? But how long can I do that? With a monthly income of a couple of thousand bucks, how can I afford to be that extravagant? No, nothing would happen. Otherwise, all these fellow passengers of mine would not have boarded the train. They must have sensed that after the bomb blast last week, everything was normal. But then, everything is always normal before it becomes abnormal. After all, before a blast, there is no blast. And no fear. No anxiety. But how can we say that? There was fear and anxiety on every face and in all eyes. Like me, all around me seemed to be thinking—would this be their last ride? I shuddered at the realization how a blast in your city rips your confidence apart.

How it reduces you to a nervous wreck who has no option but to move on with his daily life! Even if it takes him to death!

By using the episode in a narrative form, the paragraph builds up the environment of threat, fear, anxiety, and panic that lurks beneath the apparent calmness and normalcy after the incident of a bomb blast in the city. While establishing the fear and nervousness of a person by citing an episode, the author is able to illustrate the central idea of the paragraph which is pushed to the end of the construction. As we can make out, the central idea in the paragraph is to depict how an incident of a bomb blast in the city induces fear and anxiety in the minds of the people. However, before we are introduced to the central idea: *how a blast in your city rips your confidence apart! How it reduces you to a nervous wreck who has no option but to move on with his daily life!*, we are made to read through the thought process of a traveller who goes through great anxiety while boarding a city train after a tragic incident of a blast that has recently occurred in the city, shattering the commoners' assurance and composure while performing their day-to-day activities.

Thus by employing examples, facts, figures, analogies, enumeration, comparisons, contrasts, definition, causes, effects, etc., paragraphs on different issues and topics are constructed. Many a time, you will find authors combining a variety of such devices in order to structure a paragraph. Therefore, it is important to learn to use these strategies as effectively and appropriately as possible.

Just as it is important to understand how to build a paragraph through these devices, it is also of crucial importance to learn how to provide transitions in a paragraph.

6.4 USING TRANSITIONS AND CONNECTING DEVICES

Transitions are the expressions which connect different ideas expressed in a paragraph. Without learning to use them accurately, it is impossible to develop an impressive paragraph. For instance, read the paragraph given below and decide whether the transitions provided are apt and relevant:

Those who believe in God seem to be aware of His presence around them. Moreover, skeptics suggest that it is one thing to believe in God and quite another to be aware of His presence. They feel that but it is quite easy to keep oneself in illusion, ignorance, and darkness, and quite difficult to be aware, awake, and alive. Nevertheless, they feel that God is not a matter of belief and God is a power, a source of energy of which we need to be conscious about.

The second sentence starts with 'Moreover'. Do you think it is appropriately placed? *Moreover* is additive in nature. It adds to the preceding argument. When we read the paragraph, it becomes obvious that the statement contradicts the claims made in the first statement. Therefore, we need *however* and not *moreover*. Similarly, the choice of *and* in place of *but* further in the same sentence is also misplaced. In the third sentence, we need a concessional connective *though* and not *but* which is used to introduce a contrastive idea. Further in the sentence *and* is again wrongly placed and we need either *yet* or just a comma to contradict the preceding idea. Even in the last sentence *nevertheless* is quite misplaced as we need something that reinforces the continuing argument.

Look at the revised version of the paragraph and see how the transitions are properly used:

Those who believe in God seem to be aware of His presence around them. **However**, skeptics suggest that it is one thing to believe in God **but** quite another to be aware of His presence. They feel that **though** it is quite easy to keep oneself in illusion, ignorance, and darkness, **yet** it is quite difficult to be aware, awake, and alive. **In fact**, they feel that God is not a matter of belief **as** God is a power, a source of energy of which we need to be conscious about.

In fact, different types of transitional words and phrases are meant for different purposes. Look at the table given below; see the transitional and connecting devices listed; and observe the purpose for which they are used in a sentence:

Transitional and Connecting Devices	Purpose
Therefore, consequently, as a result	To establish cause and effect
While, meanwhile, in the meantime, simultaneously, even as	To suggest simultaneous actions
For instance, for example, again, such as, specifically, especially, to illustrate	To cite examples and illustrations
However, in contrast, on the other hand, but, though, although, nevertheless, notwithstanding, despite, in spite of, yet, surprisingly however, alternatively	To contrast the preceding idea
Finally, to conclude, in conclusion, thus, so, on the whole, therefore	To wind up an idea
And, moreover, more importantly, over and above, furthermore, in addition to, further, besides, last but not the least, again, first of all, secondly, finally	To add ideas
To sum up, to summarize, in a nutshell, in brief, in short	To summarize the foregoing discussion
In the same way/fashion/manner, similarly, likewise, by the same logic/account/token	To suggest similarity; add similar ideas
Because, since, as, for, on account of, due to the fact that, for that reason, because of, thanks to/thanks largely to	To highlight the cause and reason
For the same reason, to emphasize, most significantly/importantly, first and foremost, not to mention/forget, in fact, indeed, by all means, undoubtedly, to be sure	To emphasize the point in discussion
To clarify, conversely, namely, in other words, that is to say, to put it in simpler terms, to rephrase it	To clarify the preceding argument
Without doubt, clearly, obviously, evidently, clearly enough, in no uncertain terms, of course, needless to say	To establish a point of view
Having said that, even though, there is no denying the fact that, admittedly, to be honest, may be, possibly	To concede an idea
Accordingly, purposefully, for this reason, for this purpose, so that, in order to	To highlight the purpose for which an argument is made

EXERCISE 6.2

Use the following transitional/connecting devices in sentences of your own:

Hence, furthermore, nevertheless, even if, however, although, for, but, as, not to forget, notwithstanding, by all means, for instance, after all, in other words

EXERCISE 6.3

Read the paragraph given below and develop it with the help of appropriate transitional/connecting devices:

One of the challenges of having your parents and kids with you is to choose the role that you should perform. You are parents. You are kids. You have parents. You have kids. These two roles clash. Confusion arises. You start playing confusing roles. You start parenting your parents. You parent your kids. You develop the habit of doing that. Your parents want to parent you. They want to see you as parents. Some parents like that. Some don't. They require that. They are kids. They are parents. You get frustrated. You think, 'What am I? A parent? A child?'

EXERCISE 6.4

Read the following introducer and terminator of a paragraph and develop the rest of it:

Eyes are considered the most significant organ of the human body ... Hence, use your eyes well to win the audience.

6.5 EXTENDED DEFINITIONS

As the title suggests, an *extended definition* is written to explain a complex term used in a book, research paper, or a report. In fact, some of the terms may be so crucial as well as complex that without defining them or placing them in the context in which we expect our readers to do, it becomes difficult for us to establish proper communication with them. An extended definition often includes the literal meaning of the term used with all its characteristic features. Although it may be written in a variety of ways, the basic purpose of an extended definition however is to define, explicate, and establish the basic features of a term before the writer ventures to take it up further.

An extended definition often appears in the beginning of a work, often immediately following the term when it is introduced for the first time. For example, a research article on 'ethical relativism' would require the author to first define the term suggesting that 'ethical relativism is a methodical principle of interpreting mortality based on the assumption that moral ideas and standards are mere conventions' and then only build the discussion further. Similarly, a report on 'spectroscopy' needs to first establish that 'spectroscopy is a branch of analysis devoted to identifying elements and compounds and elucidating atomic and molecular structures' before proceeding further with the rest of the discussion. When required to use extended definitions in your writings, keep in mind the following tips:

- Use extended definitions for the terms generally perceived to be complex, intriguing, or multifaceted.
- Whenever required to give extended definitions, provide them when the term is used for the first time in the discussion.
- Rely on definitions given in the encyclopaedia, dictionaries, or standard books. In case the definition is picked up from the Internet, try to cross-check it with a standard source before using it in your work.
- Give all the characteristic features of the term besides providing the definition. In encyclopaedia and dictionaries, the definitions given are at times too compact to be understood well by the reader.

Therefore, it is only when such a term is explained with the help of its characteristic features that the readers are able to perceive it in the sense it is required to be seen. Moreover, one can always suggest a deviation from the commonly perceived understanding of a term. In this case also, characterizing a particular term in which it is required to be observed by the reader helps us achieve a common frame of reference with the reader.

6.6 FEATURES OF A PARAGRAPH

In the following section, let us learn the key features of a good paragraph with the help of a few examples.

6.6.1 Unity

Unity in a paragraph stands for the togetherness of ideas. Ideally, a paragraph should have one central idea—outlined through the topic sentence—and the subordinating ideas which help the main idea to come to the fore. This means that if the writer finds it important to introduce another equally important idea, he/she should switch over to another paragraph. This sometimes does not happen and hence it affects the unity of a paragraph.

Read the following paragraph and figure out whether it maintains unity in the ideas expressed:

Reading books is a great hobby. Coming from great minds, books are generally the storehouse of wisdom. Reading books helps us grow intellectually. Reading gives us ideas and ideas change the world. Reading is also helpful in making us more articulate and spontaneous in expressions. These days, however, the habit of reading books is declining. Children today prefer watching television to reading books. Television charms them with striking images. Somebody has correctly called it an *idiot box*. After all, what is there to watch on television? In the name of entertainment, it offers us loud and meaningless programmes. The so-called family serials are horrible to sit through, and idiotic masala movies are repeated endlessly. On television, you can't even watch the news; for more than the information, what you get is sensationalism.

Though the passage starts quite well, it loses unity of thought immediately after the first few sentences. The paragraph starts with the idea that reading books is a great hobby. The sentences that follow try to establish why the author feels so. It keeps building on the same theme until the author finds television to be responsible for the declining reading habits. From this point onwards, the paragraph loses the original track altogether and starts discussing only television, highlighting the weaknesses of this medium. Even if the details related to television are to be tagged along with the main idea, the author cannot afford to singularly leave out the thematic core of the paragraph, which has something to do with books and reading habits. Since the passage focuses far too exclusively on television and its drawbacks, it tends to lose the central idea altogether. Read the revised version of the paragraph to know how to maintain the main argument.

Reading books is a great hobby. Coming from great minds, books are generally the storehouse of wisdom. Reading books helps us grow intellectually. Reading gives us ideas and ideas change the world. Reading is also helpful in making us more articulate and spontaneous in expressions. These days, however, the habit of reading books is declining. Children today prefer watching television to reading books. Television charms them with striking images. So, unlike books, it captures the attention of young minds quite immediately. Books require reading, which demand concentration and effort. Alternatively, television offers them entertainment, though loud and meaningless, without demanding any effort from them in return. Moreover, books generally don't have to offer to their readers the sensational stuff that the television so readily supplies in order to capture the attention of young, innocent minds.

EXERCISE 6.5

Read the following paragraph, try to make out where it tends to lose unity of thought and expression, and rewrite it making it effective:

A life without ambition is a like a train without an engine. Just as it is the engine that drives the train, it is human beings' ambition that drives their lives. By all means, ambition occupies a central position in human efforts. Some theorists refuse to believe that ambition has crucial significance in human life. They feel that if we want to be happy, we must have no ambition whatsoever. They often quote the *Gita* that urges us to concentrate on our work without bothering about the result. Of course, the *Gita* is the most authentic work on spirituality, teaching us invaluable things. But it is not possible in life to just do our work and forget about the result of the work that we keep doing. Who would like to do a job that doesn't give them money or status or satisfaction? We are humans and we need something to keep us moving. It is really not possible to agree to the suggestion of the theorists who give no credit to ambition in human life.

6.6.2 Coherence

Maintaining *coherence* in a paragraph is different from maintaining *unity* in it. Look at the following paragraph and find out what it lacks:

I really appreciate the idea of arranging a trip to Srinagar for our school children. Certainly, it is a wonderful idea. Srinagar is a beautiful place and our students must be able to see that before they leave the campus. Since the journey is a long one, we can arrange a good, luxury bus for our students. They can watch mesmerizing sights on the way. The whole trip may consume some ten days or so. With their exams slated in March next year, there is nothing much to worry about losing precious time. And seeing a beautiful place like Srinagar is no wastage of time whatsoever. Staying our students should also not be a problem. We have good hotels in Srinagar. We can book one good one. After all, our students belong to well-off families and no student would mind sparing a couple of thousands for a trip to Srinagar. With sporadic violence and militancy, it is no longer a safe place but. Though March is far off, don't you feel that they will miss the crucial ten days on their run up to the board exams?

As we read this paragraph, we can figure out that the author seems to review the proposal whether to send the children of his/her school to Srinagar. In that sense, though loosely, the paragraph does hang onto the same idea and hence can be said to have maintained unity of idea. What it grossly lacks is coherence. In the beginning, the author appreciates the idea of taking the school children to Srinagar. Towards the end however, he/she seems to be arguing against the idea of taking students to Srinagar because of *sporadic violence* and *board exams*. In between, the author talks about the various arrangements and facilities required for the trip for a while before jumping to 'sporadic violence and militancy'.

Nothing, however, seems to move in a coherent manner in the above paragraph. If the author intends to argue against the idea of taking the students to Srinagar, it seems absurd on his/her part to begin with all accolades such as: *I really appreciate the idea of arranging a trip to Srinagar for our school children. Certainly, it is a wonderful idea.* Not only this, he/she also finds it almost mandatory on his/her part to take children to a beautiful place like Srinagar as he/she writes *Srinagar is a beautiful place and our students must be able to see that before they leave the campus.* Further into the passage, the author starts moving from one idea to the other mentioning *good, luxury bus, mesmerizing sights, good hotels, and the well-off families of students who will not mind sparing a couple of thousands.* In a way, the author seems to be quite excited at the idea of arranging a trip to Srinagar *before they leave the campus.*

While discussing all this however, the author does not focus much on the continuity of thought and hence the passage staggers incoherently from one point to the other. Towards the end, the paragraph scrambles into complete incoherence as the author changes his/her perspective quite abruptly on the issue: *With sporadic violence and militancy, it is no longer a safe place but. Though March is far off, don't you feel that they will miss the crucial ten days on their run up to the board exams?*

Look at the revised version of the paragraph and make out how the same idea can be expressed without lapsing into incoherence.

I appreciate the idea of arranging a trip to Srinagar for our school children. Srinagar is a beautiful place and it would be nice if our students are able to see the mesmerizing sights of the place before they leave the school campus. However, with sporadic violence and militancy, it is no longer a safe place for such adventures. Moreover, for the students appearing for the board exams next March, a ten-day trip might be a little too long. Regarding other arrangements however, there doesn't seem to be much to worry about. For the trip, a luxury bus can be arranged and students can be lodged in a good hotel there. Since most of our students come from well-off families, they would be able to bear the cost of expenses the proposed trip is likely to incur.

EXERCISE 6.6

Improve the paragraph given below making it more coherent:

One of the most challenging issues of urban living is to find suitable gifts for suitable people on suitable occasions. Suitable occasions exist in plenty and suitable people too are quite in multitude. I don't mean to say that suitable gifts are in any dearth. How can they be? They are far too in abundance. In the world of consumerism, they cannot be expected to be in any dearth! The only thing in dearth is your ability to choose the suitable gift that suits your pocket too. That seems to be found wanting, on the last days of the month when mostly it looks like a flat toothpaste. The situation requires you to squeeze it with all your might for you to manage to look presentable to others with polished teeth and a plastic smile on your face. All this for you to be able to say suitable words to suitable people on suitable occasions with suitable gifts in your hand!

6.6.3 Expansion and Emphasis

Alongside maintaining coherence and unity, it is also required that the idea that is introduced in a sentence is properly expanded and emphasized. Some paragraphs fail to click with the reader, simply because the idea that is generated in the passage is not taken to its logical conclusion. Read the following passage and see what it actually lacks—unity, coherence, or expansion.

At times, it is just a single sentence that makes all the difference. Look at the following example:

Global warming refers to a gradual warming of the earth. Though many scientists believe that global warming is a natural phenomenon, most of us are aware of the fact that many human actions such as emitting carbon dioxide and other gases into the atmosphere, cutting down trees, excessive consumption of water, petrol, and other natural resources, besides unplanned, unnatural, and mechanical development have contributed heavily to the triggering or escalation of the process. The consequences are for all of us to both witness and withstand. Each summer, temperatures are seen rising steadily above the normal. Besides this, we are beginning to witness a large number of natural calamities in the form of floods, droughts, tsunamis, and cyclonic storms, taking place all across the world. The number of patients suffering from skin cancer is increasing by the day. All this and a lot more establish the pattern of global warming for sure. Now the question arises: can we do something to stop this?

The paragraph does an admirable job in establishing a relationship between global warming and the human practices that cause it. However, it fails to strike an emphatic message simply because it does not reinforce the idea for which it is constructed in the first place.

Take a look at the passage once more and now form an opinion about it:

Global warming refers to a gradual warming of the earth. Though many scientists believe that global warming is a natural phenomenon, most of us are aware of the fact that many human actions such as emitting carbon dioxide and other gases into the atmosphere, cutting down trees, excessive consumption of water, petrol, and other natural resources, besides unplanned, unnatural, and mechanical development have contributed heavily to the triggering or escalation of the process. The consequences are for all of us to both witness and withstand. Each summer, temperatures are seen rising steadily above the normal. Besides this, we are beginning to witness a large number of natural calamities in the form of floods, droughts, tsunamis, and cyclonic storms, taking place all across the world. The number of patients suffering from skin cancer is increasing by the day. All this and a lot more establish the pattern of global warming for sure. Now the question arises: can we do something to stop this? The answer is YES, we can; and therefore, we should.

The only difference in these two versions of the same paragraph is the last part that attempts to inspire the reader into action. It is only because of the last two sentences in the paragraph that the author registers a change in the tone and makes the passage look like a part of some persuasive and instructive piece of speech or writing. Without this ending in place, the remaining passage of course would seem as though the author intends to share a piece of bad news with the reader. Hence, many a time, it is the proper expansion and emphasis of the ideas intended that secures the real purpose.

Thus, it is extremely important for us to keep in mind the significance of unity, coherence, expansion, and emphasis while we venture to construct effective paragraphs.

6.7 DESCRIPTIVE WRITING TECHNIQUES

Broadly speaking, paragraph writing can be divided into four kinds—expository, narrative, persuasive, and descriptive.

Expository Expository paragraphs are used for defining and introducing different concepts and ideas to the reader. For example, when you say 'Democracy is a form of governance in which people's urge for freedom and equality is respected', the statement is expository and defining in nature. If a paragraph is built on these lines, it is known as an expository piece of writing.

Narrative This writing technique is very commonly employed by creative writers. It is essentially a story telling technique. For example, it is quite common to read something like 'When I entered the room, it seemed unusually quiet. They were all sitting there. Not speaking. Just looking down, with their heads buried in their knees. More than the surprise, it gave me a shock, and a wave of trepidation swept through me.'

Persuasive Persuasive writing is very commonly employed by marketing people. It is the heart and soul of write-ups such as sales letters and business proposals. In such writings, you often come across expressions such as 'All that you have to spare is a meagre amount of 500 rupees per month to buy a life-long pleasure that comes with travelling and visiting unseen places. Just pay peanuts and let us do the rest. For almost nothing, the company takes care of all your travel programmes; gets the booking of your travel tickets done through our agent; fixes hotels for you and arranges tour guides...' Of course, writing like this is done in order to promote the sales or services of a product, scheme, or proposal.

Descriptive Of all the writing techniques, descriptive writing is the one that is most commonly used in writing. It is quite extensively used for describing some idea, object, process, procedure, event, product, features, functions, etc. Regardless of the profession, all of us have to use descriptive writing in order to make an idea, object, process, event, feature, or function known to others. Since we all have to employ descriptive writing techniques, it won't be out of context for us to learn them in some detail.

Given below are the tips for making your descriptive writing effective:

- Create a picture of the object/person/place/thing in your mind.
- Memorize the object of description.
- Visualize its features intimately.
- Employ memory and imagination.
- Create an intimate image of the object of description in your mind.
- Provide verbal structure to the object imagined.
- Make your description interesting and innovative.
- Use vivid and lucid language to communicate the idea.
- Choose words which strike clear, unambiguous images in the mind of the reader.
- Be intimate and warm in your approach.
- Use catchy, informal phrases to capture the attention of the reader.
- Use humour and wit, if possible.

Let us see an example of a descriptive paragraph.

Description of a Pet

If you intend to pay us a visit; don't hesitate doing it; at least not because of the fact that we have a dog. That too, a female one; the one you generally call a bitch. For more than anyone of us, she will be the one to receive you with open arms. Like any other dog, our Genie reacts to a doorbell call in a swift way. The moment a knock is heard or the call bell is rung, Genie's ears spring out of their drooping confines. Her eyes open and her neck arches upward. In a split second, she props herself on her all fours. In anticipation, her tail begins to wag. She knows not who might be at the door—a friend or foe, a family member or a stranger. To Genie, it doesn't matter who calls on us, at what time, or for what purpose. She is there to receive all those who come knocking. Though she cannot open the door herself, she makes up for the loss the moment anyone of us lets the latch go off its hook and the door opens. For without wasting even a single moment, she raises her mighty—and potentially threatening figure, to those who see her for the first time—to all those who use their sweet will to come to us. While she does so, her arms rest lovingly on the chest of the caller, her tongue licks the person wherever he/she can afford to let her do so, and her tail, swirling like a perpetually moving broom as a non-stop sign of welcome to the guest, sweeps the floor beneath her at a frantic pace!

Please refer to Chapter 5 on *Nature and Style of Sensible Writing* for further details on 'Descriptive Writing Techniques'.

Apart from writing descriptive paragraphs, you would be often required to write argumentative and analytical paragraphs. Therefore, it is desirable that these two types be discussed in some detail.

6.8 ARGUMENTATIVE PARAGRAPH

An *argumentative paragraph* argues against the view that is generally established. Authors writing such paragraphs normally choose to maintain a forceful and emphatic tone to contend the view that is normally taken for granted.

Look at the following paragraph and observe the style and tone adopted by the author:

Loyalty is one of the most complex and debatable issues in human life. Generally regarded as a great attribute, loyalty stands as a firm evidence of a person's socially approved demeanour. In delicate matters such as love, friendship, and marriage, it is seen as a single most important yardstick to judge someone's trustworthiness and dependence. This, however, is not the only side of the coin. At times, loyalty becomes a crippling factor in our life. It stops people from realizing their true potential. Particularly in the life of a creative and imaginative individual, maintaining loyalty to a system seems like an unnecessary append-age. This is so because creative souls tend to think beyond the existing frames. History is replete with instances where the creative people's imagination has challenged the existing codes and have preferred listening to their inner urge rather than sticking to a patterned existence. Though disapproved initially, such rebellion is often seen as an achievement and a hallmark of a person's courage. Regardless of the fact whether such 'disloyalties' are appreciated or disparaged, it is such rebellion alone that makes human life so creative, interesting, and enigmatic. Aware of the immense possibilities in not adhering to a loyal social system, creative souls often see *loyalty* only as a disruptive force that unnecessarily intends to act as an impediment in the march of a soul's innermost urge to realize its true potential.

See how carefully the author builds up the thesis to base his/her argument. As we can see that the paragraph is about *whether loyalty is a virtue or a disruptive force* and the author seems to contend the traditional view that loyalty is always a virtue. However, rather than trying to achieve this objective in a hurry he/she concedes the view that loyalty does matter in certain aspects of human behaviour before moving on to establish the paramount importance of a non-conformist, uncompromising, and creative urge in human endeavours.

Therefore, while writing an argumentative paragraph, which finally forms a part of some issue or argumentative essay, you need to agree first so as to disagree later on. This is important because a style in writings where the author jumps to his/her beliefs without paying any attention to the counter view is not generally appreciated. In fact, if you do so, you are likely to sound prejudiced and parochial in your view.

Hence, allow the argument to develop naturally out of the discussion rather than forcing it straightaway in a paragraph.

In short, keep in mind the following while writing an argumentative paragraph:

- State the established/opposing/counter view in the beginning.
- Highlight its possible advantages, if any.
- Introduce your view logically.
- Give proper examples to substantiate the details.
- Sound convincing and forceful.
- Avoid sweeping statements and hasty generalizations.
- Don't sound derogatory and insulting in an attempt to establish your argument.

EXERCISE 6.7

Given below is a paragraph written to argue against the view 'money cannot buy happiness'. Trace what is wrong with it and rewrite it to make it sound like a well-written argumentative paragraph:

After all what is there in life without money? I don't think anyone will move even a single inch without the help of movement of the golden wheel of rupee. Money is all important in all walks of life and gives you everything that you can think of getting in this world; it gives you power; it gives you status and position; it gives you respect and recognition; it gives you pleasure and enjoyment. Take money away from human affairs and all his affairs cease to be. You are anything and everything with money. Without it, you are nothing. With money you can buy your comforts; move round the world; become educated and important in life; stay healthy and fit; get popularity and fame and what not? As regards its buying happiness is concerned, tell me what do you mean by happiness. Does poverty give that? Are you any happier when you don't have money and feel hungry, embarrassed, low, defeated, and humiliated in a world that thrives on the power of money? If you are not happy when you are comfortable, recognized, powerful, and respected, you will never be. Then it is not just money but nothing else as well that can give you happiness.

6.9 ANALYTICAL PARAGRAPH

An *analytical paragraph* analyses a situation with the help of facts, figures, and information and tries to draw inferences on the basis of these.

Read the example below and observe how the author analyses the issue of *gender disparity* with the help of facts and figures:

In a highly stratified society like India, there are numerous layers of differentiations apart from those concerning caste and class. Gender is now recognized as a more pervasive and distinct category of social stratification. The literacy rate among the tribals is not only low but also shows a high level of gender disparity. During 1971, female literacy among tribals was 4.85 per cent at the all-India level and only 0.49 per cent in Rajasthan. By 1981, it had increased to 8.05 per cent at the all-India level and 1.2 per cent in Rajasthan. Despite massive efforts by government and non-government agencies, it was still 19 per cent at the all-India level and just 4.42 per cent in Rajasthan in 1991. The states of Andhra Pradesh with 8.68 per cent and Rajasthan with 4.42 per cent have remained at the bottom of the tribal female literacy table. On the other hand, states like Mizoram (78.74%), Nagaland (54.51%), Sikkim (50.37%), and Kerala (51.07%) have more than 50 per cent literacy among the tribal female population. It is significant that Andhra Pradesh, which has a lower tribal literacy than Rajasthan, has higher literacy among the tribal female population.

Read another example of an analytical paragraph. In the paragraph given below, the author analyses the situation without using any statistics and figures:

Instead of the promising and romantic images of prosperity in Punjab, the film studiously takes us away to a nondescript village where wintry fog captures the drying edges of unproductive shrubs all around. Also inhabited by a sizeable population of Dalits, it is the land of inequalities which demands a pitched battle for existence from all those who fail to prove that they are more equal than others. Mutely therefore, they are made to witness their houses being demolished, their lands being sold to factories, gun shots being fired in the night, and their existence being pushed to an extreme. Tormented both by social ostracism and economic strife, they are left with no other option but to fall prey to the luring city lights and grope for a survival strategy within its sucking tentacles.

The above example illustrates how without data, figures, and statistics, analytical paragraphs can be composed. In an analytical paragraph therefore, it is not mandatory for us to be elaborate all the time. A tidy and precise analysis should be preferred to the detailed statistical data if situation so warrants.

In short, remember to keep the following points in mind while writing an analytical paragraph:

- Present the situation not only as it is but also as it should be.
- Interpret the data or situation with the help of situations, data, facts, comparison, and contrasts.
- Be elaborate while interpreting data and succinct while analysing a situation without it.
- Don't sound equivocal and far too philosophical in tone and style.
- Present both the sides of the coin.
- Choose direct and emphatic word order.

EXERCISE 6.8

Construct an analytical paragraph on *terrorism* with the help of the outline provided below:

Terrorism, an expression of violent dissent—dissatisfied minority group—seeks its course through coercion—creating a sense of fear—reckless killings—hijacking and blowing of aircraft—Government's indulgence—cross-border terrorism—weakens the country.

ANSWER KEY

Exercise 6.1

1. Developer
2. Introducer
3. Terminator
4. Developer
5. Developer
6. Introducer
7. Terminator
8. Developer
9. Developer
10. Developer

Exercise 6.2

1. **Hence**, it is not possible for us to reconcile to our fate all that tamely.
2. **Furthermore**, you can pick up from this book how to use water colours effectively.
3. **Nevertheless**, nothing can finally be said about the patients who have heart problems.
4. **Even if** we go by the data, it is hard to justify the steps proposed by the committee.
5. **However**, it is not possible for India to allow America to intervene in all its matters.
6. **Although** they claim so much, nothing substantial has yet been achieved in this matter.
7. He never tried to be an entrepreneur **for** he was not sure of his management skills.
8. **But** in all probability, recession is likely to worsen.
9. **As** they approached the house, they saw the thief running away.
10. Cricket has brought us many laurels. Winning from the 1983 World Cup to the T20 World Cup in 2007, and the ICC World Cup 2011, it has won us moments of pride and glory, **not to forget** of course the many victories registered against archrivals like Pakistan, Australia, and Sri Lanka.
11. **Notwithstanding** lofty claims by the government, child labour in India is not likely to vanish any time sooner.

12. **By all means**, the king wanted his daughter to laugh.
13. **For instance**, it is Hamlet who needs to act but he doesn't and not King Lear who does.
14. **After all**, there is no way by which you can make the unwilling souls listen to you.
15. **In other words**, it is our thinking that makes us happy and not our situation.

Exercise 6.3

One of the challenges of having your parents and kids with you **simultaneously** is to choose the role that you should perform. You are parents **and also** kids. **So**, you have to act like kids with your parents **whereas** you have to remain parents to your kids. It is not as easy as it sounds. **It is so** because while playing parents to your kids, you start patronizing your parents as well. **Sometimes**, it is required **and also** desired by the parents. **However**, not all parents can appreciate such behaviour **despite the fact** that they require some parenting. **At times**, confusion gets to your nerves and you start wondering whether you are c parent or a child.

Exercise 6.4

Eyes are considered the most significant organ of the human body. Placed close to our brain, they are the focal point of our consciousness. It is said that eyes are the windows of the soul. There is no emotion and no expression that a human eye cannot transmit effectively. Therefore, in terms of non-verbal communication, eyes acquire a place of crucial importance. If as a speaker your eyes seem to be dull and blank, it is not really possible for you to create a positive impact on your listeners. In fact, it is impossible to keep dull eyes and reveal intensity through your voice or other body organs. Imagine a face that is bright but has dull eyes. You can't, because it is simply not possible. On the other hand, it is quite natural to have bright eyes and a lively face. It is so because when your eyes shine, your face expresses the positivity that is so crucial while making a speech. Hence, use your eyes well to win the audience.

Exercise 6.5

A life without ambition is like a train without an engine. Just as it is the engine that drives the train, it is human beings' ambition that drives their lives. So, by all means, ambition occupies a central position in human efforts. Some theorists, however, refuse to believe that ambition has crucial significance in human life. Quoting the spiritual text, the *Gita*, they feel that if we want to be happy we must have no ambition whatsoever. There is no denying the fact that the *Gita* is the most authentic book on spirituality, and what it teaches us is invaluable. For common mortals, however, it is not possible to involve themselves in action without desiring a result. Since ordinary people are normally goaded while they are able to see the result in sight, it is not possible for us to forgo human ambition.

Exercise 6.6

One of the most challenging issues of urban living is to find suitable gifts for suitable people on suitable occasions. And suitable occasions exist in plenty and suitable people too are quite in multitude. Of course, I don't mean to say that there is any dearth of suitable gifts. How can they be? In fact, they are far too in abundance. The only thing in dearth of is your ability to choose the suitable gift that suits your pocket too. Often, only that seems to be found wanting. Particularly, on the last days of the month when it looks like a flat toothpaste. In such situations, you are required to squeeze it with all your might to manage to look presentable to others, with polished teeth and a plastic smile on your face. All this for you to be able to say suitable words to suitable people on suitable occasions with suitable gifts in your hand!

Exercise 6.7

I agree with the view that money is not all that one needs to have in life. I also agree that it cannot buy happiness for us. But it can buy all the things that can be bought. I don't think anyone will move even a single inch without the help of the movement of the golden wheel of the rupee. Money is important in all walks of life and gives you everything that you can think of getting in this world; it gives you power; it gives you status and position; it gives you respect and recognition; it gives you pleasure and enjoyment. With money you can buy your comforts, move round the world, become educated and important in life, stay healthy and fit, get popularity and fame, and what not? As regards its buying happiness is concerned, tell me what do you mean by happiness? Does poverty give that? Are you any happier when you don't have money and feel hungry, embarrassed, low, defeated, and humiliated in a world that thrives on the power of money? If you are not happy when you are comfortable, recognized, powerful, and respected, you will never be. Then it is not just money but nothing else as well that can give you happiness. In fact, it is wrong to blame money for not being able to buy us happiness. Happiness is a matter of inner experience and it depends much on our attitude and way of thinking. So, if we are not happy, we are to blame, not money.

Exercise 6.8

Terrorism is an expression of violent dissent. The dissatisfied minority groups, whose views are not entertained by the majority, resort to it at times. Terrorism seeks to achieve its course through coercion, the motto being—the end justifies the means. Creating a sense of fear by reckless killings and wounding of innocent citizens, wilful destruction of public and private property, hijacking and blowing up of aircraft, and kidnapping and assassinating political personalities, it has now acquired international dimension. Intelligence reports reveal informal contact between terrorist groups of different countries for the purpose of financing, gun running, guerrilla training, and providing shelter to the terrorists. Many governments also indulge in the act of terrorism directly or indirectly, by dispatching miscreants across borders, aiding, abetting, or providing logistical support to the terrorists of other states. This type of cross-border terrorism is employed either to weaken another enemy state across the border or to promote certain other political goals.

7 ESSAY WRITING

LEARNING OBJECTIVES

After reading this chapter, you will be able to understand
- different types of essays
- characteristic features of an essay
- stages in essay writing
- components of an essay
- guiding principles for writing effective essays

As we all know, essay is a written composition in which the author shares his/her knowledge about a certain topic, reveals to the reader his/her perspective on the issue being discussed, and offers criticism and comments on the situation or the issue. The writing of an essay, therefore, requires the author to display not only his/her knowledge of the subject but also the maturity of vision, clarity of thought, and felicity of expression. Besides these, the author should also be able to weave together the different parts of an idea into a thread of unity. The task, though difficult, is not impossible to achieve and turns in hefty returns to the aspirant who commits himself/herself to the arduous but exciting prospect of writing an essay. However, before taking up the task of writing an essay, let us see the different types of essays we generally come across.

7.1 TYPES OF ESSAYS

The word 'essay' comes from the French expression *essai* which means an effort or a verbal sketch which reveals to us the author's perspective on a given subject. In all the different types of essays that we get to read, this basic feature of essays is more or less commonly reflected. It is so because essays are written to establish a point of view. Within this common frame, there exist certain distinct features which may help us classify essays in different types. Some of these different categories of essays have been enumerated below:

7.1.1 Argumentative Essays

An essay that is written to contend an established view is argumentative in nature and is known as *argumentative essay*. Read, for example, the beginning of an essay:

> Cancer is generally regarded as a disease of severe physiological disorder. Most of us believe that the malignant growth of tumour is caused by the chaotic and aggressive disorder in the human metabolism system which leads to an aggressive growth of dead cells in our body. Cancer thus is essentially seen as a disease caused by some physical disorder. The recent studies, however, suggest that cancer can be rooted in our attitude and can be linked to the way we think, feel, and perceive the world around us…

By linking cancer to a negative feeling, attitude, and mindset, the author in the above extract of the essay contends the established view. Consider the opening of another essay of similar type:

Myths have always been regarded as a complex and intriguing aspect in human life. In the modern scientific world, they are essentially seen as something unscientific and meaningless. However, after studying the myths scientifically, only a simpleton would find them irrational or worthless. Moreover, it is wrong to analyse myths on the yardstick of their factual accuracy as they were designed to serve a greater, deeper purpose.

In an argumentative essay therefore, the author is often keen to challenge the established notion. Because of this, such essays are also known as *point-of-view essays*. While writing an essay of this type, we need to establish the argument that is reason-based and not governed by our subjective opinions or emotions. In such an essay, it is always helpful to state the rationale behind the existing idea before suggesting the alternative view.

7.1.2 Analytical Essays

An *analytical essay* often reviews a book, movie, topic, situation, or a given text by bringing to the fore its subtle nuances. Take a look at the following extract from one such essay:

Set in the turbulence of partition times, the novel brings to the fore the lurking sense of insecurity and incertitude that ticks the characters in the story. As the plot develops, the initial calm suggesting harmony and peace gives way to discord and desperation that gets infused in the people of both the communities. The novel is remarkable for its ruthless yet objective depiction of reality as lack of political will and administrative commitment leads to aggravation of the situation. The minute details with which the novel observes a sense of restlessness and nervous anxiety that sets in the environment are suggestive of the author's psychological penetration into the working of mind.

While writing an analytical essay, we need to carefully observe the finer aspects of a work of art, situation, text, book, or topic and highlight all its subtleties. In an analytical essay, the data and material collected play an important role as they often form the basis of an analysis. Read the extract taken from such an essay:

In terms of sex ratio, both Haryana and Punjab seem to fare rather poorly. According to Census 2011 both these states have the worst sex ratio in the country. The picture appears really skewed in the 0–6 age group. The Census showed that the child sex ratio (0–6 years) in the state was a dismal 819 in Haryana, while the national average stood at 927. Barring a few districts such as Gurgaon and Faridabad, the rest of the districts in the state of Haryana show a pathetic situation with regard to sex ratio. And this is the situation even after a whole lot of different schemes launched by the state governments to stop female foeticide.

7.1.3 Descriptive Essays

A *descriptive essay* is written to get the reader the specific and concrete details of a situation or an object. In descriptive essays, the author primarily harps on his/her senses to help the reader visualize, feel, or enjoy the object of description. At times, descriptive essays become overtly subjective as the author intends the reader to comprehend a situation through his/her observation. Subjectively written at times, descriptive essays are quite often a reflection of the author's personality. Take a look at a part of one such essay:

The scene at the airport is so very special. You don't generally see so many people presenting themselves in such a disciplined way. So you see people standing in a long queue without trying to jump it; you see them patiently waiting for their baggage to be weighed and checked. You also see them moving through the security check-ups without grumbling or frowning. So much so that you can see some people maintaining their sense of humour even while being 'felt' by the security personnel. One thing that keeps airports strikingly different from other public places is the fact that the number of people going around with a smile on their face far exceeds than at any other similar terminus such as a railway station or a bus stand. Now that everyone is aware of the pleasant smile of the airhostesses and stewards, but it is only at an airport that even a bearded man behind a window or the one with a bushy moustache at a security point smiles at you before they let you go off to embrace the huge, silver bird waiting to take you to cloud nine.

7.1.4 Expository Essays

Unlike an argumentative essay, an *expository essay* is meant to explain a topic without giving the author's opinion. The purpose of an expository essay is to acquaint the reader with the knowledge that the author possesses. An expository essay is essentially designed to convey a piece of information with the reader so that he/she comes to know about a situation, topic, fact, or state. The tone of an expository essay is often detached, objective, and matter of fact as rather than establishing the author's point of view, it is meant to share with the reader the information and knowledge that the author possesses. At times, authors use expository paragraphs to form the part of the essay which may be argumentative, analytical, or reflective in design. Take a look at how the following expository paragraph takes off on a discussion on health insurance:

Health insurance refers to a system for the advance financing of medical expenses through contribution. When proposed as a public policy by a government, people have the facility to pay their contribution or taxes into a common fund to pay for all or part of health services specified in an insurance policy or law. The key features of health insurance are advance payment of premiums or taxes, pooling of funds, and eligibility for benefits. Known as public health insurance, this form of health insurance may apply to a limited or comprehensive range of medical services and may provide for full or partial payment of the costs of specific services. Benefits under such a scheme may range from the right to certain medical services or reimbursement of the insured for specified medical costs. Unlike public health insurance which is run by a government, private health insurance is organized and administered by an insurance company or other private agencies. It makes provision for accumulation of funds by the regular and systematic contributions made by the policy holders. Offered with a wide range of flexibilities, private policy holders are required to pay for a certain period of time towards health insurance and are offered reimbursement or cash-free facilities as per the terms and conditions initially agreed upon.

7.1.5 Reflective/Philosophical Essays

A *reflective* or *philosophical essay* is meant to discuss a profound and deep issue. In such essays, the authors discuss universal human issues, such as life, death, love, faith, truth, etc. Since the subject matter of a philosophical essay is universal, the authors rise above the immediate and mundane, universalizing the personal. Take a look at the following extract that can form a part of one such essay:

A deeper look into the equation makes us believe that it is the presence of the *other* that makes us feel good or bad about ourselves. For example, just think of a world in which no one salutes a rich man and none denigrates the poor. Would people still be after money? Of course, the money required for physical survival and comfortable living would continue to be important. But the subtler form of authority, the one that comes through economic superiority—and hence the mad rush for it—would be lost. Going further, let's think of some more such propositions: Let there be a crown and no one around to appreciate. Let there be a big house, a dashing car moving with a sleek arrogance but just shut the eye that envies them. Let there be a *topper* in the class of one. Let there be the most coveted position but eliminate the crowd that knows that they all wanted them, each of them, but none could make it. Do this simple thing—wipe out the possibility of the *others* and see what happens. We cease to be superiors. In a way, our superiority depends on someone else's inferiority. The moment the *other* is swept away from imagination, the whole edifice of our superiority collapses into absurdity and meaninglessness.

Though in a philosophical and reflective essay the author highlights his/her own perspective on a given issue, the broadness of the subject matter requires an objective and detached approach with which universal issues are viewed. Therefore, for writing such essays, we need to reflect a comprehensive and unemotional perspective. Consider one such extract that can become a part of a philosophical and reflective essay:

One of the most visible offshoots of capitalism, consumerism seems to have swamped the entire country. Regardless of the fact whether you visit a small town or a metro city therefore, a staggering spurt of shopping malls, departmental stores, and chains of retail shopping centres can be seen in almost all across the country. With the rise of such places in cities, the shopping patterns of people are also changing. Now, people don't just buy things that they want, but also those that they happen to see on display. So, what rules the roost is not their *need* but the *desire* to possess something on display. Needless to say, that in this subtle game of capitalistic coercion, scintillating display, luring packaging, attractive offers, and action inducing advertisement play a subtle but decisive role.

7.2 CHARACTERISTIC FEATURES OF AN ESSAY

Though different types of essays can be written in a variety of ways, following are some of the characteristic features of a well-written essay:

- A good essay is the result of a careful planning and selection of material. Since an essay relates to a specific situation, problem, or fact, it selects the matter that is required to be selected and rejects what is redundant. Hence, good essays are never produced abruptly but sculpted with careful consideration and thought.
- A good essay is comprehensive in its approach and vision. A well-written essay highlights all the aspects related to the issue under discussion by highlighting the various aspects of the problem or issue.
- Though an essay is a reflection of the author's perspective and at times also throws light on his/her personality, it is considered most appropriate and relevant when written in an objective and detached manner.
- A good essay is normally well-balanced and not lopsided. A well-crafted essay strikes a balance in its different parts and a good writer of essays gives due importance to each of its various parts.
- Coherence is another feature of a good essay as the different parts of an essay are well-coalesced into one another. Any part that sticks out like a loose end of a thread is likely to spoil the shape and coherence of a good passage. A good essay, rather than focusing on any individual aspect of the problem, always creates the impact of one organic whole on the reader.
- A good essay reflects consistency and logical sequence of ideas in a composed and controlled manner. Though emphatic and powerful, the expressions and words chosen to discuss an issue are not ornate or bombastic. In a well-written essay, exaggerations and hyperboles have no role to play.

- A good essay is always written without ambiguities, verbal juggleries, and equivocations. The style of a good essay is therefore direct, simple, vigorous, and lucid.
- Just like the other components of an essay, its title is also chosen very carefully.

Having established the basic nature and features of an essay, let us learn something about the process of writing. As suggested earlier, a good essay is the result of a careful planning and we need to pass through several stages before actually starting the process of composing an essay. The following section discusses these stages required for writing an effective essay.

7.3 STAGES IN ESSAY WRITING

Following are the different stages in writing of an essay:

Collecting the material A good essay is the result of careful research. Therefore, before writing an essay on some topic, we need to collect the relevant material required to be studied so that the essay we compose is authentic, substantial, and convincing. Without proper data and understanding of the relevant details, we are likely to produce a perspective that would seem subjective, trivial, and prejudiced.

Defining the scope Since an essay is always specific and to the point, it is important for us to define the scope of our presentation of the idea in question. While defining the scope, we need to look carefully at the title of the essay. For example, when we have to write on *Terrorism in Modern World,* we need to give a worldwide view of the perspective and while discussing *The Terrorism in India,* we need to restrict our scope and limit it to India alone.

Making an outline An outline of an essay relates to its skeletal form. It consists of the main and sub-points of our essay. An outline is always helpful as it keeps us focused and systematic in taking up the various issues involved in an essay. A good outline helps us express ourselves in a coherent way. Having selected or rejected certain ideas at the stage of preparing an outline, we can certainly avoid the danger of running into writing something redundant and missing out on an important aspect related to the issue.

Making the first draft Since essay is a detailed composition, it is generally best produced after revision and editing. That is why, it is quite often observed that the essays submitted after revision and editing are much better than those which are submitted without these. However, in competitive exams, it is not possible for us to write the draft fully, and give the final version after revision. Even then, it is always handy to jot down the sequence in which we plan to take up the different ideas that are going to form the fulcrum of our essay. Without the main points in our mind, it is not possible to maintain coherence and unity in the ideas expressed. Therefore, if not the entire first draft, it is quite worthwhile to prepare a brief rough sketch before launching ourselves into the actual process of composing an essay.

Revising and editing In situations where a revised and edited version is possible to be submitted, good authors take a second look at their initial draft before sending their essays for final consideration. While revising our essay, we must pay careful attention to maintaining logical development of the idea throughout our effort. Besides the content and the style, the natural evolution of a thesis is what makes an essay eminently readable. Therefore, we need to ruthlessly edit our essays by expurgating the logical inconsistencies that may creep in. A lot of revision also takes place while reshaping the matter and rephrasing the material. Any lopsided views and subjective ideas need to be pruned while writing an essay. Also, we need to write in a style that is devoid of affectation, exaggerations, and prejudices. Moreover, the style chosen has to be compact, direct, and shorn of bombastic words, clichés, and jargon. Remember that any ambiguity in style and substance is likely to erode the impact of the overall presentation and hence it must be carefully avoided.

7.4 COMPONENTS COMPRISING AN ESSAY

Regardless of its type, a good essay can be divided into three distinct parts:

(a) Introduction

(b) Development of an idea

(c) Conclusion

Take a look at the introduction of an essay and judge whether you find it effective:

When it comes to analysing a prospect such as *India's Progress: A Myth or Reality?* it appears that the word *progress* is not good enough. It is so because *progress* means something positive and good but in many ways our country is either not progressing or just becoming worse. Take for instance, the case of growing fundamentalism among several sections of the society and also the gap between the rich and the poor that seems to widen up all the time.

The introduction of the essay appears to be too abrupt to be impressive. Rather than introducing, the author here seems to be discussing the idea and starts giving the different aspects of the issue straightaway. Such beginnings do not allow the reader to feel settled with the topic. Consider another beginning that alternatively introduces the idea:

Progress is a multi-dimensional term and is generally confused with other similar terms such as 'evolution', 'growth', and 'development'. In the past, it has often been suggested that our country, in the name of development, has only managed a lopsided development. To be able to evaluate whether India has not just *evolved* and *developed* but has also *progressed*, we need to take into consideration the quantitative and qualitative aspects of the country's development over the years.

With this introduction, the essay seems to have begun well. The author tries to put the word *progress* in its right perspective and takes the reader further into the discussion. Therefore, we need to avoid an introduction that plunges into the discussion straightaway. However, a hasty discussion is not the only way in which an introduction is spoiled. At times, introductions written in essays have been found to be too long, irrelevant, flashy, or abstruse to be appropriate. Therefore, while writing the introductory part of the essay, keep in mind the following points:

- Keep your introduction brief and effective.
- Avoid starting abruptly or too philosophically.
- Define or explain the title in a precise, specific way.
- Use quotations, dictionary meanings, statements, or sayings to introduce the reader to the main idea.
- Don't take sides on an issue or sound prejudiced in your approach.
- Avoid jargons, clichés, and bombastic beginnings.

Once the beginning is set, we can move on to the main body of the essay. It is in this part of the discussion that we compare and contrast, challenge and question, reveal and establish, and hence, bring into view the different nuances of the main idea. Quite often, this part of the essay runs into several paragraphs with each of those consisting of a topic sentence, a set of developers, and a terminator. To be able to come out well in this part of the essay, we need to keep in mind the following ideas:

- Evaluate all the possible aspects of a problem, topic, or issue.
- Give due importance to each aspect; don't appear prejudiced or biased in your approach.
- Relate all your ideas to one another.
- Connect the concluding part of the essay to the perspectives broached up in the introduction.

- Avoid a miscellany of too long or too short paragraphs in this part of the essay; let there be a semblance of equality in the length and size of different paragraphs.
- It is in this section that the author attempts to convince the reader of his/her perspective on the issue; therefore, analyse the different aspects of the problem exhaustively and leave nothing to chance.
- Use supporting material to augment and develop ideas. For carrying conviction, use brief or extended examples, facts, comparison, contrasts, expert testimony, and other such devices to make the text look comprehensive and authentic.
- Let the main body lead the reader systematically, convincingly, and automatically to the conclusion of the essay.

Let us take a look at the main body of an essay on the value of sports in life:

> The physical benefits of sports are well known. Participation in sports builds the stamina and makes the player strong. Sports such as swimming, football, hockey, volleyball, tennis, badminton, and basketball that require running, stretching, bending, and constant physical movement help us develop resistance and improve reflexes. Physical activity helps us develop immunity; keep the body fit and fine; take up physical strain as and when required. It is only through physically fit countrymen that we can take our country to great heights of success, growth, and development besides getting us the brave soldiers who protect our national territories and international boundaries.
>
> Sports help us not just physically but psychologically as well. They help us maintain mental and emotional balance. Since sports require competition and constant effort to win, they lead us to a positive attitude. Participating in sports leads to purgation of unwanted emotions. It gives us a sense of well-being and helps us maintain a positive mindset. As it is aptly said, *a healthy mind lives in a healthy body*, participating in games and sports helps us attain both a healthy mind and maintain a healthy body. Even in terms of social adjustment, sports and games play a crucial role. Someone who has participated in sports and games knows the importance of team spirit, discipline, cooperation, fairness, and cheerfulness and displays these traits both in his/her personal and professional activities. Such people respond to challenges of life with a spirit of competitiveness and enthusiasm and finally achieve their goals both at the personal and professional front.
>
> Realizing this magical importance of sports, human civilizations have always assigned to games and sports vital importance. Historically, sports have swayed our imagination since time immemorial. Long ago, the Greeks realized the importance of sports in life and started a festival every fourth year that included contests of sports, music, and literature. It was these ancient games which were revived in 1896 in Athens and are now known as the prestigious Olympic Games, which involve thousands of players in numerous sports events every fourth year. Besides these, there are World Cups in sports such as football, hockey, and cricket. Table tennis, badminton, volleyball, and basketball players keep competing in other premier championships. The Commonwealth Games and Asian Games give opportunities to players from different nations to prove their mettle in a variety of sporting and athletic events.

Just as the introductory part or the main body of the essay, the conclusion of an essay is also quite crucial. In fact, many a time poor conclusion can adversely affect the overall impact of an essay. In order to come up with a good conclusion, bear in mind the following suggestions:

- Conclusion is meant to reinforce the idea already illustrated and established in the main body; avoid therefore developing any new idea in the concluding part of the essay.
- Avoid feeble endings; pack it with a punch of force and vigour.

- An unrelated or irrelevant ending makes an essay look ludicrous at times; hence, let the conclusion naturally emerge out of the discussion.
- Keep your conclusion crisp and in cohesion with other parts of the essay.

Take a look at the conclusion of an essay on superstitions in society.

In essence it seems that lack of education and superstitions are deeply intertwined. The poorer a society is in terms of education, the greater will be the prevalence of superstitions in its circles. It is only through education that we can purge a society of its superstitions. As individuals in a society become truly educated, they develop scientific temperament; are able to see through false notions and fake beliefs imposed on them through rituals and customs and hence, can steer clear of them. Therefore, in order to keep our society away from the canker of superstitions, we need to make constant efforts in providing education to as many people as possible, broaden their knowledge, and make them see the futility of the mental cobwebs that assault them in the form of superstitions. The task seems to be challenging but is not impossible to achieve as the darkness of superstitions can certainly be eliminated by spreading the light of awareness and knowledge through education.

7.5 ESSAY WRITING—GUIDING PRINCIPLES

Having understood the nature and features of an essay, let us now learn how to write effective essays. Here are some of the principles following which we can develop essays of different types.

Work hard on the introduction Just as is the case with other compositions, a good beginning is quite crucial to writing an effective essay. A good, imaginative start can help us capture the attention of the reader. For example, let us understand which of the two beginnings given below appears to be more appropriate on the issue *Freedom of Press: An Indian Perspective*:

Freedom of press is crucial and seen as part of a nation's freedom. Even after so many years of independence, press has not been able to assert itself in our country. Though there are reports that question the policies of the government and attack the ills of the political and bureaucratic system every now and then, we are yet to see a press that is fully independent of its view and can interfere directly into government's policies and play a constructive role in nation building.

An introduction of this sort is certainly not appropriate. It hardly broaches the main idea and in fact seems to end the discussion even before the discussion gets started. Rather than introducing, this piece of writing seems to wind up a discussion and hence need to be avoided. Take a look at the revised version of the same:

Freedom of press is often equated with the freedom of a nation. It is believed that the extent to which press enjoys its freedom in a country determines the extent of freedom the people of that particular nation experience. Freedom of press is crucial to the growth, development, and progress of a nation. In India, press has the constitutional freedom to express its voice. Representing the voice of people, the press in India has always played a significant role expressing the views of the masses on matters of importance and general concern. Despite having achieved that, press in India has not been able to assert its prowess as a tool of change.

Make the main body look authentic and unified Developing the idea broached in the introduction, the main body of an essay actually is its most expanded part. Since it constitutes the main argument of the whole idea, the main body may also be seen as the most important part of an essay. Running into a couple of or several paragraphs, the main body is expected to look authentic and unified. Without an authentic and compact main body, an essay is likely to sound hollow and trivial. In order to achieve unity and provide authenticity to this part, authors tend to divide the main body of their essay into different thought units and construct a separate paragraph on each of them. Before writing this part of the essay, it is quite useful to prepare a small outline by dividing the main idea into sub-topics. For instance, an outline such as the one that follows might be designed before we launch ourselves into writing the main body of our essay on a topic such as the one that follows:

The Problem of Brain Drain

- *Causes of Brain Drain*
  Lucrative Jobs
  Better Opportunities and Life Style
  Freedom of Work
  Lack of Corruption
  Better Facilities and Working Conditions
  Charm of Foreign Tag
  Enhanced Social Status
- *Recent Trends*
  Statistics in the Past Two Decades
  Future Projections
  Suggested Remedies
  Better Work Environment
  Freedom for Creativity and Innovation
  Improved Infrastructure and Facilities

Once we are sure of *what* to write, we can start thinking of *how* to write that. As already suggested, the main body of an essay constitutes different paragraphs, each of which has its own *introducer*, a couple of *developers*, and a *terminator*. Every paragraph deals with a separate sub-topic within the broad range of the principal or main idea. In order to lend credence to the thought, writers often use devices such as comparisons, contrasts, analogies, examples, instances, statistics, quotations, enumerations, definitions, etc. Using strategies such as these provides conviction and authenticity to the content of the essay and it is difficult to conceive of a topic that can be developed into a cogent and substantial essay without employing such techniques.

Just as it is important to provide convincing details and sound authentic while writing an essay, it is also equally important to make the essay coherent and well-knit. A loosely constructed essay is generally the one that does not convey the central idea with concentration and effect and where the sub-topics are fragmented arbitrarily. In such essays, the different parts appear to be disjointed from one another. Such an essay leaves a poor impact on the reader and fails to convince him/her about the author's perspective on the issue. Therefore, we must pay special attention to put the different parts of an essay in consonance with one another. Linkers and connectives help in putting different ideas in accordance with one another.

Use connectives and linkers appropriately Take a look at how by using linkers, different ideas in an essay on a topic such as the one cited below can be presented:

Media: Uses and Abuses

- *Though* media is often accused of using unfair means or sensationalism, its advantages cannot be overlooked.
- *Besides* popularizing vulgarity and buffoonery, media can also be accused of having changed the cultural ethos of modern generations.
- *Moreover*, by reporting about the corruption cases, media brings to the fore the ugliness of the system that often remains hidden from our view.
- *However*, rather than highlighting reality, most of the new channels today focus on showing what can keep their audience hooked to their programmes through alluring advertisements, catchy cover stories, sensational sting operations, and violent crime sequences.
- *Further*, the different forms of media should be alerted and made more conscious about their constructive role in the society.

Using transitions, connectives, and linkers, such as *therefore, in addition to, apart from, in fact, although, nevertheless, notwithstanding,* etc. apart from those used in the above sentences, provides logical link and consistency to the whole idea besides developing it in a coherent and convincing manner. Since connectives provide order and consistency to an idea, it is important to use them appropriately.

Let us understand through an example how lack of coherence can spoil the impact of the main body of an essay:

Corruption in India

The roots of corruption in our country have become so entrenched that it seems difficult and even impossible to uproot it. In a post-independent India, corruption has made heavy inroads in all aspects of our life and has permeated the social, political, economic, and religious fabric of our society. The pains of the masses are further aggravated by corruption rampant in government offices. Moreover, there are smugglers who go on increasing the tentacles of corruption in our country.

As far as trade in India is concerned, there too corruption rules the roost. Corrupt traders keep hoarding the essential commodities and create artificial shortage of a commodity. Because of this, the commodity becomes rare to find anywhere and then the corrupt hoarders increase the price and accumulate huge amount of money. Not only these but black marketers also introduce the spurious goods to replace the original items and thus innocent people end up buying the fake item at an exorbitant rate.

The above part lacks both coherence and unity. The first paragraph starts by introducing corruption in a post-independent India but then suddenly jumps to the idea that '...the pains of the masses are further aggravated by corruption in government offices'. Again, the idea that there are smugglers who go on increasing the tentacles of corruption in our country, appears to be too sudden, shallow, and unpremeditated. All such chinks in the construction clearly illustrate lack of coherence in the organization of the paragraph as there seems no consistent development of a principal idea that a good paragraph aspires to achieve. The structure seems flawed also in terms of unity as the second paragraph starts abruptly with the idea 'As far as trade in India is concerned, there too corruption rules the roost...'.

Take a look at how a revised version of the same seems more compact, unified, and coherent:

The roots of corruption in our country have become so entrenched that it seems difficult and even impossible to uproot it. In a post-independent India, corruption has made heavy inroads into all aspects of our life and has permeated the social, political, economic, and religious fabric of our society. For decades now, corruption has reflected itself in a variety of ways. The problems of black marketing, bribery, scams, and adulteration raise their ugly face only because of corruption in our society. Moreover, other problems such as poverty, inflation, lack of governance, and lawlessness can also be seen as other ramifications of this hydra-headed problem.

For example, if we look into the nuances of trade in India, corruption rules the roost. Corrupt traders keep hoarding the essential commodities and create artificial shortage of everyday household commodities. Because of this artificially created scarcity, the essential commodities disappear from the market every now and then. With the rise in demand, the corrupt hoarders increase the price and accumulate huge amount of money. The masses have to pay the increased price for buying the essential household commodities. This really affects their monthly budget which, for millions and millions in India, is always tenuous and dwindling. Not only these but black marketers also introduce spurious goods to replace the original items and thus the poor, innocent people end up buying the fake items at an exorbitant rate.

As can be seen in the revised version, first the different forms of corruption are highlighted in one paragraph and the one that follows takes up one particular form of corruption and explores its impact on commoners. It is evident therefore that maintaining coherence and unity in an essay becomes one of its important features and the essay that lacks in this aspect fails to create the right kind of impact on the reader.

Keep the conclusion short and effective Though conclusion of an essay comes at the end of it, its importance cannot be undermined. In fact, quite a few essays fail to click with the reader because of a poor and ineffective conclusion. Take a look at the following paragraph that comes at the end of an essay on corruption in India:

Recently, even health and educational institutes seem to have been involved in widespread corruption. There have been instances of fake degrees, illegal approvals, and unlawful admissions in various institutes across the country. In our country, corruption has made every illegal activity seem fairly common; criminals can commit a heinous crime and can roam around freely; smugglers and peddlers can freely sneak through barriers; engineers can make bridges that can collapse any day; transporters can run buses on roads without permit; employees can be selected, promoted, or transferred by greasing the palms of those concerned; doctors can sell kidneys of their patients; teachers can change grades and marks they have awarded to students. In these ways and many more, corruption is rampant in our country. Seeing this, one can only wonder what sustains our country despite this widespread wave of corruption that sweeps almost all aspects of our social, political, economic, and religious life.

A conclusion like this may seem relevant but it hardly seems impressive and forceful. A paragraph like this should be placed in the main body of the essay. Moreover, the concluding sentence expresses a despair and helplessness which is bound to create a pessimistic impact on the reader. Consider an alternative conclusion for the essay on the same topic:

Observed thus, it is apparent that corruption in India is one of the most challenging problems that our country faces. It is also clear from the discussion above that unless corrupt practices are stopped in our country, millions among us will be forced to lead a substandard, dissatisfied, and miserable life. However, since corruption emanates from loss of values and ethics, we must make untiring efforts in reviving them in all aspects of our life. Individually, each of us needs to set a high standard of personal conduct and judge ourselves scrupulously. Since a society is made up of individuals only, if the individual changes, so will the society and the country with the passage of time.

While writing the conclusion for an essay, keep in mind the following points:
- The conclusion of an essay should be short, crisp, and effective.
- While writing a conclusion, do not start elaborating a particular point.
- No new ideas should be added in a conclusion.
- The conclusion of an essay should essentially be in consonance with the discussion.
- Your conclusion should not sound too pessimistic and gloomy.
- In conclusions, writers are expected to summarize their own ideas; therefore, avoid quotations from other sources while making final statements.
- Give convincing ideas in conclusions; avoid making sweeping statements.

Write in an effective style Just as keeping an essay well-structured is important, so is writing its contents in an effective and appropriate way. The style of an essay is, in fact, as important as its contents. Therefore, writing in a style that is direct, emphatic, and elegant becomes crucial to the overall impact of an essay. At times, essays are spoiled because of a style that is circumlocutory, bombastic, and ornate. We should bear in mind however that using unnecessary frills and verbose expressions is likely to create a negative impact on the reader. Given below are some of the principles for composing an essay in an effective style:

Avoid ostentatious and showy beginnings Since essays are supposed to be written on serious issues of relevance and significance, the style chosen for these should also be sober and graceful. While writing an essay, we need to avoid ostentatious or shocking beginnings. Though we can use a statement which is arresting and interesting for the reader, a conversational or anecdotal opening is generally avoided in essays. Take a look at the following example and see how ridiculous the beginning seems to be for the essay on ragging in colleges.

> A friend of mine is scared today. He applied for admission to a college of repute in our city. Is he scared of the possibility of not getting a seat in the prestigious institute? Has he not managed admission there? Well, the answer is yes, he has! Then why should he be scared? It is so because the college is notorious for its reputation for ragging. The guys and girls getting into the first year of their degree programme are invariably in for a 'treat' and it is that 'treat' which gives my friend a scary feeling.

Beginnings such as the above may suit a speech but do not go well with the tone required for an essay. Consider alternatively beginning the essay as suggested below:

> Though started as a healthy convention of introducing the juniors to their seniors in academic institutes, *ragging* today has come to mean something really unpleasant and undesirable. A by-product of modernization, ragging has come to convey constant harassment, pressure, and torture of juniors by their seniors in colleges, institutes, and universities. Every other day, we get to know some frightening story through some report in a newspaper or a cover story on a television news channel in which a youth is reported to have committed suicide following constant torture inflicted in the name of ragging by the seniors. So much so that ragging is now regarded as an offence that is punishable by law.

At times, openings are rendered ineffective not because they sound unreal and artificial but also because they sound too passive and ineffectual. Written in a laid-back manner, some of the essays start on a note that does not stimulate the imagination of the reader at all. Take a look at one such beginning and observe how dull it sounds:

> It is commonly believed that the right place of woman is within the four walls of her house. There is a general perception in society that man should earn the livelihood for the family and woman should look after the household affairs. It is suggested that mixing these roles leads to chaos and confusion in the society and leads to family discords, insecurity in children, unnecessary ego clashes between husband and wife, and also an increasing consumerism which is a direct offshoot of woman's economic independence.

A beginning such as the one cited above seems far from being impressive as the writer uses a series of laid-back expressions such as 'it is believed…', 'there is a general perception…', and 'it is suggested that…'. This makes the passage take off on a drab and passive note. Consider the following opening which can suitably begin the essay in a more emphatic manner:

> One of the important debates of our times has been the role of Indian women in society. Traditionalists in our country have always questioned the concept of woman's equality with man in social, political, economic, and intellectual spheres. Their view has, however, been challenged in the changing times and reformists have aggressively pressed for the economic and social freedom for women in India. Moreover, since woman's freedom is now a worldwide phenomenon, it has found favours for its growth and development in India as well. Despite this global support for the movement, some segments of the society continue to react retrogressively to the idea of woman's equality to man in India. A critical and objective analysis is likely to throw up some interesting facts for our observation in this regard.

Use examples, statistics, and quotations sparingly Though examples, quotations, and statistics are required to be used in essays, their use must not be over-exercised. It is so because essays are essentially lengthy discourses and are required to present the author's views on a subject. Therefore, rather than harping excessively on statistics, examples, and quotations, we should try to present a comprehensive picture of the situation through these. Just as an essay without such supporting material would seem rather flimsy and too personal, the one that primarily rests on these would appear to be unoriginal and borrowed.

Choose elaborate sentence structure Since writing essays is indicative of one intellectual pursuit, it must be written in an effective manner. A poorly written essay hardly appears to be a reflection of someone's intellectuality. Therefore, using a jerky and choppy sentence structure shows the writer of an essay in poor light. Take a look at the following extract of an essay on the importance of co-education.

> The strict puritans won't have it. They would believe their morality being questioned. Girls should not study with boys, they believe. It spoils both boys and girls. In their view concentrating in girls' presence is hard for boys. Similarly for girls learning without being nervous or scared, is not possible in boys' company. Hence those against it, oppose co-education. They believe studying together would lead to several problems. It would lead to illicit affair. It will lead to poor academic performance. It would lead to hasty marriages. It would lead to early exposure to sexual life. Therefore, fastidious puritans emphasize segregation of boys and girls during their school and higher education.

As can be observed, the style of the extract is far from being impressive. The writer uses a prose that stumbles, stops, and resumes every now and then. The jerky, choppy prose tends to sound not only repetitive but also immature and unpolished. See how the revised version of the same extract brings maturity and focus in expression:

> Puritans generally oppose the idea of co-education. In their view, educating boys and girls together leads to several problems such as distraction from studies, poor academic performance, premature exposure to the opposite sex, immature love affairs, and hasty love marriages. Fearing such offshoots of co-education, puritans suggest educating boys and girls separately during their schooling and higher education.

Choose common, familiar words At times, essays tend to lose their appeal as writers choose to describe their views in a bombastic and pompous manner. Choice of long and unfamiliar words over simple everyday expressions leads to ambiguity in style and suggests artificiality. Reading pompous prose gives the reader an impression of vanity and unnecessary pretensions and such an essay fails to convince the reader of the writer's views. While writing an essay, we must bear in mind that a piece of writing that is not understood can hardly be appreciated. Therefore, there is no point in being pompous and artificial. Prefer writing familiar and common words instead of artificial, bombastic expressions. This builds immediate rapport with the reader and convinces him/her of the writer's views on a given subject. Take a look at how unusual expressions, circumlocution, and flowery style of writing create a befuddling impact on the reader:

> Sartre once said that when two people interact, there should be subject-to-subject correspondence between them. Groping around, what one generally excavates is a subject and object relation that seems to characterize the nuances of their mutual relationship. It means that governed by an imperceptible emotion of ravaging hatred and revulsion coupled with a spree to dominate and coerce, man wishes to manoeuvre and manipulate all the time so that all others in his existential vicinity should seem sufficiently dwarfed and thereby he be declared a winner. All human growth, development, and achievement therefore seem to have been built on the debris of countless corpses not seemingly unlike him. The difference between the vanquished and the victorious seems to be minimum as all men venture into dislodging the others and getting themselves perched on the seat of success. Digging their graves thus would be unearthing their shrouded gambits—some camouflaged in grins of achievement and some others masked in smirks of failure.

The paragraph above seems to start on the right note. Soon afterwards however, it starts losing itself in the labyrinth of ideas as from one abstruse sentence we keep moving on to the other of the same type. The deliberate use of unfamiliar and uncommon words and verbose and roundabout expressions render the content in the passage all the more confusing. A consciously carved style of this type seems belaboured and pompous affecting the overall understanding of the passage. See how the revised version of the same passage communicates the same idea with ease and clarity:

> Sartre once said that when two people interact, there should be subject-to-subject correspondence between them. What is observed in human relations however is a subject and object relation. It means that when two people share a relationship, they tend to dominate each other. It seems that because of a desire to dominate and control, we try to manipulate and manoeuvre others. This desire to coerce others can also be attributed to a deep-seated hatred or disliking for the others. In any case, in order to attain greatness or victorious status, we want to crush many others into a vanquished lot. Seen thus, all our development and achievement seems to be a sad tale of fierce struggle among human beings that quite a few lose and only a few others win.

Avoid being unnecessarily equivocal or obscure Obscurity is one of the avoidable traits of many an essay that writers of philosophical and metaphysical bent tend to slip into. Since philosophical indeterminism often leads to obscurity and confusion, an essay addressing such profound issues needs to be written in a style that is lucid and transparent. Even if the subject matter is profound and eludes direct interpretation, one needs to strive for clarity and lucidity in one's expressions. Writing in a deliberately profound manner and dropping unresolved equivocations and leaving the reader baffled with metaphysical overtones is likely to have an adverse effect on the readability of an essay. A large number of essays are not read by readers simply because they sound far too arcane, abstruse, and obscure in their choice of vocabulary, syntax, or sentence construction. Take a look at how obscurity affects the expression in the following extract from an essay:

The deliberate, purposeful embroidering of God's immanence in man's life fills in the fathomless vacuum, the scorching sense of emptiness he feels himself being confronted with once the thought of insubstantiality of all his achievements, futility of all his endeavours, and incertitude of all his plans confronts him with all the darker, gloomy shades of reality. Snubbed into an existential predicament and assured of nothing else except the triviality and mortality of his own existence, man gropes for an assurance and permanence that the existence of his creator, God would ascribe to him. Deeply disquieted about his own sense of transience and a sloppy, ephemeral existence, it is in His presence that man seeks permanence and continuity of life. God is man's assurance to himself that even when he is reduced to ashes or dust, he would continue to exist, if not here on this land of mortality then in the sweet continuity of heaven. That seems like a great snubbing of nature, the powerful but unruly, unintelligent daughter of God who most foolishly seeks to destroy her father's most loved and a chosen creature on this planet by drawing curtains on his physical existence. How else otherwise would you vouchsafe or pontificate such madness on the part of nature? If nature were not insane, she would have shown more reverence for the most gifted creature of God. Then she would not have destroyed man. She would have preserved him, as a representative species of God Himself. So an angry man, deeply annoyed at having been treated in the same way like any other creature, any other modest and mortal creature on the earth, decides to not only discard nature and cling to God but also pledges to destroy his destroyer, nature.

A write-up such as this is bound to leave a reader confused, bewildered, and exasperated. The writer expresses a complex idea in a style that is equally mystifying and confusing. Take a look at the revised version of the text to understand what the passage actually intends to communicate:

It is a deep-seated sense of insecurity in human beings that turns them against nature and makes them search for meaning, permanence, and immortality through their creations. Impelled by their own transience, humans tend to seek immortality by creating an image of God which gives them a sense of assurance that even after death they will continue to exist in heaven.

Thus, by observing the principles of clarity, coherence, and consistency, we can write effective essays.

EXERCISE 7.1

Write an essay in about 300 words on each of the following topics:

1. Generation Gap
2. Population Explosion
3. Value of Discipline in Life
4. The Great Indian Dream
5. Indian Cinema: An Escape from Reality?
6. Man vs Machine
7. Global Warming
8. The Menace of Corruption
9. Rituals and Religion
10. Science and Spirituality
11. Exodus from Villages in India
12. The Plight of Slum Dwellers
13. Can We Achieve Peace through Atoms?
14. Has Dowry System Ended in India?
15. The Role of Media
16. Mobile Revolution
17. The Role of Multinationals in Indian Economy
18. Gender Discrimination in Modern India
19. The Menace of Drug Addiction
20. Social Networking Sites: A Bane or Boon for the Youth?

8 PRÉCIS WRITING

LEARNING OBJECTIVES

After reading this chapter, you will be able to understand
- major forms of condensation practised by professionals
- principles for writing an effective précis
- seven-step ladder to writing a good précis

Just as it is difficult to be simple in life, it is difficult to be precise in what we speak and write. In fact, it is difficult to be elaborate for those who struggle with language in the sense of not having enough words, expressions, and ideas. But for those who have a good number of words at their disposal and have no dearth of expressions and ideas, it is difficult to be precise and brief. Therefore, at times, you see some of the people around you complaining that *it was not possible for them to deliver a two-minute speech though they could fairly well deliver a ten-minute talk!* However, in professional situations, one must be in a position to express oneself not just elaborately but also briefly.

Just to illustrate the view—imagine that you are a marketing executive in your company. The chief of the marketing division has called for a meeting. You have recently read an article in a business magazine which speaks about latest innovations in the field of marketing. You want to discuss some of these innovations in the meeting. Now what would you do? Will you carry the article to the meeting and read it aloud to the other members in the meeting? Or will you take down important ideas, make a summary, and highlight each of the points one by one? Obviously, it is only the second method that would work.

And you would be required to be brief and precise in such a situation. However, before we understand how to condense, we need to get acquainted with the major forms of condensation that are frequently used by us in our academic and professional life. Given below are the major forms of condensation required and practised by a professional:

- Précis
- Summary
- Abstract
- Synopsis
- Paraphrasing

Précis

Among all the major forms of condensation, précis is the most commonly required form of condensation in professional situations. Keeping its importance in view, several public and private sector organizations too expect the prospective incumbents to display their understanding and skill in composing an effective précis. Broadly speaking, précis is a short and concise account of some text, which gives all its important points but none of its details. Since the purpose of a précis is to briefly restate the idea expressed in the original write-up, it does not include any superfluous or illustrative material which may be a part of the original. Different in style and the number of words used, a précis follows and maintains the view of the author.

Summary

A summary is often written and included in the reports prepared by professionals. Summaries are also written to briefly present the main findings of a study, a journalistic article, or a geographical survey. Whatever may be the purpose, a summary is quite useful as it presents the entire matter in a nutshell. While writing a summary, the author does not add, develop, or delete any idea. A summary is often shorn of examples and illustrations, and emphasizes the main arguments and conclusions of the original. More often than not, it follows the sequence of the ideas as expressed in the original and detailed work.

Abstract

Shorter than a summary, an abstract is written to highlight the purpose, scope, and significance of a work. It is often preferred to a summary in technical and specialized forms of communication. Therefore, you often come across an abstract published along with a research article in journals and magazines.

Synopsis

A synopsis is a condensed and shortened version of an article, a research paper, a chapter from a book, a report, or a book itself. It highlights in brief all the essential features of the original document. Normally, a synopsis is required to be submitted to universities when research proposals, dissertations, and theses are proposed to be written by researchers. In a synopsis, the researcher is required to highlight the purpose, scope, and significance of the research. It also includes a reference to the methods adopted for data collection and the research gap that determines the objective of the research.

Paraphrasing

Although paraphrasing is not necessarily a condensed form of the original document, it is often believed to be the one. Therefore, it is advisable to understand the nature and purpose of a paraphrased text. The purpose of a paraphrase is to reproduce the author's ideas in your own words. So, you may employ as many words as the author has chosen to express himself/herself. Paraphrasing of write-ups is done in order to convey to the reader in simpler terms an idea which, otherwise, appears to be too ambiguous, arcane, philosophical, or poetic to follow. Many a time, you come across a paraphrased text of a classic. It is meant to bring the texts written in different times and languages to readers who can only follow a simpler and familiar version of it.

8.1 ESSENTIALS OF PRÉCIS WRITING

Among all the major forms of condensation, précis is most commonly required to be read and written, both by a student and a professional. It is a short and concise account of some text, which gives all its important points but none of its details. Since the purpose of a précis is to briefly restate the idea expressed in the original write-up, it does not include any superfluous or illustrative material which may be a part of the original. A précis follows and maintains the view of the author.

8.1.1 Some Working Principles

Keep in mind the following principles for writing an effective précis:

Be brief and precise Writing a précis is like reproducing the soul of the matter in a condensed and precise form. Therefore, it needs to be concise, precise, and focused. Normally, the length of the original passage is reduced to its one-third in the précis.

Be complete While reproducing an idea, we cannot leave out any of its vital aspects. Therefore, before we launch ourselves into writing a précis, we must carefully read the passage, notice all the important points, and incorporate all of them in our précis. A précis should, in fact, be as complete and comprehensive as the original one, albeit it should be expressed in a less number of words.

Be choosy Although it is not possible for us to leave out any important idea from the original, it is expected that we carefully choose only the material that is an indispensable part of the whole argument. In order to achieve a good précis of the original, we need to discard all the extraneous and superfluous material present in the form of examples, illustrations, instances, quotations, citations, anecdotes, parables, and any other such material that is included in the original to substantiate the basic idea.

Be original A good précis is both creative and original. Of course, while writing a précis, you are not expected to distort or modify the author's view. You are also not expected to add any idea of your own or leave out some important idea of the author, but at the same time, you are required to express the author's views in your own words. Therefore, try to use your own expressions while rewriting what the author has expressed in the original.

Be coherent While writing a précis, we normally follow the order that the author has chosen to arrange his/her ideas. However, since a précis is not a pale imitation of the original, a good précis always has a coherent structure of its own. In any case, it should not look as though some unrelated and disjointed sentences have been yoked together. Remember, the purpose of a précis is to help the reader gather the whole idea in a compact, complete, and coherent way. An incoherent or incomplete imitation of the original would, therefore, be of little worth to the reader.

Be clear In addition to completeness and coherence, clarity too is an important attribute of a well-written précis. While writing a précis, however, this element is sometimes lost as we tend to overemphasize the need to compress the ideas expressed in the original. Since a précis has to serve as a substitute for the original, we cannot afford any type of vagueness to punctuate the reader's comprehension of our précis.

8.2 SEVEN-STEP LADDER TO WRITING AN EFFECTIVE PRÉCIS

Having learnt about some essential features and principles that characterize a good précis, let us focus on the process of writing a précis. Writing a précis has some steps and stages. Follow a seven-step ladder, as discussed below, to be able to produce an effective précis:

Read and comprehend Read the original piece of writing as many times as you can, ensuring that you have understood what the author has expressed in his/her words.

Prepare a skeleton of the main ideas Having read and understood a passage, identify all the main and subordinate ideas and jot them down one by one. This gives you a clear view of all the ideas that are to be incorporated while writing the précis.

Assimilate the essentials Writing a good précis is to recapture the soul of what the author has said in your own words. For this, you need to not only understand the original passage and jot down its main points, but also assimilate the whole thought embedded in it. To achieve this, you need to focus on each of the points selected by you and rephrase them in your words. This will help you reshape the overall idea of the original passage in your words without distorting or losing its sense.

Think of a title Once you have understood the passage, focus on the central idea and think of a suitable title based on it. Thinking of a title and assigning it to a passage is essential as it keeps your thoughts focused on the core of the issue.

Prepare the first draft While preparing the first draft, remember to neither delete any important idea nor add anything of your own. Focus on the ideas observed and assimilated thus far and try to capture the spirit of the original in presenting it briefly.

Review and compare Having written it once, read your version with a view to observing whether it matches the original. While doing so, ask yourself questions such as—*Does my précis capture the essence of the original passage? Does my précis include all the important ideas expressed in the original? Has any idea been unnecessarily added, repeated, or deleted? Does it follow a coherent structure? Does it have clarity and compactness of expression? Does it use linkers and punctuation marks correctly?* etc.

At this stage, you can also count the number of words in your précis. Compare the length of your passage to that of the original. See if you can manage to do away with some more words or add a few more, depending upon whether it sounds redundant or obscure.

Edit and revise Having reviewed your first effort critically, you can now revise your draft and shape it as the final version of your précis. At this final step of précis writing, incorporate all the alterations, modifications, and changes you thought of while reviewing your first draft.

8.3 WRITING PRÉCIS OF GIVEN PASSAGES

Having learnt about the principles of writing a précis, let us practise by working out some passages:

PRACTICE TEST I

Recently, I came across a photograph of a tech CEO wearing the same outfit that she had worn in some other event a fortnight ago. Have you ever given a thought to the fact that some successful people choose to wear the same kind of outfit every day?

Wearing the same kind of outfit every day allows for fewer decisions to be made in the morning. There is a term called 'decision fatigue syndrome' for the deteriorating quality of decisions made by a person after a long session of decision making. For people who make a significant number of decisions every day, the removal of even one decision in their routine—for example, choosing clothes to wear in the morning—leaves them with more mental space and gives them better productivity throughout the day.

Writer Joshua Becker experimented with Project 333 a few years ago—a personal challenge of wearing only 33 clothing articles for a period of 3 months. It was a simple project, which proved life changing and beneficial. He realized the Gift of Time was the greatest benefit of limiting his wardrobe. Getting ready in the morning became easier, quicker, and more efficient.

'Wasted Energy' has been defined distinctly by Christopher Nolan. Large wardrobes not only require more decision making, they also require comparatively more maintenance, more organization and more shuffling around. In comparison, a capsule wardrobe may not mean less laundry; however, it surely results in both easier storage and laundry.

Our closets are full of rarely worn clothes and shoes. An average American family spends $1,700 per year on clothes. But if we adopt an iconic uniform or live with a smaller wardrobe, it automatically removes most of the unnecessary expenses from our trial-and-error clothing purchases. Moreover, a lot of time is wasted shopping for items only to return later.

Some time ago, Drew Barrymore wrote in an article for Refinery 29 about her new stage of life and her relationship with clothes. 'For starters, I'm almost 40, and the 20's clothes don't make sense anymore. And, after two babies, the 30's clothes don't fit anymore. I am at a clothing crossroads, and it's a painful one at times.' Drew put herself on a closet diet by limiting her wardrobe and buying items very thoughtfully. Months later, her closet was 'sane and happy'. It was no longer a battle to get dressed and the diet made her fashion sense 'now calmer and more peaceful'.

As a society, we are drowning in our possessions and people are trying to find freedom and rescue. They are searching for new solutions. This is the reason the capsule wardrobe movement is growing. Those who follow this minimalistic approach in their wardrobe and clothing choices get better productivity, lesser stress, lesser distraction, lesser expenses and much more peace.

(No. of Words: 468)

Suggested Précis

Title: Wardrobe Management

Instead of maintaining a large wardrobe, managing a smaller wardrobe has several advantages. Large wardrobes demand greater time, energy, and a lot of shuffling around of clothes for proper storage. Filling our wardrobes with unnecessary clothes also leads to needless expenses, unnecessary distractions, and enhanced stress levels. In comparison, smaller wardrobes require less space, time, money, and energy on our part. Moreover, maintaining a smaller wardrobe allows us greater mental space and adds to our efficiency on a day-to-day basis. That is why, most successful people are often seen wearing similar outfit everyday, which helps them fight better the *decision fatigue syndrome*. While unnecessary proliferation of mindless possessions costs us a lot and causes suffocation and fatigue, various experiments done by people reveal how by being a minimalist and preferring a *capsule wardrobe* to a massive one, we can attain a peaceful and more productive life.

(No. of Words: 151)

PRACTICE TEST II

In every age and stage of our lives, music is a boon. However, some researchers at Yale University have discovered it to be a greater blessing in the old age. Lancet, a medical journal, recently published an extensive study on the health benefits of music in old age. Music can help drive away 'old age blues' felt by most senior citizens. The study encourages senior citizens to listen to the music of their choice, and urges them to play a musical instrument if they can.

Somerset Maugham, the great novelist and raconteur, was a medical doctor who never practised medicine. To cope with loneliness in old age, he learnt to play the violin and lived near a hundred years. To overcome his sporadic schizophrenic episodes, Bertrand Russel used to listen to Beethoven's symphonies regularly. He lived a long and productive life on earth. Alfred Tennyson (1809–1892), the Victorian English poet reinvented his poetry when he started playing the piano at 70, after feeling that he was losing his poetic prowess.

The human brain has glial cells and neurons which tend to relate to the rhythms of music. This phenomenon is known as 'neural dance' in neuro-biology. These days, many old-age centers and hospitals in the West have skilled musicians and special rooms for listening to slow and lifting melodies.

Sigmund Freud always counselled his senior patients to listen to Sebastian Bach's compositions as they would make geriatric patients feel happy and cheerful.

Contrary to the popular belief that the Mughal emperor Aurangzeb detested music and barred it during his reign, the chronicler Khafif Khan revealed in his court dispatches that Aurangzeb's chronic insomnia when he was 78 years old was treated by the court musician Ahmad Rasool Khan. Ahmad Rasool Khan would play a three-stringed sarangi-type instrument (called *Wazaaf* in Persian) to make the ruler sleep and sing *Khayal* (a Hindustani music form) as he was a deft vocalist too. Aurangzeb gifted 14 villages near Badayun (in what is today Uttar Pradesh) to the talented musician who comforted the emperor by making him sleep. Aurangzeb passed away at the age of 89.

During old age, human brain remains in an agitated state and also suffers from unpleasant nostalgia. Music helps attain selective amnesia which makes the listener forget the unpleasant memories that keep gnawing. It's called in medical jargon the 'musical lobotomy of memory' or MLM.

Music revives the frayed nerves in old age. Shakespeare called old age the 'second childhood' of a person. Researchers like Statham and Barnes noticed that the mature members of retirement homes often behave and fight like children. This child-like behaviour among old people in retirement homes was attributed to the degeneration of cells and the weakening of the neuro-response. Music proves immensely helpful here by giving them a sense of friendliness and maturity, which is called 'musical maturity' (MM).

Retirement homes in the US and the UK have incorporated music sessions (both vocal and instrumental) in the daily lives of their members. It helps their minds to stay calm and composed! Violinists Yehudi Menuhin and Massimo Quarta always made time to play for the old and disabled people.

(No. of Words: 525)

Suggested Précis

Titles: i) Music—A Blessing in the Old Age

ii) Fighting Maladies with Melodies in Old Age

Though helpful at every stage of our life, music is particularly helpful in old age. Researches have established that music helps people fight *old-age blues* and recommend listening to music or playing some musical instrument in old age to overcome loneliness and lift their moods. It is so because the human brain has glial cells and neurons which tend to relate to the rhythms of music. Insight into the lives of many a great litterateur and powerful emperors helps us observe how for them music has been instrumental in containing schizophrenic episodes, reviving poetic intensity, and dealing with insomnia. In old age, human brain remains in a disturbed state and suffers from unpleasant memories. Music helps aged people attain selective amnesia and forget such bad memories. Moreover, the degeneration of cells and the weakening of the neuro-response leads to a child-like behaviour in old people. Music assigns to them a sense of friendliness and maturity and helps them remain calm, composed, and cheerful. Keeping its enormous advantages, old-age homes in the West have incorporated vocal and instrumental music sessions in the daily routine of the inhabitants.

(No. of Words: 186)

EXERCISE 8.1

1. Define a 'précis' and discuss its characteristic features.

2. 'Writing a précis does not mean resorting to a pale imitation of the original, but involving yourself in a creative process.' Do you subscribe to the view? Discuss and substantiate.

3. What is the seven-step ladder to writing an effective précis? Discuss and illustrate with appropriate examples.

4. Write a note of about 200 words on each of the following words:
   (a) Summary   (b) Abstract
   (c) Précis   (d) Synopsis

5. 'The art of condensation is an essential element in our writing skills.' Discuss and substantiate.

6. What are the necessary tenets for writing an effective précis? Discuss and exemplify.

7. Condense each of the following short passages retaining the main idea and using a minimum number of words:

   (i) When one does not really understand the true purpose of life, one is not in a position to really figure out how to focus on the actions to be carried out. That's what happens to most of us. We live and keep involving ourselves in actions which may not necessarily define us. Such a life is like a rudderless drift in a dark, befuddling ocean where you sail and sail, and still don't know where to shore up.

   (ii) 'We pine for what is not there,' says Keats and thus, like an enlightened soul, captures the cause behind perennial human suffering. Throughout our lives, we keep chasing a falling star; running after a goal, the completion of which should give us a sense of fulfilment and achievement. However, the misery lies in the fact that what is chased and achieved becomes immediately tasteless and redundant. No longer interested in what we possess, we hurtle ourselves into achieving what we don't have.

   (iii) Despite all our claims to be able to cobble up an educated and intellectual society, it seems we are hardly inching closer to one. There could be various reasons, ways, and instances to vouchsafe a view like this. One of the quickest ways to figure out the pulse of the nation: it won't be a bad idea to watch the most favoured and popular serials that swarm hundreds of channels on your television screen. Look at the lurid content, the slipshod presentation, the melodrama, the abundance of gimmicks, vulgarity, and cheapness that characterize most of these programmes. And then you realize, with a gasp of sigh, that we are hardly headed towards any awareness, education, or enlightenment.

   (iv) One of the dubious distinctions of our society surely is to be one of the most corrupt countries in the world. Corruption today has become an integral part of our system. If you want to get anything done, you need to bribe a person. It doesn't matter whether the matter is right or wrong, small or special; you need to grease a bureaucratic palm in order to get a file moving off its blocks. For those who cannot afford to fall in line with such unsaid expectations, there hardly is a ray of hope. After all, their wishes may soar but the files won't register a budge unless sufficiently winged on currency notes.

   (v) Adults are scared of death, as children are scared of darkness, so says Bacon, the legendary Renaissance English essayist. It is, however, just not children who are scared of darkness. After all how many of us can claim that darkness does not frighten us? Imagine yourself being caught in the darkness of night with no one around you! Even if you are trapped within your own house that you have lived in for years and years together, you don't really enjoy seeing your large, lonely shadow against your own walls. Similarly, not many of us feel like walking alone in long streets with no light around. And even if the grown-ups choose to watch late night horror movies in big theatres, a realization that they have to cross a long, unknown, dark street all alone after the show is over can give them a cold shiver down their spines.

   (vi) Superstition is one of the peculiar features of human life. Normally, the word is conceived, viewed, and interpreted in ancient terms and with the rise of the scientific spirit and a general sense of awareness all around, one would imagine that its tentacles on us are ebbing away. A closer look into the behaviour of even the most educated, affluent, and respected though hardly endorses such surmises. On the contrary, there is a spurt of superstitious beliefs all around us. No marriages are solemnized today without the matching of 'gunas' of the girl and the boy. Nobody is prepared to believe that it is a 'kundli' generated through an engineered software after all that is actually calling the shots. We would love to see 'the hand of God', in all the things that happen around us. If, by chance, the Gods fail to win matches for us, it is an octopus or a parakeet that can decide the matter.

(vii) Whether science is a friend or a foe has been one of the raging debates for many decades now. Gradually, however, the debate is giving way to the belief that it does not matter whether it is a friend or a foe. We all now understand that it is not just difficult but almost impossible for us to conceive of a world without the machines, motors, and computers that do not just make our life much more comfortable but almost define our existence. At the same time, we are also aware of the damage that the proliferation and advancement of science and technology has caused to the environment. The real issue for us today, therefore, is not whether to see science as a friend or a foe but to be able to survive without science and still not leave it.

(viii) Looking at the variegated shades and hues of Indian cinema in Hindi, one wonders what happened to the stream of 'parallel cinema' that characterized many movies made in the 1970s and early 1980s. Those were the days when you could see directors such as Shyam Benegal, Sai

Paranjpe, Aparna Sen, Basu Chatterjee, Basu Bhatacharya, Gulzar, Saeed Mirza, Ketan Mehta, and the likes of them raising pertinent socio-political issues, capturing realities in an intense, artistic manner, and attempting to redefine the codes and ethos that always torment the creative souls. In retrospect, they seemed much like a ruthless continuation of cinema as a means of expression of self-conceived reality and propagation of ideas, an experiment that was almost poetically presented in the 1950s and 60s by movie makers such as Bimal Roy, Hrishikesh Mukherjee, Gurudutt, Mehboob, K. Asif, and Raj Kapoor.

(ix) Whether humanity would survive global warming or not is only a matter of speculation for us. The depleting water resources, the rising temperature, the melting glaciers and strange climatic phenomena recorded in the last couple of decades, however, does not augur well. Besides, the burgeoning population, the staggering amount of inventions, and growing consumerism have only been adding many more twists and turns to the plot that now looks increasingly tragic. Of course, predictions have always been made about the catastrophe striking us, and since most of these have not materialized, we tend to believe that what is doing rounds in the media is just an unfounded and exaggerated projection of the whole situation. We may choose the position we may like to but we must know that though ignoring a rumour is judicious, ignoring reality is no wisdom.

(x) One of the toughest things to do today is to be a child. These days, children are expected to be mature, disciplined, focused, sensible, assiduous, competitive, and above all successful. So, they are supposed to be all, but not a child. Childhood today is devoid of innocence; they cannot expose their ignorance in the quizzes they have to participate in. They cannot score poor marks in exams because they were charmed by a particular sport and followed it both in their congested streets and on a television screen. Whether willing or not, they all have to live up to one single dream of their parents—they have to be successful. One really wonders what has happened to all our intelligence. By making a child chase his tail in a rat race, we are hardly making him successful. Though in an effort to do so, we ourselves are being hopelessly petulant and childish.

8. Read the following long passages and write a précis for each of them. Also assign a suitable title to every passage and write the number of words you have used in making a précis of the original:

Passage I

There was much coughing breathlessness and vomiting on the part of the Sri Lankan cricketers during a recent cricket match played in Delhi—the beautiful Indian capital with a hard to match Air Quality Index (AQI). I fail to understand why the Sri Lankans were bent on embarrassing themselves by creating such drama around their so called 'difficulty in breathing', or was the embarrassment directed towards the host. Really! Did they think that their mask wearing and this very public display of uneasiness would embarrass us? Do they not know that it's very hard to put Indians in a self-conscious position? Is it not known to them that Indians prefer to embrace their uniqueness than be embarrassed by it?

The Sri Lankans' ancestors have borne witness to our victory over them twice—once to Rajendra Chola, the great Indian emperor of whose kingdom was Sri Lanka an integral part and once to Lord Rama. Trying to embarrass us publicly by performing such acts isn't going to cut the mark.

I know what you are thinking—but Delhi's air is bad, haven't you read. I have read and I would like to clear the air here by saying that I am not going to apologize for Delhi's air quality. I would rather wear it as a badge of honour of our burgeoning economic growth, which mind you went back to being a glorious 6.3% some time back. So no Sir (or Madam or others—choose whichever label you like), but I am not embarrassed by Delhi's plunging to the depth of darkness AQI because I have already said—we Indians are hard to embarrass. Moreover, this is not something to brush under the carpet. Can't you see the benefit of this smog! This smog is what makes us adaptable and confident to breathe in air of any quality anywhere in the world, irrespective of whether it is polluted or clean.

Yes, when the AQI is in double digits, it does cause some discomfort. But really, it was pretty much Bradmanesque when the AQI hit 350 during the last Delhi winter. The more the double digits, the more confident your lungs are. In fact, it is in cities like Helsinki with outrageous AQI of 10, that your lungs will feel less than normal. Once I too had the misfortune of visiting Helsinki and I couldn't take it.

The moment I landed, the lightness of the air and the lack of any particulate matter made me breathless and I began to vomit right then and there. It was only when the authorities took me to the especially designed gas chamber connected to the chimney of a petrochemical factory that I began to feel normal. The doctors told me that my lungs could not register the air due to its foreign nature of being light and clean, which lead to the breathlessness. Only after staying in the chamber for a couple of hours did I start to feel normal again and could continue with my journey. Fun fact—did you know that such gas chambers were especially designed for travellers from Delhi; and you say the world doesn't treat us right.

But all this was a while back, today the world is aware that the Earth's air quality is inversely proportional to India and China's economic growth. As both the heftily growing economies move closer towards their target of 14% growth rates, we know that the planet would soon be rid of Helsinkiesque air. And this is not a bad thing.

(No. of Words: 587)

Passage II

If earth is struck by a catastrophic event of the same proportions as the asteroid that wiped out dinosaurs approximately 66 million years ago, the highest chance for survival of human life might be on another planet. Mars, in spite of its present hostile environment, is a lot similar to Earth. It is conceivably the most worthwhile candidate for terraformation and eventual human colonization. Terraformation of Mars is not a simple task. It's a long-term, gigantic engineering project that can take over a 1,000 or more years to be completed. What is the benefit here? A new home for us! It's a backup home for the blunders we've made on Earth.

Futurism prepared an infographic that provides a reasonably practical guide for the terraformation of Mars in four phases: Warming, Watering, Fertilizing and Populating. Although the task is supposedly doable, there are several challenges, including the cost (trillions of dollars), protection from cosmic rays (on Mars and while travelling to the planet), limited gravity on the planet, a thin atmosphere, and the absence of a magnetosphere and active plate tectonics. Additionally, is it justified to alter a planet biologically? Do we have the authority to do this? Which countries can be included in the mission? And would they be able to combine their efforts amicably? How would 'countries' be defined and managed on Mars?

Perhaps Mars is our best option but we shouldn't underestimate Saturn's icy moon, Enceladus, or its biggest moon, Titan. We can also think about Jupiter's moons—Europa and Ganymede. Despite the location, terraforming a far-off planet or moon would possibly follow a similar phased approach.

Due to its likenesses to earth, many researchers believe that Mars is a possible candidate for terraformation. We know that the planet lies within the habitable zone. So how can we make it habitable? It is a 1000+ year planetary engineering venture.

We'd start by exploding thermonuclear weapons over the planet's polar ice caps. This would help release carbon dioxide trapped inside the dry ice

on the surface. The resulting greenhouse effect would thicken the atmosphere slowly. Incoming solar rays would get trapped and heat the planet.

Firstly, we would need to mount enormous orbital mirrors to focus sunlight over the permafrost on the surface of Mars. Planetary seas would start forming as the melted water accumulates. As an outcome of the efforts to create an atmosphere, rainwater would fall from the sky. Icy asteroids would melt on impact if they are redirected towards the planet's surface.

Genetically-engineered organisms such as algae, bacteria and plants would be developed on earth and deployed to Mars to form organic soil and release oxygen. We could also plant fruits, vegetables and grains once oxygen levels are regulated.

The first set of residents would be robots. The idea would be to prepare Mars for human life. Automated 3D printers would be used to build houses and other structures using surface materials. Humans would arrive only after the basic infrastructure is set up. A genetically diverse population of 10,000+ would be required to moderate the threat of plagues and diseases.

It will be tough to sustain an atmosphere and ozone layer, which protects life from harmful solar radiation, due to the lack of magnetosphere. The nonexistence of plate tectonics on Mars would make it extremely problematic to introduce and isolate the proper mixture of greenhouse gases that human life needs to stay alive. Lower gravity would lead to higher health risks such as bone demineralization, muscle atrophy and immune system defects in people.

Once the terraformation commences, it would take hundreds of years before the planet becomes hospitable where habitants wouldn't need to wear shielding suits or oxygen masks. Several to and fro trips and trillions of dollars would be required to transport people and supplies. People would live in a dome at first, but over the time Mars could be terraformed to function like Earth, and we would be able to walk around outside without any protective gear. All in all, Mars is a fixer-upper of a home.

(No. of Words: 673)

9

UNIT III: LISTENING SKILLS

LISTENING SKILLS AND COMPREHENSION

LEARNING OBJECTIVES

After reading this chapter, you will be able to understand
- differences between poor and effective listening
- disadvantages of poor listening and advantages of effective listening
- different types of listening
- barriers to effective listening
- five important steps to active listening
- techniques for effective listening

Manish Duggal, Saavi Jain, and Saurabh Mishra went to attend a session on Effective Blog Writing conducted by Anna Rutherford of *Blogoworld*, New Delhi. Take a look at how each of them felt about the session afterwards:

Saavi: 'I really liked the session today. It was so informative, wasn't it?'

Saurabh: 'Really? Well ... I didn't listen to what she was saying ... I kept wondering how come she, despite being a Swiss, has a company in India.'

Saavi: 'So more than the topic of discussion, you were more interested in exploring the *whys* and *hows* of her choices!'

Saurabh: 'Sort of ... you know I kept thinking ... if a Swiss can start a company in India, why can't an Indian start a company in Switzerland!'

Manish: 'You incorrigible entrepreneur in the making! Always obsessed with settling abroad!'

Saavi: 'Quite right Manish ... he is always lost in such reveries! Anyway, I hope you too enjoyed the talk, right Manish?

Manish: 'I am afraid I too didn't pay attention to what she was saying. To be frank with you, I found it trivial and boring.'

Saavi: 'Trivial and boring! Strange! But why?'

Manish: 'See, mostly she talked about things that we already know. So, there was hardly anything new or interesting. So, I dozed off while she was speaking.'

The above conversation clearly reveals that though all the three friends went to attend the same talk, their observations about it are not the same. It is so because only one of them paid attention to the speaker and listened carefully, while the other two just faked listening. This is a very common problem. Have you ever tried to find out why it is so?

Actually, listening is an everyday affair. Despite that, or probably owing to that, many of us shirk listening. And when we cannot avoid listening, we just fake listening while letting our mind wander anywhere else. That's how quite a few speakers find their listeners yawning, whispering, nudging each other, looking outside, or keeping a poker face.

Following are the reasons for listening to be regarded as a boring and avoidable activity:

9.1 WHY DO WE AVOID LISTENING?

- Human brain can process around 500–700 words per minute while a speaker does not normally speak more than 120–150 words per minute. A mind not engaged properly is likely to wander aimlessly.
- Despite the fact that listening is a very crucial language skill, we get little or no training in developing effective listening techniques.
- Listening is usually taken for granted. It is presumed that by making a child sit while being spoken to, we can also make him/her listen. Forced into listening, the child sits, but does not listen to the teacher or the parent.
- By virtue of its being used as a forced exercise, listening is often regarded as an unpleasant task. Faulty school system in which a child is forced to listen to lessons after lessons creates aversion to listening.

Thus, in the name of *listening,* what people do most of the time is *hearing.* All of this leads to poor listening habits. Poor listening is fraught with many disadvantages both at the professional and the personal fronts. Some of these are mentioned below:

9.2 DISADVANTAGES OF POOR LISTENING

- Leads to poor comprehension of facts, situations, and people.
- Leads to poor speaking ability.
- Results in loss of relationships.
- Results in loss of trust and credibility.
- Establishes one's lack of commitment to discussion.
- Keeps one in darkness about others.
- Leads to parochial vision.
- Keeps one's growth stunted in professional and personal life.

Though poor listening habits are widespread, it is not easy to detect them. Therefore, for becoming a good listener, let us identify how poor listening differs from effective listening:

9.3 POOR LISTENING VS EFFECTIVE LISTENING

The major differences between a poor listener and an effective listener are as follows:

Poor Listener	Effective Listener
Either tries to blame the speaker or considers the subject to be dry.	Thinks and mentally summarizes; weighs the evidence; analyses and evaluates.
Gets distracted easily.	Fights against distractions and knows how to concentrate.

Poor Listener	Effective Listener
Finds it difficult to listen to complex material; has the tendency to read light and recreational materials.	Keeps listening on a regular basis; not averse to listening even if the task requires critical listening.
Tends to enter into unnecessary arguments.	Takes notes and organizes important information.
Jumps to pre-conceived notions about the ideas being conveyed.	Avoids pre-conceived notions. Critically evaluates the information being conveyed before drawing inferences.
Pays too much attention to appearance and delivery.	Pays proper attention to the body language, tone, and style, along with the message being conveyed by the speaker.
Waits for his/her turn to speak.	Patiently listens to the speaker and responds as and when required.

9.4 ADVANTAGES OF EFFECTIVE LISTENING

- Good listeners usually become effective speakers.
- Listening is a vital skill which helps in enhancing our learning. It increases knowledge, develops critical thinking, and broadens opportunities.
- Listening skills help us build effective relationships in our personal as well as professional life.
- Effective listening prevents miscommunication.
- It facilitates problem solving both in our personal life and at workplace.
- It helps in sharing emotions, ideas, and experiences.
- It also improves decision-making and critical thinking.

9.5 TYPES OF LISTENING

In order to hone our listening ability, it is advisable to know the different types of listening that we need to employ on different occasions.

Content/Informative listening In this type of listening, the primary focus is on understanding the message or information conveyed. We listen to reports, briefings, instructions, speeches, and conversations to obtain the desired information.

Empathetic/Therapeutic/Relationship listening Mostly used in times of crisis, this type of listening is employed while listening to someone's feelings of sorrows, regret, grief, and anguish. Besides being used in close circles, empathetic listening is employed in professional situations as well. Counsellors, doctors, psychiatrists, and good leaders use this type of listening in their professions.

Appreciative listening This type of listening is employed while listening to music or watching a movie or listening to a famous speech to draw pleasure from the melody, tone, cadence, and intensity employed by the singer/speaker.

Analytical listening The purpose of this type of listening is two-fold. On one hand, the listener tries to absorb the message and on the other, he/she attempts to analyse the ideas or facts and make critical judgements. In fact, this type of listening helps the listener evaluate the strength of argument, accuracy of evidence or facts, validity of inferences, and gaps in thinking. Thus, this kind of listening particularly helps in becoming a good professional.

9.6 BARRIERS TO EFFECTIVE LISTENING

We will discuss the various barriers that stop us from being good listeners. If you recognize that you have some/any of these problems, make an effort to overcome these barriers to listening:

Forged attention Compelled into listening at an early age, many of us become poor listeners. Such listeners pretend to listen; they sit through presentations, but let their minds wander anywhere.

Remedy Avoid fake listening, show genuine interest as each speaker teaches us something or the other.

Premature evaluation of the subject matter and speaker Evaluating someone's personality, knowledge, nature, or the subject being discussed often works as a strong barrier to effective listening.

Remedy Don't prejudge any person or topic on the basis of the speaker's personality, nation, race, or gender.

Poor interpersonal relations Human beings base their reactions on the type of relationship they have with the other person. Lack of trust in the speaker, or a sense of superiority or inferiority, prevents people from having proper involvement in the listening task.

Remedy Don't let your past impression of a person spoil your interpretation of his/her present message.

Overexcitement Whenever we listen to someone/something that we are ardently in love with or averse to, listening becomes biased. Admirers tend to over-idealize someone's virtuosity while critics tend to over-criticize the flaws of the speaker.

Remedy Listening requires focused, objective attention on the message being conveyed. Avoid letting your personal biases, likings, and dislikings mar your objective listening.

Different language variety and accent Listening to a different accent and language style may lead to lack of comprehension and it eventually turns the audience away from the message of the speech.

Remedy Try to get varied exposure into listening to speakers of different nations and accents, even with the help of available online material.

Distractions Some listeners have very poor concentration while listening. They actually get distracted even with the slightest sounds of opening and closing of doors, people whispering to each other, or vehicles outside.

Remedy As listeners, we should concentrate on the message rather than these distractions, as these are not under our control.

Evading the difficult types We usually listen to whatever is easy and familiar, and avoid whatever seems to be difficult and unfamiliar. Poor listeners become easy victims of this in classrooms, meetings, interviews, or group discussions.

Remedy Listen to all sorts of topics and all types of speakers. In order to help us achieve our goal, what we have to do is to train ourselves; and for that, we should be patient enough to listen to others.

Non-attentive state of mind The listener often fails to listen to the speaker's message because he/she is preoccupied with certain thoughts, or is tense or exhausted. He/she may be anxious or perturbed due to some reason.

Remedy This problem demands a readiness or willingness on the part of the listener for proper comprehension of the information being delivered.

Different levels of perception The speaker at times presumes that all his/her listeners have the same level of understanding that he/she enjoys. This leads to sharing of redundant or complex information.

Remedy If the message seems to be redundant, use it for extra knowledge and if the speaker is too obscure, make every effort to comprehend the content through the non-verbal and paralinguistic cues of his/her message.

9.7 FIVE STEPS TO ACTIVE LISTENING

Following are the five steps that will help us develop active listening skills:
- Grasp not only the content but also the other associated verbal, non-verbal, and paralinguistic cues.
- Constantly anticipate and summarize the speaker's ideas.
- Take down notes.
- Link what you are listening with what you already know.
- Ask and answer questions in your mind for clarity in your understanding of the subject of discussion.

9.8 TECHNIQUES FOR EFFECTIVE LISTENING

Following are the important techniques for effective listening:
- To improve your listening skills, you should have an open mind.
- You should sit alert and look at the speaker with a view to establishing your interest in him/her.
- The effectiveness of listening generally depends on the intensity of the interest taken. So, take interest in the discussion or talk.
- Do not prejudge the speaker or his/her message, until you have listened to it completely.
- Employ your critical thinking while you are listening.
- Stop talking and do not interrupt the speaker unnecessarily.
- Observe the non-verbal clues of the speaker, as this will enable you to grasp the message completely.
- Take advantage of the *lag time* that we get in terms of small pauses in between the different thought processes.
- Ask relevant questions to yourself, so that you remain on track with the ideas presented by the speaker.
- Take down notes or paraphrase the message in simple words. This will certainly enable you to grasp it quicker.

9.9 PRACTISING LISTENING ACTIVITIES

The listening activities provided here offer a wide range of listening practices. They cover a variety of formal and informal styles of language, from speeches, interviews, and presentations to conversations. The passages are of varying lengths, so as to train you in the listening of different types of conversations, talks, and lectures.

Instruction to Teachers

Please read out to students the following extracts, speeches, and passages and then ask them to answer the questions that follow.

EXERCISE 9.1

Your teacher will read out the following passage, which is an extract from a speech. Listen very carefully and answer the questions that follow:

That evening, when I stood in front of the mirror, I could see the meaning of the smirk on his face for me. Without saying much, he just had gestured me to roll up my pants upto the knees. When I obeyed, a twisted smirk displayed on his lips that had turned swarthy—probably with years into smoking. With cold stern look in his eyes, his message was loud and clear, 'You want to scale Rocky Zeniths? With this prosthetic leg?' Ladies and Gentlemen, these were the words that pierced through my heart and filled me with deepest sorrows. Back home that evening, taking a compulsive look into the mirror, tears initially had filled my eyes, but then it was the same evening when I had taken a resolve to prove Mr Mattoo wrong

Tick the most suitable choice in the following questions:

1. The speech seems to have been delivered by a/an _____.
   (a) Doctor
   (b) Engineer
   (c) Teacher
   (d) Mountaineer

2. *Rocky Zeniths* seems to refer to some
   (a) Water bodies
   (b) Mountain ranges
   (c) Dark forest
   (d) Verdant valleys

3. The purpose of the speech seems to be to
   (a) Inform the audience
   (b) Highlight how callous Mr Mattoo was
   (c) Arouse their sympathy for him/her
   (d) Inspire the audience

4. Which of the following is the appropriate replacement for the word *swarthy* as used in the speech?
   (a) Rosy   (b) Blue
   (c) Dark   (d) Red

5. The above description helps us figure out that Mr Mattoo was a
   (a) Film director
   (b) Mountaineering coach
   (c) Army officer
   (d) Government official

EXERCISE 9.2

Listen carefully to the small conversations below and answer the questions that follow:

1. Varsha: How can you leave your room like that all the time? Do you think your mother is sitting here to do all the cleaning and mopping for you?

   Ashima: Why are you raising your voice that much? After all, I too do so many things for you!

Question: What do you infer from Ashima's response?

(a) She is really apologetic about her habits.

(b) She is carefree but wants to learn from her mistakes.

(c) She is careless and doesn't want to improve.

(d) She is selfish and self-centred.

2. Boss: Chetana, can you look into the matter and submit your report by April end?

   Chetana: I can of course try, Ma'am. However, in that case, I would like you to guide me about how to manage the Soft Skills Training Programme.

   Question: From Chetana's response it becomes apparent that

   (a) Chetana holds a managerial position in the company and is supervising some soft skills development programme.

   (b) Chetana is a newcomer and is undergoing some soft skills development programme.

   (c) Chetana is a work shirker and is looking for an excuse.

   (d) Chetana is a workaholic and looks forward to taking up new challenges.

3. Reporter: Captain, your fans now have a feeling that your chances of winning the World Cup are almost negligible. With one more loss, you are out of the championship.

   Captain: You are right, that's a tough situation to be in. Having said that, I would also like to add that no one knows about the future. So, let's see what happens in the next game.

   Question: From the captain's answer, we can infer that

   (a) He/She is very optimistic and is likely to inspire his/her team to a win in the next match.

   (b) He/She is rather despaired with the team's poor run in the tournament and does not see it winning the championship.

(c) He/She is somewhat unsure about his/her team's chances of winning the next match.

(d) He/She is wise enough not to predict the future.

4. Interviewer: What do you know about our organization?

   Interviewee: Your organization, Ma'am? I think it somewhat deals with developing some software in the education field.

   Question: From the candidate's answer, it can be inferred that

   (a) He/She doesn't seem to have prepared well for the interview.

   (b) He/She seems to be prepared for the questions he/she is likely to face during an interview.

   (c) He/She is likely to leave a positive impression on the interviewer.

   (d) He/She is keen to join the company.

5. At a Group Discussion:

   Participant 1: I think not corruption, but population is India's greatest problem. If we take care of our population, we can deal with every other problem in the country.

   Participant 2: Oh, come on! I think population is just a lame excuse; can't you see how China has become a great country with more population than us. So, Mr ... if they can grow, we too can!

   Question: From Participant 2's answer it can be inferred that he/she is

   (a) Courteous and accommodates others' views.

   (b) Boorish and dismissive of other's view.

   (c) Knowledgeable and well read.

   (d) Aware of what's happening in other countries.

EXERCISE 9.3

Listen carefully to Robert Waldinger's ted talks on 'What Makes a Good Life? Lessons from the Longest Study on Happiness' and then answer the questions given below. Follow the link to facilitate the action: https://www.ted.com/.../robert_waldinger_what_makes_a_good_life_lessons_from_the_longest_study_on_happiness

1. According to the speaker, _____ people consider richness to be the goal of their life?

2. The speaker says that he is the _____ director of the agency conducting the research.

3. The subjects of the study were divided in which of the following two groups?
   (a) Army people and college girls
   (b) Second year college students and boys from disadvantaged families in Boston
   (c) 724 ninety-year-old men and young boys
   (d) Old women and children from California

4. By saying that memory can be *downright creative*, the speaker intends to suggest which of the following?
   (a) Memory can serve as a means to conduct data for research.
   (b) It can effectively contribute to the research.
   (c) It can give an imaginative and unreal picture of facts.
   (d) It can make facts look interesting and more useful.

5. What does the speaker say is the finding of the study?
   _____
   _____
   _____
   _____

6. What type of people are healthier and happier?
   (a) People who work harder
   (b) People who have good close relationships

(c) People who are famous and rich
(d) People who have higher goals in life

7. Why does the speaker consider the experience of loneliness to be *toxic*?
   _____
   _____
   _____
   _____

8. How does the author consider relationships to be *messy* and *complicated*?
   _____
   _____
   _____
   _____
   _____

9. Which of the following authors does the speaker quote at the end of his speech?
   (a) William Shakespeare
   (b) Mark Twain
   (c) Charles Dickens
   (d) Bertrand Russell

10. What according to the speaker takes a toll on the health of the people and why?
    _____
    _____
    _____
    _____

EXERCISE 9.4

Listen to Muniba Mazari's speech on 'Why am I Even Alive?' and answer the questions given below. Follow the link to facilitate the action: https://www.youtube.com/watch?v=LIF5BnugxYM

1. At the beginning of her speech, the speaker begins with a disclaimer. Which of the following is that disclaimer?
   (a) That she is not a great speaker
   (b) That she is not a story teller
   (c) That she is not a motivated speaker
   (d) That she is not a motivational speaker

2. According to the speaker, real happiness lies in
   (a) Inner peace
   (b) Gratitude
   (c) Following your intuition
   (d) Making good relations in life

3. After how many years of her marriage did the speaker meet with the car accident?
   (a) 9 years
   (b) 3 years
   (c) 2 years
   (d) 1 year

4. Which, according to the speaker, is not a common fear?
   (a) Fear of dying
   (b) Fear of losing people
   (c) Fear of the unknown
   (d) Fear of the known

5. What according to the speaker was her greatest fear? How did she overcome it?

   _____

   _____

   _____

   _____

6. 'These scars are my medals, and I wear them with pride.' This refers to whom in the speech:

   (a) Walid Khan
   (b) Wahid Khan
   (c) The speaker herself
   (d) A little child in Peshawar Army School

7. According to the speech, who helps the speaker realize that *her glass was not half empty but half full?*
   (a) Her mother
   (b) Her proctor in her school
   (c) Her son
   (d) Her husband

8. Why does the speaker say that failure should be an option in life?

   _____

   _____

   _____

   _____

   _____

9. Which of the following is not the reason for the speaker not joining the polio campaign?
   (a) The speaker's contempt in being treated with pity and sympathy
   (b) The speaker's lack of trust in such campaign
   (c) The speaker's preference for privacy
   (d) The speaker's preference for being a public figure

10. Towards the end of her speech, the speaker says that

    We all are _____ and that is _____.

ANSWER KEY

Exercise 9.1

1. d   **2.** b   **3.** d   **4.** c   **5.** b

Exercise 9.2

1. c   **2.** a   **3.** c   **4.** a   **5.** b

Exercise 9.3

1. over 80% of the

2. fourth

3. b

4. c

5. According to the speaker, the findings of the study are: good relationships keep us healthier and happier; social connections are really good for human beings as people who stay connected with their families, friends, and communities are happy and physically strong and that loneliness kills us.

6. b

7. The speaker considers loneliness to be toxic because lonely people are less happier and furthermore, the functioning of their brain deteriorates faster. Due to this, their health declines in early mid life itself and they live shorter lives.

8. The speaker considers relationships to be messy and complicated because the hard work of tending to families and friends is not only unattractive but also never ending.

9. b

10. The speaker says that family feuds, bickering, and grudges take a terrible toll on people's lives.

Exercise 9.4

1. d

2. b

3. c

4. a

5. The speaker's biggest fear was the fear of being divorced. She overcame it by recognizing it and—in her own words—by liberating herself, by letting her husband free, and by becoming mentally and emotionally strong.

6. a

7. c

8. The speaker says that failure should be an option in life because when we fail, we get an opportunity to confront the situation and overcome the challenges. By failing and getting up to fight out the situations, we become stronger in life.

9. c

10. perfectly imperfect; all right.

10

EFFECTIVE READING AND COMPREHENSION SKILLS

LEARNING OBJECTIVES

After reading this chapter, you will be able to understand
- need for developing efficient reading skills
- benefits of effective reading
- differences between effective and ineffective readers
- basic steps to effective reading
- different types of questions in reading comprehension passages
- tips on improving reading comprehension skills
- obstacles in becoming effective readers

Of all the language skills namely listening, reading, speaking, and writing, it is the reading skill that is most crucial and significant. It is so because by being a good reader, one can overcome the lack of listening and speaking opportunities. A good reader, therefore, is likely to become a good speaker and writer with passage of time. Moreover, with great deal of emphasis on reading comprehension skills in hosts of competitive exams in the country, it becomes imperative on our part to pay attention to developing effective reading comprehension skills.

10.1 NEED FOR DEVELOPING EFFICIENT READING SKILLS

You definitely know how to read. But the question is whether you know how to read skilfully and artfully. Skilful reading is reading for specific information for a better learning experience in a short span of time. Though complex, skilled reading is not difficult. It is an art which can be learnt easily by using a systematic approach and by undergoing formal training. This chapter will help you in learning this art. You will surely be able to know how to use diverse ways so that you can enhance your effectiveness and make your future reading experience more rewarding and enriching.

Have you ever noticed that we do not approach a novel, or a report, or a personal letter, or an email in a similar manner? In fact, the truth is that while reading, you employ different reading speeds and different approaches to them. However, it is also true that different people have varied speeds of reading and understanding. So, as a student, who has to read much for academic pursuance, and as a future professional, there is a dire need to learn the skills and techniques of artful reading. Before we talk about these techniques and types, let us know the major benefits that you may achieve by developing the art of efficient and artful reading.

10.2 BENEFITS OF EFFECTIVE READING

Here are the benefits of effective reading:
- Effective reading can provide you with a 'comprehensible input' from the book or document that you read.
- It can enhance your general ability to use other language skills such as listening, speaking, and writing.
- It can enhance your vocabulary, that is, you can always learn new words, phrases, and expressions.

- Effective reading also helps you keep your mind focused on the material and prevents it from unnecessary distractions.
- Moreover, this enables you to extract useful information much more efficiently within a limited time.
- It can help you consolidate both previously learned language and knowledge.
- It helps in building confidence as you start reading longer, and later, voluminous texts.
- It gives you pleasure and relaxation as books are the best and most reliable friends.
- Effective reading facilitates the development of various other skills, such as making predictions, comparing and contrasting facts, creating samples, hypothesizing, reorganizing the message as transmitted by the text, improving your critical thinking, and hence developing a sharp acumen with passage of time.

10.3 DIFFERENCES BETWEEN EFFICIENT AND INEFFICIENT READERS

The following table helps you understand the differences between efficient and inefficient readers:

An Efficient Reader	An Inefficient Reader
Always reads for ideas or information	Tries to read words
Reads group of words/multi-phrases	Reads word by word
Quickly adjusts his/her speed of reading to the nature of the text	Reads the text from the beginning till the end
Sets the purpose of reading right in the beginning	Reads everything and deliberately goes slow while reading
Reads smoothly	Reads the information again and again to figure out a clear understanding of the text
Visualizes ideas	Vocalizes or sub-vocalizes words while reading
Has a good vocabulary in that subject	Has limited vocabulary which hampers his/her speed and understanding
Continuously keeps improving his/her pace of reading	Rarely attempts speed reading
Properly tries to sort out the material as critical, interesting, analytical, etc.	Reads everything indiscriminately

10.4 FOUR BASIC STEPS TO EFFECTIVE READING

While reading a text to learn something, you need to follow the following four basic steps:

- *Figure out the purpose for reading a particular text.* You can identify suitable reading strategies and use your background knowledge of the topic in order to anticipate the contents.
- *Spot the parts of the text relevant to the identified purpose and ignore the rest.* This selectivity enables you to focus on particular elements of information from the text. So, you are able to sift the information, which in turn reduces the amount of information you have to hold in short-term memory.
- *Choose the appropriate reading strategy that suits your purpose.* Select the strategy that is suited to the reading task in that particular context and use that strategy in an interactive manner. This will develop your understanding as well as confidence.

- *Test or assess your comprehension during reading and also when the reading task is completed.* Monitoring comprehension helps you make out the inconsistencies and discrepancies in total comprehension of the text. At this step, you can also learn to use alternative strategies.

Given below are some of the strategies with which we can deal with reading comprehension passages more effectively.

10.5 GETTING ACQUAINTED WITH MAJOR TYPES OF QUESTIONS

Questions related to the main idea

- The passage is primarily concerned with...
- The author's primary purpose in this passage is to...
- Which of the following statements best expresses the main idea of the passage?

Questions related to specific details

- Which of the following statements is (are) best supported by the passage?
- Which of the following is NOT cited in the passage as an evidence of...

Inference-related questions

- Which of the following statements about ... can be inferred from the passage?
- The author in the passage implies that...
- It can be inferred from the passage that...

Application-related questions

- With which of the following statements would the author of the passage be most likely to agree?
- The author's argument would be most weakened by the discovery of which of the following?
- With which of the following statements is the author most likely to agree?
- With which of the following statements is the author most likely to disagree?

Questions related to tone/attitude/style

- The author's attitude towards the issue can be best described as...
- Which of the following best describes the author's tone in the passage?

Meaning-related questions

- The word ... as used in the passage, means...
- Which of the following is an antonym/synonym for the highlighted word in the passage?

10.6 TIPS TO IMPROVE READING COMPREHENSION SKILLS

- Locate the central idea.
- Carefully observe the common thread.
- Ask the pertinent question—Why this passage/poem?
- Look for the author's point of view, if any.
- Hunt for views and counter-views.

- Be mindful of linkers—*but, however, so,* etc.
- Read painstakingly the beginnings and endings of the passage.
- Read carefully the beginning and ending of each para/stanza.
- Never lose sight of the central idea.
- Figure out the nature of the passage/poem while reading.
- Pay attention to thoughts that follow linkers such as *but, however, hence, thus, nevertheless, though, yet, since, therefore, moreover, apart from, besides, in order to, so that, as, because, for, as far/long as, further, regarding, regardless of, with regard to, as regards, in fact, despite, in spite of, notwithstanding,* etc.
- Grasp and mark important elements.
- Relate significant statements.
- Get involved in the passage: try to anticipate the arguments/statements/events.
- Think simultaneously about the purpose/tone.
- Ask yourself: Does the author intend to explain/argue/describe/justify/contradict, etc.?
- Pay attention to connotative meaning too.
- Infer and analyse.
- See the passage/poem evolving.
- Interpret difficult expressions contextually.
- Read between and beyond the lines.
- Develop eye span.
- Think of a title and the summary of the passage.
- Observe and infer what the passage/poem implies.

10.7 STUMBLING BLOCKS IN BECOMING AN EFFECTIVE READER

- Lack of concentration
- Reading aloud
- Turning the head from side to side
- Moving the lips
- Pointing at words with pen or finger
- Eye fixation

- Regression
- Indiscriminate use of dictionary
- Lack of reading habits
- Disinterest
- Lack of concentration

EXERCISE 10.1

Going further, attempt the following passages/poems/speeches and answer the questions that follow each of them:

Passage I

One of the not so futile debates in modern society is whether *I create my destiny or my destiny creates me*. Many people believe that life moves according to a pre-ordained plan as all of us are regulated, governed, and controlled by some supreme power and authority that guides our entire course of life.

Therefore, whatever we witness, enjoy or suffer in life conducts itself on the missive of a design above us. Those with firm faith in such belief system suggest that humans cannot and do not have in them to make or mar their own destiny. They simply are the carriers of a divine order and whatever the supreme power intends them to do, they do. They often suggest that one should not worry, feel depressed, or experience frustration as whatever happens is already pre-determined and the only thing they can do is to carry out the divine wish to the best of their abilities and leave everything else to God.

Such people are sharply criticized for their 'passive' or 'fatalistic' approach to life by the other lot that gives humans greater authority and power to decide their fate. They firmly believe that human beings can change their destiny by positive thinking and powerful actions. The number of believers in such notion is growing day by day. All over the world, therefore, there has been a staggering spurt of books, discourses, seminars, speeches, debates on such subjects in the last couple of decades. The stakeholders of such perception firmly trace back all the patterns and events of our life to our thoughts. They believe that thoughts trigger actions and actions sculpt destiny. So, if the quality of thought is poor, negative, or bad, so will be the ensuing action and equally frustrating will be the experiences, incidents, and events that unfold in our life. Interestingly, as our society becomes increasingly complex, the number of believers in such ideology is growing manifold. Notwithstanding the outcome of such debates, we stand poised to gain from both the perspectives. If we choose to follow the first, we can lead a fearless, peaceful, and quiet life of contentment while if we go by the other, we can create in us a powerful fusion of positive thoughts and rightful actions and can rewrite our destinies despite all the odds, upheavals, and challenges of life.

Questions

1. The author of the passage seems to believe that our society is becoming
   (a) Increasingly debatable
   (b) Spiritually enlightened
   (c) Aggressively contentious
   (d) Increasingly complex

2. Which of the following seems to be the central idea of the passage?
   (a) The debate between the believers and non-believers is too complicated to resolve
   (b) Humans have in them the capacity to use both approaches to their advantage
   (c) Leading a life of passion, positive thinking, and rightful action is very important
   (d) One should not strive hard in life and can lead a life of contentment and quiet satisfaction

3. The tone of this passage is
   (a) Analytical   (b) Informative
   (c) Contentious   (d) Critical

4. Towards the end of the passage, the author uses the phrase 'the other' to refer to which of the following categories of people?
   (a) The one that sees the hand of God in everything that happens to us
   (b) The one that firmly believes in the power of positive thinking
   (c) The one that has the ability to understand the divine message
   (d) The one that does not have the ability to understand the divine message

5. The author of the passage does not seem to agree with which of the following statements?
   (a) The debate between destiny and human action is futile and endless
   (b) Positive approach can help us in all life situations
   (c) More than the debate, we must focus on gaining from both the approaches
   (d) Rightful actions often ensue from positive mental frame

Passage II

In India, women have traditionally been accused of being great gossip-mongers. The perceptions about *girls being chatty* all the time and *housewives hanging out of their balconies* to have a conversation with their neighbouring female-folk firmly remains etched in the perception of their male counterparts. Have we ever paused and questioned—what is the rationality behind such perception? Is there any evidence that establishes that because of their biological make-up, women have some sort of a larger tongue that makes them glib talkers? Are the boys studying in schools and colleges any less 'chatty' than the girls sitting beside them?

A feminist perspective on this issue helps us observe that all such images are created without much logic or rationality and seem to have been founded in a biased and discriminating male thought process. By labelling women as 'glib talkers' and 'chatter boxes', men in the society intend to keep women to a subordinated position. By suggesting that women can 'just talk', the patriarchal mind-set intends to keep them fastened to a less relevant role in the society. However, just as they have broken many such shackles, time is not far when women will be able to emancipate themselves from all such bigotry and ill-founded inferences. Though such archetypes are hard to do away with, a growing understanding of science and human psychology seems to reflect a glimmer of hope across this dark tunnel of discrimination and marginalization.

Questions

1. The above passage seems to be primarily concerned with the idea that
   (a) Women have the tendency to hang out of their balconies to just talk and gossip with their neighbours
   (b) Women have often been discriminated by their male counterparts
   (c) Patriarchy purposefully attempts to subordinate women by terming them as 'glib talkers'
   (d) Women have the tendency to be chatty and loquacious all the time

2. Which according to the passage is not the purpose of writing this passage?
   (a) It is by no means established that women talk more than men
   (b) That women talk more is an irrational and illogical belief system
   (c) There should be proper research to establish that women are by nature talkative and garrulous
   (d) Patriarchal mind-set intends to keep women fastened to a less important role by suggesting that they can just talk and do nothing much

3. What according to the author is the ill-founded inference of the society?
   (a) Women have the tendency to speak more than men
   (b) College girls are chatty while housewives are glib talkers
   (c) Women get subordinated when their male counterparts term them as 'chatter boxes'
   (d) Patriarchy will be reinforced if women are seen as talkative individuals

4. The tone of the passage seems to be
   (a) Acrimonious   (b) Censorious
   (c) Critical   (d) Satirical

5. The author ends this passage on a note of
   (a) Criticism   (b) Humour
   (c) Despair   (d) Optimism

Passage III

It gives me immense pleasure that I stand here before you to share my views on this significant day. At the outset, I congratulate you in having chosen a profession which is noble in its pursuit and sublime in its vision. It is teaching that not only changes the life of those who take it up but also the lives of thousands of their students and hence that of a nation. It is so because in changing the lives of students, a teacher does in fact help in changing the life of a nation. It is he who—through his students—brings about the most fundamental changes in the overall tapestry of the surroundings around him.

Further, I feel that despite all the changes in society, the teacher does hold the same pivotal place even today. And I do believe that all of you sitting here are capable of being the torchbearer, the flame with which thousands of other similar flames can be ignited. Despite all this, when I speak these words, I understand that some of you may not agree to such views. It is so because a teacher today does not feel comfortable while listening to such seemingly utopian ideas. He fails to align to such romantic notions that he is the harbinger of any change. Though he really still is—and would remain forever that—he does not view it as a necessary reason for him to have chosen this profession.

It is so because the phenomenal changes around us are making us feel more like a trainer than being a teacher—somebody whom the world knows as a guru—the eternal guide, philosopher, and source of inspiration for his disciple. The rapid commercialization of education has brought about many transformations in the sphere of education and one of the major changes that we witness today is the transformed relationship between the teacher and the taught. For a majority of our students we are now just a resource and a trainer. So, most of us don't not feel the honour and dignity that had traditionally been the hallmark of the teaching profession.

Despite all this, all is not lost to us. In the vast expanse of our society it is still the teacher who to them is the torchbearer of new directions, hopes, and vision. Therefore, Ladies and Gentlemen, do not feel disheartened by the lack of aptitude in your students or too much of attitude of your bosses. Take pride in being a teacher for it is the teacher to whom the entire society looks up. So my dear friends, let's continue to be worthy recipients of such honour with our dedication and commitment to our profession.

Questions

1. The main purpose of this passage is to highlight that
   (a) Teaching is a noble profession but teachers find themselves helpless in present circumstances
   (b) Teachers need to continue doing their work honestly despite the changing around them
   (c) Teachers today are no longer gurus but are only trainers and they should accept this change
   (d) Teachers today do not wish to be seen as living some idealistic life

2. According to the passage, which of the following can be attributed for the change of the teacher's role in society?
   (a) Commercialization of education
   (b) Excessive greed of teachers
   (c) Aptitude of students
   (d) Intervention of technology in the classroom

3. The above passage seems to have been extracted from a/an
   (a) Newspaper article
   (b) Research paper
   (c) Speech
   (d) Editorial in the newspaper

4. The author/speaker of the passage seems to agree to all except that
   (a) Teachers play a crucial role in changing the lives of their teachers
   (b) Teachers are still the torchbearers of change in the society
   (c) The relationship between the teacher and the taught has changed substantially
   (d) Honour and dignity are no longer associated with the teaching profession

5. The passage ends on a note of
   (a) Caution   (b) Inspiration
   (c) Sarcasm   (d) Didacticism

Passage IV

Is playing sports a purely physical aspect of life? Has it something to do with our intellectual pursuits or spiritual drives? Conventionally speaking, sports are primarily required to keep our body fit, muscles strong, and our human frame slim. Therefore, associating any intellectual or spiritual pursuit hidden in a sporting endeavour seems to be too far-fetched and idealistic.

A deeper look into the numerous advantages of sports helps us see their role far beyond physical boundaries. Of course sports keep us fit but not just that. They do much more for us. Playing sports on a regular basis helps us feel light not just in body also in mind. It helps us improve our focus and concentration. Since while playing we need to be competitive, it renews and reinforces our strength to confront the challenges of life. Hence, indulging in a sporting feast on a regular basis gives us mental toughness and endows in us a spirit of courage. Not only that, the need to remain focused on a task while playing makes us stick to the present. Therefore, the regret of our past actions and worry about future challenges do not normally bother a sportsperson. While playing, one develops a meditative state of mind which keeps us stable, strong, and satisfied with whatever we have achieved in life.

Therefore, viewing sports only as a physical activity is just suggestive of our limited understanding of their relevance in our life. In fact, in an age characterized by competitiveness, anxiety, and loneliness sports acquire monumental significance as they keep our spirits soaring and soul replenished with zeal, enthusiasm, positivity, and equilibrium. If such are not the pursuits of our intellectual and spiritual drives, what are they?

Questions

1. The main idea in the passage is to establish that
   (a) Associating any intellectual or spiritual pursuit with sports is far-fetched

   (b) More research needs to be done to establish a greater role of sports in human life

   (c) Playing sports gives us mental equilibrium that we intend to attain through intellectual and spiritual pursuits

   (d) Since playing sports is to be in the company of others, it does not let us feel our loneliness

2. The purpose of this passage is to
   (a) Suggest that without sports life is incomplete and worthless

   (b) Establish that besides physical advantages, sports can give us intellectual and spiritual nourishment as well

   (c) State facts to highlight that a sporting activity is better than intellectual and spiritual drives of human beings

   (d) Establish that if you keep playing sports, you will never regret your past actions

3. The tone of this passage is
   (a) Argumentative   (b) Informative
   (c) Sarcastic   (d) Matter of fact

4. By putting questions in the beginning, the author of the passage intends to
   (a) Highlight how sports are more advantageous to human beings than their intellectual pursuits

   (b) Question the relevance of sports in our life

   (c) Provide a counter-narrative highlighting the enormous benefits of sports in our life

   (d) Contradict a conventional opinion that sports have unlimited value in our life

5. The author of the passage does not seem to agree with which of the following?
   (a) A complex and competitive age such as ours needs a sporting activity rather than a spiritual drive

   (b) Sports endow in us courage and a spirit of enthusiasm

   (c) Sports are capable of assigning to us a meditative state of mind

   (d) Sports help us focus on the present moment

Passage V

Despite all the improvement in the medical facilities in our country, the medical services and facilities are far from being satisfactory. It is due to an acute shortage of qualified doctors available to treat and operate the patients. The fact that our population is becoming manifold all the time does not mean that the number of doctors and specialists too is increasing. Just see how deplorable the medical statistics are. According to an estimate, there are only 2,000 cardiac surgeons, whereas the number of heart patients in the country is in millions. Similarly, while we need roughly 4 lakh gynaecologists and paediatricians, we just have around one lakh of them put together in the entire country.

Adding insult to injury, most of them live in cities and towns, whereas 60 per cent of children born in the country are in rural India. So, during pregnancy and after delivery, a large number of young mothers suffer from multiple complications which lead to the birth of unhealthy babies and deprives scores of young women in the country from staying healthy and contributing to the growth of the society.

Suffering endlessly due to ill health, ignorance, and shortage of medical care, these women often turn to superstitions and start drifting towards the quacks readily available in their vicinity. However, rather than helping them, these charlatans just exploit and misuse them. They often rob them of their money and jewellery and sometimes, even honour. Caught up in a vicious circle of wrong medication, ignorance superstitions, and exploitation hence, they are forced to lead a life of trauma, fear, and unhappiness. Now all this can stop provided we have the requisite number of qualified and trained doctors in the country and they are made to serve in the rural part of the country for a majority of their service time.

Questions

1. According to the passage, the medical facilities in the country are
   (a) Disastrous   (b) Disruptive
   (c) Deplorable   (d) Deprived

2. The word 'charlatan' seems to refer to
   (a) The babies who are not properly treated in their childhood
   (b) The fake doctors who give people wrong medication
   (c) The mothers who are ignorant
   (d) The doctors who live in cities and towns

3. With which of the following the author of the passage does not seem to agree?
   (a) Number of pediatricians in the rural areas is more than that of gynaecologists
   (b) Most of the doctors live in cities and towns
   (c) Lack of medical facilities often leads to poor physical as well mental health of the people
   (d) Lack of medical facilities in the rural areas leads to several physical and psychological health problems

4. The passage has been written to
   (a) Highlight how in rural India, women lead a life of suffering and trauma
   (b) Suggest why doctors do not wish to serve in villages
   (c) Reveal why superstitions and fears are widespread in rural India
   (d) Bring to the fore the poor medical conditions in the villages of our country

5. The tone of the passage is
   (a) Factual
   (b) Critical
   (c) Analytical
   (d) Informative

Passage VI

Rosemary Fell was not exactly beautiful. No, you couldn't have called her beautiful. Pretty? Well, if you took her to pieces ... But why be so cruel as to take anyone to pieces? She was young, brilliant, extremely modem, exquisitely well dressed, amazingly well read in the newest of the new books, and her parties were the most delicious mixture of the really important people and ... artists—quaint creatures, discoveries of hers, some of them too terrifying for words, but others quite presentable and amusing. Rosemary had been married two years. She had a duck of a boy. No, not Peter—Michael. And her husband absolutely adored her. They were rich, really rich, not just comfortably well off, which is odious and stuffy and sounds like one's grandparents. But if Rosemary wanted to shop she would go to Paris as you and I would go to Bond Street. If she wanted to buy flowers, the car pulled up at that perfect shop in Regent Street, and Rosemary inside the shop just gazed in her dazzled, rather exotic way, and said: 'I want those and those and those. Give me four bunches of those. And that jar of roses. Yes, I'll have all the roses in the jar. No, no lilac. I hate lilac. It's got no shape.' The attendant bowed and put the lilac out of sight, as though this was only too true; lilac was dreadfully shapeless. 'Give me those stumpy little tulips. Those red and white ones.' And she was followed to the car by a thin shop-girl staggering under an immense white paper armful that looked like a baby in long clothes ....

(From Katherine Mansfield's 'A Cup of Tea'.)

Questions

1. From the above passage, one can infer that Rosemary Fell was
   (a) Talkative   (b) Extravagant
   (c) Frugal   (d) Arrogant

2. By saying that Rosemary Fell 'had a duck of a boy', the author intends to convey that
   (a) The name of her husband was boy
   (b) The name of her son was duck

   (c) Her husband was dominated by her
   (d) Her husband was uncontrollable like a duck

3. By describing some of Rosemary's guests to be 'too terrifying for words', the author suggests that they were
   (a) Difficult to be described
   (b) Terrified by words
   (c) Too terrified to find right words
   (d) Too terrified of her richness

4. The above passage is _____ in nature. Fill in the blank with the appropriate option:
   (a) Critical   (b) Stylistic
   (c) Humorous   (d) Descriptive

5. With which of the following does the author not seem to agree?
   (a) Rosemary Fell was extremely rich
   (b) Rosemary was fond of shopping
   (c) Rosemary Fell expected her things to be carried to the car by others
   (d) She bought only a few, selected items whenever she shopped

Passage VII

All this while the storm increased, and the sea went very high, though nothing like what I have seen many times since; no, nor what I saw a few days after; but it was enough to affect me then, who was but a young sailor, and had never known anything of the matter. I expected every wave would have swallowed us up, and that every time the ship fell down, as I thought it did, in the trough or hollow of the sea, we should never rise more; in this agony of mind, I made many vows and resolutions that if it would please God to spare my life in this one voyage, if ever I got once my foot upon dry land again, I would go directly home to my father, and never set it into a ship again while I lived; that I would take his advice, and never run myself into such miseries as these any more. Now I saw plainly the goodness of his observations about the middle station of life, how easy, how comfortably he had lived all his days, and never had been exposed to tempests at sea or troubles on shore; and I resolved that I would, like a true repenting prodigal, go home to my father. These wise and sober thoughts continued all the while the storm lasted, and indeed some time after; but the next day the wind was abated, and the sea calmer, and I began to be a little inured to it; however, I was very grave for all that day, being also a little sea-sick still; but towards night the weather cleared up, the wind was quite over, and a charming fine evening followed; the sun went down perfectly clear, and rose so the next morning; and having little or no wind, and a smooth sea, the sun shining upon it, the sight was, as I thought, the most delightful that ever I saw.

(From Daniel Dafoe's 'Robinson Crusoe')

Questions

1. The above passage seems to have been taken from some
   (a) Suspense thriller
   (b) Political treatise
   (c) Comic piece of writing
   (d) Adventurous tale

2. The passage highlights that while recalling his father's advice the speaker feels
   (a) Repentance   (b) Rejoice
   (c) Retribution   (d) Rewarded

3. What does towards the end of the passage lead to a change in the thinking pattern of the speaker?
   (a) A metamorphosis of heart
   (b) Change in the climatic conditions
   (c) Goodness of his father's observations
   (d) Gravity of the situation

4. The passage has been written in which of the following styles?
   (a) Adventurous   (b) Humorous
   (c) Narrative   (d) Informative

5. With which of the following is the author least likely to agree?
   (a) Sea is full of adventures and lots of challenges
   (b) Weather, like human fate, is capricious and can change any time
   (c) Children often remember the counsel of their parents in times of adversities
   (d) Children should never venture out on their adventures without the company of their parents

Passage VIII

The postmaster first took up his duties in the village of Ulapur. Though the village was a small one, there was an indigo factory nearby, and the proprietor, an Englishman, had managed to get a post office established.

Our postmaster belonged to Calcutta. He felt like a fish out of water in this remote village. His office and living-room were in a dark thatched shed, not far from a green, slimy pond, surrounded on all sides by a dense growth.

The men employed in the indigo factory had no leisure; moreover, they were hardly desirable companions for decent folk. Nor is a Calcutta boy an adept in the art of associating with others. Among strangers he appears either proud or ill at ease. At any rate, the postmaster had but little company; nor had he much to do.

At times he tried his hand at writing a verse or two. That the movement of the leaves and the clouds of the sky were enough to fill life with joy—such were the sentiments to which he sought to give expression. But God knows that the poor fellow would have felt it as the gift of a new life, if some genie of the Arabian Nights had in one night swept away the trees, leaves and all, and replaced them with a macadamised road, hiding the clouds from view with rows of tall houses.

The postmaster's salary was small. He had to cook his own meals, which he used to share with Ratan, an orphan girl of the village, who did odd jobs for him.

When in the evening the smoke began to curl up from the village cowsheds, and the cicalas chirped in every bush; when the mendicants of the Baül sect sang their shrill songs in their daily meeting-place, when any poet, who had attempted to watch the movement of the leaves in the dense bamboo thickets, would have felt a ghostly shiver run down his back, the postmaster would light his little lamp, and call out 'Ratan'.

Ratan would sit outside waiting for this call, and, instead of coming in at once, would reply, 'Did you call me, sir?'

'What are you doing?' the postmaster would ask.

'I must be going to light the kitchen fire,' would be the answer.

And the postmaster would say: 'Oh, let the kitchen fire be for awhile; light me my pipe first.'

At last Ratan would enter, with puffed-out cheeks, vigorously blowing into a flame a live coal to light the tobacco. This would give the postmaster an opportunity of conversing. 'Well, Ratan,' perhaps he would begin, 'do you remember anything of your mother?' That was a fertile subject. Ratan partly remembered, and partly didn't. Her father had been fonder of her than her mother; him she recollected more vividly. He used to come home in the evening after his work, and one or two evenings stood out more clearly than others, like pictures in her memory. Ratan would sit on the floor near the postmaster's feet, as memories crowded in upon her. She called to mind a little brother that she had—and how on some bygone cloudy day she had played at fishing with him on the edge of the pond, with a twig for a make-believe fishing-rod. Such little incidents would drive out greater events from her mind. Thus, as they talked, it would often get very late, and the postmaster would feel too lazy to do any cooking at all. Ratan would then hastily light the fire, and toast some unleavened

bread, which, with the cold remnants of the morning meal, was enough for their supper.

On some evenings, seated at his desk in the corner of the big empty shed, the postmaster too would call up memories of his own home, of his mother and his sister, of those for whom in his exile his heart was sad,—memories which were always haunting him, but which he could not talk about with the men of the factory, though he found himself naturally recalling them aloud in the presence of the simple little girl. And so it came about that the girl would allude to his people as mother, brother, and sister, as if she had known them all her life. In fact, she had a complete picture of each one of them painted in her little heart.

(From Rabindranath Tagore's 'The Postmaster')

Questions

1. From the passage it can be inferred that Ratan was
   (a) A boy whose job was to guard the postmaster's house
   (b) A girl whose job was to serve in his post office
   (c) A girl whose job was to do household chores
   (d) A boy whose job was to cook food for the postmaster

2. It can be concluded from the passage that the roads in the village where the postmaster worked were
   (a) Fully macadamized and newly laid
   (b) Virtually non-existent
   (c) Inspirational for the postmaster to write verse on them
   (d) Miraculously produced by a genie

3. With which of the following does the author not seem to agree?
   (a) Ratan and the postmaster shared memories of the past

(b) Ratan was talkative and did not listen to the postmaster

(c) The postmaster felt lonely in the remote village and missed his family members

(d) Of both the parents, Ratan was more liked by her/his father

4. The above passage is written in which of the following styles?
   (a) Informative   (b) Interpretive
   (c) Satirical   (d) Narrative

5. With which of the following does the author seem to agree?
   (a) The mendicants of the Baul sect were melodious singers
   (b) Ratan never smoked in his hut
   (c) The postmaster looked forward to a chat with Ratan in the evenings
   (d) Young boys from Calcultta are very affable and can get along strangers easily

Passage IX

My Last Duchess

FERRARA

That's my last Duchess painted on the wall,
Looking as if she were alive. I call
That piece a wonder, now; Fra Pandolf's hands
Worked busily a day, and there she stands.
Will't please you sit and look at her? I said
'Fra Pandolf' by design, for never read
Strangers like you that pictured countenance,
The depth and passion of its earnest glance,
But to myself they turned (since none puts by
The curtain I have drawn for you, but I)
And seemed as they would ask me, if they durst,
How such a glance came there; so, not the first
Are you to turn and ask thus. Sir, 'twas not
Her husband's presence only, called that spot

Of joy into the Duchess' cheek; perhaps
Fra Pandolf chanced to say, 'Her mantle laps
Over my lady's wrist too much,' or 'Paint
Must never hope to reproduce the faint
Half-flush that dies along her throat.' Such stuff
Was courtesy, she thought, and cause enough
For calling up that spot of joy. She had
A heart—how shall I say?—too soon made glad,
Too easily impressed; she liked whate'er
She looked on, and her looks went everywhere.
Sir, 'twas all one! My favour at her breast,
The dropping of the daylight in the West,
The bough of cherries some officious fool
Broke in the orchard for her, the white mule
She rode with round the terrace—all and each
Would draw from her alike the approving speech,
Or blush, at least. She thanked men—good! but thanked
Somehow—I know not how—as if she ranked
My gift of a nine-hundred-years-old name
With anybody's gift. Who'd stoop to blame
This sort of trifling? Even had you skill
In speech—which I have not—to make your will
Quite clear to such an one, and say, 'Just this
Or that in you disgusts me; here you miss,
Or there exceed the mark'—and if she let
Herself be lessoned so, nor plainly set
Her wits to yours, forsooth, and made excuse—
E'en then would be some stooping; and I choose
Never to stoop. Oh, sir, she smiled, no doubt,
Whene'er I passed her; but who passed without
Much the same smile? This grew; I gave commands;
Then all smiles stopped together. There she stands
As if alive. Will't please you rise? We'll meet
The company below, then. I repeat,
The Count your master's known munificence

Is ample warrant that no just pretense
Of mine for dowry will be disallowed;
Though his fair daughter's self, as I avowed
At starting, is my object. Nay, we'll go
Together down, sir. Notice Neptune, though,
Taming a sea-horse, thought a rarity,
Which Claus of Innsbruck cast in bronze for me!

(From Robert Browning's 'My Last Duchess')

Questions

1. By reading the above poem it can be inferred that Fra Pandolf was a
   (a) Sculptor
   (b) Duchess's lover
   (c) Friend
   (d) Painter

2. The poem has been written to reveal
   (a) The speaker's character
   (b) The listener's character
   (c) The Duchess's character
   (d) Fra Pandolf's character

3. It can be inferred from the poem that
   (a) The Duke is kind and gentle
   (b) The Duchess is clever and crafty
   (c) The Duchess is promiscuous by nature
   (d) The Duke is diabolical and cruel

4. In saying that 'I gave commands; then all smiles stopped together,' the Duke seems to suggest that
   (a) He put his wife behind bars
   (b) He put his wife to death
   (c) He put his wife away from others
   (d) He put his wife in an asylum

5. With which of the following is the poet least likely to agree?
   (a) The Duke is greedy and keen to get married again
   (b) The Duke is haughty and arrogant
   (c) The Duke is hospitable and considerate
   (d) The Duke is dictatorial and ruthless by nature

ANSWER KEY

Exercise 10.1

Passage I

1. d   2. b   3. a   4. b   5. a

Passage II

1. c   2. c   3. a   4. c   5. d

Passage III

1. b   2. a   3. c   4. d   5. b

Passage IV

1. c   2. b   3. a   4. c   5. a

Passage V

1. c   2. b   3. a   4. d   5. c

Passage VI

1. b   2. c   3. a   4. d   5. d

Passage VII

1. d   2. a   3. b   4. c   5. d

Passage VIII

1. c   2. b   3. b   4. d   5. c

Passage IX

1. d   2. a   3. d   4. b   5. c

11

UNIT V: ORAL COMMUNICATION

PHONETICS AND SPOKEN ENGLISH

LEARNING OBJECTIVES

After reading this chapter, you will be able to understand
- various reasons for incorrect pronunciation
- standard variety of British, American, and Indian English
- how to correctly produce vowel and consonant sounds
- what a syllable is and how words are divided into different syllables
- rules of word stress and intonation in the English language
- use of contrastive stress in sentences

We are all aware that some speakers of the English language attract us with their good command of language. Among other things, it is their pronunciation that creates the right kind of impact on us as listeners. It is absolutely essential on the part of every speaker of English, as is the case with any other language, to speak with the right pronunciation. Since we are not native speakers of English, there exists a very serious problem with regard to the pronunciation of the Indian speaker's English.

Because of a variety of English spoken in different parts of the world, there is no purity of either language or pronunciation. Therefore, we often come across alternate pronunciations and mispronunciations. However, no matter how common the incorrect pronunciation is, you always need to strive to acquire correct pronunciation.

11.1 REASONS FOR INCORRECT PRONUNCIATION

Let us first understand the two major reasons which lead us to acquire incorrect pronunciation:

1. In a native/first language situation, from a very early stage children learn to respond to sounds and tones which their elders habitually use while talking to them. In due course, children start learning English in English speaking countries; they tend to speak in the mother tongue accent. But in our country, where English is used as a second language, children listen to wrong sounds and tones spoken by their teachers/grown ups in their environment and tend to pick up faulty pronunciation. This happens mainly due to their lack of sufficient exposure to the right variety of the language.

2. Moreover, we tend to speak English as we speak our mother tongue; therefore, we tend to commit mistakes due to its influence.

11.2 RECEIVED PRONUNCIATION (RP)

You must be wondering what standard English is, considering this language is spoken the world over. Your confusion is justified, as English is spoken as a first or second language by a very large number of people throughout the world. In some countries such as the UK, the USA, Canada, and Australia, English is the native or first language. In other countries such as India, Pakistan, Sri Lanka, Bangladesh, etc., English is spoken as a non-native or second language. As there is such a wide range of variation in pronunciation and accent, it is essential for us to follow a standard. One native regional accent that has gained social prestige is the Received Pronunciation of English (RP for short). It is the pronunciation of the people of south-east England and is used by educated English speakers. It is now equated with the correct pronunciation of English.

Before we start learning the sounds of English, let us first clear a great misconception that exists among us about the sounds of English.

11.3 MISCONCEPTION ABOUT SOUNDS

In our school days, we were told that there are twenty six sounds in the English language as there are twenty six letters in it. Even today, the same thing is being taught in a large number of schools. Because of this misconception, most of the Indian students fail to get acquainted with the right English pronunciation and accent. There are actually *forty four* sounds in the English language even though there are only twenty six letters in it.

For instance, pronounce the following words:

- Cat
- Keen

- Occasion
- Chemistry

What do you observe? Here, the /k/ sound is used for *c* in cat, *k* in keen, *cc* in occasion, and *ch* in chemistry. In English, different letters can give the same sound. It is also possible that the same letters in English give different sounds in words. For example:

chemist and **ch**aracter   **ch** gives /k/

whereas

chest and **ch**eese   **ch** gives /tʃ/

We hope you have now understood that alphabet is different from sound. Therefore, let us stop erring at least on this front, and master these forty four sounds straightaway.

11.4 TRANSCRIPTION

Since there are standard sounds in English, these are put together with standard symbols. These symbols are called the *International Phonetic Alphabet* symbols or in short IPA. You should familiarize yourself with these symbols as you will find that they are used in dictionaries for indicating the correct pronunciation of words. These symbols are given in the ensuing section of the chapter. Using standard symbols for standard sounds is known as *transcription*. We shall learn how to transcribe words and sentences later.

11.5 SOUNDS

There are two types of sounds, which are

1. Vowels   2. Consonants

Now, most of us remember our teachers telling us that there are five vowels—a, e, i, o, and u—in English. But indeed there are as many as twenty vowel sounds in English. Out of these twenty vowel sounds, twelve are *pure* vowels and eight of them are *diphthongal glides*. It means that out of these twenty vowel sounds, eight are a combination of two vowel sounds. In phonetics, when there is a glide from one vowel sound to another vowel sound, it is called a *diphthong*. Apart from these twenty vowels, there are twenty four consonant sounds as shown in Fig. 11.1.

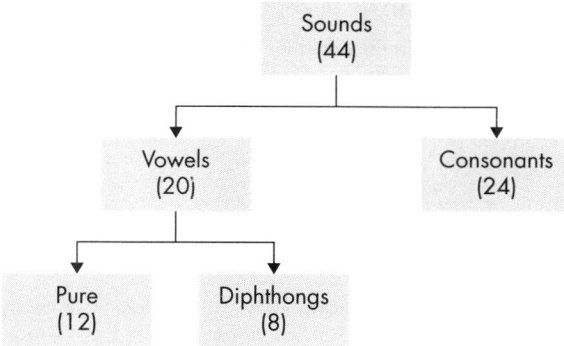

Figure 11.1 Classification of Sounds in English

So, let us learn how to correctly pronounce all the twenty vowels of English, and the symbols they are transcribed with.

11.5.1 Vowels

A vowel is a sound in spoken language, such as the English 'Ah!' [a] or oh! [o], pronounced with an open vocal tract so that there is no build-up of air pressure at any point above the glottis. This contrasts with consonants, such as English 'Sh!' [ʃ], where there is a constriction or closure at some point along the vocal tract.

Pure vowels A vowel sound whose quality does not change over the duration of the vowel is called a pure vowel. There are 12 pure vowel sounds in English which are given below with examples.

Sounds	Position	Examples
/iː/	Initial	each, eat
	Medial	these, seed, seen, cream, dream, shield, peach, thief, piece, deceive, seize, complete, replete, feel, peep, beat, heat, sheep, need, peel, leave, deal
	Final	pea, key, see, knee, plea
/ɪ/	Initial	it, in, is, intelligent, index, individual, induct, inch
	Medial	silk, thick, fill, slip, sip, hit, bit, begin, ticket, silk, cliff, city, build, busy, hills, live
	Final	duty, beauty, lonely, promptly, quickly
/e/	Initial	enter, exit, empire, entire, any
	Medial	bed, dead, head, many, said, fell, let, test, met, tell, bury, friend, leisure, melt, rest, set, wet, breath, feather, bend, men, led, red, wet, pet
	Final	**Does not occur in the final position**

Sounds	Position	Examples
/æ/	Initial	axe, actor, apple, at, an
	Medial	bank, man, sad, fan, mass, rank, sad, tax, cattle, back, mango, gradual, sand, stand, battle, cash, bag, back
	Final	**Does not occur in the final position**
/ʌ/	Initial	utter, under, understand, undo, umbrella, unable, unborn
	Medial	bus, dull, dust, gun, hunt, munch, much, pump, run, son, come, done, month, double, enough, trouble, young, blood, does, butter, country, couple, study, cup, bun
	Final	**Does not occur in the final position**
/ɑː/	Initial	art, answer, aunt
	Medial	card, farm, hard, large, march, fast, task, master, pass, dance, branch, path, bath, staff, calm, half, laugh, bath, drama, last, rather, clerk, heart
	Final	car, jar, mar, bar, tar, far, mortar
/ɒ/	Initial	office, oxygen, object, October, odd
	Medial	hot, bottle, dog, fond, lock, not, pot, solve, borrow, quality, want, because, shone, gone, off, God, knowledge, socks, robbed, cost, top
	Final	**Does not occur in the final position**
/ɔː/	Initial	all, awkward, ought, audition, August, audible
	Medial	ball, call, hall, corn, morning, north, pour, nor, water, door, thought, cause, fault, chalk, board, warm
	Final	saw, raw, claw, paw, more, sore
/ʊ/	Initial	**Does not occur in the initial position**
	Medial	book, cook, took, wood, cushion, push, could, would, should, woman, foot, good, look, hook, crook, bullet, wool
	Final	**Does not occur in the final position**
/uː/	Initial	oodles, ooze, oops
	Medial	rule, approve, groove, suit, lose, foolish, move, goose, beautiful, pupil, June, soon, group, wound, fruit, juice, tooth, choose
	Final	sue, new, you, shoe, two
/ɜː/	Initial	early, earn, urge, urgent, earnest, earth
	Medial	third, murder, surface, turn, nurse, purple, bird, stern, circle, dirt, thirst, burn, hurt, heard, learn, search, journey, flirt, skirt
	Final	Sir, fur, cur, whirr, her
/ə/	Initial	about, ago, allow, ahead
	Medial	sentence, liberty, condition, factory, society, famous, gentleman, human, substance
	Final	motor, colour, doctor, beggar, collar, dollar, finger

Diphthongs

Sounds	Examples
/eɪ/	bait, mail, fail, train, age, may, say, pray, jail, aim, straight, eight, grey, weight, great, waste, date, paste, rate, drain, trail, hail, vain, pain
/aɪ/	ice, fine, pipe, nice, write, rival, silence, tidy, type, cry, dry, fly, reply, satisfy, die, flies, high, might, right, tight, child, kind, buy, island, height
/ɔɪ/	spoil, loin, boil, choice, noise, oil, point, annoy, boy, toil, toy, foil, employ, join, soil
/əʊ/	roll, slow, home, bone, nose, rope, both, open, go, no, so, social, bold, most, post, know, narrow, window, boat, soap, shoulder
/aʊ/	sound, mouth, out, round, allow, cow, town, now, down, mouse, doubt, house, trounce, trousers, about, bound, around, crowd, town
/ɪə/	here, appear, period, mere, cheer, tear (noun), jeer, queer, career, dear, near, fear, deer, serious, zero, clear, idea, real, fierce, dear
/eə/	their, wear, there, air, chair, fair, pair, hair, bare, care, share, various, bear, tear(verb), prayer, dare, rare
/ʊə/	cruel, poor, sure, tour, actual, pure, fuel, tour, virtuous

11.5.2 Consonants

As discussed at the beginning of the chapter, there are as many as forty four sounds in English, and we have already known twenty vowel sounds. We are obviously thus left with twenty four consonant sounds. A consonant is a speech sound that is articulated with complete or partial closure of the vocal tract. Examples are /p/, pronounced with the lips; /t/, pronounced with the front of the tongue; /k/, pronounced with the back of the tongue; /h/, pronounced in the throat; /f/ and /s/, pronounced by forcing air through a narrow channel; and /m/ and /n/, which have air flowing through the nose. Some of the words using these and other consonant sounds in English are listed below:

Sounds	Examples	Sounds	Examples
/p/	pit, spill, keep	/f/	fat, feather, half
/b/	bit, imbibe, jumble	/v/	vat, wave, velvet
/t/	tin, after, what	/θ/	thin, thank, wrath
/d/	din, lead, order	/ð/	then, feather, breathe
/k/	cut, character, leak	/s/	sap, sound, pistol, cross
/g/	gut, girl, eager	/z/	zap, zing, maze, gaze
/tʃ/	cheap, nature, watch	/ʃ/	she, nation, shout
/dʒ/	jeep, jealous, judge	/ʒ/	measure, pleasure, treasure
/m/	map, remind, mime	/h/	harm, house
/n/	nap, near, line, Christian	/r/	run, ruin, craze
/ŋ/	bang, song, bring, singing	/w/	we, wicked, watch
/l/	left, relate, detail	/j/	yes, yell, yesterday

11.5.3 Consonant Cluster (CC)

A *consonant cluster* in a word is a group of two or more consonants with no vowels in between them. The consonant sounds that come before a vowel sound are called **onset**, the ones that come after a vowel sound **coda**, and the consonant cluster between vowel sounds is known as **medial**.

Examples

black, **br**ead, **tr**ick, **tw**in, **fl**at, **spl**ash, **spr**ing, **str**ong, **scr**eam – the highlighted consonant sounds are **onset**

le**ngth**, six**ths**, bur**sts**, glim**pse**, a**stray** – the highlighted consonant sounds are **coda**

hand**spr**ing, sigh**tscr**een, a**br**idge, dra**st**ic, per**qu**isite – the highlighted consonant sounds are **medial**

EXERCISE 11.1

Identify the sounds represented by the underlined letter(s) in the following words:

Example: o<u>cc</u>asion = /k/

1. Curi<u>ou</u>s _____
2. B<u>oa</u>t _____
3. Dish<u>o</u>nest _____
4. Trage<u>d</u>y _____
5. Bird<u>s</u> _____
6. Tru<u>n</u>k _____
7. App<u>r</u>ove _____
8. Aw<u>ar</u>e _____
9. Expl<u>oi</u>t _____
10. Dear<u>th</u> _____

EXERCISE 11.2

Give two examples in orthography for each of the following:

1. Words with two syllables _____ _____
2. Words ending in /dʒ/ _____ _____
3. Words ending in /g/ _____ _____
4. Words beginning with /ð/ _____ _____

EXERCISE 11.3

What phonetic symbol/symbols would be used for the underlined letter(s) in each of the following words?

1. fa<u>th</u>om _____
2. voca<u>bu</u>lary _____
3. noi<u>se</u>s _____
4. val<u>ve</u>s _____
5. lib<u>e</u>rty _____
6. rai<u>sed</u> _____
7. di<u>a</u>mond _____
8. occurr<u>ence</u> _____

11.6 PROBLEMS OF INDIAN ENGLISH

In Indian English, /z/ and /s/ are not used correctly and this leads to confusion between pairs such as the ones given below:

/z/	/s/
eyes	ice
falls	false

/z/	/s/
fears	fierce
his	hiss
knees	niece

Some Hindi speakers interchange the sounds /s/ and /ʃ/ and that leads to confusion in pairs such as the following:

/ʃ/	/s/
shave	save
she	see
sheet	seat
shine	sign

In order to discriminate between these two sounds, we need to repeatedly speak out tongue-twisters such as the one given below:

She sells sea shells on the sea shore.

Further, most Indian speakers are unaware of the difference between the consonant sounds /v/ and /w/. That is why, the following pairs are often confused:

/w/	/v/
while	vile
west	vest
why	vie

In fact, both these sounds are used indiscriminately by most of us, and careful practice to achieve a distinction between them is mandatory.

11.7 SYLLABLE

A *syllable* is a basic unit of spoken language, which consists of an uninterrupted sound that can be used to make up words. In other words, a syllable always has one vowel sound. So a word has as many syllables as there are vowel sounds. While denoting the syllabic structure of a word, 'C' is used for consonant sounds and 'V' is used for vowel sounds.

Let us look at the structure of a few words:

Train	/treɪn/
Cold	/kəʊld/

For example, 'man', 'code', 'eye', 'lead', 'strength', and 'sixths' are a few of many English words that have one syllable each.

A-go, ho-tel, free-dom, and a-gree are examples of words with two syllables.

Syl-la-ble, dic-tion-ary, and re-la-tion are examples of words with three syllables.

11.7.1 Rules for Counting Syllables

To find the number of syllables in a word, use the following steps:

1. Count the vowel sounds in the word.
2. Subtract any silent vowel, such as the silent /ə/ at the end of a word.
3. Count diphthongs as only one vowel sound.
4. The number of vowel sounds is the same as the number of syllables.

This means that the number of syllables that you hear when you pronounce a word is the same as the number of vowel sounds heard. For example:

1. Words such as *came, rule, blue,* and *name* have two vowels, but the *e* is silent. Therefore, there is only one vowel sound and thereby one syllable in each of these words.

2. The word *outside* has four vowels, but the *e* is silent and the *ou* is a diphthong which counts as only one sound, so this word has only two vowel sounds, and therefore two syllables in this word. Look at its syllabic structure:

11.7.2 Dividing Words into Syllables

Given below are some of the words with their syllabic division, phonemic transcription, and syllabic structure:

Sl. No.	Word	Transcription	Syllabic Structure
1.	Clap	/klæp/	CCVC
2.	Hope	/həʊp/	CVC
3.	Late	/leɪt/	CVC
4.	Fauna	/ˈfɔː-nə/	CV-CV
5.	Scream	/skriːm/	CCCVC
6.	Remember	/rɪ-ˈmem-bə/	CV-CVC-CV
7.	Telephone	/ˈte-lɪ-fəʊn/	CV-CV-CVC
8.	Despite	/dɪs-ˈpaɪt/	CVC-CVC
9.	Quality	/ˈkwɒ-lə-tɪ/	CCV-CV-CV
10.	Potato	/pə-ˈteɪ-təʊ/	CV-CV-CV
11.	Policeman	/pə-ˈliːs-mən/	CV-CVC-CVC
12.	College	/ˈkɒ-lɪdʒ/	CV-CVC
13.	University	/ˌjuː-nɪ-ˈvɜː-sə-tɪ/	CV-CV-CV-CV-CV
14.	Considering	/kən-ˈsɪ-də-rɪŋ/	CVC-CV-CV-CVC
15.	Ability	/ə-ˈbɪ-lə-tɪ/	V-CV-CV-CV
16.	Passenger	/ˈpæ-sɪn-dʒə/	CV-CVC-CV

Sl. No.	Word	Transcription	Syllabic Structure
17.	Imagine	/ɪ-'mæ-dʒɪn/	V-CV-CVC
18.	Languages	/'læŋg-wɪ-dʒɪz/	CVCC-CV-CVC
19.	Atlantic	/ət-'læn-tɪk/	VC-CVC-CVC
20.	Psychologists	/saɪ-'kɒ-lə-dʒɪsts/	CV-CV-CV-CVCCC
21.	Apologize	/ə-'pɒ-lə-dʒaɪz/	V-CV-CV-CVC
22.	Listlessness	/'lɪst-lɪs-nɪs/	CVCC-CVC-CVC
23.	Disdainfully	/dɪs-'deɪn-fʊ-lɪ/	CVC-CVC-CV-CV
24.	Disembarkment	/ˌdɪs-ɪm-'baːk-mənt/	CVC-VC-CVC-CVCC
25.	Iconoclastic	/aɪ-ˌkɒ-nəʊ-'klæs-tɪk/	VC-CV-CV-CCVC-CVC

EXERCISE 11.4

Show the division of syllables in the following words:

1. offer _____
2. sudden _____
3. different _____
4. September _____
5. January _____
6. children _____
7. college _____
8. disappear _____
9. accident _____
10. proper _____
11. neighbour _____
12. confident _____
13. introduction _____
14. faithfully _____
15. dentist _____

EXERCISE 11.5

Show the division of syllables in the following words:

1. window _____
2. sympathy _____
3. perhaps _____
4. information _____
6. telephone _____
8. electrician _____
5. activity _____
7. management _____
9. disappearance _____
10. concentrate _____

EXERCISE 11.6

Identify the words with one syllable from the list of words:

1. fulfil
2. awesome
3. space
4. phonetics
5. book
6. grass
7. roman
8. home
9. your
10. plant
11. conquer
12. folder
13. prepare
14. said
15. you

11.8 WORD STRESS

Are you now prepared to transcribe the words as per the RP sounds of English? Not yet. In fact, before we move on to learn how to transcribe the words, we need to know where to stress a word. Did you know that English is an accent-based language, and that in a word not all the syllables are pronounced with equal emphasis? For example, in the word *ability* it is -*bi* and not '*a*' that is heard prominently. If you look up in the dictionary for this word, it would be seen something like /ə'bɪlətɪ/. Notice the little mark "'" after /ə/ and before -/bɪlətɪ/. This is known as *word stress*. Now this stress changes the way a word is to be pronounced. For example, if you look up the word *convict*, it would be shown to have been transcribed as /'kɒnvɪkt/ and /kən'vɪkt/. In the first case, it is stressed initially while in the second instance the stress is on -/vɪkt/. Because of the shift in the stress, the corresponding vowel sound and consequently the pronunciation changes completely. Therefore, it is imperative for us to be aware of the rules that decide which word is to be stressed where. However, since there are only a few rules pertaining to word stress, it is advisable to refer to a standard dictionary to find out where a particular word receives its primary and secondary stress. Therefore, rather than being an exhaustive list covering all possible accentual patterns, the rules that follow can only give you an idea about how certain words in English are stressed.

Let us see the various word stress rules with examples. In English there are a large number of words with two syllables and in these words the stress depends on whether the word is used as a noun or a verb.

(a) When the word is used as a noun or adjective, the stress is on the first syllable. When the word is used as a verb, the stress is on the second syllable. Here are a few examples:

Noun/Adjective	Verb	Noun/Adjective	Verb
'produce	pro'duce	'record	re'cord
'object	ob'ject	'perfect	per'fect
'subject	sub'ject		

(b) Words with weak prefixes are accented on the root. For example:

a'go	be'low	re'duce	ad'mit
a'bove	re'vise	de'velop	be'gin
a'bout	be'neath		

(c) Verbs of two syllables beginning with the prefix dis- are stressed on the last syllable. For example:

dis'arm	dis'pel	dis'close	dis'turb
dis'guise	dis'tress	dis'miss	dis'may

(d) Verbs that have two syllables and end in -ate, -ise/ize, -ct are stressed on the last syllable. For example:

at'tract	nar'rate	de'bate	bap'tize
cre'mate	in'ject	cap'size	

(e) Words ending in -ion are stressed on the last but one syllable. For example:

appli'cation	intro'duction	assimi'lation	exami'nation
simplifi'cation	pro'duction	expla'nation	repe'tition

(f) Words ending in -ic/-ical/-ically, -ial/-ially, and -ian are stressed on the syllable before the suffix.

charis'matic	me'morial	'special	sub'stantial
li'brarian	mu'sician	es'sential	of'ficially

(g) Words ending in -ious and -eous are stressed on the last but one or penultimate syllable. For example:

'curious	mys'terious	la'borious	re'bellious
spon'taneous	cou'rageous	s'purious	'serious

(h) Words ending in -ate, -ise/-ize, -fy are stressed on the third syllable from the end. For example:

'duplicate	'modernize	'justify	'cultivate
'beautify	'educate	'criticize	'satisfy

(i) Words ending in -ity, -cracy, and -crat are stressed on the third syllable from the end. For example:

a'bility	de'mocracy	au'tocracy	curi'osity
crea'tivity	sim'plicity	e'quality	possi'bility
'autocrat	bu'reaucracy	mag'nanimity	ratio'nality

(j) Words ending in -graph, -graphy, -meter, and -logy are stressed on the third syllable from the end. For example:

'autograph	psy'chology	bi'ography	zo'ology
crimi'nology	bi'ology	'paragraph	pa'rameter
'photograph	anthro'pology	ba'rometer	soci'ology

(k) Words ending with the suffixes -aire, -eer, -ental, -ential, -ese, -ese, -esce, -escence, -escent, -esque, -ique, -ee, -ette, -ete, and -ade are stressed on the suffix. For example:

pio'neer	ca'reer	millio'naire	question'naire
pay'ee	barri'cade	de'lete	exi'stential
ga'zette	com'plete	mi'stique	ado'lescent
re'plete	gro'tesque	billion'naire	pictu'resque

(l) In case of compound words, i.e., words that are made up of two words and are written as one word, the stress is on the first element. For example:

'blacksmith	'dining-room	'tea-party	'blackbird

However, in compound words with -ever and -self, the stress is usually on the second element. For example:

how'ever	when'ever	him'self	her'self

Sometimes both the elements are stressed, but the primary stress remains on the second element. For example:

after'noon	old-'fashioned	absent-'minded

Note The inflectional suffixes such as -es, -ing, and -ed and the derivational suffixes -age, -ance, -en, -er, -ess, -ful, -hood, -ice, -ish, -ive, -less, -ly, -ment, -ness, -or, -ship, -ter, -ure, and -zen do not affect the stress. For example:

'match	'matches	'want	'wanted
'box	'boxes	'fine	'finely
'write	'writer	'god	'goddess
'play	'player	'waiter	'waitress
'aim	'aimless	'bad	'badly
'good	'goodness	'child	'childish
'bright	'brighten	'care	'careful
'bitter	'bitterness	'blood	'bloody
'create	'creator	'home	'homeless
'city	'citizen	'laugh	'laughter

11.9 HOW TO TRANSCRIBE

Now that you are familiar with the stress rules for words, let us start learning how to transcribe words.

Step 1 Always begin by dividing a word into parts. For example:

daughter	>	two parts of the word—daugh and ter
explain	>	two parts of the word—ex and plain
dominate	>	three parts of the word—do, mi, and nate

Step 2 This division is based on the two distinct vowel sounds in the words *daughter* and *explain*, whereas *dominate* has three vowel sounds.

The number of vowel sounds determine the number of syllables in a word. So, while transcribing a word, you need to divide the word into syllables.

Step 3 Then, fix the stress and finally go on to transcribe the word.

Now look at the following examples carefully. The exercise given below should be a handy help in getting you acquainted with how to transcribe the words properly:

daughter	/'dɔːtə/	dictionary	/'dɪkʃənrɪ/
explain	/ɪk'spleɪn/	advance	/əd'vaːns/
dominate	/'domɪneɪt/	arrange	/ə'reɪndʒ/
guide	/'gaɪd/	picture	/'pɪktʃə/

EXERCISE 11.7

Transcribe the following words (division of syllable also shown) using IPA symbols:

Word	Division	Transcription	Word	Division	Transcription
1. image	i-mage		2. society	so-ci-e-ty	
3. observe	ob-serve		4. development	de-ve-lop-ment	

Word	Division	Transcription	Word	Division	Transcription
5. breakfast	break-fast		6. famous	fa-mous	
7. creature	crea-ture		8. sure	sure	
9. nuisance	nui-sance		10. heard	heard	
11. morning	mor-ning		12. master	mas-ter	
13. enough	e-nough		14. force	force	
15. serious	se-rious		16. human	hu-man	
17. because	be-cause		18. surface	sur-face	
19. hunger	hun-ger		20. measure	mea-sure	
21. island	is-land		22. silence	si-lence	
23. wear (V)	wear		24. bottle	bo-ttle	
25. character	cha-rac-ter		26. musician	mu-si-cian	
27. occasion	o-cca-sion				

EXERCISE 11.8

Now keeping in mind the rules of word stress and recalling the forty four sounds you have learnt, transcribe the following words, marking the stress on the right place:

Word	Transcription	Word	Transcription
1. computer		2. justify	
3. suicide		4. army	
5. yellow		6. win	
7. beautiful		8. dictation	
9. reality		10. war	
11. obtain		12. bird	
13. possibility		14. frustration	
15. tour		16. flight	
17. pencil		18. item	
19. barrage		20. uncle	
21. dictionary		22. statement	
23. freedom		24. firm	
25. envelop (V)		26. terminate	
27. regularize		28. women	
29. skirt		30. approach	

Word	Transcription	Word	Transcription
31. eyes		32. master	
33. laughter		34. registration	
35. father		36. remember	
37. dumb		38. isolation	
39. quality			

11.10 WEAK FORMS

The functional words are generally used in their weak form in connected speech.

Example

In the following sentence, the first 'do' is a weak form and the second is stressed.

What do you want to do this evening?

/'wɒt dəju 'wɔ:nttə'du: ðɪs i:vnɪŋ/

Note Functional words, such as prepositions, conjunctions, auxiliaries, and articles are often pronounced in their weak forms, since they do not carry the main content, and are therefore not normally stressed.

Determiners/Quantifiers

Orthography	Strong Form(s)	Weak Form(s)
the	ði:	ðɪ, ðə
a/an	an	ə, ən
some	sʌm	səm, sm

Pronouns

Orthography	Strong Form(s)	Weak Form(s)
his	hɪz	ɪz
him	hɪm	ɪm
her	hɜ:	ə
you	ju:	jʊ, jə
your	jo:	jə
she	ʃi:	ʃɪ
he	hi:	ɪ
we	wi:	wɪ
them	ðem	ðəm, əm
us	ʌs	əs, s

Prepositions

Orthography	Strong Form(s)	Weak Form(s)
than	ðan	ðən
at	æt	ət
for	fɔː	fə
from	frɒm	frəm, fəm, fm
of	ɒv	əv, v
to	tuː	tə, tʊ
as	æz	əz, z
there	ðeə	ðə

Conjunctions

Orthography	Strong Form(s)	Weak Form(s)
and	ænd	ənd, ən, nd, n
but	bʌt	bət
that	ðat	ðət

Auxiliaries

Orthography	Strong Form(s)	Weak Form(s)
can	kan	kən, kn
could	kʊd	kəd
have	hæv	əv, v
has	hæz	əz, z
had	hæd	əd, d
will	wɪl	l
shall	ʃal	ʃəl, ʃl, l
should	ʃʊd	ʃəd
must	mʌst	məs, məst
do	duː	də, d
does	dʌz	dəz, z
am	æm	əm, m
are	ɑː	ə
was	wɒz	wəz
were	wɜː	wə

11.11 STRESS, INTONATION, AND RHYTHM

Stress, rhythm, and intonation are inextricably linked. It is almost impossible to speak of any one of these aspects of spoken English without referring to the others. However, it is necessary for the sake of clarity to deal with each one individually. Look at the following sentence.

There was an elephant at the corner of the street.

So in the sentence we have three words 'e-le-phant', '**cor**-ner', and '**street**' (highlighted syllables are stressed) stressed and rest are unstressed syllables.

By now you must have understood how in the spoken variety of English, words are divided into syllables, some of which are stressed and others are left unstressed. Similarly in connected speech also, some parts of a sentence are stressed more than the others. This practice of stressing some part of a sentence and leaving the other unstressed provides to English language a particular rhythm. In English, rhythm acquires special significance since it provides to it a distinct musicality. While speaking English therefore, we are required to employ the rhythmic rise and fall in our speech so that our expression carries the whole import of message being conveyed. Further, the use of rhythm in our speech helps the listener sustain his/her interest in what is being communicated to him/her.

In other words, in the spoken variety of English, there is a clear propensity to pronounce stressed syllables according to a relatively regular rhythm which is organized around the stressed syllables. As known, English is a stress-timed language which tends toward a regular rhythm of broadly equal-length beats on stressed syllables, the unstressed syllables being 'compressed/squeezed in' to fit the available time, and frequently reduced to a weak form. It means that the stressed syllables follow each other at intervals of about the same length, which sounds like a pulsating rhythm. This is how rhythm is created.

Then, of course, you have to decide on the appropriate *intonation*. What sort of tone do you use? If the sentence is a simple statement, 'There was an **e**lephant at the **cor** ner of the **street**.' the appropriate intonation is a falling tone on the last stressed syllable.

In day to day conversation, when we hear someone speaking, we observe that the person does not speak on the same note throughout. We find frequent rises and falls in the person's voice. This variation in the pitch patterns of voice is called *intonation*. While speaking, we glide over the less important words such as pronouns, articles, auxiliary verbs, prepositions, and conjunctions which are called *functional words* in English, whereas nouns, principal verbs, adjectives, and adverbs which are called *content words* are stressed more. This *quality of quickly gliding over less important words is the characteristic feature of connected speech.*

The syllable on which there is change in pitch is marked in the following ways in English.

11.11.1 Rules for Intonation

[`] **Falling tone**

(a) **Statements have a falling tone at the end**. It signals a sense of finality, completion, or belief in the content of the utterance, and so on. For example:
  (i) I went to `Delhi.
  (ii) They have saved enough money to buy a `new car.

(b) **WH-question** (who? what? why? when? where? how?) **have a falling tone at the end**. For example:
  (i) How did you spend your va`cation?
  (ii) When did he `come?

(c) **Tag questions take the falling tone.**
  (i) He was operated on ˋyesterday, ˋwasn't he?
  (ii) Radha comes here ˋevery day, ˋdoesn't she?

(d) **Imperative statements have a falling tone.**
  (i) Go and see a ˋdoctor.
  (ii) Come and wash your ˋface.

[´] **Rising tone**

(a) **Yes–No questions** (question you can answer with 'yes' or 'no') **usually have a rising tone.** For example:
  (i) Could you pass me the curd, please?
  (ii) Was it expensive?

(b) **Rising intonation is used at the end of the questions which do not have an interrogative word.** For example:
  (i) You are coming tomorrow?
  (ii) He has enough money to buy a new house?

(c) **Requests have a rising tone too.**
  (i) Please post this letter.
  (ii) Please calm down.

[ˇ] **Falling-rising tone**

  Fall-rise signals dependency, continuity, and non-finality. For example:
  (i) Private ˇenterprises are mostly successful.
  (ii) Preˇsumably he thinks he can.

EXERCISE 11.9

Read the following sentences and mark the tones that you will use while speaking:

1. No. The woman with the plastic bag.

   _____

2. That's the person who robbed the bank!

   _____

3. Do you mean the man with the black pants?

   _____

4. He drove to work after he had finished working in the garden.

   _____

5. Suresh bought new shoes today.

   _____

6. Hey, have you seen the new film with Bruce Willis?

   _____

7. Do you want some coffee?

   _____

8. Would you like some ice cream and cake?

___

9. Is he going to the dentist?

___

10. Yes. He has a toothache.

___

11. Usually, he comes on Sundays.

___

12. She's totally confused, isn't she?

___

13. I would be really happy if I could get more input on this.

___

14. I want a purse on my birthday.

___

15. Occasionally, I plan my budget.

___

11.11.2 Contrastive Stress in Sentences

Contrastive stress is used to contrast a word or syllable with an alternative word or syllable which is normally unstressed otherwise. It is used with determiners such as 'this', 'that', 'these' and 'those'.

Examples

*I prefer **this** purse not the other one.*

*Do you want these or **those** curtains?*

Contrastive stress is also used to bring out a given word in a sentence which also slightly changes the meaning.

- **She** came to the gym yesterday. (It was **she**, not someone else.)
- She **walked** to the gym yesterday. (He **walked** rather than drove.)
- She came to the **gym** yesterday. (It was **gym** not a meeting or something else.)
- She came to the gym **yesterday**. (It was **yesterday** not two weeks ago or some other time.)

11.12 DIFFERENCE BETWEEN BRITISH, AMERICAN, AND INDIAN SPOKEN ENGLISH

Nowadays, English is probably the most frequently spoken language in the world, either as mother tongue, official language, or foreign language. Speaking English has become more than a trend or a fashion. But the question is what kind of English do we speak? Since it is the language of the professional world, it is essential for all of us to know the differences between the three major varieties of English. When a person does not understand the differences, you may hear him or her using phrases such as 'pardon', 'come again', or 'I didn't get you'. These ruin the effectiveness of communication. Therefore, it is essential for us to understand these three varieties of English viz. British, American and Indian, briefly.

British English (BrE) is the form of English used in the United Kingdom, and includes all English dialects used there. The pronunciation of standard English is called *Received Pronunciation (RP)*. It is referred to colloquially as 'the Queen's English', 'Oxford, English', and 'BBC English'. *American English (AmE)* is the form of English used in the United States. Though Indians speak British English, yet because of the regional language or vernacular which an Indian speaks brings a significant change in the pronunciation and usage of English language. Thus, *Indian English (IE)* is considered a group of English dialects, or regional language varieties, spoken primarily on the Indian subcontinent. Indian English has generally absorbed the idiomatic forms derived from Indian literary languages and vernaculars.

Now let us take up a few examples which help us understand how, if you are not familiar with correct words, may lead to some confusion while communicating across cultures. Sometimes, the spelling of the words may be the same but they are pronounced differently. For example, 'schedule' is pronounced /skedʒuːꞁ/ and 'vitamin' is pronounced /vaɪtamɪn/ in American English whereas in British English they are pronounced /ʃeduːꞁ/ and /vɪtamɪn/ respectively. Given below are a few more such examples:

- vase: **/vaːz/** as in cars (BrE); **/vaːs/** as in face (AmE)
- route: **/ruːt/** as in shoot (BrE); **/raʊt/** as in shout (AmE)
- ate: **/et/** as in let (BrE), **/eɪt/** as in late (AmE)
- leisure: as in /leʒə/ (BrE); /lɪʒər/ with /lɪ/ as in she (AmE)

11.12.1 Other Differences in Pronunciation

- In BrE /aː/ before -f, -s, -m, -n is pronounced /æ/ in AmE, eg. ask, task, after, pass, calf.
- In BrE /ɒ/ in words such as not, block, cross, stop, college is pronounced /aː/ in AmE.
- AmE does not drop the /r/ sound in words like better, perceive, bird, here, poor, chair, dare whereas BrE does.
- BrE /juː/ after consonants /d/, /t/, /n/ is pronounced /uː/ in AmE, eg. duty, tune, new.
- The past tense forms of the two following verbs are pronounced differently.

BrE | **AmE**
- shine – shone /ʃɒn/ shine – shone /ʃoʊn/
- eat – ate /et/ eat – ate /eit/

- Here are a few examples of words which are pronounced differently in AmE than in BrE.

Word	BrE	AmE
resource	/rɪsɔːs/	/riːsɔːrs/
figure	/fɪgə/	/fɪgjər/
either	/aɪðə/	/iːðər/
research	/rɪsɜːtʃ/	/riːsɜːrtʃ/
glacier	/gꞁæsɪə/	/gꞁeɪʃər/
Asia	/eɪʒə/	/eɪʃə/
can't	/kaːnt/	/kænt/

- The BrE /əʊ/ is pronounced as /b/ in AmE in words such as go, no, crow, romantic.
- Words pronounced with /æ/ in AmE with /aː/ in BrE: bath, lath, path, aunt, plant, can't, advantage Exceptions: hath, maths, athlete, ant, banter, scant, mantle.

11.12.2 Characteristics of Indian English (IE)

- Many Indian English speakers do not make a clear distinction between $/\text{ɒ}/$ and $/\text{ɔ:}/$. Eg. cot, caught.
- Unlike British speakers, some Indian speakers, especially in the South, often do not pronounce the rounded $/\text{ɒ}/$ or $/\text{ɔ:}/$, and substitute $/\text{a}/$ instead. Eg. in South India *coffee* will be pronounced *kaafi*, *copy* will be *kaapi*.
- Words such as *class, staff,* and *last* would be pronounced $/\text{klɑ:s}/$, $/\text{stɑ:f}/$, and $/\text{lɑ:st}/$ in British English, whereas they are pronounced $/\text{klæ:s}/$, $/\text{stæ:f}/$, and $/\text{læ:st}/$ in American English.
- Standard Hindi and most other vernaculars (except Punjabi, Marathi, and Bengali) do not differentiate between $/\text{v}/$ and $/\text{w}/$ sounds.
- The voiceless plosives $/\text{p}/$, $/\text{t}/$, $/\text{k}/$ are always unaspirated in Indian English which are aspirated in RP. For example 'pin' is pronounced $/\text{pɪn}/$ in Indian English but $/\text{p}^h\text{ɪn}/$ in British and American English.
- Unlike native speakers, Indian English speakers do not make use of the consonant sound $/\text{ʒ}/$. Instead, the sounds $/\text{dʒ}/$, $/\text{z}/$ are used by Indian speakers of English.

EXERCISE 11.10

1. Identify the consonant cluster in the following words. Also, name the type of consonant cluster:

   price _____   green _____
   practice _____   private _____
   appropriate _____ cry _____
   break _____   crazy _____
   journalism _____   great _____
   bring _____   students _____
   advance _____   understand _____
   brother _____   grow _____
   transcript _____   scratch _____
   create _____   scream _____

2. Transcribe the following words into phonetic script using IPA symbols:

   1. joy _____   2. conquest _____
   3. doctor _____   4. therefore _____
   5. office _____   6. excellent _____
   7. ghosts _____   8. attached _____
   9. decision _____ 10. examination _____

3. Transcribe the following words:

   1. sorrow _____   2. machine _____
   3. sorry _____   4. design _____
   5. child _____   6. motivate _____
   7. rest _____   8. reason _____
   9. service _____   10. awareness _____

11. battle _____   12. fancy _____
13. market _____   14. huge _____
15. fear _____   16. cultivate _____
17. taste _____   18. relatives _____
19. hopeless _____   20. about _____
21. thought _____   22. stupidity _____
23. sensational _____ 24. purchase _____
25. notion _____   26. quickly _____
27. musician _____   28. writing _____
29. engineer _____   30. manager _____
31. object (Verb) ___ 32. opponent _____
33. magician _____   34. report _____
35. doctor _____   36. employee _____

4. Mark stress in the following words as shown in the example below:

   Example: Object(n) = ′Object

   1. atmosphere _____   2. comment _____
   3. contribute _____   4. demonstration _____
   5. support _____   6. complicate _____
   7. electricity _____ 8. photography _____
   9. industrial _____   10. departmental _____

5. What is onset? Provide five words with onset.

6. What is a consonant cluster and how do they contribute to study for effective speaking? Support your answer with appropriate examples.

7. Differentiate between onset and coda. Provide three examples for each.

8. What is intonation? What is the difference between intonation and word stress?

9. What is a syllable and how are words divided into different syllables?

10. What is the difference between a vowel and a consonant sound?

11. What is a diphthong? How are diphthongs different from vowel sounds?

12. How are sounds different from alphabet in English?

13. What is the difference in the pronunciation of the following words in British English and American English?

Calf, Graph, Giraffe, Half, Laugh, Staff, After, Craft, Draft, Laughter, Raft, Shaft, Sample, Example

ANSWER KEY

Exercise 11.1

1. ɪə   **2.** /əʊ/   **3.** /ɒ/   **4.** /ə/   **5.** /z/   **6.** /ŋ/   **7.** /uː/   **8.** /eə(r)/   **9.** /ɔɪ/   **10.** /θ/

Exercise 11.2

1. ago   below   **2.** judge   nudge   **3.** big   fig   **4.** then   thus

Exercise 11.3

1. /ð/   **2.** /bʊ/   **3.** /zɪz/   **4.** /vz/   **5.** /ə/   **6.** /zd/   **7.** /aɪ/   **8.** /əns/

Exercise 11.4

1. of-fer   **2.** sud-den   **3.** dif-fer-ent   **4.** Sep-tem-ber   **5.** Jan-u-ary   **6.** chil-dren   **7.** col-lege
8. dis-ap-pear   **9.** ac-ci-dent   **10.** pro-per   **11.** neigh-bour   **12.** con-fi-dent   **13.** in-tro-duc-tion
14. faith-ful-ly   **15.** den-tist

Exercise 11.5

1. win-dow   **2.** sym-pa-thy   **3.** per-haps   **4.** in-for-ma-tion   **5.** ac-ti-vi-ty   **6.** te-le-phone
7. ma-nage-ment   **8.** e-lec-tri-cian   **9.** dis-ap-pear-ance   **10.** con-cen-trate

Exercise 11.6

3, 5, 6, 8, 9, 10, 14, and 15 are the words with one syllable and the rest have more than one syllable.

Exercise 11.7

1. /ˈɪmɪdʒ/   **2.** /səˈsaɪətɪ/   **3.** /əbzˈɜːˈv/   **4.** /dɪˈveləpmənt/   **5.** /ˈbrekfəst/

6. /ˈfeɪməs   **7.** /ˈkriːtʃə/   **8.** /ʃʊə/   **9.** /ˈnjuːsns/   **10.** /ˈhɜːd/

11. /ˈmɔːnɪŋ/   **12.** /ˈmaːstə/   **13.** /ɪˈnʌf/   **14.** /ˈfɔːs/   **15.** /ˈsɪərɪəs/

16. /ˈhjuːmən/   **17.** /brˈkɒz/   **18.** /ˈsɜːfɪs/   **19.** /ˈhʌŋə/   **20.** /ˈmeʒə/

21. /ˈaɪlənd/   **22.** /ˈsaɪləns/   **23.** /ˈweə/   **24.** /ˈbɒtl/   **25.** /ˈkærəktə/

26. /mjuːˈzɪʃən/   **27.** /əˈkeɪʒn/

Exercise 11.8

1. /kəm'pjuːtə/
2. /'dʒʌstɪfaɪ/
3. /'suːɪsaɪd/
4. /'aːmɪ/
5. /'jeləʊ/
6. /'wɪn/
7. /'bjuːtəfʊl/
8. /dɪk'teɪʃn/
9. /'rɪəltɪ/
10. /'wɔː/
11. /əb'teɪn/
12. /'bɜːd/
13. /pɒsɪ'bɪlɪtɪ/
14. /frʌ'streɪʃn/
15. /'tʊə/
16. /'flaɪt/
17. /'pensl/
18. /'aɪtəm/
19. /'bæraːʒ/
20. /'ʌŋkl/
21. /d'ɪkʃənrɪ/
22. /'steɪtmənt/
23. /'friːdəm/
24. /'fɜːm/
25. /ɪn'veləp/
26. /'tɜːmɪneɪt/
27. /'regjʊləraɪz/
28. /'wɪmɪn/
29. /'skɜːt/
30. /ə'prəʊtʃ/
31. /'aɪz/
32. /'maːstə/
33. /'laːftə/
34. /redʒɪ'streɪʃn/
35. /'faːðə/
36. /rɪ'membə/
37. /'dʌm/
38. /aɪsə'leɪʃn/
39. /'kwɒlɪtɪ/

Exercise 11.9

1. `No. The woman with the plastic `**bag**. (Both the highlighted words have falling tone.)
2. That's the person who robbed the `**bank**! (falling tone)
3. Do you mean the man with the ḅlack pants? (rising tone)
4. He drove to `**work** after he had finished working in the `**garden**. (Both the highlighted words have falling tone.)
5. Suresh bought new `**shoes** today. (falling tone)
6. Hey, have you seen the ṇew film with Bruce Willis? (rising tone)
7. Do you want some ҫoffee? (rising tone)
8. Would you like some iҫe cream and cake? (rising tone)
9. Is he going to the ḍentist? (rising tone)
10. `Yes. He has a `**toothache**. (Both the highlighted words have falling tone.)
11. Us̆ually, he comes on `Sundays. (falling rising tone)
12. She's totally con`fused, `isn't **she**? (falling tone)
13. I would be rĕally happy if I could get more input on this. (falling rising tone)
14. I want a purse on my `**birthday**. (falling tone)
15. Očcasionally, I plan my `budget. (falling rising tone)

Exercise 11.10

1.

Word	Consonant Cluster	Word	Consonant Cluster
Price	onset	green	onset
practice	onset	private	onset
Appropriate	medial	cry	onset
break	onset	crazy	onset
journalism	coda	great	onset
bring	onset	students	onset, coda
advance	coda	understand	medial
brother	onset	grow	onset
transcript	coda	scratch	onset
create	onset	scream	onset
		screen	onset

@ Please refer to the Online Resource Centre for audios on phonetics.

12 CONVERSATIONS AND DIALOGUES: EVERYDAY SPEAKING SITUATIONS

LEARNING OBJECTIVES

After reading this chapter, you will be able to understand
- purpose and advantages of general conversations
- features of a good conversation
- tips for improving conversations
- how to participate in short conversations
- how seeking and offering help/advice, agreeing and disagreeing, and giving instructions in everyday situations can be handled better
- nuances of situational dialogues

Conversation is perhaps one of the most commonly employed methods of self-expression that characterizes our everyday speech-making activity. Although conversations occur normally and naturally to us, most of us tend to take for granted our ability to make our conversations work. However, like any other form of communication, conversations require effort, focus, and practice. Before talking about how to become a good conversationalist, let us know the basic aims of conversations.

12.1 PURPOSE OF GENERAL CONVERSATIONS

Broadly speaking, conversations are held for the following purposes:

12.1.1 Self-expression and Interaction

The first aim of a conversation is self-expression and interaction with other people. We spend time with people whom we like and whose company we find stimulating. This is the driving force behind all our social activities. Whenever we have an opportunity to interact with people over dinner, a party, or some occasion, we wish to express ourselves, share our ideas, and get acknowledged as a good conversationalist.

12.1.2 Getting to Know the Other Person Better

The second purpose of conversation is to get to know the other person better. In all kinds of personal and professional situations, we are required to understand the other person, family, or organization you are dealing with. Conversations play a huge part in arriving at a proper understanding about the world around us.

12.1.3 Building Trust and Credibility

The third aim of conversation is to build trust and credibility with the people whom we meet. It is only possible with the kind of conversations we have with one another. In our professional lives, particularly for better teamwork, we need to converse well with others. People who get along very well almost invariably spend a lot of time talking about various subjects.

12.2 ADVANTAGES OF CONVERSATIONS

Given below are some of the advantages of conversations:

- Conversations help you make new friends.
- Good conversational ability makes you feel happy, confident, and connected.
- Through conversations, you learn about things, people, and places.
- If you are a good conversationalist, you become very popular among your friends, relatives, and classmates.
- Effective conversational skills add to your career growth.

However, it is not just important to be a conversationalist; we need to be an effective conversationalist.

12.3 FEATURES OF A GOOD CONVERSATION

Here are some of the important characteristics of a good conversation. A good piece of conversation

- is truly interactive in nature;
- allows everyone to share, participate, and interact freely;
- is clearly, concisely, and precisely worded;
- is devoid of confusion and ambiguity.

12.4 TIPS FOR IMPROVING CONVERSATIONS

Given below are some of the important tips for becoming a good conversationalist:

12.4.1 Begin by Using Pleasantries

Without pleasantries, all conversations would appear to be abrupt, choppy, and discourteous. In themselves, pleasantries may not add anything to the conversations, but they provide your conversation a smooth beginning.

A boy (starting quite brusquely): I want to know the status of my application. When are we going to get the electricity connection?
The woman at the desk (equally dismissive): I don't know; go to the inquiry window outside.

Don't you think that the boy needed to be a little more polite in his query? See how the same person asks the same question differently:

The same boy (politely this time): Good morning, Madam.
The same woman (this time equally
polite and positive): Good morning.
The boy (very courteously): Madam, may I know the status of our application for getting electricity connection?
The woman (equally polite): When did you apply?
The boy: Madam, nearly a month back.
The woman: In which area is this electricity connection required?
The boy: Madam, our house is in Bhankrota.
The woman: Bhankrota ... fine. Please go to the next room; and ask Mr Madam Lal Tripathi. It is he who looks after the electricity connections for the entire Bhankrota and Mahapura area.
The boy (feeling obliged and courteous): Thank you very much, Madam.
The woman (warmly): You're welcome.

Let us observe how the conversation between these two strangers appears to be without proper greetings and pleasantries:

Speaker 1: (pulling in his car near a kiosk and asking): Will this road lead to Valmiki Chowk?
Speaker 2: (equally rude and dismissive): I don't know.

Do you think the other person would have replied the same way had the question been asked somewhat differently? Find out how different the conversation sounds with a little bit of politeness and a brief exchange of greetings. Alternatively, the same enquiry can be posed thus:

Speaker 1: (this time he asks in a polite manner): Excuse me, I wish to go to Adarsh Hospital, near Valmiki Chowk. Do you think I am on the right path?

See how different can the response be:

Speaker 2: For Valmiki Chowk you have to keep driving straight for two kilometres. Then you will see a T-point. Take right turn from there. Valmiki Chowk is hardly 300 meters from there.

So, remember to use pleasantries, especially when you have to talk to a stranger. By being blunt in our everyday interactions, we can neither create good impression on the listener nor get the desired information easily.

Given below is a small interaction presumably at an airport. Carefully observe how lack of pleasantries renders the entire interaction blunt, rude, and choppy:

Speaker 1: How do I get the boarding pass?
Speaker 2: Go and ask the lady on the counter.

Speaker 1: (a bit irritated): Don't you know?
Speaker 2: (sharply): Even if I know, I am not obliged to tell you! Go to any of those counters there. It is their job to answer queries, not mine!

Do you see how by shooting query without any pleasantries elicits an undesirable response?

EXERCISE 12.1

Going ahead, rewrite the conversation cited above keeping in view the importance of pleasantries and courtesy in mind:

_____   _____
_____   _____
_____   _____
_____   _____
_____   _____

12.4.2 Listen More than You Speak

As you have heard many times earlier, we come to this world with two ears and one mouth and we should use them in the same proportion. In conversations, this simply means that you should listen twice as much as you talk if you want to develop a reputation for being a person worthy of a conversation.

12.4.3 Reciprocate Warmly

Reciprocation plays a crucial role in all human interactions. Devoid of it, the conversation is reduced to the level of an empty claptrap. Take a look at the following conversation to understand this:

Employee 1: Amit, do you know that Mr Sharma is leaving our company next month?
Employee 2: Is he, why?

Employee 1: He has got into Reliance. He's going to join the refinery in Jamnagar.
Employee 2: Okay.

Employee 1: They say it is the biggest refinery in entire Asia.
Employee 2: Maybe.

Employee 1: We are giving Mr Sharma a send off.
Employee 2: Okay.

Employee 1: The party has been arranged at the Taj Sheraton.
Employee 2: Okay.

Employee 1: Which sari do you think I should wear?
Employee 2: Whichever you like.

Did you notice that the conversation fails to click as Employee 2 in the dialogue is hardly keen to talk to the lady?

Going further, listen to this conversation taking place between two friends Garima and Gaurav. Observe how lack of interest and reciprocation by one of the speakers sinks the entire conversation:

Garima: Gaurav, do you know that our university is planning to organize a book fair?
Gaurav: When?

Garima: On 8th March.
Gaurav: Okay in March.

Garima: Yes, on the day the world celebrates International Women's Day.
Gaurav: Okay.

Garima: I am so excited.
Gaurav: Why?

Garima: You know, I'll be a part of the organizing committee. Madam Bhargava told me so.
Gaurav: Okay.

Garima: I am excited about seeing so many of the books at the same place. Moreover, I am going to study how the reader's age determines his/her interest in books.
Gaurav: I see.

Garima: On the basis of the data collected during book fair, I plan to submit a paper.
Gaurav: Okay.

 **EXERCISE 12.2**

Assuming yourself to be Gaurav in the above conversation, rewrite his response so as to reveal his enthusiastic participation in the conversation:

_____   _____

_____   _____

_____   _____

_____   _____

_____   _____

_____   _____

12.4.4 Ask Open-ended Questions

The art of good conversation rests very much on your ability in asking relevant questions and responding attentively. You can garnish conversations with your insights, ideas, and opinions, but you perfect the art and skill of conversation by perfecting the art and skill of asking good, well-worded questions that direct the conversation and give other people an opportunity to express themselves.

For making your conversations work, ask open-ended questions that cannot be answered with a simple 'yes' or 'no'. Open-ended questions encourage the speaker to expand on his/her thoughts and comments. Ask questions such as 'What do you mean by … exactly?', 'Let me see if I've got this right. What you're saying is …' 'What do you think of it, precisely speaking?', 'This is amazing. What next?', 'How did it happen?', etc.

12.4.5 Be Courteous and Polite

All conversations require courtesy and politeness. Take a look at the following conversation and see if it sounds courteous enough:

Ritik: Madam, I have brought this poster. Can you put it up on the notice board of your college?
Receptionist: What kind of poster?

Ritik: Our college is organizing a debate competition; it is the poster for that.
Receptionist: Which college are you from?

Ritik: St Patrick College, Ghaziabad.
Receptionist: We can't put up notices of other colleges on our notice board.

Ritik: But why?
Receptionist: Our university authorities do not permit us.

Ritik: Who are those authorities?
Receptionist: See Mister, I don't think I need to answer such questions. Please leave the counter. I have other things to do.

The conversation does not sound all that pleasant, does it? Remember that courtesy demands nothing on our part, but can always make us sound pleasant and approachable. Follow the same conversation and observe how the introduction of courtesy can change the entire nature of the conversation this time:

Ritik (polite and humble): Good Morning, Madam.
Receptionist: Yes? How can I help you?

Ritik: Madam, I am from St Patrick College, Ghaziabad. Our college is organizing a National Debate Competition. Madam, we are looking forward to students from all good universities and colleges.
Receptionist: Okay. So, what can we do for you?

Ritik: Madam, I have brought the brochures and posters of the event. I also have the invitation letter from the Organizing Coordinator for the Head of the Department of your university. So, Madam, I would like to meet him and request for sending some students for participation.
Receptionist: Sorry, the Head of the Department is out of station. He has gone to Ahmedabad to attend a conference.

Ritik: In that case, is it possible for me to meet some other faculty member from the English department?
Receptionist: You can meet Dr Vibha Mishra.

Ritik: Okay, Madam, where can I meet her?
Receptionist: She sits upstairs. Her chamber is in the corridor on the right hand side.

Ritik: Thank you, Madam. And one more thing—can we get this poster put up on the notice board?
Receptionist: I would suggest that you first meet Dr Vibha Madam. Once she approves this idea, I'll get this poster put up on the notice board.

Ritik: Thank you very much Madam. You have been really accommodating. Thanks a lot indeed!
Receptionist: You are welcome!

12.4.6 Resist the Urge to Dominate

In order to be an excellent conversationalist, you must resist the urge to dominate the discussion. The best conversationalists seem to be easy-going, cheerful, and genuinely interested in the other person. They seem to be quite content with listening when other people are talking, and they make their own contributions to the conversations with remarks, comments, and point that are pertinent, short, and to the point.

12.4.7 Listen to Others Attentively

Listening is the most important of all skills for a successful conversation. Since everyone enjoys talking, it takes a real effort to practise excellent listening and to make that a habit.

The major reason why most people are poor listeners is that they are busy preparing a reply while the other person is still speaking. They are very much like boxers, waiting for the other person to let their guard down so that they can jump in with a quick verbal punch and take over the conversation. The best listeners seem to have developed the knack of making the person who is speaking feel as if they were very attentive, connected, and empathetic throughout.

12.4.8 Use Appropriate Body Language

You should also nod and smile when you agree to what the person is saying. Be active rather than passive. Suggest non-verbally also that you are totally engaged in the conversation. Throughout the conversation, maintain an eye contact while the other person is talking. A short pause, of three to five seconds, is a very classy thing to do in a conversation. This helps you avoid running the risk of interrupting if the other person wants to still continue. Moreover, you understand what he or she is saying with greater clarity. By pausing, you mark yourself as an effective conversationalist.

12.4.9 Be Specific and Use Vivid Language

Sometimes, conversations fail to leave the desired impact simply because the language employed is not clear, precise, or vivid enough. Lack of clarity in your expression reveals confusion and uncertainty.

Observe the conversation that follows and decide if the manager's deputy knows his job and people well enough to become a good professional. Observe carefully the lack of clarity in the deputy's response, something that his manager tries to induce in him all through the conversation:

Manager: We should send our front desk staff for training.
Deputy: Yes, Sir, we can.

Manager: They have to work on their communication skills ... they terribly lack that.
Deputy: Sure, Sir, they do lack that.

Manager: When do we send them?
Deputy: Any time, Sir ... the day you tell me, I'll send them for training.

Manager: And for how many days?
Deputy: Probably a month, Sir.

Manager: A month! That would be too much!
Deputy: Yeah, Sir ... Maybe we can send them for a fortnight.

Manager: Do you think they require that long a period at training?
Deputy: Yeah, Sir ... but maybe a week would do.

Manager: See, I feel they only need some polishing.
Deputy: You are right, Sir.

Manager: Should we send them together?
Deputy: Yes, Sir, together they will learn better.

Manager: But in their absence who will run the front desk business?
Deputy: Yes, Sir, you are right Sir ... business will suffer if they all go together.

Manager: Which month do you think will suit them?
Deputy: Any month, Sir.

Manager: But I believe that January would be better. We don't have many people walking in during that period. So, maybe we can retain one or two and the remaining staff can complete the training during that period.
Deputy: And when they return, the remaining two can be relieved for their training.

Manager: Exactly.

As you can see, the deputy hardly seems to have any concrete or independent idea. He/She just seems to be adding lamely to the ideas of his/her senior.

EXERCISE 12.3

Going further, rewrite this conversation revising particularly the dialogues of the Deputy in the conversation:

_____   _____
_____   _____
_____   _____
_____   _____
_____   _____

12.4.10 Paraphrase the Speaker's Words

By paraphrasing the speaker's words, you exhibit that you are genuinely paying attention and making every effort to understand his/her thoughts or feelings. This way, they will find you genuinely interested and sincere in holding a conversation.

12.4.11 Apply the Three Cs

The final key to becoming a great conversationalist is to practise the friendship factor. The friendship factor is based on the three Cs—*care*, *courtesy*, and *consideration*.

You must have heard what is generally quoted to emphasize empathy in human behaviour—'People don't care how much you know until they know how much you care.' It is rightly said that whenever you show another person that you genuinely care about him/her, you come across better as a good conversationalist and friend. Moreover, courtesy is a magical quality that makes people want to be around you. All good conversationalists make others feel calm and comfortable in their presence. They never do or say anything that could hurt or offend the other person in any way.

Let's not forget that if we respect others and are considerate towards them, we are respected and considered highly by other people. Whenever you treat another person as an important and worthwhile human being, you give them a feeling that you value them. This attitude helps you become not just a better human being, but also a better conversationalist.

Keeping the above instructions in mind, evaluate how effective the following conversations are. Also observe the expressions and strategies employed by people in conversations for making their interactions work:

12.5 PARTICIPATING IN SHORT CONVERSATIONS

Situation 1: A Meeting at a Market Place

Shreya: Hi, Janaki! Is it you?
Janaki: Hello, Shreya! How are you?

Shreya: Quite fine and all the more happy seeing you in the market! What are you doing here?
Janaki: Well, you know my elder brother is getting engaged next week. So, Mom asked me to buy some good crockery.

Shreya: That's being a nice girl! By the way, congratulations!
Janaki: Thank you! And you will have to come that day.

Shreya: When is it?
Janaki: On 12th November.

Shreya: On 12th November … Okay.
Janaki: Sure?

Shreya: Of course. I never miss a chance to go to a party.
Janaki: It will be a delight for us.

Shreya: Sure, it will be. Okay, bye for now.
Janaki: Bye. See you.

While looking at the above situation, you can see how two friends begin by greeting each other and then go on to discuss an event that is scheduled to take place. As you can see the above situation employs various common expressions such as *hi, hello, how are you, well, thank you, sure, of course, bye,* and *see you* which form a large part of such exchanges of greetings and information between two friends.

Situation 2: Discussing Exam Result

Vivek: Hi, Jatin!
Jatin: Hello, dear.

Vivek: What's going on?
Jatin: Nothing.

Vivek: Why do you look so sad?
Jatin: Nothing.

Vivek: Tell me dear! You don't seem to be happy. What's the matter?
Jatin: Actually, I got my result for the interview that I appeared in the last month.

Vivek: And …?
Jatin: I did not get the job.

Vivek: Sorry to learn that. But what do you think went wrong?
Jatin: Everything, I think. I was not confident while speaking. I was nervous while answering subject-related questions even when I knew the concepts.

Vivek: But why did that happen to you? You are quite good in your subjects.
Jatin: I know. But somehow, I feel very nervous while speaking before others, particularly when I have to converse in English.

Vivek: It's good that you understand where the shoe pinches. So, you can work on your language then.
Jatin: Yes, that's what I am going to do for the next three months or so.

Vivek: Then, where is the need to be so worried? Cheer up, man!
Jatin: Thanks dear for listening to me and encouraging me.

Vivek: You're welcome anytime.

The conversation above helps us observe how two friends who are known to each other need not exchange linguistic niceties but feel deeply for each other. The seemingly blunt expressions such as *nothing, I did not get the job*, etc. only convey the sense of anxiety that one of the friends seems to be experiencing. There also are some apparently incomplete but very meaningful expressions such as *And...? Everything, I think,* etc. Also notice the use of other common expressions such as *thanks for listening, sorry to learn that, you're welcome anytime*, etc. Such short expressions help us maintain courtesy in our expressions.

12.6 MAKING REQUESTS

We often need other people to help us emerge out of difficulties. Thus, giving and getting help is a very common phenomenon in human civilization. Since, most of such help is sought in language, it is important for us to understand the expressions in English that help us convey our need clearly and emphatically to others.

Look at the following situations and observe how different sets of expressions constitute our desire to seek and offer help during our everyday interactions:

Situation 1: In a Railway Compartment

Rakesh (about 25-year-old waking up an old man): Uncle? Hello, Uncle ...
Atma Ram (about 60-year-old with a start): Uhh ...! What is there? Who ... Who're you? What do you want?

Rakesh: Sorry, Uncle! I woke you up. Will you please move a bit?
Atma Ram: Why? Is it your seat?

Rakesh: No, Uncle. But if you move a bit to your right, there will be enough room for me to sit.
Atma Ram: But, why should I move? It's a reserved seat.

Rakesh: I know, Uncle.
Atma Ram: Then, why didn't you reserve your seat?

Rakesh: Actually, Uncle I had no plans to travel. But I got a phone from home that my father is in hospital. That's why I had to start immediately.
Atma Ram: Where are you going?

Rakesh: To Lucknow, Uncle. You know, it is a 15-hour journey from here.
Atma Ram: Have you bought a ticket?

Rakesh: Of course, Uncle! Shall I show you that?
Atma Ram: No, I don't need to see that. Okay, you may sit. But you will have to go if the ticket checker raises an objection to this.

Rakesh: By all means, Uncle. Thank you so much! You are so kind!

You can easily observe the sense of politeness and gratitude expressed by Rakesh as he profusely uses courteous expressions such as *sorry uncle, will you please..., by all means, thank you so much, you are so kind,* etc. The other speaker, Atma Ram, on the other hand uses expressions which convey unwillingness initially to share his berth and irritation at having been roused from his sleep. The choice of expressions such as *What is there?, What do you want?, Why, is it your seat?, Why should I move?, Why didn't you reserve a seat?*, etc. clearly convey the old man's resistance. The expressions that follow reveal his soft side and consideration as well, as he says *Okay, you may sit,* before asserting *but you will have to go if the ticket checker raises an objection to this.*

This way, we may see an entire gamut of emotions being expressed and this becomes possible for the speakers as they use expressions which reveal them.

Let's take a look at another situation where a request is made but is not accepted:

Situation 2: Making a Request

Suresh (about 30-year-old): Good evening, Uncle!
Muthuswamy (about 50 years): Yes ...?

Suresh: Uncle, may I leave my bag here?
Muthuswamy: Bag! Why?

Suresh: Actually, Uncle I have to go and get my ticket.
Muthuswamy: Then? What's the problem?

Suresh: Uncle, my bag is very heavy.
Muthuswamy: So?

Suresh: Just that. Can I leave it here?
Muthuswamy: No, no ...!

Suresh: Please!
Muthuswamy: Why don't you carry it? You are a young man.

Suresh: I want to ... but it is very heavy.
Muthuswamy: No, you can't leave it here. No way!

Suresh: But why?
Muthuswamy: Simply because it may contain something. I don't know you, do I?

Suresh: But it has nothing. It just contains some parts of a machine. I am a mechanical engineer.
Muthuswamy: No ... No! I don't want to get into this.

Suresh: Okay. Thanks for nothing!

You can easily imagine the plight of the young man provided he is speaking the truth. Repeatedly he uses polite, courteous, and even pleading expressions but the person on the other hand is in a denial mode and keeps resisting by using a series of rude expressions such as *Then, what's the problem?, So?, No, no ...!, No, but you can't leave it here. No way!, No... I don't want to get into this,* etc. All such expressions not only convey his resistance but also establish his rudeness in this particular context. We may therefore be well aware of the words and expressions we use as they not only convey our emotions but also define us in some way.

Let's go further and see the words, phrases, and expressions we generally use while seeking and giving advice.

12.7 SEEKING AND GIVING ADVICE

Situation: An Anxious Mother and a Counselor

Mother: Good morning, Madam!
Counsellor: Very good morning! Please come inside and have a seat.

Mother: Thank you.
Counsellor: Yes, Madam. May I know how I can help you?

Mother: Actually, I am Parthav's mother … He is a student in your school.
Counsellor: In which class?

Mother: He is in VIII standard.
Counsellor (after confirming Parthav's name on her laptop): Yes. Parthav Ghosh … VIII A?

Mother: Yes.
Counsellor: So, how is he doing?

Mother: Not well … That's why I have come to you.
Counsellor: Why? But he has got very good marks in II Unit Test.

Mother: Do you feel 86% is good?
Counsellor: Yes … Of course, it's in fact a very good percentage. After all, the topper got 92% only.

Mother: You may think like that. But his father is not happy with Parthav's result.
Counsellor: See, Madam. Every child has his/her own potential. It is wrong to force a child to go beyond his or her capacity.

Mother: Can't you help Parthav get better? Can't you counsel him?
Counsellor: I don't think he requires any counselling. He is doing quite fine in his studies. He is a well behaved, cheerful boy. He participates in many sports and extra-curricular activities.

Mother: But, Madam, his father is not happy with his marks.
Counsellor: That's not Parthav's problem then. The boy is doing quite well. Expecting him to do any better would in no way help him. It would only put pressure on him.

Mother: So, what to do? How do I convince his father?
Counsellor: We can think of a way, but first of all, are you convinced?

Mother: Yes … in fact, I too feel that way. He is a nice boy, very loving, respectful, and friendly. And also hard working …
Counsellor: That's it. If you are convinced, you can certainly convince your husband.

Mother: But what if he doesn't understand?
Counsellor: No problem. You can bring him here. I'll help him understand.

Mother: Oh, that will be good! Thank you very much, Madam!
Counsellor: You are most welcome, Madam.

Mother: Okay, Good Day!
Counsellor: Good Day, Madam.

You can easily observe the touch of hesitation in the mother's choice of words as she begins by gingerly putting *Actually, I am Parthiv's mother…*, *Not well … that's why I have come to you*, and goes on to reflect her anxiety in revealing *But Madam, his father is not happy with his marks*, *But what if he doesn't understand*, etc. The counsellor's choice of expressions suggests her clarity, confidence, and composure. Some such expressions may be noted as *Yes, of course …*, *That's not Parthiv's problem then …*, *That's it…*, etc. We may also observe a touch of assertion in her expressions as she assures the anxious wife by saying *No, problem. You can bring him here. I'll help him understand.*

It is in this way that we can discern how language is capable of conveying varying emotions at the same time. Though primarily we see the mother and the counsellor engaged in the task of seeking and giving advice respectively, we may also see the concept of doubt, confusion, and hesitation on one hand and that of conviction, confidence, and assertion coming to the fore through the same discussion.

Moving further, let's see what type of expressions help us in agreeing or disagreeing to others' perspectives:

12.8 AGREEING AND DISAGREEING

Situation: Parents Discussing Daughter's Higher Education

Madhu: Dear, what do you think Shruti should do after her 10+2?
Mohan: What is there to discuss? She has appeared in AIEEE, RPET, BITSAT and many other engineering entrance exams. She will get into one of the good colleges and do her engineering.

Madhu: No, but that doesn't seem to be working.
Mohan: What? What do you mean by that?

Madhu: See, I don't find her really interested in doing engineering.
Mohan: But she herself chose sciences. What will she do after an intermediate with PCM?

Madhu: Can't she pursue a BSc or a BA degree?
Mohan: Well, what's this all about? Why should she do BSc or BA when she can get into a good engineering college?

Madhu: I don't think like that. She should study the subjects she likes and the ones that we think are right for her.
Mohan: Well, dear ... What's going on here? Has she told you that she doesn't want to go for an engineering degree?

Madhu: No, nothing like that.
Mohan: Then? Why are you suggesting a change of course for her?

Madhu: It is because she has great interest in Physics and English. She is always so inquisitive to read about the universe. Then, she also reads lots of novels, plays, and short stories.
Mohan: Madhu, I think you have not seen her studying Maths and Chemistry. I have seen her studying these subjects keenly as well.

Madhu: No doubt, she does that. But, those subjects she reads when she has some homework to do or to appear in the unit test. Otherwise, she picks up a book of fiction or something related to Physics.
Mohan: See, dear, you are the best judge. You spend more time with her than I do. But what I feel is that there is no career after BSc or BA.

Madhu: I don't think that's a right perspective. Today, we have a whole lot of openings in Physics. She can even become a researcher or a scientist.
Mohan: And in English? What will she do with a BA degree?

Madhu: A lot! She can prepare for her IAS. Or a professor. We know how capable she is!
Mohan: Well that she certainly is. Little girl! How studious she is!

Madhu: Yeah ... an intelligent daughter of an intelligent father!
Mohan: Intelligent! Me! Oh, great. But Madhu, I somehow feel that she should not do a BA.

Madhu: But why so? See, if not sciences, she can go for BA (Hons) in English. After that she can do her Masters and Doctorate and can get into an academic career.
Mohan: And teaching is a good profession.

Madhu: Not just that. Our country needs a large number of quality teachers.
Mohan: That way you are right. Okay … I am fine with it.

Madhu: So, shall we discuss all these options with her over dinner tonight?
Mohan: No problem. Let's do that. That will help her decide how to proceed further in her studies.

Madhu: Sure, it would.
Mohan: Okay, dear. Let me now proceed for office. It's already 9.30.

Madhu: Okay, dear. Take care.
Mohan: Okay, bye.

Madhu: Bye, bye …

We easily perceive a change in the tone and tenor of this discussion as it unfolds between a husband and his wife. Initially, the husband seems to be dismissive of his wife's view as he bluntly puts: *What's there to discuss …, What do you mean by that …?, What's going on here …?* Gradually, however, he is able to see the worth of her perspective as his expressions begin to suggest a distinct change in his attitude towards their daughter's choice of career.

Let's take a look at another concept and see how the aspect of giving instructions and directions is taken care of through the choice of certain words and expressions.

12.9 GIVING INSTRUCTIONS

Situation: First Day in Office

Ashish: May I come in, Sir?
Satinder Sethi (the Manager): Yes, come in please.

Ashish: Good morning, Sir!
Mr Sethi: Very good morning, young man. How are you?

Ashish: Very fine, Sir. Thank you.
Mr Sethi: Welcome to the MegaSoft world.

Ashish: Thank you very much indeed Sir for helping me see this day. I am very happy to be here.
Mr Sethi: So am I. It's good that you have come to join. Have you brought your appointment letter?

Ashish: Sure, Sir. Here it is.
Mr Sethi: Good. See, you will be joining the advertising and publicity branch.

Ashish: Oh, that would be great!
MrSethi: It's good to see your enthusiasm. See, Ashish that branch is headed by Ms Nandita Chatterjee. She is a very talented and efficient officer. You will be helping her by giving new concepts for the whole lot of advertising work we do for so many of our multinational clients.

Ashish: I'll be very keen to contribute as best as I can.

Mr Sethi: Good. Look, boy, Ms Chatterjee will brief you about your roles and responsibilities. But before that, I would like you to bear in mind the principles that define and drive our organization.

Ashish: I would be grateful if I am made aware of those.

Mr Sethi: See, our first and foremost principle that we follow here is of maintaining total transparency. You will see this visible in all our transactions within and outside organization. In a way, we believe in trusting each other in the company and also the world beyond it.

Ashish: That's wonderful.

Mr Sethi: But that concept also brings with it the sense of responsibility, belongingness, and fairness that we need to maintain both within and outside office.

Ashish: Of course. That should even otherwise be the approach.

Mr Sethi: True. Further, as an organization, we work in a relaxed and pleasant environment. What we have here is work bound responsibility and not time bound duty.

Ashish: How do I understand that, Sir?

Mr Sethi: It is this way: we all have been given some specific tasks. A deadline is decided and the task is allotted to individuals and groups. Then each person has to work and contribute his/her mite according to the timeline given to them.

Ashish: Sir, may I know it through some example to understand it fully?

Mr Sethi: Okay. See, supposing Ms Chatterjee gives you a task. Say, it is designing five captivating creatives for New Lead India, which is one of our major clients. Say, she asks you to complete the exercise in three days. Now, she will not see when you come and when you go; she won't also mind if you are seen enjoying your time with others or overstaying in the cafeteria after the lunch break. However, at the end of the day, she would like the work to reach her table, efficiently, intelligently, and neatly done.

Ashish: I think that's a very positive way to get the best work from people. It helps you approach your work in a relaxed manner.

Mr Sethi: That's the reason we have that. But at the same time, it gives us a lot of responsibility. When the organization trusts its people, they too need to live up to this feeling of mutual trust and cooperation.

Ashish: I assure you, Sir ... I'll never let down the hope, trust, and responsibility given to me.

Mr Sethi: Okay, dear. Good luck to you! You can meet Ms Chatterjee and submit your joining report to her.

Ashish: Thank you very much, Sir. Have a Good Day!

You may observe the choice of language used by Ashish to convey his earnestness and allegiance on the first day of his job whereas the language employed by Mr Sethi, though courteous, is assertive and instructive. This brings us to understand how instructions can be conveyed while maintaining politeness and courtesy. The way the instructions have been given through a judicious mix of politeness and order, the message has been conveyed in an indirect manner.

12.10 SITUATIONAL DIALOGUES

Having learnt about conversations, why should we learn about dialogues? Are they same or different? If they are different, how are they different from each other?

Yes, they are same as long as the nature and style are concerned. However, they serve different purposes. In order to understand this in greater detail, let us first understand what dialogues are and how they are written or crafted.

12.10.1 Definition

A dialogue is a verbal exchange between two or more people that is reported in a drama, movie, or narrative. So, dialogues are spoken words between two or more characters which serve a purpose within a story.

It is believed that all dialogues should accomplish at least one of the following three things:

- Moving the story forward
- Contributing to characterization
- Giving information

Thus, it can be understood that in creative writing, dialogue serves the interest of pushing the story and action forward. Better writing involves a dialogue that contributes to characterization, where what a character says relates to his/her action. Dialogues thus help the authors forecast events which are to come, and make these events more vivid when they do arrive. They also give life to characters and establish the kind of relationship that exists between them.

It is useful to learn how to construct dialogues. It helps you perform better whenever you wish to participate in a role playing exercise or perform on stage. Moreover, it also helps you appraise the dialogues spoken by characters on stage, in movies, and in fiction. Most importantly, learning to appreciate the art of speaking and constructing dialogues helps you improve your overall communication skills.

12.10.2 Tips for Writing Dialogues

Following are some important tips for writing dialogues:

- Dialogues should have a certain verisimilitude. It should seem real to the reader.
- When composing a dialogue, put the words of each speaker within quotation marks, and indicate a change in speaker by starting a new paragraph.
- Use contracted forms of words such as *don't, shouldn't, can't* unless a character is very stuffy or speaks in a very formal context.
- Internal/inner dialogue/interior monologue or silent thinking is required to appear more natural and may even be composed in an abrupt, repetitive, choppy, and cluttered manner, if the situation so warrants.
- Let your characters at times break off sentences, repeat themselves, struggle with words, or express themselves in small utterances and phrases rather than expressing themselves in elaborate, well-constructed sentences. You might think of these as *verbless sentences*—at times they become ideal in composing dialogues.
- Have characters interrupt one another. This will provide authenticity and verisimilitude to your dialogue.

- Use the occasional *um* or *er*, if a character is being particularly hesitant, in order to make him/her sound authentic and real.
- Provide the name of the speaker after every five to six pieces of dialogue in your script; otherwise readers may find themselves flipping pages to find out who actually said what.
- Remember to show who is speaking; it need not be a 'he said' or a 'she said', an action works just as well, provided we are told who is doing it and how.
- Providing non-verbal cues within parentheses with dialogues makes the scene appear closer to reality.

12.10.3 Giving Characters Distinct Speech Patterns

Some factors should be taken into consideration when finding each character's 'voice' as well as their personality. These are as follows:

- Educational background of the character
- Likes and dislikes
- Inherent complexities, contradictions, and inconsistencies
- Place they belong to
- Speech habits and other behavioural patterns
- Age
- Occupation

All these will decide whether your character is well-defined or long-winded, whether they use technical terms or that of a lay person. The factors will also determine the sort of slang that your characters use. Thus, composing dialogues requires us to imagine characters, scenes, and situations creatively and making characters express themselves in a realistic language.

 **EXERCISE 12.4**

Imagine that Rajat and Raghav are talking about the last cricket test match played between India and South Africa at Johhensberg in the 2018 series. A part of the conversation has been drafted. Now draft the remaining part of the conversation in the space provided below:

Rajat: Hello, Raghav! _____; you seem to be beaming with happiness.

Raghav: Of course, _____.

Rajat: _____, India's win at Wanderers has thrilled the entire nation.

Raghav: Most remarkably, India _____.

Rajat: What sort of odds?

Raghav: _____. _____2–0 down in the series; their openers _____ horribly; and the other batsmen _____ the South African pace attack.

Rajat: Yeah ... _____ Achilles' Heel on overseas tours.

Raghav: _____... nice expression. _____ mean?

Rajat: _____? _____; some characteristically weak point.

Raghav: But you know _____, they could _____.

Rajat: _____. _____
_____ they won the last test.

Raghav: But it was not a batting track you know; _____.

Rajat: I _____. I admit that the pitch at Wanderers was not helpful for batting; _____? _____ came a cropper even there.

Raghav: You really seem to know English well ... _____
—came a cropper—does it mean to fail?

Rajat: _____ miserably. _____ lacked discipline and application. See how in all the matches, they kept on losing _____
_____ irresponsibly.

Raghav: _____. _____KL Rahul and Murli Vijay gave away their wickets. Even other _____ getting out.

Rajat: _____, their bowlers did exceedingly well.

Raghav: _____phenomenal! Look at Shami and Bumrah... _____ brilliantly.

Rajat: _____ both Bhuvneshwar Kumar and Ishant Sharma _____
_____.

Raghav: Not to forget Ashwin..._____ supporting pace bowling.

Rajat: _____ performs everywhere. _____
_____ Akram, Ambrose, McGrath _____
_____ placid Indian tracks.

Raghav: But why doesn't this rule apply to batsmen?

Rajat: _____?

Raghav: See, just as a good bowler performs everywhere; a _____
_____.

Rajat: _____ I am saying ..._____ discipline and application. Playing _____ patience, perseverance, and commitment.

Raghav: You're right. Kohli, Pandya, Bhuvneshwar Kumar, and Rahane _____
_____applied themselves.

Rajat: Kohli did well almost every time he went out to bat. Unfortunately, other _____
_____ Rohit Sharma, Rahul and Vijay could not _____.

Raghav: Nevertheless, _____ well for India.

Rajat: Yeah, for sure. A 2–1 _____ _____ 3–0 whitewash. _____, I have class.

Raghav: Okay _____.

Rajat: Sure, bye for now.

EXERCISE 12.5

Imagine that Sumit and Manish are friends and Sumit has been offered a job by some multinational company. His selection is confirmed but he has not received his appointment letter as the CEO of the company is on leave. Meanwhile, his friend Manish has been asking for a treat. Given below are the dialogues spoken by Sumit. Write in the space provided below the part of conversation for Manish:

Sumit: Hello, Manish!
Manish: _____! _____.

Sumit: Is it? Anything special?
Manish: _____, _____!

Sumit: Oh, you seem to be really excited; what's happened?
Manish: _____! _____?

Sumit: Treat? Oh, that.
Manish: _____! _____? _____.

Sumit: Sure, Manish, but let the letter come.
Manish: _____! _____. _____?

Sumit: Not really, but you know the HR Manager had told me that I would be receiving the appointment letter by 15th February or so; but, already it is the first week of March.
Manish: _____?

Sumit: Yeah, I called her last week.
Manish: _____?

Sumit: She said that the letter will come from the headquarters in Netherlands.
Manish: _____?

Sumit: She said that Mr Stanley is holidaying in US.
Manish: _____?

Sumit: The CEO of the company.
Manish: _____?

Sumit: No idea. The HR told me that it was what was holding it back.
Manish: _____?

Sumit: Yeah, she told me that my appointment has already been approved by Mr Khosla, the Business Head in India. She also told me that my appointment letter has been printed and sent for the CEO's signature.
Manish: _____? _____; _____
_____.

Sumit: I hope so.
Manish: _____? _____!

Sumit: Lugubrious? What do you mean by that?
Manish: _____. _____

_____. _____

___? _____.

Sumit: Yeah, Manish. You are right; I am getting unnecessarily worried.
Manish (with a chuckle): _____.

Sumit: Sure, dear; I'll certainly throw a big treat.
Manish: _____. _____Shubham? We'll enjoy together.

Sumit: Okay. Let's go.

ANSWER KEY

Exercise 12.1

Speaker 1: Excuse me, Sir.
Speaker 2: Yes, please.

Speaker 1: Sir, if you don't mind, I would like to seek your help?
Speaker 2: Yes, yes, please tell me what I can do for you?

Speaker1: Sir, actually I am boarding a plane for the first time. I was told that I have to get a boarding pass and get through the security check-up procedure. But I don't know how and where to begin from.
Speaker 2: Okay that; don't worry. First you put your luggage on this conveyor belt. Once your luggage is cleared, you take it from that side ... over there.

Speaker 1: Okay Sir, then?
Speaker 2: Then you move with your e-ticket to the counter there. Yours is which flight?

Speaker 1: Jet Airways. I am going to Mumbai.
Speaker 2: Then, you see there ... the fourth counter is for Jet Airways. Take your ticket there. They will give you the boarding pass and the seat number.

Speaker 1: After that, Sir?
Speaker 2: Then, you go through the remaining security checks.

Speaker 1: Then, Sir?
Speaker 2: Then you will be through to the boarding area. You will wait there for a while and after the boarding is announced for your flight, you will proceed for that.

Speaker 1: Oh, that means it is not very cumbersome.
Speaker 2: Not at all, it's quite easy and comfortable.

Speaker 1: Oh, thanks a lot indeed, Sir! Sorry to have bothered you!
Speaker 2: Not at all, it was a pleasure! Wish you a pleasant maiden flight!

Speaker 1: Thank you, Sir!

Exercise 12.2

Garima: Gaurav, do you know that our university is planning to organize a book fair.
Gaurav: Is it? Well, that's really good. So, when is it?

Garima: On 8 March.
Gaurav: Really? That makes it really special. 8th March is Women's Day as well, isn't it?

Garima: Yes; on the day the world celebrates International Women's Day.
Gaurav: So, how do you look forward to the event?

Garima: I am so excited.
Gaurav: What makes you so excited?

Garima: You know, I'll be a part of the organizing committee. Madam Bhargava told me so.
Gaurav: Congratulations!

Garima: I am also excited about seeing so many of the books at the same place. Moreover, I am going to study how the reader's age determines his/her interest in books.
Gaurav: Oh! That's great! But what are you going to do with the data?

Garima: On the basis of the data collected during book fair, I plan to submit a paper.
Gaurav: Well, that's like a studious Garima as ever! Wish you all the best!

Exercise 12.3

Manager: We can send our front desk staff for training.
Deputy (with promptness in voice): Yes, Sir … I too feel the same … they need to be trained. And more than anything else, they need training in effective communication skills.

Manager: You are right … so when can we send them?
Deputy (sounds prepared, clear, and purposeful in is approach): Sir, I have worked out a plan for that. Actually, I noticed that our staff lacks these skills quite a few months back. I have identified the personnel and the type of training they require … In fact, I have prepared a report on that and would like to submit that to you.

Manager (judging his deputy's preparedness): But I don't want a report that just contains problems … I need solutions too.
Deputy (not nervous, quite clear, and well prepared): Sure, Sir. The report analyses the whole situation and also gives some solutions.

Manager: So, you too believe that they need some such training?
Deputy (confidence in voice): Sir, I believe that out of fifteen people, ten would certainly require training.

Manager: And how long should the period be?
Deputy (sounds methodical, purposeful, and focused): Sir, I have categorized these ten people in three brackets. One such lot requires intensive training for a month or so. This bunch has five people. Three of them require a training of a fortnight or so. The other two can come up well even with a week-long training.

Manager: So, where do you propose to send them?
Deputy (confident because of the homework done well in advance): Sir, I have identified three spoken English and personality development institutes located in Patel Nagar; they have good faculty and they charge a reasonable fee.

Manager: But our work will suffer if we send them for as long as a month.
Deputy (expresses clarity and confidence in voice): No, Sir. I have worked out the training schedule in such a way that we will have at least eight people looking after the front desk operations even during the training period.

Manager: How will you do that?
Deputy (speaks with conviction and planning): Sir, not all of them will be sent for training together. I have given the proposed training programme in detail, and since most of them would be sent alternatively, the front desk operation will not suffer even for a single day.

Manager: When can we start?
Deputy: I would suggest that we send the first batch by 1 July.

Manager: Roughly, when will it be over?
Deputy: By August end.

Manager: Have you worked out the cost to company?
Deputy: Yes Sir, the whole training programme will cost us about ₹35,000.

Manager: That sounds affordable ... When can I see the report?
Deputy: Right away Sir, I have brought it.

Manager: Good, you have planned smartly.
Deputy: Thank you very much, Sir.

Exercise 12.4

Rajat: Hello, Raghav! I don't have to ask you how you are; you seem to be beaming with happiness.
Raghav: Of course, there is every reason for me to be happy.

Rajat: Why not, why not, India's win at Wanderers has thrilled the entire nation.
Raghav: Most remarkably, India has won this match against all odds.

Rajat: What sort of odds?
Raghav: All types. You know they were 2–0 down in the series; their openers were performing horribly; and the other batsmen too were not able to face the South African pace attack.

Rajat: Yeah ... this has always been India's Achilles' Heel in overseas match.
Raghav: Achilles' Heel ... nice expression. What does it mean?

Rajat: Don't you know? It means an inherent weakness; some characteristically weak point.
Raghav: But you know this time around, they could overcome that.

Rajat: I don't think so. It is not because of their batting but the excellent bowling with which they won the last test.
Raghav: But it was not a batting track you know; so they could not have done any better.

Rajat: I can agree with you to some extent. I admit that the pitch at Wanderers was not helpful for batting; but what about the other two pitches? Indian batsmen came a cropper even there.
Raghav: You really seem to know English well ... you are using another good expression—came a cropper—does it mean to fail?

Rajat: Yes, it means to fail miserably. What I feel is that Indian batsmen lacked discipline and application. See how in all the matches, they kept on losing their wickets by playing irresponsibly.
Raghav: You are right. Both KL Rahul and Murli Vijay gave away their wickets. Even other batsmen kept playing rash strokes and getting out.

Rajat: Yeah; in comparison, their bowlers did exceedingly well.
Raghav: Bowlers were phenomenal! Look at Shami and Bumrah ... they bowled brilliantly.

Rajat: Not just that... both Bhuvneshwar Kumar and Ishant Sharma too bowled superbly.
Raghav: Not to forget Ashwin...he did so well on tracks that were supporting pace bowling.

Rajat: A good bowler performs everywhere. You know how earlier greats such as Akram, Ambrose, McGrath have been successful even on placid Indian tracks.
Raghav: But why doesn't this rule apply to batsmen?

Rajat: Which rule?
Raghav: See, just as a good bowler performs everywhere; a good batsman too should bat well on all tracks.

Rajat: That's what I am saying ... they lacked discipline and application. Playing test matches requires more patience, perseverance, and commitment.
Raghav: You're right. Kohli, Pandya, Bhuvneshwar Kumar, and Rahane all did well when they applied themselves.

Rajat: Kohli did well almost every time he went out to bat. Unfortunately, other batsmen including Rohit Sharma, Rahul, and Vijay could not do well enough to win India the series.
Raghav: Nevertheless, the series ended well for India.

Rajat: Yeah, for sure. A 2–1 loss is much more respectable than a 3-0 whitewash. Okay dear, I have a class.
Raghav: Okay; see you soon.

Rajat: Sure, bye for now.

Exercise 12.5

Sumit: Hello, Manish!
Manish: Hi, Sumit! It's great that you came, I was about to call you.

Sumit: Is it? Anything special?
Manish: Of course, everything is special!

Sumit: Oh, you seem to be really excited; what's happened?
Manish: Now, don't you pretend! When are you giving us a treat?

Sumit: Treat? Oh, that.
Manish: Yes, that! So, when are we getting the treat? Shubham too was asking about it.

Sumit: Sure, Manish, but let the letter come.
Manish: Oh, don't worry! Letter too will come. Is there any doubt about that?

Sumit: Not really, but you know the HR Manager had told me that I would be receiving the appointment letter by 15th February or so; but, already it is the first week of March.
Manish: Have you spoken to her?

Sumit: Yeah, I called her last week.
Manish: Then? What did she say?

Sumit: She said that the letter will come from the headquarters in Netherlands.
Manish: What did she say about the delay?

Sumit: She said that Mr Stanley is holidaying in US.
Manish: Who is Stanley?

Sumit: The CEO of the company.
Manish: So, when is he going to be back?

Sumit: No idea. The HR told me that it was what was holding it back.
Manish: Otherwise, the appointment is final?

Sumit: Yeah, she told me that my appointment has already been approved by Mr Khosla, the Business Head in India. She also told me that my appointment letter has been printed and sent for the CEO's signature.
Manish: Then, why are you getting so anxious? The letter will come; it's just a matter of time.

Sumit: I hope so.
Manish: What hope so? Don't you sound lugubrious!

Sumit: Lugubrious? What do you mean by that?
Manish: What I mean to say is that when the appointment letter has already been printed, it is bound to come. Maybe a couple of days here or there. But where is the element of doubt? So, there is no reason for you keep a sad and worried face.

Sumit: Yeah, Manish. You are right; I am getting unnecessarily worried.
Manish (with a chuckle): Don't worry; we are not going to let you off without a treat.

Sumit: Sure, dear; I'll certainly throw a big treat.
Manish: Okay; let's have fun meanwhile. Shall we go to Shubham. We'll enjoy together.

Sumit: Okay. Let's go.

 Please refer to the Online Resource Centre for audios on conversations.

13

UNIT VI: COMMUNICATION AT WORKPLACE

JOB INTERVIEWS

LEARNING OBJECTIVES

After reading this chapter, you will be able to understand
- definition of interview
- process and stages of job interviews
- types of interviews and questions related to them
- desirable qualities of interview candidates
- how to prepare for successful job interviews
- importance of using proper verbal and non-verbal cues during job interviews
- how confidence helps in facing interviews
- tips for success of an interviewee

MT College of Engineering and Management is quite a busy place these days like all other colleges. The students in their last semester are undergoing the placements. They are preparing their level best. Some of the students of the college have been picked by the companies, but some others have not been so lucky. Amit Dubey is also one of them. He has become depressed for he has not been selected by any of the companies. His academic record is very good. But why is it so that he is unable to make it in the interviews? He has already been interviewed by three companies. This failure is bothering him so much that he has become a diffident person and is also suffering from insomnia. However, the solution to the problem does not lie in getting disturbed.

Having come to know about this, Siddhant, his senior, met him and tried to know about the questions that were asked and how Amit had responded. To Siddhant's surprise, the answers given by Amit were not all that bad. He analysed the whole situation and tried to make him understand the proper use of body language, how to improve his enthusiasm level, and develop the art of becoming assertive while answering. After a rigorous training of two weeks, he got through an interview in one of the multinational companies, with a handsome salary package.

Amit Dubey's case establishes the fact that in order to emerge successful in job interviews, some special preparation is required. There certainly are certain traits that are desirable in job interviews and some others that are not so. Getting to know what stands us in good stead in job interviews is quite important to us. However, before going further, let us understand what an interview is and how it is conducted.

13.1 DEFINITION OF INTERVIEW

The word 'interview' comes from 'inter' and 'view'. 'Inter' means *in between*, and 'view' means *to see*. In fact, an interview is a process in which the employer gets an opportunity to see whether the candidate is suitable for the position vacant, and the candidate tries to prove that he/she possesses the desired skills and knowledge.

The crux of the matter is that your prospective employer is interested in you only if you have the desired skills, qualification, and knowledge. Therefore, before you appear for an interview, you have to make sure that you possess these. Further, it is crucial that you are well prepared, so that you can confidently stake your claims for the slated position. In fact, it would be quite worthwhile to understand the whole process of the interview so that you can prepare yourself for all its stages.

13.2 PROCESS OF JOB INTERVIEW

Even if many of us are not sure of how to perform during an interview, most of us are aware of the process. During the interview process, the employer attempts to determine whether the applicant is suitable for the job or not. In a typical job interview, there is a panel which consists of three to four people who sit on one side of the table and a candidate who sits on the other side. During a job interview, the interviewers ask the candidate questions about his/her job history, personality, work style, and other factors relevant to the job. For instance, a few common interview questions are 'Tell me about yourself', 'What are your strengths and weaknesses?', 'Why should we hire you?', 'How will you contribute to our company?', etc. All such questions aim at finding out your strengths, your motivation to work, and your suitability for the job. You will usually be given a chance to ask questions at the end of the interview. These questions are strongly encouraged since they allow the interviewee to acquire more information about the job and the company, but they can also exhibit the candidate's confidence and strong interest in the company.

Though the interview process appears to be simple, it involves a lot of money on the part of the company. In fact, most of the companies want to select the candidates they are interviewing, simply because they do not want to repeat the costly affair. This gives the candidates an advantage, as the panel interviewing them is keen to see them succeeding and not failing. So, if you do reasonably well and showcase your potential appropriately, the chances for success are much higher than those of failure. At the same time, the companies do not want to select a wrong candidate, as righting a wrong would result in further wastage of time, money, and energy on their part. In many companies, therefore, you can observe that the duration of an interview is increasing, particularly for high ranked positions, and the interview process may involve analytical tasks, group activities, presentation exercises, and psycho-metric tests, besides the usual interaction between the candidate and the selection panel. Therefore, it is advisable to approach interviews seriously and be prepared, because interviews are becoming grilling and challenging with the passage of time.

Keeping the above mentioned facts in mind, the first thing you should do is to keep your résumé updated and practise the frequently asked interview questions. These simple exercises can be very effective and can go a long way in getting the most out of your interview. Broadly speaking, we can say that this is a three-step process which includes the following steps:

- Gathering information
- Getting ready both with the technical and HR questions
- Performing well both verbally and non-verbally

The interview process requires you to first gather information regarding the company you intend to be associated with. It is essential for you to know the total turnover, the products and services, number of employees, its branches, work culture, and future plans of your prospective company. This will enable you to establish a quick rapport with the panel members and exhibit to them your keenness to be associated with the company.

The next stage of preparation requires you to go prepared with suitable answers for all the commonly asked questions. Besides these, also be prepared with the subject related/technical questions relevant to your field of interest, study, and research.

And finally, you need to be prepared well for performing both verbally and non-verbally during the interview. A good level of confidence, fluency in English, and a good display of appropriate body language collectively help you leave a favourable impression on the interview panel. It is possible that you might be asked to ask a question. Be ready with one, and think about your closing remarks when the interviewers tell you that your interview is over.

By following all these steps, try to achieve the following objectives by the end of the interview:

- Make it clear that you want the job.
- Set the stage for the next step.
- Create a final good impression.
- Get an actual offer.

13.3 STAGES IN JOB INTERVIEWS

Before you appear for your first job interview, it is advisable to know the various stages through which your suitability for the job is assessed. These stages may include the following steps/stages of screening:

- Screening of application
- Group discussion (GD)
- Appraisal of curriculum vitae (CV)
- Negotiations
- Competency tests/technical know-how
- Medical test
- Psychological tests/aptitude test

13.4 TYPES OF INTERVIEWS AND QUESTIONS RELATED TO THEM

There are various types of interviews that are held for different fields and positions. Here are a few types which are held for middle-level managers and fresh engineers.

Telephonic/Phone interview A common initial form of interview is the telephonic interview. This is an interview conducted over the telephone or a mobile phone. This is especially common when the candidate does not live near the prospective employer and also has the advantage of keeping costs low for both sides. In case of a large number of candidates, this method is used as a tool for the first round of screening. Though a telephonic interview sounds easy when compared to a face-to-face interview, the task requires thorough preparation on the part of the candidate. In this type of interview, the candidate's voice plays a key role.

At times, telephonic interviews may finally decide a candidate's suitability for a position. Mostly, however, it is followed by other rounds of the interview which aim at finding out a candidate's suitability for the job from various perspectives. At times, these rounds may not be preceded by a telephonic interview at all.

Technical interview This is an essential round of screening. In this part of the interview, the experts on the panel try to assess your knowledge in the subject domain. They ask you questions related to various fundamental concepts involved, their application, and your ability to relate your knowledge in other related fields. Look at a few technical questions:

Question: What is the name of the first clone? Do you think cloning is dangerous for mankind?

Answer: It was Dorset sheep which was named Dolly. This was created in Roslin Institute, Edinburg, 1992. This new genetic technology was a major breakthrough, but surely unrestricted cloning is dangerous for mankind for obvious reasons. The probabilities of its misuse are more serious. The responsibilities of children and parents, the concept of identity, etc. will become the points of bitterness. It will collapse the social order and will give rise to many legal problems. So I feel cloning can do more harm than good to society.

Question: How do aeroplanes fly?

Answer: Sir, in the flying of an aeroplane, the theorem of Bernolli is applicable, and by virtue of the drag and lift force it goes in the air.

Question: What do you mean by the term 'lead bank'? Is it anyway applicable in the industrial area?

Answer: Sir, this is a concept related to area banking. Each bank is specified a district in which it has to survey the district and prepare a development programme, including the credit scheme and other requirements. Coming to the second part of the question—yes, it exists in the industrial area as well. When two banks jointly fund an industrial project, the bank which has the major share is considered to be the lead bank.

Behavioural interview A common type of job interview in the modern workplace is *behavioural interview*. This type of interview is based on the notion that a candidate's past behaviour is the best indicator of his/her future performance. In behavioural interviews, the interviewer asks the candidates to recall specific instances where they were faced with a set of circumstances, and how they reacted. Typical behavioural interview questions are usually worded like this:

- Tell me about a project you worked on where the requirements changed midstream. What did you do?
- Tell me about a time when you took the lead on a project. What did you do?
- Describe the worst project you worked on.

Question: Describe a time you had to work with someone you didn't like.

Answer: Sir, everyone has his/her own likes and dislikes. However, one has to work even when you do not like a person because of certain things which you do not appreciate in him/her. This situation calls for tremendous patience and understanding. This happened with me when I was to give a team presentation with a classmate who had a laidback attitude. This was a real challenge for me because I am a hard worker and I am quite committed to my work. However, this gave me an opportunity to understand him well. That teammate was actually sharp and intelligent but lazy and complacent. So, I motivated him to share his inputs by having discussions with him on the project. Slowly he started participating wholeheartedly. In the end, we delivered an excellent presentation and I found a friend in the person whom I did not like sometime back.

Stress/Skeet shoot interview The candidate is asked a series of questions by panellists in rapid succession to test his/her ability to handle stress-filled situations. While answering these questions you need to be mentally alert since you are asked more than one question at a time. You should stay calm during such sessions. Stress interviews might involve testing an applicant's behaviour in a busy environment. Questions about handling work overload, dealing with multiple projects, and handling conflict are normally asked in such type of interviews.

Another type of stress interview may involve only a single interviewer who behaves in an uninterested or hostile manner. For example, the interviewer may not make eye contact, may roll his eyes, or sigh at the candidate's answers, interrupt, turn his back, take phone calls during the interview, or ask questions in a demeaning or challenging style. The goal is to assess how the interviewee handles pressure or to purposely evoke emotional responses.

Psychometric/Aptitude test In order to judge a candidate personally, sometimes, psychometric tests are administered. Gradually, the test is becoming a part of the whole selection procedure in interviews. In this test, almost fifty to sixty questions are asked to assess whether the candidate has the desired aptitude and knowledge. If the candidate clears this round, he/she is asked to appear for a GD round, and finally an HR round.

13.5 DESIRABLE QUALITIES OF CANDIDATES

While appearing at job interviews, the prospective candidates must aim at reflecting the following traits:

- Clarity of thought
- Presence of mind
- Balanced point of view
- Composure
- Logical thinking
- Maturity
- Sincerity
- Openness
- Capacity to conceptualize
- Good understanding of fundamentals
- Fluency in expression
- Effective display of body language

13.6 PREPARATION FOR SUCCESSFUL JOB INTERVIEWS

Any fact facing us is not as important as our attitude towards it, for that determines our success or failure.

–Norman Vincent Peale

Preparation for a successful job interview requires the candidate to do the following:

13.6.1 Know the Company

Researching a company about its products and services is essential before you go for an interview. This can easily be done by browsing the site of the company, by going through its brochures and report, and by getting to know the value of its shares and debentures.

History Gather information about the company you want to work for. Visit the company's website and talk to anyone you might know who works there or had worked there.

Find out details such as: What products or services does the company offer or sell? When did it start? Who are its promoters? What is the total strength of employees in the company? What is its position in the market? Who are its major competitors in the market?

Projects undertaken What are its significant projects? What kind of benefits does it reap from those projects?—These are certain questions that the candidate should seek answers for.

Growth The candidate should try to find out details such as: What are its growth prospects in future? Does it have any plans to expand in the near future? What is its growth rate?

It is important to know about the company because if the candidate does not know anything about the company, it reflects his/her lack of preparation for the interview and lack of enthusiasm in associating himself/herself with the company.

13.6.2 Know Yourself

Before you set a foot on your job-hunting expedition, take some time to know yourself. The more self-aware you are, the more confident and comfortable you will be in job interviews.

Strengths and uniqueness While preparing for an interview, you should always try to know your own strengths and weaknesses. In the following situation, you can see how impressively the interviewee responds.

Interviewer: What is your greatest strength?
Interviewee: Sir, I think my abilities to motivate people and to adapt with changing circumstances are my key strengths. I think these qualities will help me lead a team and accomplish tasks within the stipulated time.

As you can see from this example, you need to know about yourself. For this, you need to think of the possible answers for the most frequently asked questions. Read the following example carefully:

Interviewer: What is your major weakness?
Interviewee: I sometimes go into greater details of the task assigned to me which makes the task a little unmanageable at times. But, lately I have realized that I need to keep track of both my ideas and the time alloted for the task, and I am working towards being better at time management.

Here, you can see a well thought out answer. The candidate is able to tell the interviewers about one of his/her qualities even when he/she talks about his/her weakness.

Competitive advantage It is essential that you make a good lasting impression on the people who meet you at any job interview. Showing yourself as qualified for the job is one important element, but you need to win the person over and ensure that he/she is also impressed, both by your knowledge and your personality.

To be a great champion, you must believe that you are the best. If you're not, pretend you are.

–Muhammad Ali

13.6.3 Review Common Interview Questions

There are a few questions which are invariably asked in most of the interviews. A good technique is to write out your answers to the questions you anticipate and then read your polished answers out loud, over and over. Go through mock interviews with the help of your friends. Most questions will relate either to your ability to do the job or to the type of employee you will be.

Some such questions are given below. For these questions, try to find out and craft your own answers. Do not try to imitate others. A few questions have been answered, and the purpose behind these questions have also been discussed briefly to guide you, so as to help you get to know how to prepare answers for the frequently asked questions on your own.

1. **Tell me about yourself.**

Approach This is the most often asked question in interviews. You need to have a short statement prepared in your mind. Be careful that it does not sound rehearsed. Limit it to work-related items unless instructed otherwise. Talk about things you have done and jobs you have held that relate to the position you are getting interviewed for. Start with the item farthest back and work up to the present.

2. **What is your greatest strength?**

Approach This question gives you a great opportunity to highlight your best skills. Don't pick just one; focus on your top three or four strengths. Some of the qualities you can mention are persistence, dedication, punctiliousness, commitment, leadership skills, team-building skills, and organizational skills. Determine which strengths would fit best with the position for which you are applying.

Answer: Sir, as far as my strengths are concerned, I'm good at organizational skills, prioritization, and time management. But my greatest strength is my ability to effectively handle multiple projects within deadlines.

3. What is your greatest weakness?

Approach Be careful with such questions. To stand out, be more original and state a weakness, and then emphasize what you have done to overcome it. Be sure the weakness you talk about is not a key element for the position sought.

Answer: Since I am a hard worker, I've had trouble delegating duties to others. The reason being, I felt I could do things better myself. This has sometimes backfired because I ended up with more than what I could handle and consequently, the quality of my work would suffer. But I've realized this lately and attended courses in time management and learnt effective delegation techniques, and I feel I am able to overcome this weakness.

4. Are you a team player?

Approach Of course you are required to highlight that you are a team player. Be sure to have examples ready. Provide examples that establish how often you have performed for the good of the team rather than for yourself. Do not brag.

Answer: Sir, I am a good team player. I was part of a team of six members for the Automated Traffic Control System project which was to be demonstrated at the IIT Mumbai Tech Fest. This was ready well in time, but the system did not work an evening before when we were supposed to leave for Mumbai. As a first reaction, all of us felt dejected and low because we checked everything but could not trace the problem. Our project guide was out of station. We felt helpless for a while. Then I called up my uncle who is a mechanical engineer in LNT and explained to him the problem we were experiencing. He guided us in that crucial hour. We worked throughout the night and finally we could demonstrate it. I mean, I believe that the task that the team has been assigned or taken up should not suffer even if I have to walk an extra mile.

5. Explain how you would be an asset to this organization.

Approach You should be keenly looking forward to this question. It gives you a chance to highlight your best points as they relate to the position being discussed. Give a little advance thought to this relationship.

Answer: Sir, I will definitely be an asset to your organization, because I am a person who possesses skills both in networking and banking, which are the major requirements of this position. Moreover, the experience that I gained during my industrial internship in JP Morgan Stanley will help me do my work efficiently. So, in this way, I believe I will be able to contribute significantly to the growth of the organization.

6. Why should we hire you?

Approach Point out how your qualities and skills meet what the organization needs. Do not mention any other candidate's name to make a comparison.

7. Why do you want this position?

Approach Here is where your research about the company will help you stand out among the other candidates. Explain how you always have wanted the opportunity to work with a company that provides a vital public service and leads the industry in innovative products. Explain how your qualifications and goals complement the company's mission, vision, and values (use specific examples).

Answer: Sir, I have gone through the job profile that was mentioned in the advertisement. I understand that you are looking for a person who is an expert in both networking and banking. Since I have done a couple of courses in banking, and computer science is my discipline, I know networking very well. I shall be able to apply and expand on the knowledge and experience I've gained during my internship, and will be able to increase my contributions that will add value to the company.

8. Where do you see yourself five years down the line?

Approach Don't tell them that you want to be where they are sitting right now—the interviewer may feel threatened. Also, don't tell them that by that time you would be renouncing all your worldly pursuits and would set out on a search for truth. This is an opportunity for you to demonstrate your long-term planning capacities. They are asking about your career aspirations. Tell them that you see yourself in a role in which you will be handling more responsibilities effectively and capably, because the current job will provide you with a lot of learning and experience to do so.

List of questions asked frequently during interviews Following is a list of questions often asked by interviewers during interviews:

- Tell me about yourself.
- Why have you applied for this job?
- What do you know about this job or company?
- What are your major strengths?
- What is your greatest weakness?
- What type of work do you like to do best?
- What motivates you to do your best on the job?
- What do you feel has been your greatest work-related accomplishment?
- What are your interests outside of work?
- What accomplishment gave you the greatest satisfaction?
- How does your education or experience relate to this job?
- Do your skills match this job or another job more closely?
- Tell me about your ability to work under pressure.
- Where do you see yourself five years from now?
- How do you handle stressful situations?
- Describe a time you had to work with someone you did not like.
- Describe the worst project you worked on.

- Are you willing to put the interests of the organization ahead of your own?
- Tell me about a time when you had to deal with a co-worker who was not doing his/her fair share of the work. What did you do and what was the outcome?
- What is the toughest problem you've had to face, and how did you overcome it?
- Describe your management style.
- Do you have plans to go for higher studies? If yes, when do you want to do it?
- Have you appeared for any of the competitive exams such as GRE or CAT?
- How long do you plan to stay with us?
- In case you get a job in a company which offers you a higher package, what will you do?
- You have witnessed economic depression recently. Suppose it occurs again, how will you help the organization in that crucial hour?
- How do you define success?
- Who is an effective leader according to you?
- What can we learn from China's economic reforms that have taken place recently?
- Are you willing to work overtime? Nights? Weekends?
- What are your hobbies?
- Where do you see yourself five years down the line?
- Why are you here?
- What do you know about corporate social responsibility (CSR)? How can our company go for it?
- What do you think of economic reforms such as demonetization and GST? How do you think it impacts the country's economy?
- What is the major difference between a manager and a leader? Are you a manager or a leader?
- How do you see the future of Indian market in the years to come?
- What can you do for us?
- What kind of person are you?
- What salary do you expect?
- What distinguishes you from nineteen other people who have the same skills as you have?
- Can I afford you?
- Do you read newspaper every day? If yes, what is the major news item today?
- Who is your role model other than your family member(s)?
- What motivates you to work?
- How do you handle an ethical dilemma?
- Tell us a time when you had to finish too many things at a time and how you went about doing that.
- We would like to know your views regarding the naxalite problem in India?
- Why did you choose this discipline particularly?
- Imagine that you are not lucky enough to get this job and fail in the subsequent attempts, how will you take it and what will you do then?

13.6.4 Prepare Questions You Want to Ask the Interviewer

Employers are as interested in your questions as they are in your answers. Therefore, ask intelligent questions, whenever you do. This is your opportunity to separate yourself from the other interviewees. Here are a few examples of some smart questions you may ask the interviewers.

- If you hire me, what would be my first assignment?
- Would you please tell me about the people I will be working with?
- Other than yourself, who else is involved in the hiring process? Is it possible for me to meet them today?

Most importantly, you should learn from your mistakes. If you don't get an offer from this company, you will succeed another time. Do not allow rejection to defeat you.

13.7 USING PROPER VERBAL AND NON-VERBAL CUES

Using effective non-verbal communication techniques is essential for you to get your dream job. It is believed that a majority of the message you convey during your job interview is through non-verbal cues. Therefore, you need to effectively communicate your professionalism, both verbally and non-verbally. If you come to an interview reeking of cigarette smoke, chewing gum, or too much perfume, it will not help you succeed. Not being dressed appropriately, not having proper leather shoes, talking on your cell phone, or listening to an iPod while waiting to be called for the interview may also prove fatal.

What is important when being interviewed is to appear professional and attentive throughout the interview process. Here are a few verbal and non-verbal tips to be followed before, during, and after an interview:

- Before you leave for the interview, make sure you are dressed professionally, neatly groomed, and your shoes are well polished.
- When you are entering an interview room, it is always better to walk with your head up to show your confidence.
- When you enter the interview room, shake hands with your interviewer(s). Your handshake should be strong and firm. A weak, limp handshake signifies nervousness and lack of enthusiasm.
- Sit up straight with your hands relaxing completely and lean slightly forward in your chair to exhibit your confidence as well as interest.
- Don't sit on the edge of your chair. It shows that you are tense.
- Maintain an eye contact with the interviewer or interviewers while answering questions but don't stare at them constantly.
- It is also essential to have proper eye contact while your interviewer is speaking to you; it will ensure that you are listening to him/her and are able to comprehend what is being conveyed.
- Don't forget to smile occasionally since it will help you show your enthusiasm, confidence in your abilities, and interest in the job.
- Don't move your legs while sitting. It is distracting and shows how uncomfortable you are.
- Do not rest one leg or ankle on top of your other knee. It makes you look too casual or even arrogant.
- At the end of an interview, stand up and shake hands while you thank the interviewer for the opportunity.
- Avoid speaking in a monotone; express yourself all the time by bringing variation to your tone and pitch.
- Ensure that your voice does not sound apologetic or nervous.

13.8 EXHIBITING CONFIDENCE

It is very common to be nervous before an interview; so don't get intimidated by your nervousness. You are nervous because you want to do well. Therefore, being anxious can raise your energy level and may eventually help you perform better.

Remember, that lack of confidence will mess up your chances of getting the job. Make sure that you exhibit confidence when you are being interviewed for a job. The interviewer will take your lack of confidence as a sign that you may not be able to handle the job.

When your name is called, walk in confidently and briskly; this shows confidence and enthusiasm. Extend your hand first; this shows a genuine interest in the person you are greeting. Shake hands firmly with interviewers and introduce yourself in a courteous and confident manner. Tell them that you are excited about this opportunity to share your job skills with them. You should appear assertive during your job interview so that you can ace it. Keep your eyes and mind focused and maintain a charming facial expression with a genuine smile. If you believe in yourself, it will be easier for you to be yourself in the interview. If you rehearse your answers, you will feel more confident. Use a tape recorder, watch yourself in front of a mirror, or get a friend to practise with you.

And finally, practise, practise, practise—it will make a difference.

13.9 TIPS FOR SUCCESS

Following are the dos and don'ts for the success of an interviewee.

Dos

- Find out about the company.
- Practise.
- Greet interviewers enthusiastically and sit comfortably.
- Dress smartly to make a good first impression.
- Be mentally alert.
- Stay positive.
- Focus on what you have to offer, not what you want.
- Appear confident.
- Be prepared to ask the interviewer questions.
- Thank the interviewers before leaving.

Don'ts

- Don't tell lies.
- Don't blame your circumstances.
- Don't find faults with your earlier employer or company.
- Don't make tall claims about your skills.
- Don't fidget about in your chair.
- Don't use vocalized pauses while answering.
- Don't look down or make furtive eye contact with interviewers.
- Don't bluff about issues you are not aware of.
- Don't keep on simpering sheepishly or answer emotionally.
- Don't exhibit your nervousness.

EXERCISE 13.1

Answer the following questions:

1. What is a job interview? Discuss the process of a job interview in detail.

2. Imagine that you are going to sit for an interview for JP Morgan for the position of middle-level manager. Along with other frequently asked questions, prepare answers for the following questions:
   (a) Tell me about a time when you took the lead on a project. What did you do?
   (b) Describe the worst project you worked on.
   (c) Describe a time you had to work with someone you did not like.
   (d) Tell me about a time when you had to stick to a decision you had made, even though it made you very unpopular.
   (e) Give us an example of something particularly innovative that you have done, which made a dif-ference in the workplace.
   (f) What happened the last time you missed the deadline of a project?
   (g) Have you ever witnessed a person doing something that you felt was against company policy? What did you do then and why?

3. How far is body language important to succeed in an interview? Discuss in detail.

4. Your placements are going to commence next month. What preparations will you make to get through the job interview?

5. Write short notes in about 150 words each on the following:
   (a) Technical interview
   (b) Eye contact during an interview
   (c) Psychometric test
   (d) Skeet shoot interview
   (e) Phone interview

6. Discuss the ways, adopting which, you will exhibit confidence during an interview.

7. Write short notes on the following points to get ready for your interview to be held next week:
   (a) Your strengths and weaknesses
   (b) Your academic achievements
   (c) Your extracurricular activities
   (d) Your hobbies
   (e) Your unique selling proposition (USP)

8. Discuss the various qualities of a candidate that are evaluated during an interview.

9. How will you combat your nervousness before and during an interview?

10. Discuss the interview process and the various stages that a candidate has to face for getting a job.

 Please refer to the Online Resource Centre for audios on phonetics.

14 FORMAL PRESENTATIONS

LEARNING OBJECTIVES

After reading this chapter, you will be able to understand
- ways to overcome nervousness while giving presentations
- important factors that help in successful presentations

Give us a presentation on that—these six words are inevitable in the life of a professional. Regardless of who we are—whether a manager working in a multinational company, an engineer overseeing the construction of a flyover in the city, a medico studying the factors related to the germination and proliferation of swine-flu virus, or a student writing a report on the citizens' awareness about use of helmets on the road, presentations come to play an important role. In today's world, it is hard to conceive of a profession that does not require its incumbents to prepare and give presentations to a group of people.

In professional situations presentations are quite often made to

- Inform the audience about some procedure, plan, and phenomenon.
- Analyse situations, trends, and results.
- Evaluate performance, progress, and growth.
- Suggest modifications and improvements in existing practices.

Since making presentations is an integral part of a professional's life today, the task can neither be escaped nor passed on to others. Therefore, we need to learn how to make a powerful presentation. However, before we begin to learn how to make a powerful presentation, we need to overcome the sense of fear, nervousness, or inadequacy that many of us experience while making a presentation. So, let's first learn how to deal with our nervousness in public speaking situations.

14.1 OVERCOMING NERVOUSNESS

Most of us are scared of a situation in which we have to stand up in front of our audience and make a presentation. This fear is so widespread that as many as 70 per cent of the university students regard it as a very big challenge and seek to avoid the task of making a presentation as long as they can. However, just as most of our fears are baseless and can be overcome with some guidance and training, it is possible to overcome stage fright too. Here are a few suggestions which can help you overcome this fear:

- Recognize your nervousness. Don't run away from the task of accepting the fact that you feel nervous when you speak in formal situations.
- Nervousness is a normal feeling with most people who have to perform in professional situations. Not just the speakers, but even other professionals experience it from time to time. For instance, actors are nervous when they face the camera; singers are nervous when they are required to sing in front of their audience; politicians are nervous when they have to address a crowd.

- Understand what happens to you physically when you feel nervous. Actually, nervousness is a type of chemical movement which is caused by a sudden rush of adrenaline in your body.
- Recognize the fact that the flow of adrenaline in the body only gives you more glucose, which actually provides your body with greater energy.
- Regard your nervousness, therefore, as a positive phenomenon and a form of energy which you can turn to your advantage.
- Since nervousness makes you feel more energetic, you are not likely to be timid when you experience it. Thus, a moderate sense of nervousness actually helps you overcome a sense of inadequacy.
- Nervousness is experienced by those who are really keen to make a good presentation; in a way, it is an evidence of your sincerity and commitment to the task. Therefore, rather than feeling nervous about the presentation, feel excited about the task.
- Visualize yourself making a good and strong presentation. Positive imagination infuses freshness and confidence.
- Work hard on your content. If you are well prepared, you will feel excited about sharing what you know with others.
- Work hard on your opening lines and the rest of the introduction. Use humour and wit if possible. Nervousness is most disquieting during the initial part of a presentation. Once we are able to put a couple of opening sentences in the right place, we start feeling better almost instantly.
- Rather than bothering about your nervousness, focus on what you have to speak to your listeners. Once you are caught up in the task of telling the audience what you know, nervousness starts leaving you.
- Rehearse your presentation in front of your friends, parents, or siblings. Rehearsal and practice not only polishes your performance, but also makes you feel more confident and assured of yourself.
- Look at your audience; maintaining eye contact with them helps you feel rooted and related to them.
- Start your presentation with a smile and warmth. It is likely to help you negotiate your nervousness and make your audience take interest in your presentation.
- Prepare well; it is the best antidote to nervousness.

14.2 FACTORS THAT MAKE A PRESENTATION WORK

As already suggested, formal presentations are crucial in professional situations and are meant to serve a specific purpose in a given context. To be able to achieve this, we are required to render presentations that are well planned, properly substantiated, adequately convincing, and unquestionably relevant to the need of the situations. In order to make your formal presentations work, bear in mind the following points:

- Research your topic thoroughly.
- Choose an appropriate pattern of organization.
- Start innovatively.
- State facts to substantiate main ideas.
- Use examples and instances.
- Use visual aids effectively.
- Be witty and humorous.
- Employ effective body language.
- Maintain appropriate space distance.

- Make proper use of paralinguistic features.
- Use PowerPoint slides effectively.
- Make effective group presentations.

Let's study some of these points in detail:

14.2.1 Researching the Topic Thoroughly

For making a good presentation, it is important for us to collect all the facts, statistics, data, and all the other relevant details related to the topic of our presentation. A good research into the subject helps us speak with clarity, conviction, and precision. Making use of library, office records, websites, company reports, etc. and collecting all relevant facts related to the topic is an important step that helps you prepare a good, convincing presentation.

14.2.2 Choosing an Appropriate Pattern of Organization

As a speaker, the first thing that one has to do is to structure one's speech. Before presentations are delivered formally, the speaker has to decide the pattern in which the idea will be put across to the audience. There are some widely recognized patterns, and while planning to make a speech, you can choose any one of these or use some of these. Let us look at the finer aspects of all such patterns in some detail.

Chronological pattern The chronological pattern is one of the most commonly employed patterns for organizing a speech. In this pattern, we arrange ideas, keeping in mind the chronology of events. For example, if we are required to give a presentation on 'The History of Indian Cricket', 'The History of Mughal Emperors', 'The Development of Psychology', 'The Progress of Democracy in the World', etc., we are likely to choose a series of events and speak about their development over a period of time. Whenever you choose to utilize the chronological pattern, you are required to match the sequence of events and time. The presentations organized through this pattern require a clear link to be established between the events and their time sequence. Often, the style of presentation structured in this pattern is detached with more focus on sharing with audience the information on how a particular system, organization, or situation has evolved over a period of time.

Causal pattern In this pattern, the ideas are divided into two major components—causes and their effects. Normally, this pattern is chosen to highlight the relationship between a problem and the reasons for its existence. While employing this pattern, some speakers choose to reverse the pattern and highlight first the effects of a problem, and then explain the causes behind it. Some of the topics for which you may require to structure the presentation on this format are 'Corruption in the Indian Bureaucracy', 'Global Warming: Challenges and Perspectives', 'Impact of Advertisements on Young Minds', 'From the Joint Family System to the Nuclear Family Structure', 'Alcoholism: Its Causes and Effects', etc.

Unlike the presentations arranged in the chronological pattern, the presentations arranged in a causal pattern are more involved and emotive in approach. While choosing this pattern, the speaker intends to highlight the gravity of a situation by focusing either on its causes or their effects. The causal pattern is preferred in situations when the speaker intends to create a lasting impact on his/her listeners.

Spatial pattern Spatial pattern is best suited to presentations which have a geographical or structural orientation. For instance, topics such as 'Amer Fort: Its Structure and Splendour', 'The Birla Temple Jaipur: A Structural Description', 'Design of an Automatic Washing Machine', etc. would fall under this category.

Therefore, the presentations that require us to discuss the components and structure of a particular building, machine, organization, etc. are arranged in this pattern. While choosing this pattern, we can move the discussion from top to bottom or right to left or front to back. As the spatial pattern chooses to arrange the discussion in different directions, it is also referred to as *directional pattern.*

Topical pattern Another commonly employed pattern—the topical pattern—chooses to divide and arrange the different parts of a presentation into various headings and sub-headings. When the speaker has to inform the audience about the various kinds or types of something, he/she chooses this pattern. Of all the patterns, the topical pattern is the most widely utilized. Some of the topics for which you may choose the topical pattern for arranging the ideas of your presentation are 'Types of Cancers', 'Importance of Sex Education in Schools', 'Differences in Marxist and Capitalistic Economies', 'Kinds of Cyclonic Storms', etc.

Psychological pattern At times, a situation requires the speaker to structure the presentation according to the needs of his/her listeners. In such situations, the speaker arranges ideas in a manner most likely to create an immediate impact on the listeners. Essentially persuasive in appeal, the presentations structured in the psychological pattern are quite emotive in style and sense. Some of the topics speaking on which the speakers may use this pattern are 'Loneliness: A By-product of Modern Living?', 'Are We All Getting Americanized?', 'Pakistan Nuclear Programme: A Threat to Our Survival?'

14.2.3 Starting Innovatively

Good beginning is always crucial for making an effective presentation. Since listening to others is a demanding task, an interesting and innovative start is essential in order to capture the attention of the audience. If the opening itself is dull and boring, there is a very slim chance that the audience will pay attention to the rest of the presentation. Therefore, while working on your presentation, think of an innovative and interesting beginning. Avoid opening by reading out bookish definitions or verbose explanations. Given below are some of the strategies that will help you start your presentations innovatively:

- Start with an anecdote.
- Make an interesting or intriguing statement at the outset.
- Use a witty and humorous statement.
- Begin with a quotation.
- Startle the audience with some shocking facts.
- Begin with a question.

See the opening of a presentation in the following example:

Presentation on Global Warming

Ladies and Gentlemen, when I was a student of class twelve, we read *The Rime of the Ancient Mariner.* I liked the poem for its meaning and message. But most importantly, what still rings in my ears is the beginning as Coleridge opens with his famous lines: 'Water, water, everywhere/But not a drop to drink.' That great poets have a prophetic voice is better illustrated nowhere else. Friends, as I stand here to make a presentation on Global Warming, I feel we truly are heading for a time when there will be water and water everywhere but there won't be a single drop to drink.

14.2.4 Stating Facts to Substantiate Main Ideas

Ideas, without facts, seem much like opinions. In professional situations, what people want to listen to is strong, convincing ideas and not personal or prejudiced opinions. While making a presentation therefore, always remember that rather than some lopsided views and opinions, your audience is more likely to appreciate ideas which are well supported with facts and figures. Take a look at the following example and observe how convincing the speaker appears as he/she uses facts and figures to augment his/her ideas.

Situation: A Presentation on Deforestation

Friends, if no words, pictures, or statements can prove that deforestation is happening at a rapid pace, consider the following facts:

- 80% of the world's forests are gone.
- Over 40% of all tropical forests have been destroyed and an acre is lost each second.
- The United States of America, the strongest nation on earth, has less than 4% of its forests left.
- Still, Americans annually use 50 million tons of paper. This equals the consumption of more than 850 million trees.
- Every day 50 to 100 species of plants and animals become extinct.

14.2.5 Using Examples and Instances

Besides facts and figures, examples from one's personal, professional situations/life or past experiences always add to the interest of the audience. Instances, anecdotes, sayings, quotations, and personal examples, besides the relevant statistics, data, and testimony, also help you sustain the interest of your listeners in your presentation. Moreover, such strategic allusions relate the audience to the speaker and evoke strong responses from them. Read through the example below to see how a team manager convinces and inspires his/her team to work hard and keep abreast of the latest developments in their field, to be successful in their professional lives, by citing his/her own example.

Situation: Senior Quality Control Manager Addressing Young Professionals

Friends, we are in an era of cut-throat competition. People who cannot keep up with the pace will perish and only the fittest will survive. The rule of the game is to learn fast, adapt to changes quickly, and be in the know of the latest developments around you. Let me give you an example. When I came into this field, I was a complete fresher; I had no knowledge of this profession. I interacted with people who had superior knowledge in their areas and learnt a lot from them about the different processes in this organization. I worked hard on acquiring skills that were required and I kept myself updated with the changes around me. When I learnt that there was a vacancy for a specialist in quality assurance, I applied for that as I could sense that in a new role the prospects for growth are abundant. I worked on my skills and developed new quality assurance techniques by following the best practices in other established organizations. Soon we became a small team and as you can see, this team has now grown in size to a full-fledged department. Other branches of our company are replicating this concept and new quality assurance teams are functional in some branches, and in other branches this idea is in the pipeline.

See further how the speaker, by quoting relevant sources in the following example, creates the emotional impact he/she intends to leave on his/her listeners:

Situation: Director of State Women Commission Addressing Young Social Workers

Friends, if you refer to the editorial entitled *Shame!* in The Week of 30th May, you would realize that we are not reading through the stories of the dark ages when women were branded as witches and were raped, tortured, and even killed, but we are staring at these grisly facts from the present times. The title chosen by the magazine really highlights India's hidden shame and brings to the fore the fact that despite all our claims to modernity, awareness, and development, millions of women in our country continue to live even today in perpetual darkness …

It is thus important that the presentations we make have the required substantiation and authentication from sources, facts, instances, and examples.

14.2.6 Using Visual Aids Effectively

The impact of what we both hear and see is certainly more than what we just hear. In professional presentations, therefore, visuals play a crucial role. However, while using visuals, we must ensure that they integrate well with our content and are presented to the audience in an interesting and captivating manner. A well-chosen visual can immensely heighten the impact of your presentation.

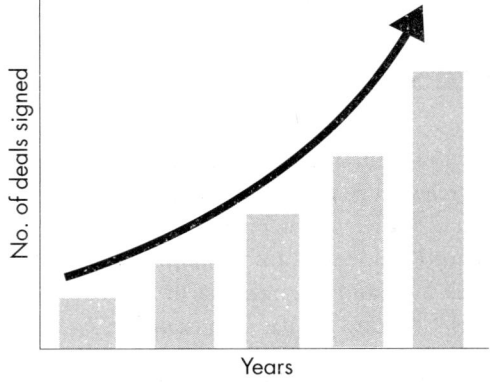

Example: Presentation on Performance

The figure clearly shows the growth in an individual's performance over the years. It is examples like these which are widely used in presentations across regions and different fields to put across information. It is seen that such tactics increase the attention of the audience and makes understanding easier.

14.2.7 Being Witty and Humorous

Wit and humour is the spice of life and is regarded as an integral part of every good presentation. Most memorable presentations become so because of the ability of the speaker to use these traits in a controlled, relevant, and effective manner. By using wit and humour, you can enliven presentations even on apparently drab and mechanical subjects. See how the speaker in this presentation uses them to induce interest in the listeners.

Situation: A Presentation on Conflict Management

Ladies and Gentlemen, every time I rise from my seat to make a presentation on Conflict Management, I dread the proposition. After all, conflict is not a nice word to begin with. In fact, the moment someone utters the word 'conflict', many unpleasant images swarm our minds. We visualize tense faces, angry looks, raised eyebrows, clenched fists, exchange of filthy words and expressions, and other such signs of conflicts. Some amongst us may also envision some spousal conflict while others might fancy a handful of soldiers brandishing swords at their opponents. In modern times, however, conflict has acquired much deeper connotations and the professionals dealing with conflict management have to manage something more profound, subtler, and indirect than the traditionally understood manifestations of conflict.

14.2.8 Employing Effective Body Language

People speak not just with the help of words but also through their expressions, gestures, postures, and movements, something what we commonly refer to as *body language*. Therefore, if you want your presentations to be effective, make good use of it. Remember that body language is universal in its appeal and you can't imagine making a good presentation with poor body language.

Let us take a look at some of the important elements of body language.

Personal appearance A good personal appearance is quite important in conveying your sense of authenticity and conviction on the day of your presentation.

In order to create a favourable impression on your audience, take care of your dress, make-up, shoes, and hair style. On the day of your presentation, pick a dress that is neatly washed, properly ironed, and fits you well. Avoid wearing clothes, ties, and footwear that make you feel uncomfortable. Taking care of your personal appearance does not mean being fashionably or glamorously dressed. So, avoid heavy make-up, gaudy clothes, and stomping shoes/sandals. On the other hand, also avoid walking in for your presentation with rumpled clothes, uncombed hair, and untended stubble.

Posture Posture refers to the way we sit, stand, and carry ourselves. Our posture communicates the way we visualize the world around us. The person who stands, sits, and walks upright commands respect and attention. Therefore, a professional has to cultivate and maintain elegance in his/her sitting, standing, and walking posture.

Given below are some important tips, following which you can maintain an impressive posture during professional meetings, interviews, group discussions, presentations, and other formal occasions:

- Look straight while walking; avoid looking down at the floor, outside the window or door, or up at the ceiling.
- Don't let your shoulders droop.
- Lift your feet clearly off the floor while walking; avoid dragging them.
- Avoid being too slow or aggressively fast while walking up to the podium or dais.
- Don't slouch while walking, or sprawl while sitting.
- Don't sit on the edge of the chair; it communicates unease and discomfiture.
- Avoid crossing your legs while sitting or standing before your audience.
- Avoid leaning on the lectern or reclining against the back of the chair.
- Keep shifting your body weight as you stand before your audience.
- Feel and communicate ease through your sitting and standing posture, and also the way you carry yourself at professional gatherings.
- Avoid keeping your feet at attention or parallel.
- Keep one foot ahead of the other; this helps you feel and appear at ease.

Gestures and hand movements Just as a picture can speak a thousand words, a gesture can also communicate all that the speaker feels, consciously or unconsciously.

Common gestures and their commonly understood meanings in our culture

- Waving indicates saying hello or goodbye.
- Making a fist indicates anger.
- Thumbs up shows appreciation or agreement.
- Pointing means showing something.
- Crossed arms indicate submissiveness, defence, and negativity.
- Hands on knees indicates readiness.
- Locking hands behind one's back indicates one's sense of authority on others.
- Rubbing the eye indicates doubt and disbelief.

A speaker's hand movements can support and emphasize his/her state of mind. Imagine a speaker who keeps rubbing his/her palms while making his presentation or keeps rubbing his/her face. What do you make of them? Do these people create a favourable impression on others? Clearly, they don't.

It is so because though the gestures do not overtly convey anything, the impact created by them is telling enough. Therefore, it is advisable to use gestures and hand movements appropriately, so that the impact created by them is graceful and suits the occasion.

Given below are a few tips which should be borne in mind while using gestures and other hand movements:

- Keep your hands in control; don't let them have a life of their own.
- Don't let your arms wave below your waist or allow them to loosely move about.
- Use graceful and socially acceptable gestures.
- Avoid aggressive and provoking gestures.
- Don't rub your palms or your face while speaking or listening to others; it suggests lack of confidence and uncertainty.
- Don't keep your arms folded against your chest; it suggests evasion and fear.
- Don't keep your hands locked behind you; it suggests concealment of your true personality.
- Avoid twitching or rubbing your nose.
- Don't scratch your forehead, or eyebrows, or head; it suggests that you are unsure of yourself.
- Don't lean on to a lectern; it reveals lack of confidence.
- Avoid keeping your hands in your pocket; it suggests that you are hiding something from others.
- Avoid playing with key rings, etc.; it distracts your listeners.
- Don't wring your hands or play with rings on your fingers.
- Don't tug on your shirt sleeves or shirt collars; it reveals your discomfiture.
- Don't scratch or crane your neck; it reveals uncertainty and doubt.

Eye contact Eyes are regarded as the window of our soul. They truthfully convey the emotions and feelings one goes through. Therefore, looking into a person's eye is the best way to understand his/her attitude or reaction to all that you speak. Hence, maintaining an eye contact with your speaker and listener is the most important part of your non-verbal communication skills.

As a professional speaker, try to look into the eyes of the people in front of you. At times, the crowd that we face is huge and we feel nervous and hence start avoiding eye contact. Remember, however, that it is bound to spoil all the impact of your otherwise well prepared presentation.

Here are a few suggestions, following which you will be able to use your eyes to support your effort in communicating your ideas effectively:

- Maintain good eye contact with your listeners.
- While addressing a large gathering, ensure that you keep looking in all directions.
- While others speak, observe them carefully and try to understand the non-verbal cues they emit.
- Exude confidence through your eyes.
- Feel warmth for your fellow listeners; it is likely to improve your eye contact with them.
- Feel and express a willingness to connect and communicate through your eyes.

Facial expressions Just as eyes are regarded as the window of the soul, the face is considered an index of our mind. If there are unpleasant, sad, and gloomy expressions on your face, you are likely to create a very negative impact on your listeners. In the entire communication process, it is the person's face that we get to see most of the time. Therefore, if a face reflects negativity of any type and expresses dejection, irritation, indifference, fear, confusion, inhibition, vulnerability, or doubt, it is likely to severely affect the effectiveness of communication.

Therefore, use your face for expressing your confidence and ease. Start with a smile; a smile can light up your face. A smile is more often than not likely to help you establish a rapport with your audience. Let your face reveal your confidence, zeal, and enthusiasm on the day of your presentation.

Given below are some tips which may help you maintain proper facial expressions while making formal presentations:

- Start with a smile but don't keep smiling throughout.
- Don't sport a frown on your face; it suggests arrogance.
- Avoid raising your eyebrows while speaking or listening to others.
- Don't purse your lips while speaking; it reveals your lack of confidence.
- Don't narrow your eyebrows; this too suggests your lack of trust in others.
- Avoid being dull in the face; express confidence and ease.
- Avoid expressing dejection, sadness, or indifference.
- Avoid reflecting strong emotions on your face.
- Let your face suggest your honesty, integrity, and conviction in what you say.
- Don't smirk; it suggests arrogance.
- Don't express any kind of disrespect or contempt for your listeners.
- Let your face suggest a willingness to associate yourself with others.

14.2.9 Maintaining Appropriate Space Distance

Have you ever observed lions and tigers in a zoo? Do they appear to be comfortable with their caged existence? Don't you often find them moving restlessly inside their cage? Tigers and lions—and none of the other animals or birds—seem to be happy inside a cage. Therefore, they appear to be restless and disquieted most of the time. The situation gets worse if many of them are put inside the same cage. You often see them attacking and mauling each other. Why does it happen? And it is not just animals or birds but also humans that detest being inside cages. We all love our freedom and want to protect it at any cost.

Observed closely however, it seems that it is not just freedom but also the sense of space that matters to us. For example, when we get into a crowded place, we do not feel comfortable. We do not want to board a crowded bus or train; sit on a waiting bench where others are sitting; stand in a long queue; sleep in a room that seems crammed and crowded with things. In fact, these are only a few instances which suggest how we all want our own territory and space to feel relaxed and enjoy a comfort that is lost if we are surrounded by things or people.

While communicating in formal situations, therefore, it becomes quite important for us to understand and respect the territories of other professionals, and see to it that they never feel intruded. In fact, if you stand too close to people while speaking to them in formal situations, they are likely to resist and resent your presence. Standing or sitting too far away from your listeners or speakers, on the other hand, is also not all that advisable. Just as standing or sitting too close to others may make them feel intruded upon, and violated or choked, standing or sitting too far away may communicate a sense of alienation and lack of warmth. Therefore, it becomes important for us to understand the different zones into which the psychological territories of human beings can be divided and choose a zone that suits us as a speaker during our presentations.

Intimate zone No stranger is welcome into the intimate zone which is shared only by spouses, lovers, children, parents, and very close relatives and friends. Anyone who tries to enter someone's intimate zone in professional situations is more likely to seem like an intruder.

Personal zone Watch carefully the distance maintained by people while they interact with one another during business gatherings, social functions, parties, and other friendly get-togethers. The distance maintained by people in a zone varies from a couple of inches to a couple of feet and is indicative of the warmth or the necessity to maintain formality in relations. When the personal and the professional relations seamlessly fuse, it becomes possible for professionals to enter each other's personal zone without appearing to be intruders.

Social zone The distance maintained between a couple of feet to several feet is suggestive of the social zone that we maintain while interacting with strangers or occasional visitors such as laundry persons, gardeners, plumbers, electricians, etc. In professional gatherings, people sometimes are seen maintaining this distance. Social distance is effectively maintained in situations where professional needs overweigh the personal.

Public zone In most professional communication situations, public zone is most commonly maintained by the speakers and their audience. Consequently, we find a defined area from where the speaker has to address his/her listeners. Though a distance of some feet is usually maintained between the speaker and the listeners while they share a public zone, the actual distance maintained differs from culture to culture. For instance, it is quite possible for a teacher in India to walk up to his/her students and reduce the distance of several foot to barely half a foot or so. It may not be possible for them to do so while addressing students in some other countries.

14.2.10 Employing Paralinguistic Features Effectively

Just as we can communicate various attitudes through our gestures, posture, expressions, and body movements, eyes, and hands, we can express emotions and feelings with the help of different aspects of our voice. Though we cannot radically change our voice, there are different aspects of voice which can be carefully worked on to create the right type of impact on our listeners while we deliver a speech, make a presentation, participate in a group discussion, or appear for a job interview.

Rate Rate refers to the number of words we utter per minute. When you speak in professional situations, try to assess whether you speak too fast or too slow. Speaking too fast is related to lack of comfort. A speaker who does not feel sure of himself/herself generally feels intimidated by the challenge of speaking in professional situations. This leads to a feeling of nervousness, and the best solution seems to speak as fast as one can and be finished with the frightening prospect of standing in front of the audience. Such a speaker, however, fails to win the audience as the breakneck speed of delivery not only reveals the speaker's lack of confidence but also makes it difficult for the audience to comprehend, assimilate, and digest what is being said by the speaker.

Just as too fast a pace causes inconvenience to the audience, so does a pace far too slow. In fact, too slow a pace of your presentation is most likely to cause monotony and boredom to such an extent that the audience start feeling sleepy and lose interest in the speech. Moreover, too slow a rate suggests lack of preparedness on the part of the speaker.

Now the question arises: How does one understand what a slow or fast rate is? Studies in this regard suggest that a rate between 125 and 150 words per minute is ideal in professional situations. However, if the matter needs deep thought and meditative attention, the rate is generally a little slower. Similarly, when we have to share something in an exciting or casual way, the rate of delivery can accelerate.

Pauses Pauses are an essential part of all human interactions. We pause between different thought units in our day-to-day interactions with others. Therefore, if we do not pause while we speak in professional situations, it only makes our presentation appear unnatural and hasty. Pauses lend credibility to the text of the speech. The speakers who pause suggest that they are quite accomplished, poised, and composed, and are not *really worried about not being able to locate an idea* once they have paused. Thus, if we pause, we display a sense of security and feeling of assurance that we know how to go further in our presentation after a pause. On the contrary, those who do not pause seem to be in a hurry. Moreover, those who rush through their presentations and are nervous about using pauses, as once they stop, they feel they would not know how to resume or reconnect.

By all means, we must use pauses while speaking in professional situations. They make our presentation sound natural. Moreover, pauses are also required for the audiences to comprehend what you say, relate it to your earlier statement, and critically participate in the act of communication.

The most crucial thing about pauses is their timing. A rightly timed pause is as important as a rightly placed word. Since a pause has to indicate either the emphasis or the conclusion of a thought unit, it is important not to put them at wrong places. Therefore, whenever you pause, pause at the conclusion of a certain thought unit and not in between. Remember, a rightly timed pause adds to the value of what you say and makes it adequately natural and emphatic. A wrongly placed pause, however, distracts the audience. Also remember that though a pause is always a natural breather, both to the speaker and to the listeners, silence—a longer pause—makes the audience feel impatient. To understand the difference between a pause and silence, let us look at a presentation situation. When a speaker comes to speak, he/she first takes his/her position, walks up to the lectern, waits for things to be in order, and then starts. All this while, nothing is spoken and heard; this is what silence is. It is a long pause which indicates the beginning of a new momentum, whereas a pause is a short silence which indicates a natural gap between different thought units, and is meant to secure emphasis at certain places.

Just as silences or wrongly placed pauses distract the audiences, so do the *vocalized pauses* which truly spoil the impact of an otherwise effective speech. Vocalized pauses are sounds such as 'umm...', 'err...', 'aa...', etc. Time and again, you hear people using them in their everyday speech. In professional situations, they act as a nuisance since they do not add to the meaning of what you say. They only suggest that we struggle with ideas and are not in control of our matter and manner. So, if we use vocalized pauses frequently in professional situations, we are likely to be mocked at.

Similar to vocalized pauses, is the overuse of repetitive expressions. Many a time, we come across a speaker who adds a phrase such as 'you know...', 'I mean...', 'actually...', 'basically...', 'in fact...', 'okay...', 'well...', or 'right...', to almost all the ideas he/she communicates. Using an expression once in a while is not distracting, but when we start putting up a string of such expressions to begin or end all that we have to say, it surely distracts the audience. In such instances, rather than focusing on your speech, some of them start looking forward to hearing that typical refrain of yours. Therefore, it is advisable not to unnecessarily become a victim of such fanciful presentation mannerisms. Use pauses but don't vocalize them. Also avoid using some particular expression repeatedly while in a professional situation.

Volume A speaker's volume often decides how he/she is likely to be received by the audience. The speaker who speaks at a low volume is likely to be seen as someone who lacks confidence, whereas a speaker whose volume is too high suggests his/her boorishness. A speaker who maintains an inadequate volume while speaking to others clearly reflects his/her lack of conviction of ideas. Such a speaker can never appear or emerge to be the master of the situation.

Now the question arises: How do we understand whether the volume we maintain is adequate or not? In order to understand this, carefully observe the reactions of the audience while you speak. If you see some smirks or mocking expressions on the faces of the people sitting in the first couple of rows, the chances are that you are speaking far too loud. On the other hand, if you observe people in the last rows craning their necks and their faces registering confused expressions, it means that you are not audible enough. Remember, maintaining an adequate volume is extremely crucial for creating the right kind of impact on your audience, and if you are found wanting in this, you are likely to be rejected by them.

Voice modulation Human voice is the most magical and versatile musical instrument in the world. If used well, our voice can convey all our moods, emotions, feelings, and views. Without proper voice modulation, however, we cannot fully express ourselves. So, modulate your voice according to the situation to create the desired impact on your listeners.

The speaker speaks the following text with enthusiasm, liveliness, and spirit in his/her voice in the example below:

Situation: A Presentation on Positive Attitude

Friends, do you know what is common among Thomas Addison, Mother Teresa, Mahatma Gandhi, Abraham Lincoln, Lance Armstrong, Madam Curie, Kapil Dev, Narayan Murthy, John Milton, and R.K. Narayan? (*The speaker speaks each of these with emphasis, holds the audience in some suspense for a while, and then breaks free.*) No, it is neither their nation nor their profession or even their sphere of action that was common among these great individuals. They all were born in different times, lived in different nations, spoke different languages, and achieved different milestones in their lives. (*The speaker pauses at each of these points of reference to highlight the differences in the backgrounds and achievements of the great people mentioned earlier.*) But then there was something still common among them. (*The pause here keeps the audience guessing before the speaker relates to the main idea.*) And it was their attitude towards life. In fact, it was their positive attitude that helped them achieve outstanding milestones in their lives.

See the following example:

Situation: A Presentation on Advantages of Vegetarianism

Not only this (*The speaker pauses slightly.*), non-vegetarian food also affects our overall system and results in other health problems such as constipation (*emphatic pause*), drowsiness, and even high blood pressure (*With a little raised voice, the speaker speaks to register the climactic effect.*) Not just that, but it also affects our mental health since we tend to have dull thinking, and we become aggressive and increasingly insensitive to other creatures including our own brethren.

In a way, being carnivorous dehumanizes us! (*The speaker ends the sentence with a rising tone to secure emphasis and attention.*)

Situation: A Presentation on Child Labour

(*The speaker speaks the following with a deep voice, maintains a slow pace, and uses pauses to emphasize successively.*):

He greets you with a faint smile on his dry lips; (*pause*) though aged twelve or thirteen, his sunken belly, and in fact the whole frail structure, can easily slip into a vest meant for a well-fed child of six or seven; he nods feebly at you; (*pause*) remains unsure of the response his desperately prompt service evokes in you; even then, he *sprints away* (*emphasizes these two words*) to the canteen counter to fetch yet another burger for you. Having known hunger at close quarters, he knows fully well that in a well-fed stomach, (*pause*) hunger never waits with patience and grace! (*The speaker ends with a rising tone to underline irony and arouse compassion in the listeners.*)

Pronunciation and articulation Pronunciation plays an important role in expressing our ideas. English is not our native language and hence the pronunciation of Indian speakers of English is different from that of the native speakers. An effort should constantly be made to make our presentation as close to standard English as possible. In terms of pronunciation, we should stick to RP English as it is recognized as the standard pronunciation of English worldwide. The chapter on *phonetics* discusses the different RP sounds of English and also gives you sufficient information regarding word stress, weak forms, and intonation patterns, following which you can make your spoken English intelligible to a native listener.

Articulation is also as important as pronunciation. To highlight the difference in these two commonly confused terms, let us consider the following words and expressions: 'psychology', 'mythology', 'rendezvous', 'clerk', 'sample', etc.: all such words and many more in English are pronounced in different ways, but there is only one standard way to pronounce these. Therefore, the difference is in the different ways of pronunciation—some acceptable and others not acceptable. However, when we listen to expressions such as 'lemme...', 'yeah...', 'dint...', etc., it is not the pronunciation but the person's articulation that is at fault.

Articulation refers to our ability to speak different sounds distinctly. If we are able to speak and enunciate different sounds in a distinct and crisp manner, our articulation is considered appropriate and impressive. On the other hand, if we mix or mumble words, it is regarded as sloppy and inelegant. Among youngsters, the problem of sloppy articulation is quite common, probably partly because of the influence of American movies and mannerisms, but mainly owing to a cyber-savvy mobile culture that believes in chopping, truncating, and abbreviating all that is elaborate and requires more effort in reading, writing, speaking, and listening.

Consequently, quite often you find a friend of yours slurring and mumbling his/her expressions and reducing 'let me' to 'lemme...', 'have to' to 'hafta...', 'I didn't...', to 'I dint...', 'yes' to 'yeah...', 'you ought to' to 'you otta…', and so on and so forth. Some of our young friends really find their own presentation becoming 'stylish', and hence 'impressive', with the help of such chopping, slurring, and mumbling expressions. A speaker who tries to sound 'trendy' and 'stylish' is likely to be rejected as someone amateurish, immature, and 'funky' by a knowledgeable audience.

14.2.11 Ending on an Emphatic Note

Just as starting innovatively is important, so is ending emphatically. In fact, many a presentation become memorable because the speaker ends the presentation on an emphatic note, which in turn leaves the audience enthralled. Ending your presentation emphatically is important also because of the fact that it is your one last chance to strike a chord with your audience. When you end your presentation with a statement such as 'In the end…', 'To conclude…', 'Finally…', 'One last word…', etc., the audience expects you to speak about the most important part of your speech. As a speaker, you cannot take lightly what to your audience appears to be a significant part of your speech. Therefore, it is quite important that you end your presentation on an emphatic note so that you can create on your listeners a lasting and impressive impact.

Given below are some such strategic endings which help the speakers achieve required emphasis and reiteration at the end of their speech:

Situation: A Presentation on Leadership

Friends, we have seen how leadership is more than what meets the eye; how leadership is not just assigning tasks to subordinates; how leadership studiously avoids being seen as dictatorship; how leadership has a vision; how it inspires others; and how it differs from simple management. Finally, we can say that a leader is the one who has not only a vision and pursues it with passion, but also the imagination to make others see and follow it.

The ending in the above example acquires emphatic connotations as first, the speaker summarizes the main ideas of his presentation and then winds up the discussion on a note of purpose and intensity.

Here is another example:

Situation: A Presentation on Drug Addiction

My friend is back from the rehabilitation centre. He intends to start his life all over again. He spends a lot of time with his Mom, Dad, and Sis. He told me that he is planning to resume his studies. Of course, with the awesome percentage that he had up to the 12th standard, getting into a degree programme is not going to be all that difficult. What, however, is going to be difficult would be to overlook the sum of losses accumulated over the four years of frenzy, madness, and the subsequent darkness and damnation in the name of drug addiction. Mercifully for my friend, his darkness and damnation were not permanent. The love and support he got from his family members was amazing. He was also lucky to get an opportunity in his life to stage a comeback. I know my friend is a lucky person. Not every other drug addict around us is as lucky as he. Scores of them, in fact, are lost to the darkness and are damned forever.

By alluding to his/her friend's example, the speaker reminds us about the tragic, dark pit that a drug addict can fall into and be perpetually lost in. Look at the profound imagery of darkness the speaker creates through a vivid language that maintains the intensity of expression throughout the ending.

14.2.12 Using PowerPoint Slides Effectively

Besides taking care of all the points mentioned above, it is also important for a professional to plan his/her presentation appropriately. One of the key areas of preparation relates to the planning of PowerPoint slides that the speaker intends his/her audience to view. Many a time, an otherwise good presentation is spoiled because of poor presentation slides. Over the years, PowerPoint slides have almost replaced all other types of presentation aids. Very often, we see speakers walking in with their laptops, connecting wires to the LCD projector and displaying the slides one by one.

Nothing seems to be wrong with this strategy, but like many other misuses of technology, a PowerPoint presentation does have its disadvantages, and if not planned properly, the slides can actually derail a presentation. Remember the tips given below as you plan your presentation on PowerPoint slides:

- Reach the presentation area much before the audience and adjust material on the laptop or pen drive well before you speak. When speakers fiddle with technological gadgets in the presence of the audience, they start getting panicky, especially if some technological glitch confronts them.
- Time your slides to perfection. It is important to know when to show a slide. At times, the discussion and the slide do not match, which looks odd and distracts the audience.
- Keep the lens of the LCD covered with its lid or a handkerchief, so that the audience do not necessarily have to look at a blank screen before you choose to show them your first slide.
- Even while displaying a slide, avoid standing or walking in front of the LCD lens. A shadow looming large on a projected slide is a sight weird enough for the audience to feel distracted.
- Don't clutter your slides with too much detail. Avoid writing long paragraphs or lengthy sentences on slides. A cluttered slide is ultimately going to irritate and distract your audience.
- Give all your material in bulleted form, with a single slide not exhibiting more than eight to ten points.
- Don't read your own slides by looking at the screen. It certainly makes you lose eye contact with your audience. Moreover, it reveals lack of preparation on your part. To aid your memory, you can keep some flash cards with you, or look at the computer screen if required. At the most, you can look at the slides perfunctorily; however, avoid reading them. Remember that you display slides for your audience and not for yourself.
- Keep your slides to the minimum number. Many a time, speakers pour slide after slide on their audience. This not only makes them feel weary of it but also causes monotony. Moreover, it also reveals that you, as a speaker, depend far too much on slides for all your ideas and discussion.
- Make your slides as captivating and innovative as possible for your audience. Avoid, however, unnecessary frills and ostentation.
- Avoid talking to your slides, it makes your audience lose interest in your presentation.

14.2.13 Making Effective Group Presentations

In present day professional situations, it is quite common for a group of people to be involved in combined projects. Many such projects require a presentation to be prepared and delivered by a group to another group of professionals. At times, all the members of the team are required to present some segment of their study, experiment, or research involved in such a group project. Such presentations made by different members of a group that jointly worked on a project are referred to as group presentations.

Apparently, a group presentation seems to be an attractive alternative to an individual presentation where the entire task is to be carried out by a single person. In a group situation, the workload is shared; and the members have to speak about only a part of the whole project. With each member having to prepare a smaller part of the entire exercise, the amount of work, the labour involved, the time spent in preparation, and above all the amount of time to be spent in front of the listening group seem less daunting and challenging This, however, is only one aspect of the reality. For, on the other side, making a group presentation becomes all the more challenging, considering the various factors which come into play.

Some such factors are enumerated below, with suggestions as to how to avoid the pitfalls which may hinder a group presentation from becoming effective and memorable:

- It is seen that a group presentation is quite often loosely structured. The group members presenting their part of the presentation are often unable to maintain continuity in the discussion. It is, therefore, important to pick up the discussion from the point where your group member has left and connect well to his/her ideas before taking the audience to newer realms.

- It is also seen that each of the group members starts with a greeting such as 'Good Morning, Ladies and Gentlemen', 'Welcome to the presentation on...', etc. As a group member speaking second or third, we must realize that the discussion has already been initiated and a series of greetings would only leave a ludicrous impact on the listeners.

- On the other extreme, quite a few speakers in a group presentation situation tend to start abruptly without making any effort to connect with the preceding speaker. Such presentations fail to leave a unified impression on the audience.

- In order to maintain continuation and connectivity to the preceding speaker, all the members of the team must thoroughly prepare the entire presentation. Remember, though each member has to present only a part of the entire presentation, all of them must be acquainted with the entire presentation.

- Once some member of your group has finished his/her part, you need to start with a brief recapitulation of what he/she has said. For instance, in a presentation on 'consumerism', one can always connect to the preceding idea by saying something like *We have just seen the advantages of a consumerist culture but not everything about consumerism is worth adulation and celebration. There are some very grave concerns associated with this phenomenon, a few of which I would be discussing with you...*

- At times, group members consciously or unconsciously end up contradicting each other. While making a group presentation, we have to keep in mind that though there are different speakers in the presentation, they are all making one single presentation. Therefore, it is important that their ideas cohere and integrate. In no way a contradictory statement such as 'I really don't agree with my friend who has presented his views prior to me...' has a place in a team presentation. Of course, the different aspects of the same issue are required to be brought into perspective, but contradicting your own team member would only serve to distract and confuse the audience.

- Improper distribution of text and slides also makes a group presentation go haywire. In a group situation, it is common that somebody starts a presentation, some others develop it, and finally some member of the team brings it to a conclusion. An unequal distribution of the task may however leave the audience bemused and distracted. For instance, a speaker getting up to say: 'Finally, I would like to end by saying that democracy is the ultimate form of governance...' would hardly make a presentation sound convincing and emphatic. Even when a member is supposed give a conclusion, it has to be well crafted and meticulously planned. Standing up as the last member in the crew and just throwing about a perfunctorily uttered concluding remark does not help. Such hasty and casual participation would only serve to harm the presentation rather than help it, as it sounds artificial and forced.

- Plan well in advance regarding who is going to start, who is going to cover which points, who is going to focus on which aspect of the problem, and who is going to give a proper, authentic conclusion to the presentation.
- Rehearse within the group so as to ensure that no member loses sight of the common thread that runs through a well-constructed presentation.
- Remember to use connectives; avoid abrupt transitions and sudden changes in thought.
- Let the entire presentation develop coherently through different speakers in your group. Don't allow inconsistencies, contradictions, and dissonance of any sort to develop alongside the discussion.
- Stick to meticulous time management. Identify the strengths and weaknesses of the group members, and share time within the group with intelligence and objectivity.

EXERCISE 14.1

Answer the following questions:

1. 'Stage fright or nervousness helps us achieve better performance in professional presentation situations.' Do you subscribe to this view? Discuss and elucidate.

2. Discuss the points you would bear in mind while making a group presentation. Provide examples to substantiate your views.

3. As a part of your class assignment, you are required to discuss a book you have recently read. Write the complete text of your presentation. Invent the necessary details.

4. Assume that you have associated yourself with Nokia as its sales executive. The company has asked you to give a presentation on the latest mobile set launched by it, to a group of potential customers. Write the text of your speech, discussing the essential features of this mobile set and describing its functions, utility, and added features.

5. 'PowerPoint slides are used not just for decorative purposes; they must be functional.' Discuss and substantiate.

6. Imagine that as an HR Manager in your company, you are required to deliver a presentation on *Impact of Social Networking on Human Relations*.

7. Imagine that you have to make a presentation on *Conflict Management*. Create an introduction for the topic.

8. Write a forceful and emphatic ending for a presentation on *Water Conservation*.

9. What tips would most help you in preparing and delivering persuasive, powerful presentations? Give proper examples to illustrate your points.

10. Imagine you have to deliver a team presentation on the topic *Global Warming*. Prepare twelve slides on the topic related to its different aspects. And prepare the full text of the presentation in about 300 words.

 Please refer to the Online Resource Centre for audios on phonetics.

RELATED TITLES